D0847862

Marshall W. Meyer
and Associates

Environments
and Organizations

Jossey-Bass Publishers
San Francisco · Washington · London · 1978

ENVIRONMENTS AND ORGANIZATIONS
Theoretical and Empirical Perspectives
by Marshall W. Meyer and Associates

Copyright © 1978 by: Jossey-Bass, Inc., Publishers
433 California Street
San Francisco, California 94104
&
Jossey-Bass Limited
28 Banner Street
London EC1Y 8QE

Library of Congress Catalogue Card Number LC 76-50706

International Standard Book Number ISBN 0-87589-374-0

Manufactured in the United States of America

JACKET DESIGN BY WILLI BAUM

HM
131
M47

FIRST EDITION

Code 7811

The Jossey-Bass Social and Behavioral Science Series

Preface

The chapters in this book represent recent work on organizations by a group of researchers brought together by common origins, common interests, and a catalyst. Our origins are in the sociological tradition of research on organizations. W. Richard Scott, William G. Ouchi, and I were students of Peter Blau at the University of Chicago; John H. Freeman and Michael T. Hannan were students of Amos H. Hawley and H. M. Blalock, Jr., at the University of North Carolina; John W. Meyer was a student of Paul F. Lazarsfeld at Columbia. Additionally, Jeffrey Pfeffer was a student of Scott at Stanford, and I was an undergraduate student of Meyer at Columbia College. Being colleagues has been as important as common origins. Scott, Meyer, Hannan, and Ouchi are faculty members of the sociology department at Stanford (Ouchi's primary appointment is in the Stanford Graduate School of Business), and Freeman was my colleague in sociology at the University of California, Riverside, until he moved to Berkeley to join Pfeffer in the Graduate School of Business Administration there.

Although the members of this group shared an interest in the broad area of organizations, we wanted to set up a more formal organization and then determine an agenda in the hope that issues of common concern would emerge. We began meeting regularly, once each academic quarter, in the winter of 1974. Two themes arose out of our early discussions. One was dissatisfaction with the state of research on organizations. The work of the University of Aston group (in Birmingham, England) and of Blau, representative of large-scale quantitative research on organizations, had fallen somewhat short of expectations. Comparing large numbers of organizations, apparently, would not easily yield results consistent with central theoretical statements that emphasized the primacy of the environment for organizations. A second theme, not wholly unrelated to the first, was a common interest in longitudinal analysis. Freeman and Hannan had conducted a panel study of school districts, Hannan and Meyer were in the midst of longitudinal research on education and political development in nation-states, and I had just completed data collection for the second wave of a panel study of local government bureaucracies. Whereas the longitudinal approach had been expected to resolve questions of causality (for example, does size precede technology or vice versa?), it soon became apparent that data collected over time captured more variation in environments and organizations than was present in data collected at any one point. As some of the chapters in *Environments and Organizations* demonstrate, the longitudinal or panel approach does reveal links between environments and organizations that would not surface in ordinary cross-sectional comparative studies.

The catalyst for our collective efforts and this book was the Problems in the Discipline program of the American Sociological Association. Beginning in 1974, the association funded grants to small groups of scholars in order to stimulate research and to enable them to gather to exchange ideas. The costs of our meetings were covered by grants from the Problems in the Discipline program for two years; these grants are gratefully acknowledged. Because we wish the American Sociological Association to continue its support of collaborative research among sociologists, the royalties from this book will be donated to the Problems in the Discipline program for as long as it continues.

Riverside, California   MARSHALL W. MEYER
February 1978

Contents

Preface   vii

The Authors   xiii

1. Introduction: Recent Developments in   1
   Organizational Research and Theory
   Marshall W. Meyer

   Part One: Theoretical Perspectives   21

2. The Micropolitics of Organizations   29
   Jeffrey Pfeffer

3. The Process of Bureaucratization   51
   Marshall W. Meyer, M. Craig Brown

4. The Structure of Educational Organizations   78
   John W. Meyer, Brian Rowan

5. Social Structure and Organizational Type   110
    William G. Ouchi, Alfred M. Jaeger

6. The Population Ecology of Organizations   131
    Michael T. Hannan, John H. Freeman

    Part Two: Empirical Research   173

7. Internal Politics of Growth and Decline   177
    Michael T. Hannan, John H. Freeman

8. Leadership and Organizational Structure   200
    Marshall W. Meyer

9. Instructional Dissensus and Institutional   233
    Consensus in Schools
    *John W. Meyer, W. Richard Scott, Sally Cole,
    Jo-Ann K. Intili*

10. Coupled Versus Uncoupled Control in   264
    Organizational Hierarchies
    William G. Ouchi

11. Organizational Effectiveness and the Quality   290
    of Surgical Care in Hospitals
    *W. Richard Scott, Ann Barry Flood, Wayne Ewy,
    William H. Forrest, Jr.*

12. Uncertainty and Social Influence in   306
    Organizational Decision Making
    Jeffrey Pfeffer, Gerald R. Salancik, Huseyin Leblebici

    Part Three: Implications   333

13. The Unit of Analysis in Organizational Research 335
    John H. Freeman

14. Strategies for Further Research: Varieties of   352
Environmental Variation
John W. Meyer

References   369

Index   395

The Authors

MARSHALL W. MEYER is professor of sociology at the University of California, Riverside. He was awarded his bachelor's degree in sociology and history at Columbia University (1964) and his master's and doctoral degrees in sociology at the University of Chicago (1965 and 1967, respectively).

Meyer, who has also taught at Harvard and Cornell, is the author or editor of several books, including *Change in Public Bureaucracies* (in press), *Theory of Organizational Structure* (1977), *Bureaucratic Structure and Authority* (1972), *Structures, Symbols, and Systems* (1971), and *Bureaucracy in Modern Society* (with P. M. Blau, 1971). He has served as associate editor of the *American Sociological Review* (1972–1975) and of *Contemporary Sociology* (1974–1977); he is currently a member of the editorial board of *Administrative Science Quarterly*.

The other researchers in the study group that generated the theory and the empirical findings reported in this book are:

JOHN H. FREEMAN, associate professor in the School of Business Administration, University of California, Berkeley.

MICHAEL T. HANNAN, associate professor of sociology, Stanford University.

JOHN W. MEYER, associate professor of sociology, Stanford University.

WILLIAM G. OUCHI, associate professor in the Graduate School of Business and the Department of Sociology, Stanford University.

JEFFREY PFEFFER, associate professor in the School of Business Administration, University of California, Berkeley.

W. RICHARD SCOTT, professor in the Department of Sociology, Graduate School of Business, School of Education, and School of Medicine, Stanford University.

The coauthors of chapters in this book include: M. Craig Brown, assistant professor of sociology, State University of New York at Albany; Sally Cole, Ph.D. candidate in sociology, Stanford University; Ann Barry Flood, postdoctoral fellow, Research Training Program in Organizations and Mental Health, Stanford University; William H. Forrest, Jr., associate professor in the Department of Anesthesia, Stanford Medical Center, Stanford University; Wayne Ewy, biostatistician, Biometrics Division, Warner-Lambert/ Parke-Davis, Ann Arbor, Michigan; Jo-Ann K. Intili, lecturer, School of Education, Stanford University; Alfred M. Jaeger, Ph.D. candidate in the Graduate School of Business, Stanford University; Huseyin Leblebici, instructor in organizational behavior, Department of Management, Middle East Technical University, Ankara, Turkey; Brian Rowan, Ph.D. candidate in sociology, Stanford University; and Gerald R. Salancik, professor of business administration, University of Illinois at Urbana-Champaign.

Environments
and Organizations

*Theoretical and
Empirical Perspectives*

1

Introduction: Recent Developments in Organizational Research and Theory

Marshall W. Meyer

Another book on organizations and their environments? For more than a decade, both research and theory have been concerned with interdependencies between environments and organizations. Publishing yet another book may signal the exhaustion of ideas in the field, but a different possibility—and the more likely one—is that continued interest, together with a stream of new research findings and theoretical syntheses, are signs of vitality. This book presents, in compact form, some of these recent developments.

The intent of this introduction is not so much to describe the following chapters as to trace the antecedents of the interest in the environment-organization nexus shared by a group of researchers. A number of factors coalesced to create a common interest in environment-organization problems; hence the research results reported here. One factor was a sense that organizational theory was progressing much faster than was empirical research. Theoretical statements taking explicit account of the environment, broadly defined, seem to have gone much beyond Weber (1946) and the precepts of the classical administrative theorists, Gulick and Urwick (1937) and others. Aldrich and Pfeffer (1976) provide an excellent review of the literature. Developments in research have also suggested environmental impacts on organizations, but, for reasons to be outlined later, the effects of organizational environments tended not to surface in the first quantitative studies of large numbers of organizations conducted during the early 1960s. As longitudinal studies and historical research emerged in the 1970s and as researchers became more comfortable with variables describing qualitative aspects of organizational environments, reliable research findings concerning effects of the environment began to emerge. A third factor is a sense among the contributors to this book that our work does represent an advance in organizational theory. Not only do we argue that organizations are creatures of their environments, but we also treat environments as more complex and variegated than they have been treated in the past. We find organizations as much—and, in some instances, more—determined by their social and political environments as by technological and economic imperatives stressed by conventional theories of organizations. In this sense, we hope to reintroduce sociological content into a literature from which it has been nearly absent for almost a decade.

Developments in Organizational Research

I begin this introductory chapter with a discussion of research methods rather than organizational theory for several reasons. First of all, while it is true that research *results* have lagged somewhat behind theoretical developments concerning organizations, the range of available research tools has tended to determine the kinds of theoretical propositions about organizations that are tested empirically. Second, research methods used by sociologists generally and methods used in organizational research have tended

to be the same. The fit between developments in general sociological theory and in organizational theory has been more tenuous,
mainly because the substance of macrosociology—the interrelations of elements of entire societies—is very different from that of
organizational theory. Additionally, the substance of organizational theory is profoundly influenced by work in other disciplines,
especially in economics, and it may have pulled somewhat away
from the mainstream of sociology. Third, it is easiest to present
research developments before turning to theory. Research methods for studying organizations have developed in an identifiable
sequence: indeed, almost in cadence. This is very different from
the pattern in theory, where things have been much less neat.

I count the following as important developments in organizational research methods: the definition of organizations, as
opposed to individual people, as the unit of analysis: the study of
many organizations using quantitative approaches as opposed to
qualitative case studies of organizations: the application of multivariate statistical techniques to organizational data; and the use of
panel studies and time series to trace changes in organizations over
lengthy intervals. Each of these developments will be discussed
separately.

Organizations as the Unit of Analysis. A fundamental shift
in thinking about organizations occurred in the late 1950s and
early 1960s. Prior to that time, sociological studies of organizations
consisted mainly of case analyses, exemplified by the work of Blau
(1955), Gouldner (1954), and Selznick (1949). The case studies
consist for the most part of qualitative description of individual
behavior in organizational settings. Quantification, where it occurred, was used mainly to illustrate patterns of interaction among
workers. Structural properties of organizations were presented almost entirely descriptively. One finds very little about organizations, although much about interpersonal and micropolitical processes, in the case studies. With some exceptions, there were few
attempts to account for the development of distinctive features of
modern organizations (for example, hierarchy of authority and
rules) in these works. Organizational attributes are presented as
constraints or elements of the context in which individual actors
functioned, but they are not causally linked to one another or to

environmental elements. It should also be noted that these early studies were published primarily in book rather than in article form. This is unimportant, save as an indication that accumulation of research results describing organizations was not possible so long as case studies dominated the field. Not only did the case studies use qualitative measures that are not easily compared across diverse organizations, but they also addressed diverse hypotheses concerning, for example, effects of impersonal rules (Blau), of managerial succession (Gouldner), and of cooptation into existing institutional structures (Selznick). Importantly, *Administrative Science Quarterly*, the first journal devoted to research on organizations and the main outlet for such studies nowadays, commenced publication in 1955.

The shift from individual persons within organizations to organizations themselves as the unit of analysis was motivated by a variety of factors, not the least of which were some very specific hypotheses to be discussed later in a section on theory. Whatever the specific hypotheses demanding organizational—as opposed to individual—data for confirmation or disconfirmation, the premise underlying them was fundamental and marked a rather radical departure from past sociological practice. The choice of organizations as the unit of analysis implied that interrelations among elements of organizations were of sociological interest in their own right, apart from the effects of these elements on individual people in organizations. This premise contrasted sharply with the social-psychological assumptions guiding most research through the 1960s. The bulk of social research, then and now, was concerned with explaining individual attitudes, opinions, predilections, and behaviors as a function of a person's social position (for example, age, ethnicity, social class) or of his or her context. Indeed, so-called contextual analysis (see Lazarsfeld and Menzel, 1961) was considered to be the "cutting edge" of sociology in the early 1960s. Examination of interrelations among structural elements of organizations was expected to yield genuinely sociological, rather than social-psychological, generalizations about organizations. Whether this actually occurred or whether naive economics was substituted for naive social psychology (see Argyris, 1972) are still open questions. However, the trend away from studies of individual people and the effects of contextual or social structural variables on individuals and toward studies of interrelations among structural variables themselves is unmistakable.

Quantitative Comparisons of Organizations. Once they had reached consensus that organizations themselves ought to be the unit of analysis for organizational research, investigators concentrated on accumulating data describing enough cases to permit quantitative comparisons. Some early "comparative" studies—in quote marks because we do *not* mean *cross-national*—studied rather small numbers of organizations intensively. Burns and Stalker (1961) had data describing twelve cases; Lawrence and Lorsch (1967) intensively studied ten cases; and the early studies of Hage and Aiken (1969) were based on information describing sixteen agencies. Quantification was not even attempted by Burns and Stalker; both the Lawrence and Lorsch and the Hage and Aiken studies used questionnaire techniques and aggregated responses by key personnel into overall organizational scores. As larger numbers of organizations began to be surveyed, single informants were substituted for multiple respondents, and accounts of formal organizational arrangements were taken as accurate descriptions of actual organizational patterns. The Aston group (see Pugh and others, 1968; Hickson, Pugh and Pheysey, 1969) and Peter Blau and his associates used essentially similar procedures to identify and question key individuals about structural arrangements in organizations. While partial attempts to corroborate informants' accounts were made, their answers for the most part remained unverified. Although this potentially raises the question of reliability of measures of organizational structure, an issue not yet considered carefully in the literature, the use of informants in place of respondents was advantageous in that it allowed cumulation of data describing relatively large numbers of organizations at reasonable cost. The Aston group's initial studies encompassed some fifty-four diverse organizations in and around Birmingham, England; Blau's major work (Blau and Schoenherr, 1971) described structural patterns in some fifty-one state and territorial employment security systems; and my study covered 254 finance agencies in the initial wave.

It should be emphasized that large numbers and large numbers of organizations are not always the same things in organizational research. A number of early studies concerning organizational questions—see especially Stinchcombe (1965), Rushing (1967), and Pondy (1969)—relied on census data describing industrial sectors, not individual organizations. The results of these studies have been quite suggestive, so much so that they are among the most frequently cited in the literature, but there is no guarantee that effects of aggregation or the "ecological fallacy" have not produced spurious results. Freeman's chapter in this book illustrates the importance of using organizations as the unit of analysis. It should also be noted that the benefits of studying very large numbers of organizations may not always justify the costs of such undertakings. Conventional survey research technology relies heavily on its ability to take probability samples from a known population of individual people, so that the larger the sample, the smaller the likely margin of error. Organizational studies, by contrast, do not draw random samples from populations. Sometimes the universe—or nearly the universe or organizations of a given type—is exhausted; sometimes a catch-as-catch-can procedure is adopted by the investigators. Often, organizational data are drawn from studies intended for other purposes and in which no claim of representativeness is made. Although organizational theorists write as if the units they are analyzing were representative of organizations generally, there is usually little empirical support for this implicit claim, and the generality of results is left for the reader to decide.

In sum, just as organizations have displaced individual people as the unit of analysis in organizational research, so also large sample studies of organizations have for the most part displaced small sample studies. The advantages of very large samples over intermediate-size samples, however, are not clear. The complexity of organizations and of their environments may be such that time and thought are probably best devoted to analyzing data rather than gathering huge samples.

The Use of Multivariate Methods. As studies involving large numbers of organizations developed, multivariate statistical techniques began to be applied to organizational data. The advantages of multiple-regression approaches over simple correlation or cross-tabulation approaches to organizational data were obvious: Not only could the effects of several independent variables be assessed simultaneously, but nonlinear and interactive models could be tested as well. The numerous articles of the Aston group, Blau and Schoenherr's book *The Structure of Organizations* (1971), and virtually all large sample organization studies published recently in leading journals used multivariate methods.

Multiple-regression techniques allow a level of precision and economy of exposition not possible with simple cross-tabulations, but they are not without restrictions. Whereas cross-tabulation and correlation analysis are not usually accompanied by specification of the mathematical form of hypothesized relations among variables and of the hypothesized direction of causation, even though such specification is implicit, regression models make these explicit. Moreover, the causal models most commonly used by sociologists require that causality be unidirectional. To be sure, recursive causal modeling does allow for detection of misspecified models when either correlated error terms or causal paths not significantly different from zero appear, but the technique generates neither a most plausible recursive model nor results clearly signaling that recursive models are inappropriate to the process being described.

The limitations imposed by recursive causal modeling might have been unimportant compared to its virtues, except for the fact that they are exactly the limitations modern organizational theories seek to overcome. Contemporary research methods most suited to testing simple cause-and-effect statements are at odds with contemporary theory emphasizing the openness and hence complexity and indeterminacy of organizations and the prevalence of feedback or homeostatic processes in them. This has resulted in a situation where a problem occupying many researchers, the effects of size on organizational structure, which is wholly appropriate for recursive causal modeling, is dismissed as wholly unimportant in a major theoretical statement (see Thompson, 1967). The lesson seems to be that multivariate techniques alone will not bring about a convergence of research and theory and, rather, that multivariate models isomorphic to the central propositions in organizational theory are required. These models often will be nonrecursive, and hence they carry even more restrictions than simple causal models. The task of methodology will be to design models that incorporate some of the subtlety and complexity of organizational theory and that at the same time are capable of empirical confirmation or disconfirmation.

Longitudinal and Historical Studies. Another innovation in organizational research has been the use of panel or longitudinal studies and, more recently, historical studies of organizations. Panel studies involving several successive surveys of a set of organizations at relatively short intervals are still the exception (see, aside from the chapters in this book, Holdoway and Blowers, 1971; Hendershot and James, 1972). Historical studies have, to date, been confined to case analyses (see, for example, Chandler, 1962; Nelson, 1975), but efforts to construct historical time series describing organizations quantitatively are now underway.

Longitudinal and quantitative historical studies of organizations, despite their cost and complexity, offer significant advantages over cross-sectional studies comparing large numbers of organizations. Most importantly, the introduction of the time element into study designs permits changes in organizations to be observed and linked to events external to the units studied. A second advantage of longitudinal and time series approaches is that they permit stronger causal inferences than cross-sectional data usually allow. The time ordering of variables is known, and, provided that one can reasonably justify the assumptions needed to identify lagged regression models, it becomes possible to test for the direction of causality as well as for simultaneity among key variables. Third, longitudinal and historical time series data open the way for studies of change in populations of organizations as well as of change in ongoing ones. Hannan and Freeman argue, in Chapter Six, that organizational change occurs as much through formation and failure of organizations as through incremental modifications of existing ones. If this is the case, then studies of populations of organizations over long intervals should reveal these processes.

If studies of organizational structures over time yield interesting results, then they may stimulate reconsideration of some fundamental issues in sociological theory. There has been a tendency to separate inquiries into the origins of organizations and institutions from research on their contemporary functioning and persistence. Lipset and others (1956), for example, explicitly separate historical from functional modes of analysis. More generally, thinking about social structural patterns and about social change have been compartmentalized. Longitudinal and historical analyses of organizations and other complex social units have the potential for integrating these disparate strands of theory by asking how much stability there has been, how much change has taken place, and under what conditions stability gives way to change and vice versa.

Developments in Organizational Theory

As already noted, organizational theory has followed an irregular course in the past fifteen years. Whereas there has been broad agreement about the most appropriate methods for studying organizations—perhaps the term *comparative* elicits more consensus than any other—there is disagreement as to the central issues in the study of organizations. One early goal of research was refinement of Weber's theory (see Udy, 1959a; Stinchcombe, 1959; and Hall, 1963); another goal was taxonomy (see Pugh and others, 1968). The impact of technology on organizations concerned other investigators (Burns and Stalker, 1961; Woodward, 1965; and Perrow, 1967), and contingency theories have emerged in an attempt to synthesize knowledge about both environmental and technological determinants of organizational structure (Lawrence and Lorsch, 1967). A central theoretical work was James D. Thompson's *Organizations in Action* (1967), which treated organizations as open systems subject to uncertainty arising in the environment and technologies but striving for closedness (and hence for certainty). Most recently, and perhaps most importantly for this book, has been the development of Blau's theory of differentiation in organizations, which gave primacy to size and treated the environment, technology, and uncertainty in organizations as less important.

No simple explanation for the discontinuities in thinking about organizations, as compared to the surface continuity in research methods, is adequate. Yet an important element has been an unintended but nonetheless marked change in the substance of research that accompanied quantification, the study of large numbers of organizations, and the employment of multivariate techniques. Briefly, the shift was this: Whereas the early studies were eclectic and thus disparate in their theoretical orientations, large-scale quantitative research comparing organizations converged quickly, if not prematurely, on one theme, namely the effects of organizational size. Blau's "Formal Theory of Differentiation in Organizations" was published in 1970 and his book with Schoenherr, *The Structure of Organizations,* in 1971. Both explained structural differentiation—and hence organizational structure generally—as a function of size and explained administrative overhead as a function of both size and differentiation. Not since Caplow's much earlier (1957) article had the size of organizations figured so centrally in theoretical statements, and most theories immediately preceding Blau's work had ignored size altogether. However, recent work by economists (see Arrow, 1974; Williamson, 1975) has reintroduced size into the theory of the firm, although not in ways that Blau anticipated.

This is not the place to consider the details of Blau's empirical research or of the inductive procedures he used in constructing his theory. Suffice it to say that there have been a number of attempts to formalize mathematically Blau's formal theory (see Meyer, 1971; Hummon, 1971; Pondy, 1975; McFarland, 1972), which, while starting from diverse assumptions, reproduced Blau's results. A recent review article by Kimberly (1976) cites some eighty studies of size and structure that again reproduce, for the most part, Blau's results. The empirical accuracy of the link between size and structural differentiation in organizations is not in question. However, its adequacy as a basis for a general theory of organizations is.

The group of researchers whose work appears in this book shared a discomfort with the theorizing of Blau and his associates. This arose, in part, from the closed-systems character of the theory. Organizational structure was explained in terms of other organizational characteristics without reference to elements in the environment. The static nature of the theory was also of concern; even though covariation of organizational properties was posited, little was said about how change occurs in organizations. But aside from these technical considerations Blau's theory was intuitively unsatisfying. Its three principal variables—size, structural differentiation, and administrative overhead—appeared to capture very little of the texture of organizational life. The volitional element —the fact that organizational structures are purposive and sometimes designed with ends other than efficiency in mind—was ignored. In a word, Blau's theory, although not wrong, seemed quite partial. It is neither to be derided nor dismissed as a "quality control check" on civil service regulations (Argyris, 1972, p. 16) because it did succeed in comparing large numbers of organizations. It is illustrative of the limitations of studying formal organizational attributes at a single point in time only and without reference to more microscopic properties of organizations as well as events occurring in their environments. The chapters in this book all represent attempts to overcome these limitations.

What, then, remain as the central theoretical issues in the sociology of organizations? My own view, and I emphasize that this does not necessarily reflect the opinions of my coauthors, is that the following questions will be central to the field in the foreseeable future. First, the theory of bureaucracy has still not been given the sustained attention it deserves, especially when compared to developments in the theory of the firm. We still have not accounted fully for the development of modern procedure-bound administrative structures. Second, what Hannan and Freeman term the *population ecology of organizations* will become an increasingly important theme, although, for reasons to be explained later, I think it will take a turn not anticipated by my colleagues. The interpenetration of societal elements and organizations may also assume some importance, as may the study of power relations in organizations: the two are closely linked. Finally, I would argue that certain issues will fall dormant shortly if they have not done so already. These include the open- versus closed-systems debate, contingency theory, and the technology-organization nexus. All of these possibilities should be discussed in some detail.

The Theory of Bureaucracy. Weber's theory of "bureaucracy" (1946) is a classic in the social sciences because it describes a fundamental transformation in Western societies, namely the substitution of large-scale, rational, "bureaucratic" forms of administration for traditional and less rational forms. Whereas the ideal-typical model outlined by Weber indicates the distinctive *features* of bureaucracies compared to earlier administrative forms—division of labor, hierarchy, administrative staff, written rules, fixed salaries, and so on—it says somewhat less about the *causes* of bureaucratization. Not surprisingly, recent research on organizations following Weber's lead has focused on interrelations among characteristics of existing organizations, rather than searching for origins.

It may be that the causes of bureaucratization lie as much in historical as in contemporary events. There is now some evidence that a series of developments, perhaps connected, perhaps not, around the turn of the century have affected organizations existing since. These events include the civil service movement, which was aimed at eliminating political spoils from government; the disappearance of inside contracting from industry; the rise of scientific management; and the reform movement, which sought fundamental structural changes in local government and extension of civil service principles. Civil services, of course, introduced the concept of "merit" personnel administration, substituting educational qualifications and objective test scores for patronage (see Chapter Three by Meyer and Brown). The inside contracting system, under which foremen contracted with factory owners and in turn recruited and paid their workers, gave way to modern hierarchy, which treated foremen and workers alike as employees of management (see Buttrick, 1952; Nelson, 1975). Scientific management (see Taylor, 1911) similarly advocated a proactive role for management and demanded expertise and specialization. The reform movement introduced expertise into local governments by hiring professional managers to substitute for elected officials and expanding civil service coverage (see Griffith, 1974). It should be noted that these changes were not always unopposed. Just as there were Taylorites and reformers, there were anti-Taylorites and antireform politicians. The controversy surrounding the transformation of organizations at the turn of the century suggests that these changes were sometimes motivated by considerations other than efficiency, even though the ideas of the Taylorites and reformers were based largely on a calculus of efficiency.

The historical argument implies that origins dominate organizations, especially large and complex ones. If this is the case, then further study of social conditions accompanying bureaucratization of both public and private enterprises is perhaps war-

ranted. Such research would not be concerned with further refinement and elaboration of Weber's ideal-typical model of
bureaucracy; rather, it would focus almost exclusively on the social,
political, and economic changes that give rise to bureaucratic structures in the first place. For example, one wonders whether "merit"
principles were, in part, a response to alliances between machine
politicians and immigrant groups that threatened WASP elites.
One wonders whether the inside contracting system was dropped
because it was inefficient or because it was so efficient that contractors made more money than factory owners (see Williamson,
1975). Whether the gospel of Taylor and the gospel of reform were
preached by the same people and hence reflected similar interest
in political beliefs also needs study. Understanding the origins
of contemporary organizational forms would help demystify current bureaucratic practices, especially the reliance on abstract rules
as a means of ensuring fairness, and it could also suggest conditions
under which the ponderousness of bureaucratic decision making
might give rise to new administrative forms.

The Dynamics of Organizational Populations. Hannan and Freeman, in Chapter Six, ask "Why are there so many kinds of organizations?" Accounting for changes in *populations* of organizations as compared to properties of individual organizations is
bound to become a central theoretical issue in the field, although
the precise direction that this theorizing will take is unclear. There
are two approaches to studying populations of organizations in the
literature so far, and no attempt has yet been made either to rec-
oncile them or to test alternative models empirically. Basically, the
models are the population ecology approach and the transaction
cost approach. A common assumption underlies both perspectives,
namely that organizational change occurs mainly through fundamental restructuring or replacement of organizations rather than
through incremental adjustment or adaptation of ongoing units.
But there are also important differences between them.

The population ecology approach focuses on a number of
organizations, a function of competitive equilibrium, and organization form—specialism versus generalism—as key attributes of
organizations. The transaction cost approach, best illustrated in
Williamson's work (1975), treats markets and internal organization
as alternative means of coordinating activity and hence is interested

mainly in organizational structure: isolated individuals contracting from one another as in classical markets, simple hierarchy, vertical integration, multiunit organization, and conglomerate. Numbers of units and their relative specialism versus generalism are, by implication, results of organizational structure in the transaction cost approach (for example, vertical integration diminishes numbers but increases generalism compared to simple hierarchy, and the conglomerate maximizes generalism). A complete theory of organizational populations will have to incorporate concepts describing numbers, specialism versus generalism, organizational structure, and other considerations, including location in the public versus the private sector.

The importance of environmental or external influences relative to internal factors may also be at issue in studies of organizational populations. The ecological approach assumes that external events determine population characteristics of organizations, but the transaction cost approach favored by economists treats organizations as maximizers and envisions both internal and external sources of organizational arrangements. Whereas competition drives out wholly inefficient organizations and political and ethical considerations limit monopolies and conglomerates, the transaction cost model also claims that organizational learning often accounts for the shifts from unitary to multiunit to conglomerate organizational forms. Needless to say, separating external from internal sources of change is not always easy. Just as internal organization can substitute for market coordination of activity, so can internal learning and anticipation substitute for direct environmental effects.

Empirical research on organizational populations is fraught with complexity. Either one must compare organizations operating in diverse environments *where environmental differences are not confounded with differences in tasks and technologies,* or organizations whose environments truly change must be examined over lengthy intervals. Historical and retrospective studies may have to take the place of prospective research designs. The organizational landscape of the society is difficult enough to describe at any one point, but describing how the landscaping changes over time with environmental variations poses even greater challenges. If the sociology of organizations is to be concerned with macroscopic issues, however, then the study of organizational populations is clearly in order.

The Intrusion of Individual Preferences and Society into Organizations. A relatively new development in organizational theory is the questioning of the rationalistic assumptions about the connectedness of structure and process to organizational goals. Sometimes the phrase "loose coupling" is used to denote disconnectedness of behavior and outcomes. Weick's (1969) characterization of rationality as "post hoc dissonance reduction" and Cohen's (Cohen, March, and Olsen, 1972) "garbage can" model of organizational decision making, elaborated in March and Olsen (1976), convey the same skepticism about supposedly rational, instrumental behavior. These accounts are, of course, somewhat metaphoric. There is little doubt that, compared to traditional administrative structures (see Dibble, 1965), contemporary organizations are rationally ordered and efficient. But theories of loose coupling are useful correctives to normative theories of organizations, which take little account of human and societal nonrationalities.

If values of rationality and efficiency insufficiently account for organizational patterns and if in fact organizational forms are explainable, then one must turn to other potential causes of organizational structures, namely the preferences of individuals who happen to be in organizations and the preferences of societies surrounding organizations. Individual preferences, of course, give rise to organizational politics and the development of power relations; the intrusion of societal elements may also create institutionalized nonrationalities. That individual preferences and societal prescriptions influence organizations is beyond dispute. Pfeffer's chapter treats organizations as arenas for interpersonal politics, and J. Meyer and Rowan's discussion of structure as myth and Ouchi's "Type Z" model show that values other than instrumental efficiency affect the design, operation, and evaluation of supposedly rational organizations. To what extent and, more importantly, under what circumstances nonrationalities penetrate organizations has not yet been the subject of much comparative organizational research, despite recent theoretical developments along these lines.

There have been diverse formulations of the problem of politics and power in organizations, and not all of them can be reviewed here. One approach, elaborated by Crozier (1964),

Thompson (1967), Hickson and others (1971), and Child (1972a), treats power as the obverse of dependence. Individuals who control scarce resources and sources of uncertainty assume power over others despite procedural safeguards intended to minimize such outcomes. This perspective on power is very much social psychological in that it identifies attributes of people—mainly, their positions and access to resources—but not organizational characteristics that stimulate or attenuate unplanned power relationships. Interestingly, economists have been as attentive to nonrationalities in organizations as sociologists. The term *power*, it should be noted, is not often used in the economics literature on organizations because power relations are considered to be only manifestations of opportunism, subgoal pursuit, or suboptimization. Basically, the economists' argument is this: The greater the accuracy of monitoring and auditing of outputs, although not necessarily of activities, and the lower the cost of obtaining information, the greater the likelihood of efficient pursuit of organizational goals as opposed to pursuit of individual preferences. Certain types of organizational structures, then, limit subgoal pursuit better than others. Williamson (1975) argues, for example, that simple hierarchies are more efficient than peer groups for most tasks because the "peak coordinator" can audit the performance of other members and reward them. Auditing and experience rating, according to Williamson, violate the spirit of peer groups but are acceptable in hierarchies. A parallel advantage of multiunit over unitary organizational structures is that the central office of the former can perform auditing and experience rating of operating divisions organized as profit centers, and it can also reward managers and deploy capital in relation to performance. Studies of the relation of organizational structure to outcomes, whether dysfunctional subgoal pursuit and power relations or desired efficiency, are quite sparse (however, see Weston and Mansinghka, 1971). Clearly, measures of organizational structure, power and outcomes will have to be brought together in empirical research. The chapter by Scott and others describes one effort at such a synthesis.

The theory of how societal preferences intrude in organizations is even less developed than work on how individual preferences displace organizational goals. Until recently, the literature consisted mainly of case studies of organizations in different societies (see Berliner, 1957; Bendix, 1956; Hartmann, 1959; Kelsall, 1955; Abegglen, 1958), which yielded valuable insights but little by way of general statements about how and when culture shapes organizations. Attempts to construct organizational theories as subtheories of cultural and social systems have proved risky. Witness the discrepancy between Crozier's (1964) explanation of French bureaucratic patterns—demands for both absolute authority and absolute autonomy for individuals give rise to a vicious circle of impersonal rules, centralization, strata isolation, and nonhierarchical power relationships—and Suleiman's (1974) recent study of elite civil servants in France, which does not find the same pattern of inefficiency and stasis, hence does not attribute much importance to these contradictory elements in French culture. Even quantitative cross-national comparisions have not yielded unambiguous results. Udy (1971) suggests that among nonindustrial societies, societal complexity diminishes rationality in organizations, as measured by specificity of goals, recruitment of workers according to skills, and production orientation. By contrast, complexity appears to promote bureaucratic elements such as hierarchy, administrative overhead, and rewards attached to office rather than output. Norr and Norr (1977), however, dispute this conclusion and show that some, although not all, of Udy's results do not hold when the level of workers' power is controlled.

Perhaps the paucity of reliable results showing societal effects on organizations, save for studies of size and structure, stems from asking the wrong questions. Since quantification of the elements of societies is elusive—indeed, it is sometimes difficult to elicit agreement as to what the elements are—comparisons of their effects are necessarily inconclusive. A better strategy may be to examine long-term trends in different societies, paying some attention to the hypothesis that the simultaneous processes of development of non-Western nations and the spread of multinational corporations has accelerated the convergence of organizational forms across diverse cultures. Research is needed to identify for what types of organizations and under what conditions cultural differences promote organizational divergence. The resurgence of ethnic identity and regionalism in the United States and elsewhere suggest that continued homogenization of culture and hence of organizational forms cannot be taken for granted.

Dead Issues. Several theoretical issues in the study of organizations are, I think, dead or dormant. It is not that these theories did not lead full and useful lives; it is rather that some issues seem to have been settled.

The Comparability of Organizations. The argument that the complexity of organizations and their environments renders them noncomparable and that therefore research is necessarily confined to idiographic case studies no longer holds credence. To be sure, comparisons of wholly disparate organizations may not yield meaningful results as easily as comparisons of fairly similar units. But the maintained hypothesis is now that almost all organizations can be compared in at least some respects.

"Open" Versus "Closed" Systems. I think the issue of open versus closed systems is closed, on the side of openness. Few researchers or theorists are likely to accept the premise that organizations, save for cloisters, can be analyzed without reference to events occurring externally, and even the cloisters are now in doubt (see Sampson, 1969). If nothing else, the studies in this book illustrate the richness and variety of findings that can emerge from organizational research when elements in the environment are considered.

Contingency Theory. There are two versions of contingency theory: one tautological and thus untestable, and one widely accepted and thus no longer controversial. The tautological version of contingency theory states that organizations whose structures best "fit" their technologies and environments are most effective. Since measures of "fit" are in practice, if not in principle, closely related to effectiveness, the proposition tends toward circularity. The second and widely accepted version of contingency theory states that empirical regularities in organizations depend on environmental and technological constraints. In other words, just as there is no one best way to organize, there may be no simple empirical generalizations holding for all organizations. This perspective is evident in chapters of this book where attention is paid to some of the special characteristics of the organizations studied and where very few unqualified theoretical generalizations are attempted.

Technological Determinism. The notion that technology is the main determinant of organizational structure seems to have fallen into disrepute, partly because of mixed empirical results, partly because technology may affect the composition of organizational populations more than it affects the structures of existing organizations. The mixed pattern of empirical results concerning technology is evident in the inability of the Aston group (Hickson, Pugh, and Pheysey, 1969) to reproduce Woodward's (1965) findings on the effects of small-batch, large-batch, and continuous-process technologies on organizational patterns and in Aldrich's rather complicated (1972) path model, which extracted some effects of technology from the Aston data, albeit not the same as Woodward's results. The utility of treating technology as a determinant of organizational populations is suggested by Stinchcombe (1965), who argues that certain types of organizations could not be founded before their technologies were invented, and by Williamson (1975), who treats technologies as sources of transaction costs, which in turn account for the existence of different organizational structures.

Conclusion

This book is not a celebration of old ideas about organizations but, rather, is an attempt to stimulate new theorizing in research endeavors. Developments in research methods—the treatment of organizations as the unit of analysis, comparative studies, the use of multivariate methods, and longitudinal and historical approaches—have contributed to understanding of the complex relations between organizations and environments, if only because they have allowed consideration of many organizational attributes varying greatly both across organizations and over time. New strands of theory—a historically based theory of bureaucracy, models of organizational populations, and inquiry into the intrusion of individual and societal preferences into supposedly rational organizations—reflect actual and anticipated research results. These ideas, of course, do not wholly displace the theories that preceded them, but the notion that complex organizations mirror interpersonal and societal complexities as well as economic and technological forces arising in their environments should be the cornerstone of a sociology of organizations.

Part One

~~~~~~~~~~~~~~~~~~~~~~~~~~~~~~~~~~~~

Theoretical
Perspectives

~~~~~~~~~~~~~~~~~~~~~~~~~~~~~~~~~~~~

The chapters contained in the first section of this book, as well as the work of other contemporary organization theorists, suggest that we are on the threshold of another major paradigm shift in the type of theoretical models that guide our investigation of the structure of organizations. Such a shift has occurred twice before in this century, and, in an odd and interesting way, history appears to be repeating itself.

At the risk of considerable oversimplification, I will argue first that theoretical models of organizations underwent a major shift about 1960, with open-systems perspectives supplanting closed-systems models. Analyses that focused primarily on the internal characteristics of organizations have increasingly given way to approaches that emphasize the importance for the organization of events and processes external to it. The environments of organizations, conceived in terms of economic, political, cultural, social, technological, and interorganizational elements, now figure importantly in the explanation of organizational structure and behavior. The title of this book attests to the importance we attribute to this change.

On either side of this watershed representing the transition from closed- to open-systems models, I believe that a second trend can be identified: a shift from rational to social models of analysis. By a rational model, I mean simply that the structure of the organization is conceived as an arrangement designed to foster the effective pursuit of specified objectives. A social model, on the other hand, emphasizes that structural arrangements primarily represent settlements of the conflicting status and power concerns of groups of participants and constituents. The shift from rational to social models has occurred twice. It occurred for the closed-systems models in the late 1930s and early 1940s, and it appears to be occurring again for the open-systems models at the present time. Table 1 summarizes this pattern and lists some representative theorists associated with each perspective.

While there are important similarities between Type 1 and 3 rational models and Type 2 and 4 social models, the differences associated with the transition from closed to open models should not be ignored. By emphasizing the recurrence of certain models, I do not mean to imply that there has been no theoretical progress during the time period surveyed. On the contrary, I do believe the later models are superior to the earlier and that this is best illustrated by briefly describing each of the four types of models (and their associated methodologies).

Table 1. Dominant Theoretical Models and Representative Theorists for Four Time Periods.

Closed-Systems Models		*Open-Systems Models*	
1900–1930	*1930–1960*	*1960–1970*	*1970–*
Rational Models	*Social Models*	*Rational Models*	*Social Models*
Type 1	*Type 2*	*Type 3*	*Type 4*
Taylor (1911)	Barnard (1938)	Udy (1959)	Hickson and others (1971)
Weber (1925)	Roethlisberger and Dickson (1939)	Woodward (1965)	March and Olsen (1976)
Fayol (1916)	Mayo (1945)	Thompson (1967)	Weick (1976)
Gulick and Urwick (1937)	Selznick (1949)	Perrow (1967)	
	McGregor (1960)	Blau and Schoenherr (1971)	

Rational Models—Type 1

Although there are important differences among them, the first group of rational theorists all conceived of organizations as tools designed to achieve preset ends. Weber (1925) attempted to identify the specific set of structural features that in combination were conducive to rational and predictable operation of complex administrative units. In contrast to Weber's more descriptive approach, administrative theorists such as Fayol (1916) and Gulick and Urwick (1937) adopted a prescriptive stance, attempting to develop general principles for improving the efficiency and effectiveness of organizations. Taylor (1911) concentrated attention on developing methodologies for improving the efficiency with which individual tasks are performed, but, although he began at the task level, the ramifications of his approach moved relentlessly up the hierarchy to include the design of larger management and control systems. These differences aside, all of these theorists viewed organizations as rather special types of social systems that were or should be consciously designed to pursue specified goals.

Social Models—Type 2

The first major challenge to the rational conception of organizations came from the empirical studies conducted over a ten-year period at the Western Electric company, Hawthorne Plant (Roethlisberger and Dickson, 1939; Mayo, 1945). These studies emphasized the extent to which nonrational factors governed the behavior of organizational participants, not only through the salience of noneconomic, "human relations" types of incentives but also through the emergence of informal systems—systems of power, status, communication, and friendship—among participants. Although some theorists, such as McGregor (1960), argued that organizational efficiency and effectiveness could be improved by redesigning formal structures to take into account the social needs of participants, most analysts viewed these concerns as operating *within* the context of the formal structure. They conceived of an infrastructure operating primarily at the level of the work group, supplementing or eroding the formal system of relationships but not seriously challenging this rational framework.

Even with the translation into English in 1946 and 1947 of Weber's writings on bureaucratic structure, a decade passed before sociologists returned to the serious examination of organizations as rational systems. Most sociologists treated Weber's work as simply a more elaborate description of the formal context in which the "more interesting" informal processes could be studied.

However, it is important to note that during the 1950s, under Merton's influence (Merton and others, 1952), a series of empirical case studies of organizations were carried out by Selznick (1949), Gouldner (1954), and Blau (1955) that foreshadowed the later, Type 4, social models. In each case, a set of social variables was examined to determine its influence on the characteristics and functioning of the formal structure. In an early study of organization-environment relations, Selznick (1949) examined the impact of the ideology and co-optation tactics of the leadership of the Tenessee Valley Authority on the goals of the organization. Gouldner (1954) focused on the impact of succession and leadership style on formalization and centralization processes within a gypsum mine and factory. And Blau (1955) studied the effect of competition and informal status processes on organizational goals and on participant conformity to formal rules. All of these studies documented the power of informal, nonrational processes to fundamentally shape the formal structures of organizations. In my opinion, these studies were important precursors of the Type 4 social models now being developed, but they were temporarily overwhelmed in the late 1950s by the resurgence of a new wave of rational system models.

Rational Models—Type 3

Like its intellectual ancestor, this newer version of organizations as rational systems presumed that organizational systems are designed to foster the rational pursuit of predetermined objectives. But there are significant differences between the research approach of these newer rationalist theorists and their predecessors. Rather than being content to describe or prescribe organizational forms, the second generation of rational system theorists set out to explain differences among organizations in formal structure. Their methodology was comparative, and for the first time the units of analysis were the organizations themselves rather than the individuals or the subgroups within them. Formal structure was viewed as the dependent variable—its characteristics to be measured and explained.

Although a few studies have examined the impact on an organization's structure of more general features of their social context (for example, Udy, 1959b; Pugh and others, 1968), most have concentrated attention on size, technology and uncertainty as the major factors accounting for structural variation (Woodward, 1965; Perrow, 1967; Thompson, 1967; Blau and Schoenherr, 1971). I have attempted to summarize some of these studies and their principal findings elsewhere (Scott, 1975) and will not replicate that effort here. What requires emphasis in the present discussion is the extent to which these theorists have clung to a rational model in their theoretical explanation of structure. Among these analysts, Thompson was the most explicit about this theoretical underpinning, prefacing all his predictions with the phrase, "under norms of rationality," but he was not alone in presuming that in organizations forces are present that act to maximize effectiveness and efficiency. Thus, in generating his predictions relating technology and structures, Perrow (1970, p. 80) observes, "We must assume here that, in the interest of efficiency, organizations wittingly or unwittingly attempt to maximize the congruence between their technology and their structure." And Blau "explains" such processes as structural differentiation and the growth of administration by positing their contribution to organizational effectiveness, as follows: "Formal organizations cope with the difficult problems large-scale operations create by subdividing responsibilities in numerous ways and thereby facilitating the work of any operating employee, manager, and subunit in the organization" (1970, p. 203). And, further, he says that administrative growth accompanies structural differentiation "because the intensified problems of coordination and communication in differentiated structures demand administrative attention" (p. 213). It is interesting to note that these assumptions are not in keeping with other facets of the work of these theorists—all three have constantly called attention to the nonrational features of organizations. In seeking a theoretical basis for the explanation of the formal structural features of organizations, however, they embraced a rational model.

Social Models—Type 4

As indicated at the outset of these comments, it now appears that social models are staging a comeback. However, as with the neorationalist models, the second generation of social models exhibit features that distinguish them from earlier versions. Not only have Type 4 social model theorists embraced the comparative methodology of the newer generation of rational system theorists, in which multiple organizations are studied, with each organization constituting a single case for analytic purposes,* but for the first time they are applying these models to the explanation of *formal* structures. This may be illustrated by the five chapters in the first section of this book.

The chapter by Ouchi and Jaeger is perhaps most similar in theoretical stance to the Type 2 social models, especially the work of Mayo (1945). Indeed, this chapter even takes on some of the prescriptive tone of these earlier writings. What distinguishes it from the earlier social models is its emphasis on formal structure— Types J and Z are structural systems as full and complete as is Type A, the conventional rational model—and its use of methods in which organizations are the units for comparison. Also, unlike the earlier models proposed by such social theorists as McGregor (1960), Ouchi and Jaeger's work embraces the contingency perspective by assuming that which structures are better depends on what the organization is attempting to do and the sociocultural conditions under which the attempt is being made.

Pfeffer's chapter provides a strong illustration of those features that distinguish current from earlier social models. The focus is on organizational structure, the approach is comparative, and the determinants of structure are sought for not in the rational plans of managers but in the political struggles among coalitions of participants. This perspective is indebted to the earlier work of Cyert and March (1963), who first argued that goal setting in organizations could usefully be conceived as the outcome of a bar-

---

*However, some analysts, such as Weick (1976) and March and Olsen (1976), are calling anew for more in-depth case studies of actual decision making and behavior and more "deep descriptions" of the context and meaning of organizational activities.

gaining process among shifting groups of dominant coalitions within organizations, and to the model proposed by Hickson and his associates (1971) accounting for the differential power of organizational actors in terms of their ability to cope effectively with contingencies in the organization's environment. In Chapter Two, Pfeffer succinctly concludes that "organizational structures are the outcomes of political contests within organizations."

The chapters by M. Meyer and Brown and by Hannan and Freeman place great emphasis on the impact of environmental factors on organizational structure. This emphasis does not distinguish them from the second group of rational system theorists, who also focus on external influences or organizational form. The distinction comes from the types of environmental factors selected for attention by the two groups of theorists and from the nature of the arguments used relating environmental variables to organizational forms. M. Meyer and Brown focus on the impact of specific circumstances present at the origin of or during the development of the structures under study. In this approach, they are following up on the insights of Stinchcombe (1965), who first noted an association between the date of an organization's founding and its structural characteristics. Taking as their subject the structure of finance departments in local governmental agencies, M. Meyer and Brown embrace a historical approach, noting the effect of civil service regulations on the development of rules and other indices of bureaucratization within these departments.

Hannan and Freeman propose the applicability of a population ecology model to explain variations in organizational structure. In so doing, they emphasize the nonadaptability of organizational structure. If organizations are the tools of action, as is claimed by rational system theorists, they side with social system theorists such as Selznick (1949) in emphasizing the "recalcitrance of the tools of action." Rather than a model in which managers design and modify organization structures in search of better performance, they posit a system in which environments select those structures best suited for survival.

In many respects, the arguments developed by J. Meyer and Rowan based on their observations of educational organizations raise the most general challenge to rational system models. They argue that in many organizations the formal structure is a "myth" having little or no connection to the actual behavior of organizational participants. This is not to say, however, that these myths, with their accompanying rituals and ceremonies, are unimportant to the survival of these organizations. Rather, when cultures place great emphasis on the importance of rational plans and structures, organizations will create "rational" structures in order to gain legitimacy and to acquire support from their environment. In previous social models, social arguments have been used to explain departures from the rational system models; in J. Meyer and Rowan's system, not only the departures but the rational system models themselves are given a social model interpretation.

Also, in common with March and Olsen (1976) and Weick (1976), Meyer and Rowan raise the question as to just how tightly connected the various structural units and levels of organizations are. Many contemporary organizations appear to consist of quite loosely coupled segments—so much so that March and his colleagues refer to them as "organized anarchies"—capable of relatively independent actions and subject to varying environmental constraints. This conception not only challenges the rational system conception of structure but also raises the issue as to how meaningful the organization is as a unit of analysis, a problem pursued by Freeman at the conclusion of this book.

The five chapters to follow differ in many respects, as the reader will discover without assistance. They do, however, appear to me to reflect a turning away from the narrower, more technocratic explanations for organization structure that dominated the scene during the decade of the 1960s to a broader, richer, and sociologically more interesting set of models. It is probably premature to declare, with Reich (1970), the dawning of Consciousness III, but there do appear to be distinct signs at the present time of the (re)greening of organization theory.

W. Richard Scott

2

The Micropolitics
of Organizations

Jeffrey Pfeffer

Research on organizational structure and writing on the related topic of organizational design has, almost without exception, been normative either in intent or in the source of theoretical hypotheses. While the use of normative models for guiding thinking and research has been found to be useful in economics (see Friedman, 1953), there is growing evidence that the models most used in studying organizational structures—variants of structural contingency theories—are not successful in consistently accounting for variation in either structures or performance. Moreover, by implicitly adopting a managerial or ownership perspective concerning the goals of the organization, such an approach tends to completely neglect one of the most important issues determining organizational structures and activities—the conflict in preferences among organizational participants and the resulting contest for control over the organization.

In this chapter, I want to examine three aspects of the study of organizational structures. First I shall briefly review the various theories of structure and design, noting how they all assume an organizational objective or set of goals, most often from a managerial or ownership point of view. Not only is this a limited perspective on organizations, but there is also increasing evidence that this perspective has only limited scientific utility. Second, I shall articulate an alternative perspective on organizational structure, proceeding from the conceptualization of organizations as political coalitions in which the question becomes not only how is the organization doing but also who is benefiting and who is losing from the organization's activities. Finally, I shall explore in a few examples some possible advantages provided by this latter perspective in analyzing structure as observed in organizations.

Normative Theories of Structure

Virtually all writing about organizational structure proceeds from a normative orientation, and this orientation takes as given or implicit the goals of the top organizational administrators or owners. Even those theories of structure not specifically directly concerned with performance assume certain performance goals from which to derive their theoretical propositions.

One of the dominant brands of theory currently used to explain organizational structure is structural contingency theory. Briefly, this theory argues that there is no single best way to organize. Rather, the appropriate organizational structure depends on the contingencies confronting the organization. These contingencies variously include the technology used by the organization, the environment in which the organization operates, the tasks performed, and the organization's size. Structure, in other words, depends on the specific circumstances the organization faces. In studies of organizational structure, predictions derived from structural contingency theory seldom account for most of the variation in observed structures, and this leads to the second part of structural contingency theory. Organizations deviate more or less from appropriate structures, and the second part of structural contingency theory, the consonance hypothesis, states that those organizations that deviate less from the optimal structure will be more effective. Effectiveness has most often been defined in terms of profits or ratings by others of the organization's performance. Structural contingency theory, then, not only posits lawful relationships between the various contingencies and structure but further hypothesizes a relationship between structure-contingency matching and performance.

The structural contingency approach has been articulated in the classic literature on organizational structure. Woodward (1965) argued that structure depended on the production technology and found support for the consonance hypothesis. Lawrence and Lorsch (1967) measured structure in terms of differentiation and integration and found that structure depended on the certainty of the organization's environment. Lawrence and Lorsch also found support for the consonance hypothesis. Duncan (1972), too, argued that structure was determined by environmental uncertainty, a position that had been articulated earlier by Burns and Stalker (1961) and Dill (1958). While not all research proceeding from this orientation has tested the consonance hypothesis, such research is still clearly within the structural contingency framework, arguing that appropriate organizational structures depend on the environment, technology, task, or size of the organization.

Structural contingency theory has been largely silent about the mechanisms that might create the fit between structure and the various presumed determinants of structure. Two possible mechanisms creating structure-contingency matching are (1) managerial adaptation to obtain higher levels of organizational performance and (2) natural selection in which those organizations with appropriate structures tend to survive. The managerial adaptation perspective is implicit in most of the existing literature. If appropriate structures enhance organizational performance, then surely managers will alter structures so that they fit the organization's contingencies. Such a perspective implicitly assumes that those designing structures are interested in enhancing organizational performance, and this further presumes that performance can be assessed, that there is reasonable agreement on the dimensions used in the assessment, and that there is either goal congruence in the organization or enough formal authority to ensure that the selected objectives are pursued. In such cases where these conditions do not hold, the adaptation mechanism is not likely to work to produce the structure-contingency matching hypothesized by the theory.

For a selection mechanism to work, it is necessary that there be failures or mortality in the organizational population and, further, that the selection mechanism select for appropriate structure-environment matching. Such a selection mechanism is likely to be observed in conditions of perfect competition, further assuming the validity of the consonance hypothesis. Under conditions of perfect competition, firms with appropriate structures will outperform those without appropriate structures, thereby attracting more resources and surviving at the expense of those performing less well. While there might be other selection rules that would also tend to favor the structure-contingency matching organizations, the literature seems to imply that performance is the critical dimension that causes appropriate structures to emerge, either through managerial adaptation or through selection.

Structural contingency theory is currently a widely accepted perspective, in spite of numerous serious theoretical and empirical problems. Not the least of these problems is the inconsistent evidence obtained in tests of the theory. Mohr (1971) found only weak support for Woodward's (1965) technology-structure hypotheses and found no support at all for the consonance hypothesis. Pennings (1975), in a study of forty stock brokerage offices, found little evidence for the ability of structural contingency theory to explain observed structure and also found no support for the consonance hypothesis. Hickson, Pugh, and Pheysey (1969) could not replicate Woodward's findings on the importance of technology and concluded that technology affected structure only in smaller organizations or in those parts of the organization directly connected to the technology and the work flow. Of course, the tests of structural contingency theory have problems themselves. Mohr (1971) examined public health agencies and found no clear evidence that there is either enough pressure for performance or selection occurring to provide mechanisms leading to the structure-contingency match. Pennings' study used forty branch offices of a single brokerage firm, which means that there may not have been enough structural variation or variation in contingencies to provide a fair test of the theory. Nonetheless, the evidence for the validity of structural contingency theory is, at this point, equivocal.

There are other problems with structural contingency theory beside inconsistent data. To state that structure is contingent begs the question, "Contingent on what?" There are about as many answers to this question as there are researchers. Some have focused on the importance of technology for determining structure (Woodward, 1965; Perrow, 1967), while others have focused on the importance of the environment (Lawrence and Lorsch, 1967; Burns and Stalker, 1961; Duncan, 1972). Still others have examined the relationship between task routineness and structure (Hage and Aiken, 1969), and the effects of size have also been explored (Hall, Haas, and Johnson, 1967; Blau, 1970). Technology has been conceptualized in terms of the variability and analyzability of the task (Perrow, 1967) and as the degree of mechanization and specialization of the production technology (Woodward, 1965), with process production being the most specialized and prototype production being the most flexible. Uncertainty has been conceptualized and measured in a variety of ways. Tosi, Aldag, and Storey (1973) found that Lawrence and Lorsch's uncertainty scales were not statistically reliable and, furthermore, were not correlated with various measures of firm and industry volatility. Downey, Hellriegel, and Slocum (1975) replicated Tosi's (Tosi, Aldag, and Storey, 1973) finding of low reliability for the Lawrence and Lorsch (1967) uncertainty measures and further demonstrated similar problems with Duncan's (1972) uncertainty scale. The two scales showed small intercorrelations and disappointingly small relationships with various criterion measures. Thus, not only has structural contingency theory faced a proliferation of dimensions and measures, but many of the measures themselves are not reliable and indicate little construct validity.

Furthermore, there has been a pronounced tendency to examine the various determinants of structure one at a time, with one study examining technology, another the environment, and still another size. The possibility exists, however, that these various determinants affect structure in an interactive, rather than an additive, fashion. This possibility is consistent with the data reported in a study of thirty-seven small manufacturing firms in Illinois (Pfeffer and Leblebici, 1973). In that study, the competitiveness of the environment was hypothesized to produce a demand for increased control and centralization. While change in product design and the production process and the number of products were expected to be associated with increased decentralization and differentiation, such effects were found only for those firms operating in less competitive environments. In the case of firms operating under more competitive circumstances, the resultant demand for control neutralized the effect of product diversity and change. The possibility of interactive structural effects has been explicitly recognized elsewhere as well, even though it has seldom been empirically investigated. For instance, Blau, Heydebrand, and Stauffer (1966, p. 180) wrote, "The complex interdependencies he (Weber) traces clearly imply that the relationships between any two characteristics of bureaucracies often depend on and are modified by a third factor or even by a combination of several others." The possibilities that the contingencies on which structure is presumed to depend interact and that the dimensions of structure themselves interact are both ideas that have received short shrift in the extant literature.

Perhaps the most important theoretical failing in structural contingency theory is that, like other theories of structure discussed hereafter, the theory presumes a goal of high organizational performance along dimensions presumed to devolve from ownership or managerial interests and, further, that structures adapt or evolve in response to these performance pressures (Child, 1972b). Structural contingency theory apparently presumes the existence of defined, consistent, agreed-on goals (or a situation in which compliance with such goals can be obtained, as through the purchase of labor power) and also the existence of either environmental or managerial forces tending to cause or select actions increasing performance. While this is one perspective on organizations, there are clearly others worthy of exploration, particularly coalitional (Cyert and March, 1963) and even more random (Cohen, March, and Olsen, 1972) models of organizations.

While sociological theories of organizational structure, such as those proposed by Blau (1970) and Thompson (1967) do not always explicitly mention performance or effectiveness, such theories tend to share implicit managerial assumptions with structural contingency theory in their development of hypotheses. Blau's studies of the effects of size on differentiation, the size of the administrative component, and the interrelationship of structural elements proceeded from requirements of organizational control necessary for effective performance. Blau, Heydebrand, and Stauffer (1966) explicitly treated costs and later the relative size of the administrative component (Blau and Schoenherr, 1971). Managerial control for performance is the glue that holds much of the theoretical reasoning together. Blau's theory is functionalism, functionalism serving organizational performance as defined by managers or top administrators. For instance, Blau, Heydebrand, and Stauffer (1966, p. 191) concluded their study of 150 public personnel agencies with the following comment: "The general conclusion suggested by the analysis is that the complex interrelations and higher-order interactions observed in the organizational structure are more likely to be functionally adapted by feedback than the separate attributes themselves . . . the complex, higher-order relationships among elements in the structure have been adapted by feedback to minimize dysfunctions."

Thompson was quite explicit about the development of structure in response to performance requirements. His numerous propositions were prefaced with the condition "under norms of rationality." Of course, rational action is only defined with respect to some goal or set of preferences. While Thompson occasionally noted that the interests of the power holders may include things other than performance, including maintaining themselves in power, his specific propositions dealing with structure assumed a performance objective. He argued, for instance, that structures develop to minimize coordination costs (Thompson, 1967, Chap. 5), with reciprocally interdependent positions grouped together first. In discussing the effect of the environment on structure, Thompson (1967, Chap. 6) argued that differentiation and decentralization arose as organizations needed to cope with heterogeneous and changing environments. Coping was being able to respond to ensure effective organizational performance under the varying environmental conditions.

It seems fair to state that prevalent theories of organizational structure ignore the question of the definition of success or effectiveness. Goals are taken for granted or assumed, and then studies proceed to derive propositions using these goals. Such an approach nowhere raises, let alone seriously examines, the question of whose interests, whose goals, and whose preferences are to prevail in organizations. If we take seriously the conceptualization of organizations as coalitions (March, 1962), then a critical issue is not just what the consequences of various structural arrangements are, but who gains and who loses from such consequences. Structure, it would appear, is not just the outcome of a managerial process in which designs are selected to ensure higher profit. Structure, rather, is itself the outcome of a process in which conflicting interests are mediated so that decisions emerge as to what criteria the organization will seek to satisfy. Organizational structures can be viewed as the outcome of a contest for control and influence occurring within organizations. Organizational structural arrangements are as likely to be the outcomes of political processes as are organizational resource allocation decisions (Pfeffer and Salancik, 1974).

One notable example of a study of structure adopting a political perspective is the examination of the size of the administrative component in school districts facing growing and declining enrollments (Freeman and Hannan, 1975). The authors argue that, in school districts with declining enrollments, the administrators would be less willing to terminate themselves or their staffs. They predict a larger effect of enrollment on administrators in the case of expanding districts, when teachers and administrators were being added, than in districts in which enrollment was declining. This was the result observed. In this instance, the source for the hypothesis is a framework emphasizing control and influence; Freeman and Hannan did not couch their argument in terms of the effects on performance of adding or terminating administrators in growing or shrinking districts.

A Political Perspective on Organizational Design

In many organizations, there are conflicts about preferences and desired courses of action. Such conflicts can arise either because there are differences in the basic preferences of organizational participants or, when preferences are shared, because there are differences in beliefs about what actions are most likely to achieve the various goals. Differences in preferences and in beliefs about the consequences of various actions can arise from different socialization and training prior to joining the organization, from the development of subunit identification and loyalty after joining the organization (March and Simon, 1958), from differences in information, and from being imbedded in different social networks both on and off the job. Almost any differentiation of function within an organization will promote some differences in orientation and perspective (Lawrence and Lorsch, 1967), and, furthermore, unless the organization attempts to recruit from a homogeneous external source it is likely to import many differences. It is fair to state that in many organizations agreement about preferences and technologies for achieving those preferences is the exception rather than the rule.

Organizations typically control resources, including labor power, and, thus, they themselves are resources that various interests would like to use (Perrow, 1972). As Perrow aptly noted, one of the functions of bureaucratic organizational structure is to ensure that individuals will not attempt to use the organization to further their own interests but rather will be controlled and managed so as to work for the organization's purposes. Needless to say, such control is only imperfectly achieved, particularly when there is legitimate disagreement concerning what the organization's purposes are and how they should be achieved.

Organizations, in this perspective, are not rational decision-making mechanisms but rather are arenas in which various persons and groups participate. Such participation is more often predicated on achieving something from the organization, either directly, as in the case of wages, or indirectly, as with the ability to control the organization's activities to advance some participants' interests. Many different interests participate, and not all are actively involved in all aspects of the organization or its decisions. Organizations are loosely coupled (Weick, 1976), in part because few participants are constantly involved or care about every dimension of the organization's operations. Cyert and March's (1963) conceptualization of organizations as coalitions is the one we are employing. As Cyert and March note, conflict need not be perfectly resolved but can be ignored, and, through the variety of possible policies, different coalition members can be induced to remain in the coalition.

Participants in the organization are likely to be interested in taking actions and making decisions that tend to favor their interests and their objectives. If every participant in the organization has similar beliefs and preferences or if there is an extraordinarily high degree of trust, such that participants assume that each is acting in each other's interests, then there need be little concern with issues of control and governance. In the likely event that such conditions are not realized, then there is concern with the distribution of influence in the organization. Each group seeks not only power but also the direct ability to affect organizational actions as it desires. Such ability is in part created through the organization's structure.

The design of an organization, its structure, is first and foremost the system of control and authority by which the organization is governed. In the organizational structure, decision discretion is allocated to various positions and the distribution of formal authority is established. Furthermore, by establishing the pattern of prescribed communication and reporting requirements, the structure provides some participants with more and better information and more central locations in the communication network. As Pettigrew (1973) found in his study of the decision to purchase a computer, the control of information is a potent source of power. Thus, organizational structures create formal power and authority by designating certain persons to do certain tasks and make certain decisions and create informal power through the effect on information and communication structures within the organization. Organizational structure is a picture of the governance of the organization and a determinant of who controls and decides organizational activities.

This argument, at once obvious, makes it apparent why organizational structures are the outcomes of political contests within organizations. Given the various participants interested in controlling the organization, the fact that their preferences and beliefs conflict so that they cannot completely trust one another, and the importance of structure to control, it is clear that the participants will contend over the allocation of discretion and resources and the control of information in organizations as they attempt to gain more influence within the organization.

The preceding reasoning implies that a theory of organizational structure should consist of the following elements: (1) the relationship between structural dimensions and the control of organizational activities, (2) the determinants of power and influence of various subunits and groups involved in the organization, and (3) the link between the power of various interests and the structural outcomes that maintain or assure their effective control over organizational activities. There is a reasonable empirical literature dealing with the determinants of power within organizations, but the literature addressing the other two points is much less adequate. We can consider each of the three elements of a theory of organizational design in turn, to see what is known and what such a theory might look like.

Structure and Organizational Control. Structure has as its basis the control of behavior. In order for coordinated action to occur among interdependent positions, it is necessary for the behavior of the various position occupants to be predictable, so that the integration of the interdependent activities becomes possible. Weber's (1946) theory of bureaucracy is an attempt to describe some principles by which persons can be convinced to perform according to the role prescriptions they are given and to act in the organization's interests rather than for themselves. This control of behavior is, after all, the reason for rules and formalized procedures, for having rewards based on organizationally relevant performance, for having careers in the work organization, for treating clients and customers equally. There has been concern with the dysfunctional consequences of behavior control, including the possibilities that overly conservative, conforming persons may result (Merton, 1940); that personal growth and adjustment may be harmed (Argyris, 1957); and that organizational effectiveness may be diminished, compared with situations in which control is more widely shared (Tannenbaum, 1968). There has been concern with the use of impersonal mechanisms of control (Blau and Scott, 1962), with the use of output versus activity control, or the control of outcome versus process (Ouchi and Maguire, 1975), and particularly with the issue of centralization of control. Decision participation has been a recommended strategy for obtaining commitment and compliance with decisions since the original Harwood study (Coch and French, 1948), with its effectiveness widely debated (Lowin, 1968).

What is strangely missing in all this literature is an assessment of the effectiveness of various types of control on specific activities. This is to be distinguished from studies assessing the effects of various controls on aggregate effectiveness measures. Rather, we are talking about the assessment of the extent to which, and under what circumstances, rules actually control behavior, decision centralization actually increases the effective control of higher-level participants, and so forth. There are, of course, differences between the formal system of controls and the actual effects on activities. Most universities, for example, have rules about professors missing classes, particularly to engage in consulting. Yet such behavior does occur. Rule interpretation, obedience, and enforcement are all problematic in actual social settings. Similarly, decision centralization requires that the person in authority have the time, the ability, and most importantly, the information necessary to make the decision and see that it is implemented. There is surprisingly little systematic attention paid to the question "If a given organizational member wants someone else to take some specific action, what is the best way to ensure that the person takes the desired action?"

The answer to the question just posed is far from obvious. There is evidence that, at least in educational organizations, rules may be used not to control behavior *within* the organization but rather to make the organization appear legitimate and acceptable to the *external* constituencies (J. Meyer and Rowan, Chapter Four). In fact, in elementary school systems, there is apparently little empirical evidence for very much control at all (J. Meyer and Rowan, 1975), at least as far as that control is relevant to the teaching activity. There are examples of high-level administrators, apparently with decision-making discretion, who are captives of their staffs or who are unobtrusively controlled by those who furnish the information on which the decisions are based. In other words, both formal rules and formal position may not be the most critical variables affecting control over organizational activities.

Pettigrew's (1973) description of a decision made by a British company to purchase a specific computer indicates the importance of information control. The department head, Kenney, was able to influence the decision taken by the board of directors, the group with the formal authority to make the decision, by systematically filtering the information from both the computer manufacturers and his own personnel. Indeed, because of Kenney's position as a gatekeeper for information, opposition to his position within his own group never was visible to the board as a whole. In this specific instance, it is reasonable to state that information control gave Kenney as much effective control over this specific organizational action as if the power to make the decision had been formally delegated to him as part of a program of decentralization.

It is likely that the relationship between structure and control is most productively examined in terms of information and the distribution of communication within social structures. Information is, after all, a prerequisite for control. For control to be exercised, one must know both what specifically is the desired action and be able to monitor whether or not the action or the desired outcome is accomplished. In the context of analyzing information flows, of course, the formal structure does not determine everything. Particularly in the case of informal communication, there may be an informal structure, involving information sharing, that is quite different from the formally designated system. However, even such informal structures are amenable to design. Communication is affected by physical distance and contact, among other things, and this can be designed into the facilities layout. Communication can be enhanced by developing perceptions of similarity and attraction, and this can be formally encouraged through socialization and the dissemination of favorable information.

It is possible that the formal rules and procedures and even, to some extent, the formal organizational structure serve more as a legitimation of the organization's activities, buttressed by mythologies concerning the need for various rules and allocations of discretion, than they serve to represent the actual pattern of control in organizations. In fact, there may be advantages in having the actual control structure fairly well hidden. Not knowing the actual sources of control in the organization makes influence attempts difficult to mount and thereby insulates those with control and enables them to maintain their discretion. It is clear that a theory of the acquisition and use of power and discretion in organizations is required in order to assess the effects of various structural arrangements on control. Such a theory is to be found currently primarily in case studies of how decisions are made and organizations operate (Cyert, Simon, and Trow, 1956; Baldridge, 1971; Pettigrew, 1973).

Determinants of Power and Influence. The second part of a theory of organizational structure from a political perspective is the determinants of political power within the organization. This part of the theory is, at present, the easiest to state and support with existing research. The strategic contingencies theory of intraorganizational power (Hickson and others, 1971) stated that power accrued to an organizational subunit to the extent the organization could cope with organizational uncertainty, that such coping capacity could not be obtained readily elsewhere, and that the uncertainty being handled was important and pervasive in the organization. This theory follows a line of thought from Crozier (1964), Thompson (1967), and Perrow (1970), all of whom, in one form or another, posited the relationship between power and uncertainty or the organization's most critical function. Salancik and Pfeffer (1974) argued that subunit power was determined by the provision of the most critical resources. In a study of the power of departments in one graduate research-oriented university, they found that subunit power was predicted best by the amount of outside grant and contract money brought in, followed closely in importance by the size and prestige of the graduate program. Information is, of course, one kind of resource, so the two perspectives on power acquisition are complementary rather than in conflict.

Empirical support for the strategic contingencies theory was found by Hinings and his associates (1974) in a study of breweries in Canada. Salancik, Pfeffer, and Kelly (in press), examining the purchase of offset printing equipment in seventeen organizations, found that the determinants of influence varied depending on whether the decision context was a new purchase, an additional purchase, or a replacement purchase. These authors noted that their findings provided support for the strategic contingencies theory prediction that influence derived from coping with the most critical uncertainty. In the three decision contexts, the source of uncertainty and the coping required differed, as did the correlates of influence.

There are some important caveats to remember in spite of the empirical support found thus far for the various models of the determinants of intraorganizational power. The most critical uncertainty or the most important resource is not a given but is itself socially determined. After all, in the university study, the university might have defined students to be the most important resource rather than research funding and national prestige. The fact that the university was a research-oriented university was both an outcome of the power distribution as well as a determinant of what resources or performances brought power in the system. Similarly, the critical organizational uncertainties are defined by the organization. Indeed, it is the ability to institutionalize power and define critical resources and contingencies that leads to the fact that influence structures are typically more stable than the environments in which the organizations exist. Thompson (1967) noted that it was in the interest of those in power to continue to define organizational problems as being within their competence and that it was not in their interest to announce loudly that the contingencies had changed and they were no longer as necessary. The Hickson (Hickson and others, 1971) and Salancik and Pfeffer (1974) hypotheses are probably correct but not complete descriptions of the process by which power is determined. What is missing is an assessment of how certain resources or uncertainties come to be viewed or defined as most critical or important.

A second problem with these studies is that the process of power acquisition is omitted. Both analyses are unduly static and deterministic—the power accrues to the subunit coping with the most critical contingency or to the one supplying the most important resources. Clearly, there must be some residual variance to be explained by the political skills of the various subunit leaders. Knowledge of subunit power distributions (Pettigrew, 1973) or skill in presenting the subunit's case can, at the margin, probably affect subunit power.

Third, the literature on determinants of power in organizations has concerned itself primarily with the determinants of power variations among subunits on the same horizontal level in the organization. Thus, comparisons are made between functional departments in business firms (Hinings and others, 1974) or between academic departments in universities (Salancik and Pfeffer, 1974). A separate issue, however, would be the determinants of the vertical distribution of power and control or the extent to which control was centralized or decentralized throughout the organization. There is some evidence that task routineness is positively related to centralization (Hage and Aiken, 1969) and that size is negatively related to centralization (M. Meyer, 1972a; Child, 1973). Furthermore, Pfeffer and Leblebici (1973) argued that competition or external pressure led to centralization, an argument made in an experimental study by Hamblin (1958).

The three variables can all be summarized under the rubric of constraints on control. I posit that power would be as centralized vertically as possible, subject to constraints. One constraint, of course, is simply information-processing capacity. Thus, larger organizations with more persons to be coordinated and more decisions to be made would, of necessity, be less centralized. Devices that increased information processing, such as computers, would be expected to lead to centralization (Whisler, 1970). Another constraint is the demands for control made by organizational participants. Participants performing routine, repetitive tasks can presumably be readily replaced and hence cannot obtain much control. Persons performing more complex, nonroutine tasks presumably are more critical to the organization and less easily replaced, and hence they can obtain more control. In times of external threat, the chief administrators can use the threat as legitimation for centralizing control. And organizational participants are probably more willing to see their discretion limited to the ultimate benefit of the entire organization.

In the instance of vertical power, then, I suggest that the determinants of power are similar to those explaining subunit power. The control over critical resources, including knowledge and expertise, and the control of critical organizational uncertainties helps to predict the extent to which power is centralized or decentralized across organizational levels, with capacity considerations also playing an important role.

The Link Between Power and Structure. The third part of a political theory of organizational structure must treat the link between power in the organization and the structural arrangements that permit that power to be used to affect organizational activities. Here again the existing literature is relatively scant. However, the evidence on administrator succession is somewhat relevant. Zald (1965) argued that administrator succession was the outcome of a political process in organizations. Once installed, of course, the chief administrator has additional power to obtain the activities desired and to guide the course of the organization. This is not to say that such discretion is unconstrained—it merely says that occupying the chief administrator position probably provides some additional structural resources for exercising control.

Thompson (1967) has argued that organizations choose administrators in part to solve currently pressing contingencies. Some support for this position was found by Pfeffer and Salancik (1977) in a study of the tenure and characteristics of chief administrators of fifty-seven hospitals. The characteristics of administrators could, in part, be explained by the hospital's ownership and funding context, while tenure could be explained in part by the competitive circumstances confronting the hospital. While the theoretical argument posited a link between context and power and then between power and administrator succession, only the context-succession relationship was actually examined.

Administrator succession may be one important outcome of power, but there are other, more structural outcomes as well. Shifts in the control over information systems, shifts in control over resources, and the gaining and losing of discretion may be observed structural consequences of changes in the distribution of influence within organizations. At the same time, such structural changes help to determine the future distribution of control within the organization. For it is the case that structure is at once both an outcome of the influence distribution and a determinant of power within the organization.

As an example, consider the changing structures of universities. While there is some variation in the course of such changes, the general tendency has been to add levels in the administrative hierarchy, administrative staff, and elaborate information systems servicing the various administrative positions. Such changes seem to have devolved from the increasing power of administrators, which has resulted from increasing external pressures, including government pressures for equal employment and financial pressures. As predicted by Hamblin (1958) and Pfeffer and Leblebici (1973), external crisis has led to a centralization of power within the organization. This centralization of control in turn has produced changes that have provided administrators with both more formal discretion and more information control. And, in turn, such new administrative systems permit the centralization of control and power to be effected.

Using a Political Perspective in Analyzing Structures

The usefulness of a theoretical perspective can be illustrated best by examining what new variables are highlighted and how previously reported data can be examined from the new position. The final theme in this chapter, then, is some possible insights gained from the political perspective on organizational structures.

Concentration of Control. If structure is the mechanism for control, the representation of control, and the mainfestation of organizational power and influence, then it is logical to presume that structure will differ depending on the distribution and particularly the concentration of power in the organization. The concentration of control has seldom been investigated as a determinant of organizational structure; yet the argument developed here would indicate it might be an important determinant of structural dimensions.

In economics, the concentration of ownership interests and its implications for the control and activities of the corporation has been of continuing interest. Recently, McEachern (1975) argued that there were three control types of organizations: (1) organizations controlled and managed by the owners, (2) those with concentrated ownership interests but managed by others, and (3) those managed by others in which there was widely diffused ownership. In a series of sophisticated empirical analyses, McEachern demonstrated differences in performance across the types of organizations and, of even greater interest, found differences in tenure for chief executives. Executives in either owner-controlled and managed or manager-controlled firms had longer tenure than managers in externally controlled firms. If the concentration of ownership has been found to affect organizational risk-return choices and executive tenure, it might be expected to affect organizational structures as well.

Specifically, concentration of ownership should permit a concentration of control in the organization manifested by (1) fewer outside directors, (2) increased centralization, (3) reduced differentiation that renders coordination and control more difficult (Hall, 1972), (4) less information sharing and more concentration of information and communication, and (5) attempts to routinize activities to reduce the number of independent centers of power within the organization. Child (1973, p. 10) reported a statistically significant correlation between concentration of ownership and centralization ($r = .47, p < .001$) and a negative association with the perceived authority of high-level managers ($r = -.32, p < .05$). Both findings are consistent with the position, taken here and also taken by McEachern, that concentrated ownership tends to lead to centralized control and reduces the discretion of managers compared to the control of the external owners.

Ownership is, of course, only one indicator of concentration of control. Another might be the extent to which resources come from a few rather than many sources. Again, the prediction would be that concentration of control, in this case effected by concentration of resource control over the focal organization, would tend to appear as concentration of power within the organization's structure. In this context, it is not surprising that as resources in education have become concentrated in the hands of a relatively few federal and state bureaucracies, centralization and increasing bureaucratization have come to characterize educational organizations. Increasing concentration of resources leads to an increasing concentration of power, and this power becomes visible in increasingly centralized organizational structures.

Routinization and Task Specialization. The two variables of routinization and task specialization, commonly used in describing organizational structures, illustrate the advantages of using variables relating to power and influence. Routinization, the extent to which an individual does the same job repeatedly or the length of time required to learn the task, is likely to be related to power. French and Raven (1968) have identified expert power, and in Hickson's (Hickson and others, 1971) strategic contingencies theory the idea of substitutability is proposed as a determinant of power. It is easier to have expert power if one is doing a complex task that is novel, nonroutine, and takes time to learn. Similarly, substitutability is increased and power diminished if one performs a routine task. Therefore, task routineness is likely to be related to the power of the persons or subunits performing the task. The finding that task routineness is related to centralization (for example, see Hage and Aiken, 1969) is explainable from a political perspective. Persons performing nonroutine tasks possess more power and can therefore demand and obtain more control and discretion in the organization. Persons performing routine tasks however, are readily replaced, have little power, and therefore have less control and discretion. Instead of viewing discretion as something delegated to enhance performance, we can view discretion as something won from a position of power.

Task specialization, sometimes also called *organizational complexity*, presents a different picture. Specialization is complexly related to power. On the one hand, specialization, by creating smaller tasks for individuals, may lead to routineness and hence to a loss of power. It is obviously easier to find someone to turn three bolts on an assembly line than to find someone who can assemble an entire car. The latter person will have more power in the organization because of the scarcity of his or her skills and therefore will be subject, one might predict, to fewer rules and will have more discretion. On the other hand, specialization need not lead to task routineness; moreover, specialization may mean the organization has fewer persons available to perform a given task. When many people do many tasks, each can substitute for the others, but when each does a different task substitutability is reduced. Furthermore, a task can be subdivided without leaving the resulting components routine, as is well illustrated by the case of medical practice. While there is increasing specialization, there is not increasing routineness. Since specialization or complexity is not related in a simple fashion to power and influence, it is not surprising that various researchers have found different relationships between specialization and structure. What we are suggesting is that by approaching variables in terms of their effects on power better predictions may be obtained as to their effects on the resulting organizational structures.

Differentiation. Differentiation—the number of subunits or vertical levels in the organization as measured by Blau (1970) or the difference in subunit time orientation, goals, and structure as measured by Lawrence and Lorsch (1967)—has been a frequently studied structural attribute. Unfortunately, neither size nor environmental contingencies completely explain organizational creation of subunits, nor do either explain varying levels in hierarchies.

The case of subunit creation is, at times, a case of protest absorption as described by Leeds (1964) with respect to internal groups and by Thompson (1967, Chap. 6) for external groups. If a group makes claims on the organization, one way of handling the claims is to create a subunit to buffer the organization and at the same time provide the group making the demands with the feeling that something has been done, since a subunit has been created. The creation of affirmative action departments, consumer affairs departments, and public relations departments are all more obvious examples of this process at work.

Indeed, any time there is conflict in goals, preferences, or values within the organization, differentiation to create subunits that are within the organization but at the same time loosely coupled to each other so that conflict need not be resolved is a possible solution. The concept of differentiation as implied by Lawrence and Lorsch (1967) is consistent with this view. The difference between the position proposed here and their position is that, while Lawrence and Lorsch argued that differentiation arose from subunits facing different subenvironments and therefore requiring different appropriate structures for good performance, I argue that differentiation results from anything, including the environment, that produces an organizational coalition in which interests and preferences conflict.

I can also see why size might be related to differentiation, although for reasons having little to do with performance as customarily measured. It might be expected that as organizations

grow they confront more and more diverse external groups interested in their activities and that more diverse interests also come
to be represented within the organization. If differentiation is, in
part, a response to a divergence of interests, and if size is associated
with diversity of interests, then the relationship between size and
differentiation may be, in part, a consequence of the relationship
of both size and differentiation to conflict and interest-group
diversity.

Conclusion

Hannan and Freeman (1976) have recently argued that one
of the problems with the study of organizational effectiveness is
that the issue of multiple, conflicting, unspecified goals is difficult
to resolve. We would assert that much the same problem confronts
the study of organizational structure and organizational design.
We must ask, explicitly, the question, "Design for whom?" Descriptively, we may be able to better account for observed structural
variations if we proceed from the realization that structures are
part of the organization's governance system and a reflection of
the power and influence processes operating within the organization. Structures cannot be explained solely in terms of the relationship to performance or output. Particularly in cases where
goals are in conflict or the connections between actions and results
are unclear, the study of organizational structure must become a
study of organizational political processes—how conflicts in preferences and beliefs are solved and how these decisions are imbedded in the control system that is the organization's structure. The
explanation and analysis of organizational structure will be enhanced if we consider not only the efficiency, performance, and
managerial aspects of structure but the politics of organizational
structures as well.

3

The Process
of Bureaucratization

Marshall W. Meyer
M. Craig Brown

Max Weber's classic essay "Bureaucracy" (1946) delineates some of
the characteristics of modern organizations that distinguish them
from traditional forms of administration. These characteristics include division of labor, hierarchy of authority, written rules and
regulations, and the like. The surface attributes of bureaucracy
identified by Weber are not to be confused with its causes, however. In comparing traditional with bureaucratic means of administration, the latter based on belief in rational-legal authority, We-

This chapter was originally published in the *American Journal of Sociology*,
September 1977. The research was supported by National Science Foundation
grants GS-33509 and SOC 73-05688 (formerly GS-39637), which are gratefully
acknowledged. Also acknowledged are the assistance of Phillip Robinette and the
aid of Judith P. Meyer in retrieving various state civil service statutes. Comments on
earlier drafts of this chapter by Edna M. Bonacich, John H. Freeman, Michael T.
Hannan, John W. Meyer, Jeffrey Pfeffer, Arthur L. Stinchcombe, and Jonathan H.
Turner are also gratefully acknowledged.

ber was clearly suggesting that bureaucratization is but one aspect of the historical trend toward rationalization in the development of all institutional forms in modern societies. The substitution of authority based on rules for authority based arbitrarily on persons is central to the development of bureaucracy. Weber identifies other preconditions of bureaucratization, including a money economy, which allows calculability of results and widespread literacy. To this list, one might add such possible causes of bureaucratization as urbanization, mobility of resources, and religious beliefs permitting trust among strangers (see Stinchcombe, 1965). The relative importance of these causes of bureaucratization is perhaps of less significance than the fact that they are external to organizations and arise largely as a result of historical processes. Rational legal authority, cash economies, widespread literacy, and other conditions contributing to the development of bureaucratic forms are characteristics of whole societies that may change over time but that need not vary from organization to organization in a society at any one point.

Contemporary research on organizations has apparently overlooked this fact in seeking to explain characteristics of bureaucracies in terms of internal characteristics while ignoring the changes in the larger social and political environments that Weber thought central to the growth of modern organizations. The reasons for concentrating on internal organizational characteristics, as opposed to external, are not difficult to identify. Quantitative research studies can take into account tangible aspects of organizational structures—size, job titles, levels of supervision, spans of control, and the like—much more easily than the less quantifiable elements of the environment which, while amorphous, may be exceedingly important. The work of Blau (1970) and his colleagues (see also M. Meyer, 1972b) exemplifies the tendency to overlook qualitative elements of organizations in focusing almost exclusively on the implications of organizational size for structural differentiation and of differentiation for administrative overhead. What is disputed is not the accuracy of the results but their importance for understanding the development of bureaucratization. A theory that explains bureaucratic structures solely in terms of size runs afoul of the fact that large organizations existed well before bureaucratization became widespread (see, for example, Dibble, 1965). A second factor limiting the usefulness of most such studies is that they present data from one point only and thus overlook the possible effects of history. Current trends in research have precluded the possibility that the greatest variations occur over time and are due to environmental shifts affecting organizations of a given type almost uniformly. Given this inattention to qualitative historical aspects of organizational environments, it is not surprising that empirical research has not addressed the question Weber raised in his classic essay: How does one explain the development of large-scale, hierarchical, and rule-bound bureaucracies?

Only a partial answer can be attempted here. Our study is limited to a single set of organizations—city, county, and state finance agencies—and to a time span of six years. It concerns only causes and consequences of formalized personnel procedures, because the origins of these rules can be identified easily and because rules vary somewhat across the agencies studied. The results of this limited study are quite suggestive, however. They indicate that the extensiveness of formal procedures in bureaucracies is due in part to the historical era in which they were founded and in part to the subsequent effects of the environment. Formalization in turn gives rise to hierarchical differentiation and differentiation to delegation of decision-making authority. The effects of origins are shown to be results of openness to environment at the time of formation. In short, the process of bureaucratization begins with environmental pressures—in this case, the civil service movement—and proceeds by developing rules to accommodate these pressures, elaborating organizational structures consistent with the rules and delegating authority as necessitated by structure. The primacy of the environment as a determining factor of bureaucratization and the dependence of organizational structure on rules embodying external demands are emphasized here.

Although centrally concerned with the process of bureaucratization, this chapter touches on several other topics. Its method is necessarily intertwined with its substance. A key question to be considered is how history can be incorporated in organizational analysis. An understanding of history requires separating the effects of time of origin from the effects of changes in organizational environments that occurred in the past and could not be observed. Origins and environments are likely to have had opposite effects and to obscure each other, but estimates of the magnitude of the impact of each are important to understanding how bureaucratization or any other organizational process takes place over a lengthy period. The substantive findings developed in this chapter are also linked closely to the types of organizations studied, which are city, county, and state departments of finance, comptrollers' offices, and departments of administration, all of which are administrative units of local governments. Because they are government organizations, finance departments are bound by certain federal statues that do not affect the private sector so directly. These statutes are crucial environmental elements, and it is unlikely that they have affected private organizations similarly. Whether the process of bureaucratization is similar for public- and private-sector organizations cannot be determined until there is comparable research on the latter. In all likelihood, similar patterns of behavior hold for both public and private organizations, but their histories and relevant environments may be so different that they do not behave in the same way at any given point.

We shall proceed by first outlining the broad hypotheses to be tested in this study and the nature of the research undertaken. The discussion will then be turned to some federal and local regulations affecting personnel matters. A complete history of civil service legislation is not possible, but important developments in it can be noted. The next section develops a model showing why effects of origins and of the environment are often confounded in organizational research, and it suggests a procedure for distinguishing between them. This procedure is then applied to data on the formalization of personnel procedures in finance agencies. In the following section, we examine the relationship among formal personnel procedures, multitier hierarchies, and decision making. The last substantitve section returns to the question of the effects of origins on organizations by examining the formalization of personnel practices in a small number of agencies that reorganized completely during the interval between the two surveys reported here. The implications of the empirical results are discussed in the concluding section.

The data in this chapter are drawn from two surveys of city, county, and state finance agencies in the United States conducted in 1966 and 1972. The nature of the surveys is reported fully in earlier articles (see Chapter Eight; M. Meyer, 1975), and elaborating the study design seems unnecessary here. The present chapter reports data on some 215 agencies that existed continuously from 1966 to 1972 and on 14 others that changed their names and reorganized between the two surveys. A point made in the earlier studies bears repeating: The data analyzed here are drawn from these two points only. A third survey of finance agencies now underway will provide additional data that can be used to replicate the results reported here.

Civil Service and Formalization of the Personnel Process

The history of the civil service movement in the United States is complex, and only the highlights can be touched on here. But one pattern is unmistakable: There has been increasing federal intervention in local government personnel practices. Of the three most significant federal acts establishing merit procedures for appointment to public office in place of the spoils system, the first, the Pendleton Act of 1882, which created the U.S. Civil Service Commission, did not mention state or local government at all. State governments fell under the purview of the 1939 amendments to the Social Security Act, and both state and local governments were subject to provisions of the Intergovernmental Personnel Act of 1970. Each of these laws was aimed at removing politics from administration by requiring impersonal procedures for the selection and the advancement of employees. The provisions of these acts should be reviewed in some detail.

The first U.S. Civil Service Act was approved by Congress in 1882 and went into effect the next year. In addition to creating a three-person Civil Service Commission, it required the president, under the advice of the commission, to "provide suitable rules for carrying this act into effect . . . as nearly as the conditions of good administration will warrant, as follows: *first* . . . open, competitive examinations . . . *second* . . . selection according to grade from those graded highest . . . *fourth* . . . a period of probation before any ab-

solute appointment . . . *fifth* . . . no person in the public service is . . .
under any obligation to contribute to any political fund or to render any political service" (U.S. Congress, 1881–1883, pp. 403–
404). The essence of a merit system of appointment for civil servants, as opposed to the old-fashioned political spoils systems, lay
in the use of written examinations and the insulation of officials
from electoral politics, two of the characteristics Weber thought
common to modern bureaucracy.

Interestingly, the Pendleton Act was much more specific in
its provisions than later statutes imposing merit requirements on
state and local governments. The Social Security Act amendments
of 1939, for example, made repeated mention of "such methods
of administration (including, after January 1, 1940, methods relating to the establishment and maintenance of personnel standards on a merit basis . . .) as are found . . . to be necessary" (U.S.
Congress, 1939, p. 1360), but the amendments did not specify what
those merit personnel standards were. They did, however, direct
the states to use merit standards in administering old-age assistance, unemployment compensation, aid to dependent children,
and grants for the blind. The Intergovernmental Personnel Act of
1970 was aimed at extending merit standards to all government
units. It created an advisory council charged with determining,
among other things, "(1) The feasibility and desirability of extending merit policies and standards to additional federal-state grant-
in-aid programs; (2) the feasibility and desirability of extending
merit policies and standards to grant-in-aid programs of a federal-
local character; (3) appropriate standards for merit personnel ad-
ministation . . . [and] (4) the feasibility and desirability of financial and other incentives to encourage state and local governments
in the development of comprehensive systems of personnel administration based on merit principles" (U.S. Congress, 1970–1971, p.
1911). The 1970 act also provided for grants-in-aid to states and
local governments for the development of merit systems and the
training of employees. But, like the 1939 Social Security Act
amendments, the legislation did not specify the means to be used
in enforcing merit principles.[1]

A number of states followed the federal lead in removing
partisan pressures from civil servants. New York adopted a merit

system in 1883, and Massachusetts did so a year later. Other states lagged considerably. Article 24 of the California constitution, which established the state civil service, was not approved until 1934. As late as 1960, eighteen of the fifty states had extended civil service coverage only to employees in agencies receiving federal grants (Mitau, 1966, p. 154). Generally, permissive legislation allowing counties and municipalities to establish merit personnel systems for their employees was passed shortly after state civil service systems were enacted. New York State had a permissive statute for cities and counties in 1909; California cities in 1935 and counties in 1939 were authorized to enact their own merit systems. By 1960, thirty-nine of the forty largest cities in the United States and three quarters of all cities with populations over 10,000 had legal provisions for civil service systems of some sort. Whether these systems were equally effective in enforcing merit practices is another matter however. As Phillips (1960, p. 387) notes, "The record, of course, shows wide variation in merit system efficiency . . . merit systems of some cities are sorry exhibits of personnel administration."

Apart from federal legislation that affected civil service procedures, the movement to reform local administration that peaked in the early 1900s also gave impetus to the formalization of personnel procedures. Cities suffered recurrent fiscal crises throughout the last third of the nineteenth century, immigration swelled urban populations (hence the demand for reliable services), and political spoils were rampant. Among other innovations, the reformers demanded expertise in place of political reliability as the criterion for appointment. As Griffith (1974, p. 15) notes, one asset of the Progressive movement was the precepts of scientific management, which strengthened the demand for fundamental structural reform in local government. The Taylorites and the Progressives were not always the same people, but they aided each other in municipal affairs.

Despite the trend toward merit personnel standards at all levels of government, there are now some pressures in the opposite direction. Cities and counties have come to rely somewhat on temporary employees whose positions are exempted from normal civil service procedures. Salaries for those positions are often funded out of federal subventions, particularly the Emergency Employ-

ment Act (EEA) of 1971, which has since expired. At the time of
the 1972 survey, EEA grants were funding a number of positions
in finance departments. In addition, there has been recognition
that inflexible merit principles should not extend to policy-making
positions. The 1970 Model Public Personnel Administration Law
as well as the report of the Advisory Council on Intergovernmental
Personnel Policy took cognizance of this. An introductory comment to the 1970 Model Public Personnel Administration Law
stated that "In order for the spirit of a merit system to be realized,
it is essential that a majority of the positions in the public service
be classified. Conversely, it is equally important that certain positions be exempted from the provisions of this act. Key policy-
determining officials such as department heads and agency heads
must be acutely sensitive to the program objectives of the chief
elected official. As a result, those persons should serve at the plea-
sure of the chief executive rather than be under the provisions of
the merit system. The selection of key policy-determining officials
by the chief executive does not constitute spoils" (National Civil
Service League, 1970, p. 6). In this respect, the 1970 Model Law
is a substantial departure from earlier versions.

Several broad conclusions can be drawn from the brief review of civil service legislation in the United States. First, most state
and local governments have adopted merit personnel policies in
place of either patronage appointments or the spoils system. The
only exceptions to this pattern are the more frequent use of temporary employees and the removal of policy-making officials from
civil service protection. The historical trend toward the imposition
of merit personnel standards constitutes an important alteration
in the political environments of local government agencies. Second,
effective merit standards usually entail substitution of impersonal
procedures such as written job descriptions and fixed probationary
periods for personal and political criteria for appointment. In
other words, merit standards promote the formalization of the
personnel process. Third, despite the ascendancy of merit principles, their application has been somewhat uneven. For this reason,
an exact correspondence between federal legislation and the actions
of state and local governments cannot be expected. Instead, considerable variation remains, and the actual procedures adopted by

local agencies in conformity with requirements for merit personnel administration are themselves of interest. An important question is whether local government units have responded uniformly and fully to the demand for personnel standards consistent with merit principles or whether their personnel procedures have remained essentially unchanged over time. If the former, one would conclude that local government units are vulnerable to certain environmental pressures; if the latter, one would think them resistant to environments and hence bound by their origins. A fundamental sociological question is whether origins or environments dominate organizations. Only an approximate answer can be developed here. The research on finance agencies suggests, however, that both have substantial effects, even though environmental shifts may in the long run have greater impact than origins.

A Model of Effects of Origins and the Environment

A fundamental problem in assessing effects of origins and environment is the lack of complete data tracing organizations from their beginnings to the present. Usually data from only one point are available, and inferences about the effects of history or age are made on the basis of contemporary differences between organizations with diverse origins. Exactly this procedure is followed by Stinchcombe (1965) in his analysis of stability of organizational types over time. Stinchcombe found small but consistent effects of era of origin on some characteristics of the labor force in several industries. The correlation between age and labor force (or organizational) structure, he surmises, can be accounted for by "the postulate that economic and technical conditions determine the appropriate organizational form for a given organizational purpose and the postulate that certain kinds of organizations . . . could not be invented before the social structure was appropriate to them" (p. 160).

This approach to the effects of age on organizations has several limitations, and we shall seek to overcome them here. One problem is that organizations are portrayed as essentially unchanging. The possibility that substantial differences due to origins are reduced over time by the environment is not considered. The source of this difficulty can be seen quite easily in Figure 1, which displays values of a hypothetical index of bureaucratization (b) for three organizations at three points. Organization 1, which was founded in era 1, has index values of b_{11}, b_{12}, b_{13} at times 1, 2, and 3, respectively; for organization 3, only b_{33} is displayed, because it did not exist in eras 1 and 2. Ignoring organization 2 for the present, Figure 1 shows the effects of origins on the index to be $b_{33} - b_{11}$. The effect of time, which is in fact a surrogate for the environment, is $b_{13} - b_{11}$ for organization 1. There is no effect of time for organization 3, because it was only recently founded. Cross-sectional data do not permit separate estimates of effects of origins and of the environment as suggested by Figure 1. Instead, only the difference, $b_{33} - b_{13}$, can be estimated. But this difference corresponds exactly to the difference between effects of origins and of the environment, $(b_{33} - b_{11}) - (b_{13} - b_{11})$, thereby confounding the two hopelessly. Since environmental effects often diminish differences due to origins,[2] Stinchcombe's data in all likelihood underestimate both the effects of origins on organizations and the amount of change occurring over time.

		Era		
		1	2	3
	1	b_{11}	b_{12}	b_{13}
Organization	2	—	b_{22}	b_{23}
	3	—	—	b_{33}

Effects of origins $= b_{33} - b_{11}$

Effects of environment $= b_{13} - b_{11}$

Difference $= b_{33} - b_{13}$

Figure 1. Hypothetical Values of Bureaucratization (b) for Three Organizations Formed in Different Eras.

Another problem with Stinchcombe's approach to the effects of history on organizations is its inability to link specified historical changes to enduring properties of organizations. This derives from his use of census data that do not reveal organizational characteristics other than labor-force composition. The importance of history for organizations can be demonstrated best if certain organizational properties varying with time of origin can be linked to specific historical developments. Showing differences between old and new organizations does not limit possible explanations for observed effects of age, but both showing that old organizations differ from new ones in some respects but not others and specifying historical changes that correspond to these differences narrow the range of possible explanations considerably and hence give greater credence to the historical argument. Indeed, it may be that age does not affect organizations much in comparison with the impact of identifiable historical events.[3]

The data available from the study of finance agencies allow us to begin to distinguish effects of origin from those of the environment, although they do not permit precise estimates. They are sufficiently detailed to allow separation of organizational properties that should have been affected by historical changes from properties for which no such effects are anticipated. For 215 departments of finance, comptrollers' offices, and the like, we have information on the year in which they were founded, formalization of personnel procedures, and organizational structure for both 1966 and 1972. These agencies existed continuously over the six-year interval between the two studies; hence changes during this time cannot be due to origins. (The 14 departments that reorganized between 1966 and 1972 will be discussed later.) The finance agencies were classified according to the era of formation—nineteenth century, 1901–1939, and 1940 and later—so that the breaks between periods correspond closely to the dates of two major federal acts affecting personnel matters and the movement to reform city administration. It should also be noted that the third important piece of legislation—the 1970 Intergovernmental Personnel Act —became law in the interval between the 1966 and 1972 studies.

The appropriateness of finance agencies for the research undertaken here should be discussed, if only briefly. Two considerations should be kept in mind. First, whereas entire local governments as wholes would seem to be the natural unit of analysis in a study of effects of federal legislation and the reform movement, this approach would pose some difficulties. In particular, identifying a single time of formation of administration agencies employing civil servants would be impossible, because these agencies are typically founded and reorganized one at a time. One could of course find times during which reorganization of offices of elected officials occurred, but these offices are usually not affected by civil service laws, and reorganization of them does not necessarily generate reorganization of administrative agencies. Second, finance agencies are not atypical of administrative bureaus of local governments, and results concerning them may be treated as representative of local administrative agencies generally. Clearly it would be desirable to have information on other types of government bureaus for this study, but these data are not at hand.

The kinds of comparisons allowed by the study design are illustrated in Figure 2. Differences appearing within the columns displayed here occurred between 1966 and 1972 and may be due to environmental shifts, although we must consider the possibility that they are due to other factors. The differences appearing across the rows are, as we have shown, due to differences between organizations at the time of their formation, less subsequent effects of the environment. If there were environmental effects between 1966 and 1972, then in all likelihood much greater effects of the

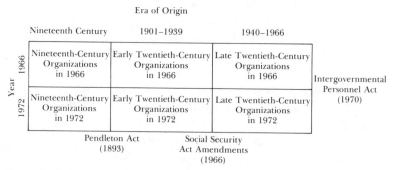

Figure 2. Study Design for Research on Finance Departments.

environment occurred between the late nineteenth century and 1966, because the interval was longer and the impact of the federal legislation probably greater.

Origins and Formalization in Finance Agencies

The information collected from finance agencies included extensive data describing procedures for hiring and evaluating personnel. We have information about whether entry-level employees are usually placed through civil service or equivalent uniform personnel codes; whether written regulations govern the criteria used in promotion decisions; the length of the probationary period, if any, for new employees; whether the department head is appointed or elected; and the number of employees covered by civil service or similar merit systems. Civil service coverage for employees, written promotion regulations, and a meaningful probationary period suggest merit personnel administration of the sort envisioned by federal and state civil service statutes. Their absence and the presence of an elected department head are indicative of the old-fashioned patronage or spoils system. These items were included in both the 1966 and 1972 surveys. In Table 1, they are cross tabulated by the era when a department was founded. The tabulations show effects of both era of formation and time of measurement, suggesting that the cross-sectional results in fact understate the true effects of origins. The tables should be reviewed in detail.

Section A of Table 1 displays percentages of departments where entry-level employees are placed through civil service or an equivalent personnel merit code. As shown, in 1966, 55 percent of nineteenth-century finance agencies, 71 percent of early twentieth-century agencies and 73 percent of those founded after 1940 hired newcomers through civil service. By 1972, these percentages had increased to 65, 72, and 84, respectively. Overall, the proportion of finance agencies placing entry-level employees through civil service increased by about 6 percent between 1966 and 1972. And in both 1966 and 1972, approximately 18 percent more of post-1940 than of nineteenth-century agencies had such

**Table 1. Measures of Formalization in 1966 and 1972 by Era
When Departments Were Founded.**

	Pre–1900	Era 1900–1939	Post–1940
	A. *Percentage of Departments Where Entry-Level Employees Are Placed Through Civil Service or Equivalent Uniform Personnel Code (EMPLACE)*		
1966	55	71	73
	(49)	(72)	(90)
1972	65	72	84
	(49)	(72)	(90)
	B. *Percentage of Departments Where Written Regulations Govern Promotion Criteria (PROMO)*		
1966	49	68	67
	(49)	(71)	(90)
1972	59	72	73
	(49)	(72)	(90)
	C. *Percentage of Departments Where Probationary Period Is Six Months or Longer (PROBAT)*		
1966	65	72	88
	(49)	(69)	(89)
1972	69	75	89
	(49)	(71)	(90)
	D. *Percentage of Departments Where Head Is Elected (HEDEL)*		
1966	74	24	7
	(49)	(71)	(90)
1972	69	22	6
	(49)	(72)	(90)
	E. *Mean Proportion of Positions Covered by Civil Service (PSCE)*		
1966	.607	.767	.746
	(47)	(70)	(88)
1972	.582	.691	.785
	(48)	(72)	(89)

Note: Figures in parentheses represent actual numbers of cases.

civil service arrangements. The same pattern obtains for the use of written regulations governing promotion criteria. There is about a 6 percent increase between 1966 and 1972 and a nearly 16 percent spread between nineteenth-century and post-1940 agencies. Differences due to time of measurement are somewhat smaller in sections C and D of Table 1, where data on the length of the probationary period for new employees and the method of selection of department head are presented. Between 1966 and 1972, there was but a 3 percent increase in the proportion of departments with lengthy probationary periods and a 2 percent decrease in elected agency heads. The differences associated with era of origin are more prominent in section D, however: Indeed, practically all of the variance in whether or not a department head is elected—although not, if he is appointed, in whether such appointment is at the discretion of the head of government or through civil service—can be explained by era of origin.[4] Finally, section E of Table 1 displays mean proportions of positions in finance agencies covered by civil service in both 1966 and 1972. Whereas time of formation is positively associated with civil service coverage—newer agencies have more employees under merit systems—somewhat fewer positions were covered in 1972 than in 1966. The reasons for this contraction of civil service have already been noted and need not be pursued further.

Because the first four items describing finance agencies' hiring and evaluation procedures are dichotomies, they were combined in an index of formalization of the personnel process. Section E of Table 1 was not included in the index, because the mean PSCE declined between 1966 and 1972. Correlations among the four items between 1966 and 1972 and their autocorrelations over time are displayed in Table 2. Generally, the correlations are modest and in the expected direction, but there are some exceptions. For example, the correlation of placement of new employees through civil service with written promotion criteria is .6136 in 1966 but plummets to .3989 in 1972. And the correlations of whether department heads are elected with length of the probationary period are not very different from zero, −.1217 in 1966 and −.0319 in 1972. The autocorrelations are also of interest. For the first three items, they range from .4348 to .6321, but for elec-

Table 2. Correlations of Items in Index of Formalization (1966/1972 Correlations).

	Emplace	Promo	Probat	Hedel
Emplace	.6321	.6136/.3989	.2568/.2884	−.2376/−.2015
Promo	—	.4348	.2683/.1828	−.1628/−.2093
Probat	—	—	.5278	−.1217/−.0319
Hedel	—	—	—	.8489

Note: Autocorrelations on major diagonal.

tion of department heads the autocorrelation is .8489. The index of formalization ranges from zero to one; its value is the proportion of the four elements of an agency's personnel procedures consistent with merit principles—entry-level placement through civil service, written regulations governing promotions, a probationary period of six months or longer, and an appointed department head. The index had mean values of .697 in 1966 and .745 in 1972.

In order to estimate effects of era of origin and year of measurement more precisely than the cross tabulations in Table 1 allow, the index of formalization was regressed on era of origin. Six cross-sectional regressions are displayed in Table 3, three each for 1966 and 1972. In these regressions, the 1966 and 1972 indices of formalization are regressed separately on era of origin. In the first two regressions, no additional variables are controlled. Each increment of era—there are two increments, since we have three eras—adds .148 to the index in 1966 and .142 in 1972. The difference between the constants in the first pair of equations, .0622, is a rough estimate of the effects of year of measurement on the index of formalization. In the third and fourth equations in Table 3, a dummy variable coded one for state finance agencies covered in the surveys and zero for others is added; in the fifth and sixth equations, a dummy variable coded one for nonsouthern states and zero otherwise is included. Neither of the added variables significantly predicts formalization of personnel practices, whereas the effects of era of origin remain. The time at which an agency was founded and subsequent environmental shifts account for formalization much better than either the level of government or geographic location.

In the last entry of Table 3, the 1966 and 1972 data are

Table 3. Regressions of Indexes of Formalization on Era of Origin and Other Environmental Variables.

Cross-Sectional Regressions

1966 formalization = .3712+.1484•era
(.0255)
1972 formalization = .4334+.1422•era
(.0225)
1966 formalization = .3057+.1539•era− .0226•state
(.0238)   (.0557)
1972 formalization = .4095+.1286•era+ .0399•state
(.0231)   (.0540)
1966 formalization = .3021+.1542•era+ .0003•nonsouthern
(.0241)   (.0431)
1972 formalization = .4135+.1281•era+ .0030•nonsouthern
(.0234)   (.0418)

Pooled Regression

Formalization = .3625+.1328•era+.0485•year
(.0160)   (.0277)

Note: Errors in parentheses.

pooled, and year of measurement is added to the model as a dummy variable coded zero for 1966 and one for 1972. The pooled regression allows estimates of the statistical significance of year of measurement and comparisons of effects of era and year on formalization. As can be seen from the error terms, the effects of era are far greater than might have occurred by chance, but the significance of year of measurement is uncertain in the pooled regression—the coefficient of year is 1.75 times its error. But the coefficient is in the expected direction, and more important, since the six-year interval between measurements is considerably shorter than the intervals between eras, which are 27 and 39 years, one would expect time of measurement to have considerably less impact than era of origin. Had the measurement interval been longer, the effects of year in all likelihood would have attained significance. While one cannot legitimately project recent trends backward to the nineteenth century, it may be reasonable to assume that the rate at which personnel procedures in local government agencies have been formalized since the turn of the century is such that changes in these procedures over time have been greater than

differences occurring across organizations at any one point due to
persistent effects of origins. To speak of stability of personnel procedures in finance agencies would be accurate for short intervals
only. The long-range effects of environmental shifts are in all likelihood far greater than origins.

Origins and Organizational Structure

Although era of origin shapes the personnel procedures
used by local government finance agencies, it does not affect their
organizational structures significantly. Table 4 displays mean size
and number of divisions, sections (that is, subunits of divisions),
and levels of supervision for the 254 departments studied in 1966
and 1972. The largest agencies are the oldest ones, but early

**Table 4. Measures of Organizational Structure in 1966 and 1972 by Era
When Departments Were Founded.**

	Pre–1900	Era 1900–1939	Post–1940
Mean size:			
1966	136.96	89.31	95.16
	(49)	(72)	(90)
1972	163.35	106.78	123.28
	(49)	(72)	(90)
Mean N operating divisions:			
1966	6.20	5.33	5.52
	(49)	(72)	(90)
1972	6.04	5.40	5.52
	(49)	(72)	(90)
Mean N sections:			
1966	12.90	10.14	11.40
	(49)	(72)	(90)
1972	12.48	11.37	13.17
	(48)	(71)	(90)
Mean N levels of supervision:			
1966	3.84	4.02	3.93
	(45)	(71)	(90)
1972	4.03	4.08	4.13
	(49)	(71)	(90)

Note: Figures in parentheses represent actual numbers.

twentieth-century departments are the smallest; even this difference is not statistically significant because of the large variance in size. Differences in numbers of operating divisions and sections are entirely artifacts of size, and the greatest level of numbers occurred, in 1966, among the early twentieth-century agencies, which are on the average the smallest. Overall, then, the organizational structure of finance agencies bears no direct relationship to the era in which they were founded. This is not surprising, given that there is no reason to anticipate such a relationship. Organizational structures, unlike personnel procedures, have not been the subject of federal legislation, and they are not directly linked to cultural and political preferences of different historical periods.

Formalization, Hierarchy, and Delegation of Authority

If origins and subsequent effects of political and social environments account for the extent of formal personnel processes but not for administrative structure in local agencies, one would expect variables describing organizational structure to have little or no effect on formalization. This expectation, however, runs counter to inferences drawn from the results of several research studies, including some publications from the 1966 survey of finance agencies. Correlations between the extensiveness of hierarchy and delegation have been observed in several studies (see Blau, 1968; M. Meyer, 1968; Pugh and others, 1968; Blau and Schoenherr, 1971; M. Meyer, 1972a), and they are replicated here. Table 5 displays the zero-order correlations of the index of formalization, the number of hierarchical levels in finance agencies, and two indicators of delegation of authority in personnel matters. The indicators of decentralization are (1) whether the department head or someone below him, such as a division head, formally recommends promotions and dismissals and (2) the relative influence of division heads in promotion decisions.[5] The 1966 and 1972 correlations are displayed to the left and right of the solidi, respectively. There are modest but positive associations of levels of supervision with decentralization in both 1966 and 1972. The correlations of levels with delegation of formal authority to rec-

Table 5. Correlations of Index of Formalization, Levels of Supervision, and Delegation of Decision-Making Authority (1966/1972 Correlations).

	Levels	Delegation 1	Delegation 2
Formalization	.2338/.2338	.0716/.1405	.0600/.0563
Levels	—	.1814/.2326	.2645/.3107

ommend promotion and dismissal are .1814 in 1966 and .2326 in 1972; the correlations of levels with division heads' influence are .2645 and .3107, respectively. In contrast, the associations of formalization with delegation of authority in 1966 and 1972 are virtually zero. Of the four correlations of formalization with delegation in Table 5, only one is significantly larger than zero, and, as can readily be seen from the table this zero-order correlation drops to nonsignificance when the number of levels is controlled.

The minuscule correlations of formalization with decentralization and the small though significant links between era and formalization and between formalization and levels of supervision suggest that formalization precedes proliferation of hierarchical levels rather than the other way around. Cross-lagged path analysis shows that neither size nor levels affect formalization over time, whereas the 1966 measure of formalization affects 1972 levels net of 1966 levels, albeit slightly. The regressions are displayed in Table 6. Unfortunately the link between levels and delegation of decision-making authority cannot be confirmed in the longitudinal analysis. Lagged regressions show no significant links between the extensiveness of hierarchy and decentralization. Decision-making practices can change rapidly, and the six-year interval between measurements may be far too long for meaningful results to appear. In sum, the cross-sectional analysis suggests links between formalization and hierarchy and between hierarchy and delegation; no direct relationship between formalization and decentralization was shown. The longitudinal analysis indicates that causality runs from formalization to hierarchy, not the reverse. While these results are not wholly conclusive, they are consistent with our expectations: hierarchy follows from extensive personnel procedures and decentralized decision making from hierarchical differentiation.

Table 6. Lagged Regressions of Formalization, Size, and Levels.

	Regressions of 1972 Formalization on 1966 Formalization, 1966 Size, and 1966 Levels of Supervision	
	Zero Order	B
1966 formalization	.7802	.7820
1966 size	.0603	(−.0182)
1966 formalization	.7802	.7651
1966 levels	.2433	(.0644)
Regressions of 1972 size:		
1966 size	.9497	.9492
1966 formalization	.1005	(.0052)
Regressions of 1972 levels:		
1966 levels	.5700	.5432
1966 formalization	.2419	.1149

Note: Coefficients in parentheses not statistically significant.

Openness to the Environment at the Time of Formation

One final question remains: How does one account for the persistent, although modest effects of era of formation on personnel procedures in finance agencies? Effects of origins, although diminished by environmental forces, do not disappear altogether; and it is not clear from the data describing modifications in on-going organizations why this should be so. Put somewhat differently, the problem is to identify what takes place at the time an organization is formed that continues to influence it throughout its existence.

A partial solution is suggested by data describing a small number of finance agencies that reorganized totally between 1966 and 1972. These fourteen departments were described in an earlier article (see M. Meyer, 1975). All changed their names and altered administrative arrangements so fully that the autocorrelations of variables describing organizational structure between 1966 and 1972 were zero. One other interesting property of these fourteen agencies was noted in the earlier article: the correlations of size with environmental demands for their services were zero in

1966 and much higher in 1972 (M. Meyer, 1975, p. 614). Not examined in that article were changes in formalization of personnel procedures. A reasonable expectation is that, just as their size moved from inconsistency to consistency with environmental demands as a result of reorganization, so did their personnel procedures. The amount of this change is critical, however. As will be remembered from Table 3, there was only a slight increase in formalization, .0622 on a 1.0 point scale, for the 215 ongoing organizations between 1966 and 1972. For agencies that reorganized totally, a somewhat greater increase in formalization was anticipated, if only because of the extent of other changes. We had not expected, however, to find that the environment had ten times as much impact on this small group of agencies as it had on ongoing organizations in the six-year interval.

Following is the pooled regression of the index of formalization on era of origin and year for the fourteen reorganized finance agencies. Errors are in parentheses.

$$\text{Formalization} = .2977 + .0320 \cdot \text{era} + .5411 \cdot \text{year}$$
$$\phantom{\text{Formalization} = .2977 + } (.0512) \phantom{\cdot \text{era} + } (.0936)$$

The regression model is the same as that at the bottom of Table 3; only the results differ. Casual inspection of these pooled regressions reveals, first, that the constant terms are somewhat lower for the reorganized cases than for the others, indicating that formalized personnel procedures were nearly absent from the former in 1966. Era of origin has a minuscule and nonsignificant effect for the reorganized cases, but this was expected because era describes the period during which the old organizations—those obliterated between 1966 and 1972—were formed. In contrast, year of measurement, which for the reorganized cases indicates whether they were formed before or after 1966, has a very large effect on formalization; the metric coefficient of year is .5411. The coefficient of year is almost an order of magnitude larger for the fourteen reorganized departments than for the 215 ongoing finance agencies. This suggests that the environment is much more intrusive when reorganization takes place than otherwise. And it helps explain why effects of era of origin appear and persist over time despite environmental forces that affect all organizations.

In brief, we would argue that the effects of origins (or what Stinchcombe, 1965, calls the correlation of age with structure) are but artifacts of the discontinuous nature of change in organizations. Organizational change involves two types of effects of the environment: gradual alterations in the internal structure of ongoing organizations and replacement of organizations that were inconsistent with external demands by new ones highly consistent with the environment. The model in Figure 3 depicts this process graphically. A hypothetical measure of bureaucratization is plotted as a function of time for a set of organizations, most of which continue but some of which are replaced at each time point. A secular trend toward bureaucratization is assumed due to environmental forces, and some of the organizations that are least bureaucratic, hence least consistent with the environment, reorganize at a level of bureaucratization higher than the others. The implications of this pattern are easily described. First, the association between age and structure can be explained entirely as the replacement of existing organizations with new ones. Second, the effects of era of origin on organizational properties increase over time and are limited only by whatever upper bound may exist for organizational age. The second implication follows directly from the first and can

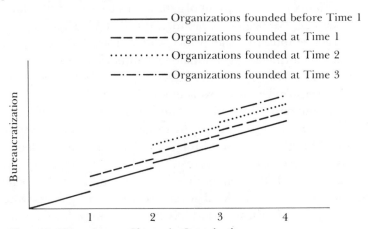

Figure 3. Discontinuous Change in Organizations.

be easily shown by combining data from the 215 continuing finance agencies with data from the fourteen reorganized cases and treating the post-1966 years as a fourth era of origin. For the 229 cases in 1966, the correlation of era with formalization of personnel procedures was .3487. In 1972—it should be noted again that the post-1966 agencies are treated as founded in a fourth era—the correlation was .4264.

The ultimate explanation for the discontinuous pattern of change in organizations lies in the nature of organization itself. At the time of formation, the elements of organizations are not separable from the larger social structures in which they are embedded and thus are wholly dependent on their environments. Once organizations are founded, however, they must remain essentially stable, if only to satisfy the expectations of members and clients. These expectations may change gradually over time, but they are revised substantially when reorganization occurs and the environment intrudes. What has not been explained is why some anachronistic organizations manage to survive while others do not. Myriad hypotheses could be put forward, but this is not the place either to propound or to explore them.

Conclusions

A number of ideas about organizations have been developed in this chapter. We began by pointing out that Weber's theory of bureaucracy emphasizes the primacy of historical forces and in particular the influence of rational-legal authority as causes of bureaucratization. Most researchers acknowledge this but have been unable to grapple with the problem empirically. We took the civil service movement in the United States as an illustration of historical change and the ascendance of rational-legal over traditional standards of authority. The history of federal civil service legislation was reviewed briefly in terms of its effects on state and local governments, and it was hypothesized that the extent of formal personnel procedures and local government finance agencies would reflect both the historical period in which they were founded and the subsequent effects of the environment. Older agencies were less formalized than the newer ones, but over time all adopted procedures more in keeping with the idea of merit personnel administration and less conducive to the political spoils system. An increase in formalization, it was shown, gives rise to multitier hierarchies, and hierarchical differentiation in turn gives rise to the delegation of personnel decisions to lower levels. A causal chain from origins and the environment to formalization to hierarchy to decentralization was thus posited.

A small number of agencies that changed their names and reorganized totally between the two surveys of finance agencies was examined to determine whether the effects of origins could be due to extreme susceptibility to environmental pressures at the time of formation. Environmental effects on personnel procedures are almost an order of magnitude greater in the reorganized agencies than in the ongoing ones. The discontinuous pattern of change explains the observed correlation between age and certain organizational properties, and we predicted that this correlation would increase over time. Our prediction was substantiated by the 1966 and 1972 data describing finance agencies.

Several implications arise from these results. First, the patterns described here need not be peculiar to finance agencies or to the history of the civil service movement in the United States. Effects of origins and the environment and the discontinuous pattern of change should be evident for diverse institutional sectors. Second, if some of the key questions in organization theory concern the effects of societal forces on organizations over time, organizational research ought to be directed toward answering these questions. Historical and longitudinal studies are required, and they must take explicit account of qualitative as well as quantitative elements of environments which have heretofore been neglected. In all likelihood, research will have to be larger in scope and longer in duration than has been usual until now. Third, the results presented here, together with those in earlier articles, suggest means for stimulating change in organizations. M. Meyer's article, "Leadership and Organizational Structure"(Chapter Eight) suggested that change in leadership and dependence of leaders on higher authority opens organizations to environmental influences. Here it has been shown that total reorganization speeds the process of accommodation to environmental pressures. These results are not surprising, but they do call into question the efficacy of attempting incremental change, the results of which are at best uncertain, compared with that of changing leaders or the total reorganization of agencies. Our results do not speak to the desirability of reorganization. For some organizations, particularly those performing mediating functions, continuity is essential. But our research suggests that, when shifts in administrative patterns are sought, they are obtained most efficiently through changes in leadership and fundamental alterations in organizational structures.

Notes

1. This is not to deny that the federal government had imposed specific merit-system requirements on state and local governments prior to the 1970 Intergovernmental Personnel Act. Quite the opposite: some 150 district personnel requirements, some of them contradictory, had already been attached to various grant-in-aid programs. These requirements were greatly simplified in the 1971 "Standards for a Merit System of Administration" promulgated by the Departments of Health, Education, and Welfare; Defense; and Labor; and further simplification was proposed by the Advisory Council on Intergovernmental Governmental Policy in its 1973 report (U.S. Senate Committee on Government Operations, 1974, pp. 4–5). The advisory council recommended that a set of uniform personnel standards be applied in the administration of all federal grants-in-aid to states and localities, with the sole exception of revenue-sharing funds.

2. Charles Bidwell has suggested that organizations in shared environments may diverge over time. He cites in private correspondence the example of midwestern colleges founded in the late nineteenth and twentieth centuries that were initially similar but became differentiated due to demands of controlling bodies, local constituencies, and the like. Divergence unrelated to time of formation, of course, cannot be captured in the model in Figure 1. It may well be that local conditions have caused some divergences in finance agencies over time, but our lack of information about these conditions renders it difficult to gauge their effects.

3. Only Starbuck (1965) has argued that age affects the degree of formalization in organizations, but there has been no empirical confirmation of this claim. While it is possible that organizational age influences bureaucratization apart from time of origin (that is, cohort) or effects of the environment (that is, period), neither the data nor justification for the strong assumptions needed to separate the effects of cohort, period, and age exists. For a discussion of the problem of cohort, year, and age, see Mason and others (1973). The literature also suggests that time of origin is more important than age. Aiken and Hage (1968, pp. 921–922) found no correlates of age in their study of sixteen health and welfare agencies; Pugh (1969, p. 94) found a negative but nonsignificant relationship of age with impersonality of origins of fifty-four diverse organizations in the Birmingham, England, area. Only Kimberly's recent (1975) study of sheltered workshops has corroborated Stinchcombe's results. Kimberly found post-World War II workshops to be more oriented toward rehabilitation than pre-World War II agencies. This in all likelihood reflects changing beliefs about the appropriate functions for sheltered workshops rather than effects of age per se.

4. Procedures for selecting department heads have been least affected by civil service laws. Environmental forces have not had much impact, and a strong

effect of era of origin occurs in section D of Table 1. It could be argued, although not proved, that the differences between the correlations of era of origin with whether the department head is elected and the correlation of era with the other items in Table 1 is indicative of the magnitude of environmental effects on the other items from the time of origin to the present.

5. The first measure of delegation is coded zero if the department head officially recommends promotions and dismissals and one if someone below him does; the second measure is coded zero if the division heads' influence in promotion decisions is less than 80 percent and one if their influence, as reported by the department head, is greater than 80 percent.

4

The Structure of Educational Organizations

John W. Meyer
Brian Rowan

Large-scale educational organizations have become dominant forms in almost all countries (Coombs, 1968). That is, not only has *formal* education become dominant, but this education is organized in

Revised version of a paper presented at the annual meetings of the American Sociological Association (ASA), San Francisco, August 1975. The work reported here was conducted in the Environment for Teaching Program of the Stanford Center for Research and Development in Teaching, under a grant from the National Institute of Education (NIE), grant number NE-C-00-3-0062. Views expressed here do not reflect NIE positions. Many colleagues in the Environment for Teaching Program, the NIE, the Organizations Training Program at Stanford, and the ASA work group on organizations and environments, offered helpful comments. In particular, detailed substantive suggestions and comments were provided by Albert Bergesen, Charles Bidwell, Terry Deal, John Freeman, Paul Hirsch, James March, Barbara Payne, Jeffrey Pfeffer, Phillip Runkel, and W. Richard Scott, and Betty Smith provided much editorial assistance.

large bureaucracies managed by political systems; no longer is it simply a matter of exchange between families and local educational organizations.

This circumstance is not surprising. Many other social activities have come under political and bureaucratic control in modern societies. It is customary to suppose that, as the scale of these activities expands, higher levels of coordination and control are required and that bureaucratic controls emerge to structure these activities efficiently. This view does not fit educational organization, however. There is a great deal of evidence that educational organizations (at least in the United States) *lack* close internal coordination, especially of the content and methods of what is presumably their main activity—instruction. Instruction tends to be removed from the control of the organizational structure, in both its bureaucratic and its collegial aspects. This property of educational organizations, among others, has led March and Olsen (1976) and Weick (1976) to apply the term "loosely coupled" to educational organizations. By this they mean that *structure is disconnected from technical (work) activity, and activity is disconnected from its effects.*

In this chapter, we offer an explanation of the rise of large-scale educational bureaucracies that consistently leave instructional activities and outcomes uncontrolled and uninspected. We argue that educational bureaucracies emerge as personnel-certifying agencies in modern societies. They use standard types of curricular topics and teachers to produce standardized types of graduates, who are then allocated to places in the economic and stratification system on the basis of their certified educational background. In such matters as controlling who belongs in a particular *ritual classification*—for example, who is a certified mathematics teacher, a fifth-grader, an English major—educational organizations are very tightly, not loosely, organized. As large-scale educational organizations develop, they take on a great deal of control over the ritual classifications of their curriculum, students, and teachers. The reason for this is that the standardized categories of teachers, students, and curricular topics give meaning and definition to the internal activities of the school. These elements are *institutionalized* in the legal and normative rules of the wider society. In fact, the ritual classifications are the basic components of the theory (or ideology) of education used by modern societies, and schools gain enormous resources by conforming to them, incorporating them, and controlling them. (J. Meyer and Rowan, 1977).

Schools less often control their instructional activities or outputs, despite periodic shifts toward "accountability." They avoid this kind of control for two reasons. First, close supervision of instructional activity and outputs can uncover inconsistencies and inefficiencies and can create more uncertainty than mere abstract and unenforced demands for conformity to bureaucratic rules. Second, in the United States centralized governmental and professional controls are weak. Schools depend heavily on local funding and support. Maintaining only nominal central control over instructional outputs and activities also maintains societal consensus about the abstract ritual classifications by making local variations in the content and effectiveness of instructional practices invisible. This also allows instructional practices, although prescribed by rules institutionalized at highly generalized levels, to become adapted to unique local circumstances.

In the American situation, attempts to tightly link the prescriptions of the central theory of education to the activities of instruction would create conflict and inconsistency and discredit and devalue the meaning of ritual classifications in society. Educators (and their social environments) therefore decouple their ritual structure from instructional activities and outcomes and resort to a "logic of confidence": Higher levels of the system organize on the *assumption* that what is going on at lower levels makes sense and conforms to rules, but they avoid inspecting it to discover or assume responsibility for inconsistencies and ineffectiveness. In this fashion, educational organizations work more smoothly than is commonly supposed, obtain high levels of external support from divergent community and state sources, and maximize the meaning and prestige of the ritual categories of people they employ and produce.

Our argument hinges on the assertion that education is highly institutionalized in modern society. Its categories of students and graduates, as well as its ritual classification of production procedures—types of teachers, topics, and schools—are all derived from highly institutionalized rules and beliefs. Educational organizations derive power and resources when such rules are institutionalized in society, and they are thus inclined to incorporate and remain in close conformity with such categorical rules.

In this chapter, we (1) describe the prevailing pattern of control in educational organizations, (2) consider the inadequacies of conventional explanations of this pattern, (3) formulate an alternative interpretation, and (4) consider some research implications and issues in organization theory that arise from the discussion.

Patterns of Control in Educational Organizations

The literature on educational organizations manifests a peculiar contradiction. On the one hand, there are depictions of the educational system as highly coordinated and controlled—to the point of restricting local innovation (for instance, Holt, 1964; Rogers, 1968). On the other hand, conventional sociological discussions hold that actual educational work—instruction—occurs in the isolation of the self-contained classroom, removed from organizational coordination and control. In this view, local innovations fail, not because the system is rigid but because the system lacks internal linkages (Lortie, 1973; Deal, Meyer, and Scott, 1975). Both of these views contain an element of truth. Instructional activities—the *work* of the organization—are coordinated quite casually in most American educational institutions. But the ritual classifications and categories that organize and give meaning to education are tightly controlled. Our first concern is to describe this situation in more detail.

Loose Coupling of Structure and Activities. Consider some of the ways in which educational organizations lack coordination and control over the technical activity within them—a situation called "loose coupling" by March and Olsen (1976) and Weick (1976).

Evaluation. Educational work takes in the isolation of the classroom, removed from organizational controls of a substantive kind (see, for instance, Bidwell, 1965; Dreeben, 1973; Lortie, 1973). Neither teaching nor its output in student socialization is subject to serious organizational evaluation and inspection (Dornbusch and Scott, 1975). The weak formal inspection of instruction is evident from a 1972 survey of San Francisco Bay area elementary schools conducted by the Environment for Teaching Program (Cohen, and others, 1976). Survey data were obtained from 34 district superintendents, 188 principals of schools within these districts, and 231 teachers in 16 of the schools. The schools were selected by stratified random sampling from the population of elementary schools in the eight counties adjoining San Francisco Bay. The data show that the inspection of instructional activity is delegated to the local school and takes place infrequently. For example, only one of the thirty-four superintendents interviewed reported that the district office evaluates teachers directly. Nor does it appear that principals and peers have the opportunity to inspect and discuss teachers' work: Of the principals surveyed, 85 percent reported that they and their teachers do not work together on a daily basis. Further, there is little evidence of interaction among teachers: A majority of the principals report that there are no day-to-day working relations among teachers within the same grade level, and 83 percent report no daily work relations among teachers of different grades. Teachers reaffirm this view of segmented teaching. Two thirds report that their teaching is observed by other teachers infrequently (once a month or less), and half report a similar infrequency of observation by their principals.

Direct inspection of the teaching task is, of course, only one means of organizational control. Organizations can also exert control by inspecting outputs (Ouchi and Maguire, 1975). Schools, for example, could determine which teachers have students that score well on standardized tests. But a striking fact about American education at all levels is that student achievement data are rarely used to evaluate the performance of teachers or schools. For example, in 1972, only one of the thirty-four superintendents in the Environment for Teaching survey reported using standardized achievement data to evaluate district schools. Many reasons have been given for this failure to employ output controls—among them, the unavailability and low reliability of the measures. These reasons are made less plausible by the fact that such measures are routinely used to assess and determine the life chances of students.

Curriculum and Technology. Another critical ingredient of organizational control—a teaching technology or even a detailed instructional program of socially agreed-on efficacy—is largely missing in schools. Routine technologies with high consensual standards of efficiency are thought, in organization theory, to create great pressures for effective control (Perrow, 1970). But in schools there are few detailed standards of instructional content or procedure. For example, 93 percent of the principals interviewed in the Environment for Teaching survey report having only general or informal curriculum guidelines, as opposed to detailed policies. Such diffuse standards are even more the case with teaching methods. Only 4 percent of the principals report that they are extremely influential in determining the instructional methods used by teachers.

There is similar lack of coordination and control over technical interdependencies. Schools appear to minimize problems of coordination that might arise from instructional practices. For example, it may seem necessary for sixth-graders to have mastered fifth-grade work, but in fact students are often processed from grade to grade with little regard for how much they have learned. In this way, schools minimize sequential interdependencies inherent in their instructional core, and teachers adapt informally to student variability. Schools also minimize the interdependence among instructional programs. Webster (1976) reports that specialized program administrators seldom interact or discuss the activities of other programs.

Authority. It also seems that educational administrators have little direct authority over instructional work. While administrators have a generalized responsibility to plan and coordinate the content and methods of instruction, their authority to carry out these activities is in fact evanescent. As an illustration, only 12 percent of the San Francisco Bay area principals say they have real decision power over the methods teachers use. On the other issues than instruction, however, principals assume real decision rights: Of those surveyed, 82 percent claim to decide about scheduling, 75 percent about pupil assignment. And 88 percent claim to decide (alone or with district consultation) about hiring.

These data and examples suggest that educational organizations only marginally control their central instructional functions —especially when it is remembered that the data concern elementary schools, which are the types of schools ordinarily thought to have the highest levels of control, as organizations, over the content and methods of instruction. But an important caveat is needed: This discussion is limited to American schooling. In contrast, schools observed in Britain show much more internal coordination. Evaluation and control are exerted under the authority of the headmaster, whose role in the school and in British society is substantial and is rooted in established tradition. Similarly, some continental educational systems also vest substantive power and authority in central ministries. Our description of the loose control of instruction, as well as our subsequent explanation, will therefore need to take into account particular features of American society and education.

The Tight Control of Ritual Classifications. The description just given has highlighted the structural looseness (Bidwell, 1965) of educational organizations. But, although the evidence seems to show loose controls in the area of instruction, there is some evidence of tight organizational controls in such areas as the credentialing and hiring of teachers, the assignment of students to classes and teachers, and scheduling. This suggests that within schools certain areas of organizational structure are more tightly controlled than others. In contrast to instructional activities, there seem to be centralized and enforced agreements about exactly what *teachers, students,* and *topics of instruction* constitute a particular *school.* Also, in the allocation of space, funds, and materials schools exercise considerable control. Teachers in different, isolated classrooms seem to teach similar topics, and students learn many of the same things. One of the main emphases in our discussion will be to explain how educational organizations, with few controls over their central activities, achieve adequate coordination, and how they persist so stably.

The tight control educational organizations maintain over the ritual or formal classification systems is central to our understanding of education as an institution. To a considerable extent, educational organizations function to maintain the *societally agreed-on rites defined in societal myths (or institutional rules) of education.* Education rests on and obtains enormous resources from central institutional rules about what valid education is. These rules define the ritual categories of teacher, student, curricular topic, and type of school. When these categories are properly assembled, education is understood to occur. But for the rites to occur in a legitimate way some general exigencies of the physical and social world require practical management. All participants assembled for their ritual performances must be properly qualified and categorized. Consider the procedures for controlling the properties of ritually defined actors, for assembling the legitimate curricular topics, and for assembling these into an accredited school.

Teacher Classifications. There are elaborate rules for classifying teachers. There are elementary school teachers, high school teachers, and college teachers—each type with its own specifications, credentials, and categories of specialists. Each type has a legitimate domain outside of which instruction would be deemed inappropriate—for example, elementary teachers do not teach college physics. Each type also possesses appropriate credentials, which are defined and controlled in an elaborate way (see Woellner, 1972, for specific descriptions). Educational organizations, then, have detailed, definitive specifications delineating which individuals may teach in which types of classes and schools.

Further, particular educational organizations maintain lists of teachers, with their formal assignments to topics, space, students, and funds. These teachers are defined by name, recorded background and training, and types of credentials. Schools are very tightly coupled organizations in defining who their teachers are and what properties these teachers have. Yet there is almost no formal control exercised to ensure that each teacher enacts the substance of the typological category in daily activity. That is, documents of what teachers *do* are either nonexistent or vacuous, while documents that *define persons as teachers* are elaborately controlled.

Student Classifications. Similarly, elaborate sets of formal rules define types of students. Students are sharply distinguished by level or grade, by programs or units completed, by subject area specialization, and even by special abilities (for instance, educationally handicapped). Student classifications are tightly contolled, and schools can define exactly which students are fifth-graders, chemistry majors, or enrollees. Adding a new type of student (for instance, economics majors or emotionally handicapped students) is an explicit and important organizational decision. But, while the documents and rules relevant to the classification of students are

explicit and carefully maintained, little formal organization ensures that students are being treated (or acting in a manner) appropriate to their type (for instance, see Hobbs, 1975). It is very
clear whether a given school has an economics major or not, but
there may be no one in the organization who keeps track of exactly
what economics majors study or learn.

Further, there are rules governing the students' entrance
into and movement through the system. Residence, age, previous
education, or ethnic background often govern entrance into a particular school, grade, or program. Changes from any ritual category—for instance, to sixth-grader or to college student—require
close coordination ensuring the propriety of the ritual transition.
However, although there is great clarity in formal assignment or
transition, few formal organizational mechanisms ensure that these
assignments are enacted substantively—for instance, that twelfth-
graders are actually doing twelfth-grade work or that third-graders
who are being promoted have actually met some standards.

Topic Classifications. Definitive sets of topics are organized in
schools and assigned to teachers, students, space, and funds. Each
school has a formalized set of curricular topics. An elementary
school, for instance, may cover the standard elementary curriculum from kindergarten through the sixth grade. A high school may
offer instruction in history and business but not in Latin. There
is a definitive agreement, built into the school's formal structure,
about what topic the school is and is not offering instruction in at
any given time. These topics are carefully documented, as are the
particular teachers who manage them and the particular students
who receive (or have received) instruction in them. But there is
extraordinarily little formal control to define exactly what any
given topic means or to ensure that specific topics are taught in the
same way. Business courses, for example, can vary greatly from
teacher to teacher. Similarly, what actually constitutes sixth-grade
mathematics can show remarkable variation from classroom to
classroom. Yet, despite the vacuity in specified content, elaborate
rules make sure that each elementary school has something called
a sixth-grade, and that this sixth-grade contains instruction in something called *sixth-grade mathematics.*

School Classifications. Finally, students, teachers, and topics are assembled into formal units by an elaborate and precise set of rules. Such units are then assigned to funds, space, and materials. The expected location of each teacher and student is recorded in detail as are the topics they will cover, and missing teachers or students are promptly recorded.

The assembly of teachers, students, and topics into classrooms creates the larger institutional classification called *school,* and although little attention may be focused on what actually goes on in these units, detailed records are kept by districts, local and state boards of education, and accrediting agencies that certify their existence as valid schools of a particular class (for instance, elementary schools or colleges). So, for example, elaborate lists of state "high schools" are kept, even though one may stress college-level work while another provides only very rudimentary instruction.

The internal and external emphasis on the formal categorical status of schools and their elements may seem at first to be a misdirected obsession. But in many ways the meaning of schooling in modern society seems to be captured by these definitions and categories. Without such general understandings, the educational system would not receive the massive social support that it does. Without such social classifications and understandings, parents and the state would not legitimately extend broad powers over children to random adult strangers. What sensible person would devote years and money to disorganized (and not demonstrably useful) study without the understanding that this is "college" or "economics"? These shared ideas of teacher, student, topic, and school— and some implicit assumptions about what will or will not go on— give schooling its social plausibility.

Conventional Explanations of the Organization of Schools

Educational organizations are formed to instruct and socialize. Their specific activity in these two areas, however, seems to be diffusely controlled, in good part outside formal organizational controls. On the other hand, the ritual classifications of schools are precisely specified, closely inspected, and tightly controlled. Our purpose here is to discuss explanations that are often used to account for this pattern of control in educational organizations. The conventional dynamic in these accounts begins with the question of what is wrong with schools and then goes on to a consideration of how it can be changed. Our problem, however, is to account for this situation, not to decry it. By way of clarification, we consider the following conventional accounts.

The Reform Perspective. Reformers abound in the world of education. They paint a picture of schools as archaic, as organizations not yet rationalized by proper output measures, evaluation systems and control structures, and therefore as systems that rely mainly on traditional types of authority among students, teachers, and school administrators. Reformers imagine that rationalized control and accounting measures can drive out less "modern" mechanisms of control once a few recalcitrant and reactionary groups are eliminated.

The difficulty with the reform view is its faith in the inevitable progression toward rationalization. This idea is not new. In many ways, it characterizes Horace Mann's ideas, and it certainly describes the perspective of the educational reformers of the late nineteenth century (for example, see Cubberly, 1916). The "new" organizational forms advocated at that time were to bring measurement, evaluation, and organizational control to instruction (Tyack, 1974). The guiding image was that of the factory, with its emphasis on organizationally controlled design and production. But a good case can be made that there is now less organizational control and evaluation of instruction than there was in the nineteenth century, before all the reforms (Tyack, 1974).

One cannot keep on asserting that the educational system is archaic, a passive anachronism itching for reform, when it seems to systematically eliminate innovations that bring inspection, evaluation, coordination, and control over instructional activities (Callahan, 1962). In any event, the view that education is weakly controlled because it lacks output measures is misdirected. Schools use elaborate tests to evaluate pupils and to shape the course of their present and future lives. But the same data are almost never aggregated and used to evaluate the performance of teachers, schools, or school systems. (Some data of this kind are made available for school and district evaluation in California, but only under the pressure of the state legislature, not the local school system.)

One other feature of the reform perspective deserves special note. Reformers tend to view American education as fragile, inept, disorganized, and on the edge of chaos and dissolution. Schools are seen to be in a poor state of organizational "health" (Miles, 1975). This is an astonishing description of a network of organizations that has grown rapidly for many decades, that obtains huge economic resources in a stable way year after year, that is protected from failure by laws that make its use compulsory, that is constantly shown by surveys to have the confidence and support of its constituency (Acland, 1975), and that is known to have high levels of job satisfaction among its participants (J. Meyer and others, 1971). Reformers may wish educational organizations were on their last legs, but all the "crises" reformers have declared have subsided quickly, and the system has remained stable.

The Decentralist Stance. Another view has it that educational organizations are oligarchic structures, headed by educational administrators and the elites that control them. In this view, educators are entrenched bureaucrats, resisting local community control and evaluation and building up their status rights and immunities in the system. This system resists accountability, the argument goes, and should be decentralized to the local level where the lay public can be involved in educational decision making (for example, see Fantini and Gittell, 1973; Rogers, 1968).

This view does not easily come into accord with the following facts. First, the American educational system has enormous popular support. This is inconsistent with the view that the system is controlled by a resistent and entrenched bureaucracy, unless one argues that the entire populace is afflicted with false consciousness in the matter. Second, even if the bureaucrats who presumably control the educational system were uninterested in effective education and were only seeking self-aggrandizement, why would they not inspect and control teachers more carefully to make sure that they conform to elite or bureaucratic interests?

In fact, the main difficulty with the decentralist's position is that it ignores the fact that local control of education in America

is not in conflict with the organizational structures we have described. We will later argue that the local community obtains important benefits from the present dearth of systematic inspection
and evaluation and that accountability could only arise from more,
not less, centralization of educational power.

The Professionalization of Teaching. It is possible to argue that
educational instruction is not controlled by central administrators
but rather by the teaching profession. In this view, schools are
loosely coupled simply because they provide a setting in which
professional teachers, thoroughly socialized to use the expert techniques of their discipline, ply their trade. Educational administrators merely form a sort of holding company to provide and maintain the facilities in which teachers work, in much the same way as
hospital administrators service doctors.

This view is not seriously maintained in most quarters.
Teachers themselves turn out not to believe this myth of professionalism. Dornbusch and Scott (1975) show that teachers report
that their training has little to do with their ability to perform effectively (in sharp contrast to nurses, for example). And in the San
Francisco Bay area survey reported earlier (Cohen and others,
1976), of the elementary teachers interviewed, 77 percent agreed
that the personality characteristics of the teacher were more important for success in teaching than any particular knowledge or
professional skills a teacher might possess.

Moreover, the school is not organized to delegate all the responsibilities for instruction to teachers. Thus, a school is unlike
a hospital, where doctors, not administrators, control task activities.
In schools, there is a more generalized locus of responsibility for
planning and coordinating instructional matters. Centralized policies about what teachers should teach, how they should teach, and
what materials they should use to teach are often developed jointly
by teachers, administrators, and sometimes parents.

Teachers, then, *appear* to be professionals because they have
much discretion within a loosely coupled system. The myth of
teacher professionalism is an interesting and important feature of
the American educational system. It does not, however, provide an
explanation for the structure of educational organizations.

Organization Theory. The most conventional idea in organizations research that could be used to explain the lack of central control over instructional activities is the idea of "goal displacement": the notion that organizations shift their control systems to focus on those outputs for which they are most accountable—in this case, the ritual classifications—and not on those which they were originally intended to maximize. This idea is, in large measure, true. But it does not go far enough. First, while both the school and the environment have evolved an elaborate scheme to control ritual classifications, the idea of goal displacement does not explain why a tacit agreement not to create an accounting scheme based on the "actual effectiveness" of these classifications evolved.

Second, in one sense goals may not be far displaced after all. We should not lose sight of the fact that a very high proportion of the resources schools receive *is* devoted to instructional activity. Teachers' salaries are a major expenditure item, as are instructional materials. Administrators and other district staff make up a very small proportion of the total employees of most school districts. The resources, in other words, continue to be focused on the instructional aspects of the system, even though achievement of instructional goals is not measured.

This fact suggests that educational organizations direct resources to their main goals but do not carefully control or evaluate the consequences of these allocations. It is as if society allocates large sums of money and large numbers of children to the schools and the schools in turn allocate these funds and children to a relatively uncontrolled and uninspected classroom. All of this seems to be done in a great act of ritual faith.

As we will see, this depiction is not inappropriate. Further, the parties involved may not be as foolish as they seem in conventional depictions of education. It is unfortunately true that most depictions of the educational system see its organizational administrators as somehow misdirected. The reformers see backwardness everywhere the magic of rationalization does not reach. The decentralists see self-aggrandizement. The myth of professionalism depicts administrators as factotums who submit to professional authority. And organization theorists see administrators who have lost sight of their original purposes. It may make sense, however, to consider another view of educational organization, one in which the participants are sensible people running a highly successful enterprise.

The Organization of Schooling: Another Interpretation

The explanation developed here begins with the context in which educational organizations are presently found. Modern education today takes place in large-scale, public bureaucracies. The rise of this kind of educational system is closely related to the worldwide trend of national development. The first step in our argument, therefore, is to relate national development to the organization of education.

The Growth of Corporate Schooling. From the preceding characterizations, we know that bureaucratic schooling has not arisen from a need to coordinate and standardize instruction, for this is precisely what modern American educational organizations do not do. Nor do these bureaucratic organizations merely fund and administer an exchange between educational professionals and families needing educational services. Educational bureaucracies present themselves not as units servicing education but as organizations that embody educational purposes in their collective structure. A theory of their emergence and dominance should explain why these bureaucracies assume jurisdiction over educational instruction.

The most plausible explanation is that modern schools produce education for *society*, not for individuals or families. In the nineteenth and twentieth centuries, national societies everywhere took over the function of defining and managing the socialization of their citizen personnel (Coombs, 1968; J. Meyer and Rubinson, 1975; Ramirez, 1974). In national societies, education is both a right and duty of citizenship (Bendix, 1964). It also becomes an important way of gaining status and respect (for example, see Blau and Duncan, 1967). For reasons that do not require elaborate discussion here, education becomes the central agency defining personnel—both citizen and elite—for the modern state and economy.

Since World War II, the trend toward corporate control of education has intensified. As nation-states have consolidated their control over a growing number of elements of social life, they have established educational systems to incorporate citizens into the political, economic, and status order of society. This incorporation is managed by a large public bureaucracy that uniformly extends its standardization and authority through all localities. Thus, educational organizations have come to be increasingly structured by centers of political authority (J. Meyer and Rubinson, 1975).

Bailyn (1960), Field (1972), M. Katz (1968), and Tyack (1974) describe the steps of this process in pretwentieth-century American history. First local, and later national, elites became concerned with the social control of peripheral citizen groups—who need control precisely because they *are* citizens. At first, the rural New Englanders who escaped from the control of clergy and town community (Bailyn, 1960), then the Irish immigrants (Field, 1972; M. Katz, 1968), and finally the great waves of nineteenth-century immigration (Tyack, 1974) created the pressures to control, standardize, and coordinate the educational system. As these steps progressed, the impetus to organize schooling on a large scale—to certify and classify pupils, to certify teachers, to accredit schools, and to control formal curriculum—gained force.

The growth of corporate control of education has major implications for educational organizations. As citizen personnel are increasingly sorted and allocated to positions in the social structure on the basis of classified or certified educational properties, the ritual classifications of education—type of student, topic, teacher, or school—come to have substantial value in what might be called the societal identity "market." A workable identity market presupposes a standardized, trustworthy currency of social typifications that is free from local anomalies. Uniform categories of instruction are therefore developed, and there is a detailed elaboration of the standardized and certified properties comprising an educational identity.

The result of this social expansion of education is a basic change in social structure. Education comes to consist, not of a series of private arrangements between teachers and students, but rather of a set of standardized public credentials used to incorporate citizen personnel into society. Society and its stratification system come to be composed of a series of typifications having educational meaning—ordinary citizens are presumed to have basic literacy. Strata above ordinary citizens are composed of high school and college graduates. The upper levels contain credentialed professionals, such as doctors and lawyers.

Thus, as societies and nation-states use education to define their basic categories of personnel, a large-scale educational bureaucracy emerges to standardize and manage the production of these categories. The credentials that give individuals status and membership in the wider collectivity must come under collective control. Such collective control would not be necessary if instruction were conceived of as a merely private matter between individuals and teachers. But, as educational organizations emerge as the credentialing agency of modern society and as modern citizens see their educational and corporate identities linked—that is, as education becomes the theory of personnel in modern society—it is consequently standardized and controlled.

Society thus becomes "schooled" (Illich, 1971). Education comes to be understood by corporate actors according to the *schooling rule:* Education is a certified teacher teaching a standardized curricular topic to a registered student in an accredited school. The nature of schooling is thus socially defined by reference to a set of standardized categories the legitimacy of which is publicly shared. As the categories and credentials of schooling gain importance in allocation and membership processes, the public comes to expect that they will be controlled and standardized. The large-scale public bureaucracy created to achieve this standardization is now normatively constrained by the expectations of the schooling rule. To a large degree, then, education is coordinated by shared social understandings that define the roles, topics, and contents of educational organizations.

The Organizational Management of Standardized Classifications. The political consolidation of society and the importance of education for the allocation of people to positions in the economic and stratification system explain the rise of large-scale educational bureaucracies. These processes also explain why educational organizations focus so tightly on the ritual classifications of education. Educational organizations are created to produce schooling for corporate society. They create standard types of graduates from standard categories of pupils using standard types of teachers and topics. As their purposes and structures are defined and institutionalized in the rules, norms, and ideologies of the wider society, the legitimacy of schools and their ability to mobilize resources depend on maintaining congruence between their structure and these socially shared categorical understandings of education (Dowling and Pfeffer, 1975; J. Meyer and Rowan, 1977; Parsons, 1956).

Consider this matter from the viewpoint of any rational college president or school superintendent. The whole school will dissolve in conflict and illegitimacy if the internal and external understanding of its accredited status is in doubt: If it has too few Ph.D.'s or properly credentialed teachers on its faculty, it may face reputational, accreditational, or even legal problems. If it has one too many "economics" courses and one too few "history" courses (leave aside their actual content), similar disasters may occur as the school falls short of externally imposed accrediting standards. No matter what they have learned, graduates may have difficulty finding jobs. No matter what the school teaches, it may not be capable of recruiting funds or teachers. Thus, the creation of institutionalized rules defining and standardizing education creates a system in which schools come to be somewhat at the mercy of the ritual classifications. Failure to incorporate certified personnel or to organize instruction around the topics outlined in accreditation rules can bring conflict and illegitimacy.

At the same time, the creation of institutionalized rules provides educational organizations with enormous resources. First, the credentials, classifications, and categories of schooling constitute a language that facilitates exchange between school and society. Social agencies often provide local schools with "categorical funding" to support the instruction of culturally disadvantaged or educationally handicapped students or to support programs in bilingual or vocational education. Second, schools can exploit the system of credentials and classifications in order to gain prestige. They can carefully attend to the social evaluations of worth given to particular ritual classifications and can maximize their honorific worth by hiring prestigious faculty, by incorporating programs that are publicly defined as "innovative," or by upgrading their status from junior college to four-year college. Finally, the school relies on the ritual classifications to provide order. Social actors derive their identities from the socially defined categories of education and become committed to upholding these identities within the context of their school activities. To the degree that actors take on the obligation to be "alive to the system, to be properly oriented and aligned in it" (Goffman, 1967), the whole educational system retains its plausibility.

In modern society, then, educational organizations have good reason to tightly control properties defined by the wider social order. By incorporating externally defined types of instruction, teachers, and students into their formal structure, schools avoid illegitimacy and discreditation. At the same time, they gain important benefits. In schools using socially agreed-on classifications, participants become committed to the organization. This is especially true when these classifications have high prestige (McCall and Simmons, 1966). And, by labeling students or instructional programs so that they conform to institutionally supported programs, schools obtain financial resources. In short, the rewards for attending to external understandings are an increased ability to mobilize societal resources for organizational purposes.

The Avoidance of Evaluation and Inspection. We have explained why schools attend to ritual classifications, but we have not explained why they do not attend (as organizations) to instruction. There are two ways that instructional activities can be controlled in modern education bureaucracies. First, many of the properties of educational identities may be certified in terms of examinations. Second, many of the ritual classifications involve a reorganization of educational activity, and some school systems organize an inspection system to make sure these implications are carried through. Thus, two basic kinds of instructional controls are available to educational organizations—the certification of status by testing, and/or the inspection of instructional activity to ensure conformity to rules.

Our explanation of the loose control of instruction in U.S. school systems must in part focus on specific features of U.S. society, since most other societies have educational bureaucracies that employ one or both forms of instructional control. In many other nations, for example, assignment to a classification such as student, graduate, or teacher is determined by various tests, most often controlled by national ministries of education. Also, national inspectors are often employed to attempt to make sure that teachers and schools conform to national standards of practice, regardless of the educational outcome. Thus, in most societies the state, through a ministry of education, controls systems of inspection or examination that manage the ritual categories of education by controlling either output or instructional procedure (Ramirez, 1974; Rubinson, 1974).

In American society, tests are used in profusion. However, most of these tests are neither national nor organizational but, rather, are devices of the individual teacher. The results seldom leave the classroom and are rarely used to measure instructional output. In the United States, the most common national tests that attempt to standardize local output differences—the Scholastic Aptitude Test (SAT) and the Graduate Record Examination (GRE) —are creatures of private organization. Further, only the New York State Board of Regents examination approximates (and at that in a pale way) an attempt to standardize curriculum throughout a political unit by using an examination system.

The apparent explanation for this lack of central control of instruction in American education is the decentralization of the system. Schools are in large part locally controlled and locally funded. While higher levels of authority in state and federal bureaucracies have made many attempts to impose evaluative standards on the educational system, the pressures of continued localism defeat them; category systems that delegate certification or evaluation rights to the schools themselves are retained. The reason for this is clear. A national evaluation system would define almost all the children in some communities as successes and almost all those in others as failures. This could work in a nationally controlled system, but it is much too dangerous in a system that depends on legitimating itself in and obtaining resources from local populations. Why, for instance, should the state of Mississippi join in a national credentialing system that might define a great proportion of its schools and graduates as failures? It is safer to adapt the substantive standards of what constitutes, say, a high school graduate to local circumstances and to specify in state laws only categories at some remove from substantive competence.

There is yet another way in which the institutional pattern of localism reduces organizational controls over instruction. In the United States, the legitimacy of local control in some measure de-professionalizes school administrators at all levels (in contrast to European models). They do not carry with them the authority of the central, national, professional, and bureaucratic structures and the elaborate ideological backing such authority brings with it. American administrators must compromise and must further lose purely professional authority by acknowledging their compromised role. They do not have tenure, and their survival is dependent on laypersons in the community, not professionals. Their educational authority of office is, therefore, lower than that of their European counterparts, especially in areas dealing with central educational matters such as instruction and curriculum. This situation is precisely analogous to the "red" versus "expert" conflict found in many organizations in communist societies, where organizational managers must often act contrary to their expert opinion in order to follow the party line. The profusion of local pressures in American society turns school administrators into "reds" as it were.

The Organizational Response:
Decoupling and The Logic of Confidence

Decoupling. American educational organizations are in business to maintain a "schooling rule" institutionalized in society. This rule specifies a series of ritual categories—teachers, students, topics and schools—that define education. Elaborate organizational controls ensure that these categories have been incorporated into the organization. But the ritual categories themselves and the system of inspection and control are formulated to avoid inspecting the actual instructional activities and outcomes of schooling. That is, a school's formal structure (its ritual classifications) is "decoupled" from technical activities and outcomes.

External features of American education, especially the local and pluralistic basis of control, help to account for this pattern. But there are more elaborate internal processes involved as well. From the viewpoint of an administrator, maintaining the credibility of his or her school and the validity of its ritual classifications is crucial to the school's success. With the confidence of the state bureaucracy, the federal government, the community, the profession, the pupils and their families, and the teachers themselves, the legitimacy of the school as a social reality can be maintained. However, if these groups decide that a school's ritual classifications are a "fraud," everything comes apart.

There are several ways in which the decoupling of structures from activities and outcomes maintains the legitimacy of educational organizations. Consider some reasons why an American administrator would avoid closely inspecting the internal processes of the school.

First, the avoidance of close inspection, especially when accompanied by elaborate displays of confidence and trust, can increase the commitments of internal participants. The agreement of teachers to participate actively in the organized social reality of the ritual classifications of education is crucial, and an administrator can trade off the matter of conformity to the details of instruction and achievement in order to obtain teachers' complicity and satisfaction. By agreeing that teachers have instructional competence and by visibly not inspecting instructional activities, an administrator shifts maximal social responsibility for upholding the rituals of instruction to the teachers. The myth of teacher professionalism and the autonomy associated with it, for example, function to increase the commitments of teachers.

A second reason for avoiding close inspection and evaluation arises from the fact that a good deal of the value of education has little to do with the efficiency of instructional activities. If education is viewed as a ceremonial enactment of the rituals of schooling, the quality of schooling can be seen to lie in its *costs:* spectacular buildings, expensive teachers in excessive number (a low student-teacher ratio), and elaborate and expensive topics (French for first-graders, or nuclear physics). To the state, the accrediting agencies, the community, and the participants themselves, costs of these kinds index the quality and meaning of a school. It therefore makes little sense to view a school as if it were producing instructional outcomes in an economic marketplace, since an economizing perspective would treat many of the critical features of a school as costly waste, as liabilities rather than assets.

It is enormously damaging for a school to view the categories that validate it, as well as the cost of their upkeep and prestige, as liabilities. The ritual of schooling is evaluated according to a logic in which quality and costs are equivocal. Expenditures per student or the number of books in the library are among common indices of educational quality, even though maximizing these indices may require a studied inattention to an economizing logic. The wise administrator will call attention to the elaborate and expensive structure of ritual classifications his school has, not to the amount of learning achieved per dollar.

Third, decoupling protects the ritual classification scheme from uncertainties arising in the technical core. In education, it is quite common that rules of practice institutionalized at state and federal levels create technical uncertainty at the local level. State-mandated curricula may be too advanced for the students at hand. And innovative state and federal programs often need to be adapted to the specific circumstances unique to the local school. Measuring what pupils actually learn in these programs or what teachers are actually teaching introduces unnecessary uncertainty, increases coordinative costs and creates doubts about the effectiveness of the status structure of the school and the categorical rules that define appropriate education.

Fourth, decoupling allows schools to adapt to inconsistent and conflicting institutionalized rules. Schools, of necessity, are plural organizations adapted to plural environments (Udy, 1971). This is especially true of American schools, with their welter of external pressure. One way to manage the uncertainty, conflict, and inconsistency created by this pluralistic situation is to buffer units from each other. Udy, in fact, sees this as a major explanation for the differentiation of modern organizations into specialized components. When differentiation is accompanied by isolation and autonomy of subunits rather than by interdependence and coordination, jurisdictional disputes among categories of professionals or incompatibilities among inconsistent programs are avoided. For example, in schools, the work of a large number of specialists— vocational educators, speech therapists, reading specialists—is organized separately and buffered from the usual classroom work.

Our point is this: By decoupling formal structures from activities, uncertainty about the effectiveness of the ritual categories is reduced. When the behavior of teachers and students is uninspected or located in isolated classrooms, the state, the community, and administrators are presented with little evidence of ineffectiveness, conflict, or inconsistency. And the teacher and student are free to work out the practicalities of their own unique relationship little disturbed by the larger social interpretation of which activity is appropriate to a given category. Further, in a pluralistic setting the number of ritual classifications institutionalized in the environment is large, and there are frequent additions and subtractions. By decoupling ritual subunits from one another, the school is able to incorporate potentially inconsistent ritual elements and to recruit support from a larger and more diverse set of constituencies.

By minimizing the resources devoted to coordination and control, the school furthers its ability to increase the ceremonial worth of its ritual categories. This strategy also cuts down the costs involved in implementing new categories and maximizes their chance of success. New programs or specialists need not be integrated into the structure; they merely need to be segmentally added to the organization. Further, new categories need not even imply a substantial reorganization of activity, as the activities of particular ritual actors and programs remain uninspected. The decoupling of the internal structure of education is therefore a successful strategy for maintaining support in a pluralistic environment.

The Logic of Confidence. The classifications of education, however, are not rules to be cynically manipulated. They are the sacred rituals that give meaning to the whole enterprise, both internally and externally. These categories are understood everywhere to *index* education. They are not understood to *be* education, but they are also not understood simply to be alienating bureaucratic constraints. So the decoupling that is characteristic of school systems must be carried out by all participants in the utmost good faith.

Interaction in school systems, therefore, is characterized both by the assumption of good faith and the actualities of decoupling. This is *the logic of confidence*: Parties bring to each other the taken-for-granted, good-faith assumption that the other is, in fact, carrying out his or her defined activity. The community and the board have confidence in the superintendent, who has confidence in the principal, who has confidence in the teachers. None of these people can say what the other does or produces (for example, see Chapter Nine), but the plausibility of their activity requires that they have confidence in each other.

The logic of confidence is what Goffman (1967) calls "face work"—the process of maintaining the other's face or identity and thus of maintaining the plausibility and legitimacy of the organization itself. Face work avoids embarrassing incidents and preserves the organization from the disruption of an implausible performance by any actor. Goffman (1967, pp. 12–18) discusses three dimensions of this face-saving procedure: *avoidance, discretion,* and *overlooking.* Decoupling promotes each of these dimensions. Avoidance is maximized when the various clusters of identities are buffered from each other, when the organization is segmentalized, and when interaction across units is minimized (as by the self-contained classroom). Discretion is maximized when inspection and control are minimized or when participants are cloaked with "professional" authority. Finally, participants often resort to overlooking embarrassing incidents or to labeling them as deviant, as characteristic of particular individuals, and therefore as nonthreatening to the integrity of the ritual classification scheme.

It must be stressed that face work and the logic of confidence are not merely personal orientations but are also institutional in character. For instance, a state creates a rule that something called "history" must be taught in high schools. This demand is not inspected or examined by organizational procedures but is controlled through confidence in teachers. Each teacher of history has been credentialed. There is an incredible sequence of confidences here, with faces being maintained up and down the line: The state has confidence in the district, the district in the school, and the school in the teacher. The teacher is deserving of confidence because an accrediting agency accredited the teacher's college. The accrediting agency did not, of course, inspect the instruction at the college but relied on the certification of its teachers, having confidence in the universities which the teachers attended. The accrediting agency also has confidence in the organization of the college—its adminstrators and departments. These people, in turn, had confidence in their teachers, which enabled them to label certain courses as *history* without inspecting them. The chain goes on and on. Nowhere (except in the concealed relation between teacher and pupil) is there any inspection. Each link is a matter of multiple exchanges of confidence.

The most visible aspect of the logic of confidence in the educational system is the myth of teacher professionalism. Even in higher education—where teachers typically have no professional training for teaching—the myth is maintained. It serves to legitimate the confidence the system places in its teachers and to provide an explanation of why this confidence is justified. This explains one of the most puzzling features of educational professionalism —why the professional status of teachers rises dramatically with the creation of an educational bureaucracy. It is conventional to assume that professionalism and bureaucracy are at odds, although the evidence rarely supports this view (Corwin, 1970). In fact, even though the ideology supporting the creation of large American educational bureaucracies argued for close control, evaluation, and inspection of teachers, it seems clear that these bureaucracies greatly lowered the amount of such control (Tyack, 1974). Prebureaucratic teachers were often under direct inspection and control of the community that hired them. The bureaucracy, justified on the grounds that it would assume responsibility for inspection and control of instruction, however, almost immediately began to inspect and control only the superficial and categorical aspects of teachers. To account for this lack of specific inspection and control of instruction, the myth of professionalism arose very early, despite the original intentions of the founders. Our argument—that professionalism serves the requirements of confidence and good faith —explains this growth: The myth of teacher professionalism helps to justify the confidence placed in teachers and to legitimate the buffering of uncertainty in the performance of pupils and teachers in educational organizations.

Overview of the Argument. With the growth of corporate society, especially the growth of nation-states, education comes into exchange with society. Schooling—the bureaucratic standardization of ritual classifications—emerges and becomes the dominant form of educational organization. Schools become organized in relation to these ritual categories in order to gain support and legitimacy. In America, the local and pluralistic control of schools causes these classifications to have little impact on the actual instructional activities of local schools. Thus the official classifications of education, although enforced in public respects, are decoupled from actual activity and can contain a good deal of internal inconsistency without harm. As a result, American schools in practice contain multiple realities, each organized with respect to different internal or exogenous pressures. These multiple realities conflict so little because they are buffered from each other by the logic of confidence that runs through the system.

In this fashion, educational organizations have enjoyed enormous success and have managed to satisfy an extraordinary range of external and internal constituents. The standardized categories of American society and its stratification system are maintained, while the practical desires of local community constituents and the wishes of teachers, who are highly satisfied with their jobs, are also catered to. As new constituents rise up and make new demands, these pressures can be accommodated within certain parts of the system with minimal impact on other parts. A great deal of adaptation and change can occur without disrupting actual activity. And, conversely, the activities of teachers and pupils can change a good deal, even though the abstract categories have remained constant.

Implications for Research and Theory

The arguments we have discussed have many implications for research on educational organizations. We see schools (and other organizations) as vitally—and in complex ways—affected by their institutional environments. Much more research is needed, carefully examining such institutional variations—among societies or among institutions within societies—and their organizational impact.

Propositions Comparing Societies. First, the formal structure of educational organizations tends to come into correspondence with environmental categories. These ritual categories, further, tend to be linked to the nation-state, implying that formal education structure ought to vary more between societies than within them. Second, educational content and instruction is organizationally most loosely coupled in societies with pluralistic systems of control, such as the United States, and is more tightly controlled in countries with centralized systems. Further, ambiguities and vacuities in the educational languages specifying the meaning and implications of the ritual elements of educational organization should be found to be greatest in pluralistic systems. Third, the more education is a national institution of central importance, the more loosely coupled its internal structure and the more control rests on the logics of confidence and of professionalization.

Propositions Comparing Education with Other Institutions. First, instructional work in institutionalized educational systems is less closely inspected or coordinated than similar work in other institutions such as businesses or armies. Second, educational structures are more responsive to even inconsistent environmental pressures than organizations in other institutional settings. In part, this is because they are buffered from their own internal technical work activity. This situation permits more internal and external constituent groups to perceive that they have power in education organizations than in other organizations.

Propositions Comparing Educational Organizations. First, the formal structure of educational organizations responds to environmental (or societal) categories. It varies less in response to variations in the actual characteristics of clienteles or of problems of instruction. Similarly, changes in environmental rules defining education produce more rapid formal structural changes than do changes in the content or methods of instruction. Second, educational organizations are internally coordinated and legitimated by their environmental categories, not primarily by their own technical activity or instructional output. Variations in their success at maintaining correspondence with environmental rules predict the success, survival, and stability of educational organizations more than do variations in their instructional effectiveness. Third, loosely coupled educational organizations structurally respond more effectively to environmental pressures and changes than do tightly coupled organizations. Instruction adapts more quickly, in such organizations, to the informal pressures of teachers and parents, while structures respond more quickly to environmental institutional categories.

Propositions Comparing Internal Components of Organization. First, in educational organizations, feedback concerning the work and output of teachers and schools tends to be eliminated, even if it happens to exist. Participants employ logic of confidence, and overlook observations of actual work and outcomes. Feedback on the categorical status of teachers, schools, students, and programs tends to be retained.

Second, educational organizations respond to external institutional pressures with programmatic or categorical change, minimizing the impact on instruction. They respond to variations in teacher or parent preference with activity change, but not necessarily with categorical change. Each part or level of the system responds relatively independently to its environment. Thus, the greatest part of organizationally planned innovation in instruction is never implemented, and the greatest part of instructional innovation is not organizationally planned.

Third, the loose coupling of instructional activity in educational organizations permits more internal and external constituent groups to perceive that they have power in this area than over other policy decisions.

Implications for Organization Theory. The arguments above have many implications for theory and research on organizations other than schools. Our arguments seem quite plausible in terms of the literature on school organization, but some of them are sharply at odds with the theory of organizations (for a more detailed suggestion, see J. Meyer and Rowan, 1977). Perhaps organization theory is imperfect. It seems unlikely that educational organizations are so extremely unusual. Indeed, a most fundamental observation in research on all sorts of organizations is that rules and behavior—the formal and the informal—are often dissociated or inconsistent. This is the same observation we have been making about schooling organizations, and it may be time to stop being surprised at it. The surprise arises, not because the observations are novel, but because researchers take too limited a view of formal organizations. They see formal structure as created to actually coordinate production in the case of market organizations and conformity in the case of political bureaucracy (see Thompson, 1967; Scott, 1975). And they are consequently surprised when formal structure and activity are loosely linked.

It is true that production requires some coordination, as political structure demands some conformity. But it is also true that the myth or social account of production and conformity is critical. Much of the value of what we purchase lies in intangibles. Much of the value of social control and order inheres in the faith that is generated. Put differently, organizations must have the *confidence* of their environments, not simply be in rational exchange with them. And those that have this confidence and legitimacy receive all sorts of social resources that provide for success and stability. That is, organizations must be legitimate, and they must contain legitimate accounts or explanations for their internal order and external products. *The formal structure of an organization is in good part a social myth and functions as a myth whatever its actual implementation.* In small part, it is a mythical account the organization attempts to institutionalize in society. In much greater part, the formal structure is taken over from the accounts already built into the environment. Incorporating the environmental myth of the organization's activities legitimates the organization both externally and internally (Dowling and Pfeffer, 1975) and stabilizes it over and above the stability generated by its network of internal relations and production. Organizations integrate themselves by incorporating the wider institutional structures as their own.

Thus, if systematic safety problems are "discovered" by the environment, safety officers are invented: Their existence explains how the organization has "taken into account" safety problems. (Who actually deals with safety is another matter.) So also with pollution control, labor relations, public relations, advertising, affirmative action, or research and development. Some of these activities may, in a day-to-day sense, actually get done: Our point here is that incorporating them in the formal structure of the organization has the function of legitimating myths and that such myths may be created quite independently of the activities they index. All these units represent the formal incorporation by the organization of environmental definitions of activities that then become part of the firm's account. Incorporating them deflects criticism from internal coalitions. It also legitimates the organization externally: Banks lend money to *modern* firms. Role handles are provided: Other organizations have someone inside the firm "with whom they can deal." The legal system may require such forms of accountability. Firms often incorporate external values in a very explicit way by attaching units and products "shadow prices" derived not from any production function but from market prices external to the firm.

The formal structure of an organization incorporates (and in some respects *is*) an environmental ideology or theory of the organization's activity. As the environmental ideology changes, so does the formal structure. No wonder the formal structure may be poorly adapted to the actual ongoing activity, which has to coordinate internal exigencies of its own.

A critical aspect of modern structure arises from the rationality of modern society and of organizations as myths. Formal organizational structures represent more than mere theories of activity: They must represent *rational, functional* theories. The structural account they present to society must give every appearance of rationality. Much of the irrationality of life in modern organizations arises because the organization itself must maintain a rational corporate persona: We must find planners and economists who will waste their time legitimating plans we have already made, accounts to justify our prices, and human relations professionals to deflect blame from our conflicts. Life in modern organizations is a constant interplay between the activities that we need to carry on and the organizational accounts we need to give.

This discussion generates several implications for organization theory. First, formal organizational structure reflects and incorporates prevailing environmental theories and categories, often without altering activity. These environmental rules constitute taken-for-granted understandings in the organization. Organizational actors are constantly in the business of managing categories abstracted directly from environmental theories.

Second, organizational structure has two faces: It conforms to environmental categories and categorical logics, and it classifies and controls activity. Organizational actors must take into account both what they are doing and the appearances of what they are doing.

Third, to accommodate both appearance and reality, organizational structure must always be partly decoupled from actual activity. Special managers may arise to adjudicate relationships between the categories of the formal structure and actual activities. Personnel officers classify persons and jobs into categories, registrars and admitting physicians institutionalize official diagnoses, accountants organize activity into budgets and budget categories, and so on. Linking the organization as a formal structure with the organization as a network of activities is a major task, and it tends to introduce inconsistencies and anomalies into both domains.

This view of organizations as constituted and coordinated at every point by taken-for-granted environmental understandings is considerably different from most prevailing views. Both "closed-systems" and "open-systems" views of organizations tend to see them as encountering the environment at their *boundaries*. We see the structure of an organization as derived from and legitimated by the environment. In this view, organizations begin to lose their status as internally interdependent systems and come to be seen as dramatic reflections of—dependent subunits within—the wider institutional environment.

5

Social Structure and Organizational Type

William G. Ouchi
Alfred M. Jaeger

"In a time of stress, like the one we have been through, a lot of people come home again to the fact that the churches and schools, the service clubs, and lodge halls hold much of our society together" (Sidey, 1975, p. 8).

It is true that society has traditionally relied on the church and the club as well as the family, the neighborhood, and the childhood friendship to provide the social support and the normative anchors that make collective life possible. Sociologists have long

The ideas expressed here were shaped through discussions with many managers and academics. We are particularly indebted to Melvin B. Lane, L. W. Lane, Jr., Patricia James Lyman, Alan Wilkins, Alice Kaplan, Raymond Price, David Gibson, and Jerry B. Johnson. This research was supported by grants from the Stanford University Research Development Fund, from the Alcoa Foundation, and from E. I. du Pont de Nemours and Company, for which we are grateful. This paper is based on "Type Z Organization: Stability in the Midst of Mobility" by William G. Ouchi and Alfred M. Jaeger, *Academy of Management Review*, in press.

contended that membership in stable primary groups is essential in every society. It is through such stable ties that basic needs are met for affiliation, for psychological security, and for more mundane forms of physical and financial support. The society that offers a rich network of these affiliative networks is a healthy one: A society in which such networks are sparse becomes anomic. This basic argument has a long history from the work of Durkheim (1933) and Tönnies ([1887] 1957), to Sumner (1907) and Wirth (1938) and more recently from Parsons (1951) and Kasarda and Janowitz (1974). It survives despite a lack of consistent empirical support. In each case, it is asserted both that urban life is antithetical to the traditional forms of primary group affiliation that are held to be necessary, and it is furthermore asserted that the absence of these institutions (club, neighborhood, church, and so on) is largely responsible for various contemporary social ills, including drug abuse, alcoholism, child abuse, and divorce (for example, see Halpern, 1972; M. Moore, 1973; Angell, 1951, 1974; Form, 1975; Srole and others, 1962).

Whether it is the effects of city size, density, and heterogeneity (Wirth, 1938); of increasingly short tenure in a single place of residence (Kasarda and Janowitz, 1974); or of factory work and technological change (Mayo, 1945), many observers have for decades agreed that the traditional sources of affiliation are disappearing. Perhaps the most discouraging scenario is that painted by Homans (1950, p. 457): "Now all the evidence of psychiatry . . . shows that membership in a group sustains a man, enables him to maintain his equilibrium under the ordinary shocks of life, and helps him to bring up children who will in turn be happy and resilient. If his group is shattered around him, if he leaves a group in which he was a valued member, and if, above all, he finds no new group to which he can relate himself, he will under stress, develop disorders of thought, feeling and behavior. . . . The cycle is vicious; loss of group membership in one generation may make men less capable of group membership in the next. The civilization that, by its very process of growth, shatters group life will leave men and women lonely and unhappy."

Although recent surveys indicate that the decline in church membership of the past twenty-five years may be ending and that the proportion of the populace that changes residence each year is showing signs of a decline, no one expects the old institutions of neighborhood, church, and extended family to return to their central importance. Faced with this situation, one cannot help but wonder what institutional forms will provide the interstices to hold American society together in the coming decades.

We contend, in this chapter, that in many cases it is the work organization that can and will take on this role. We argue that, because the work organization is not now and never was isolated from its social environs (as recommended by Udy, 1962) but rather is a reflection of its social environment (see Chapter Four), it is not at all surprising to expect the role of the work organization to evolve in this manner. As with all things, the core of this idea has been around for some time; for example, "Mayo shows us for the first time in the form of specific instances that it is within the power of industrial administrators to create within industry itself a partially effective substitute for the old stabilizing effect of the neighborhood. Given stable employment, it might make of industry (as of the small town during most of our national life) a socially satisfying way of life as well as a way of making a living" (Donham, in Mayo, 1945, p. ix).

What Donham and Mayo were describing is what we now cynically refer to as the misplaced "paternalism" of the mines, the plantations, and the small-town companies right after the industrial revolution. There is no doubt that those organizations served as a central focus in the affiliative network of their employees, and there is also little doubt that they were often run autocratically, sometimes to the point of totalitarianism. Yet there are other examples of the work organization that not only admits but even actively incorporates its social environment, while simultaneously serving as the social "glue" that holds peoples' lives together and managing to maintain individual freedoms. Lipset, Trow, and Coleman (1956) described the effects of shift work and of apprenticeship training on the development of a holistic subculture within the typesetting union. Trist and Bamforth (1951) had described a similar phenomenon in the coal mines of England, as did Gouldner (1954) in a gypsum mine. Above ground, Selznick (1949) described the blurring of the boundary between work organization and community, while Mann and Hoffman (1960) documented the effect of work flow technology in a continuous-process industry on the development of close social groupings. In each of these cases, the work organization assumed a very central role in the whole of the social existence of its members. Not coincidentally, in each case the members of the work organization were largely cut off from the possibility of interaction with other members of the community: Whether because of shift work, of being underground, or of being in a "company town," these people had little choice but to center their affiliations around their fellow workers.

Employment already defines many aspects of our lives: our socio-economic status, our children's education, the kinds and length of vacations we take, the frequency and severity with which we can afford to become ill, and even the way in which pension benefits allow us to live our retirement years. From childhood to the grave, the work organization plays a central role in identifying us and in molding our lives. We see in Japan (Abegglen, 1958), in Poland (Kolarska, 1975), and in China (Whyte, 1973) models of work organization that provide such an organization of life and of society, but we have been unwilling to borrow these models, because they do not permit the individual freedom that is quintessential to American life.

With memories of the totalitarian paternalism of the mines and the plantations still not healed by time, Americans have been reluctant to even consider the work organization as the social umbrella under which people can live lives that are free, happy, and productive. The ideology of independence that is part of the basic fabric of the American persona recoils at the thought of individual freedom subordinated to collective commitment. American heroes are the rough, tough individualists, the John Waynes, the Evel Knievels, the Gloria Steinems. Our most pitiable figures are those who lose their individuality in some larger, corporate entity and become organization men, faceless men in gray flannel suits.

Those who concern themselves with the ills of modern society (for example, Reissman, 1964; Short, 1971; Warren, 1972; Kasarda and Janowitz, 1974) universally ignore the work organization as a possible source of moral integration. This oversight is hardly surprising, since those who study organizations (for example, Udy, 1962; Thompson, 1967) actively prescribe that work organizations should seek, insofar as possible, to seal themselves off from the nonachievement-oriented social environment in which they exist. Thus it is also not surprising that a number of scholars (for example, Goode, 1960; Kahn and others, 1964) have emphasized the strains and conflicts that "inevitably" occur when one individual must simultaneously occupy roles as a member of a work organization on the one hand and of a church, family, or other nonachievement-oriented group on the other. In this chapter, we argue that the separation of work organization from community is not only not inevitable but is even uncommon and most certainly undesirable. For the American case, however, the only experiment that anyone can remember of combining work and community is that which produced the plantations and the sweatshops, a period to which no one wishes to return. The problem, then, is to discover a means through which the work organization can serve both as a social glue and as a democratic institution.

A New Organizational Form

The beginning of an answer to this question may be found in a study published by one of the authors (Johnson and Ouchi, 1974). Interviews were conducted with employees of twelve Japanese and thirteen American firms that had operations in both the United States and Japan. In Japanese companies in Japan, the now familiar characteristics first reported by Abegglen (1958) were found again to exist. These include almost total inclusion of the employee into the work organization so that the superior concerns himself with the personal and family life of each subordinate; a collective, nonindividual approach to work and to responsibility; and extremely high identification of the individual with his company. These characteristics are largely the result of the lifetime employment system that characterizes large companies in Japan (see also Cole, 1971; Dore, 1973; Nakane, 1973).

The surprising finding of the study was that Japanese companies that have opened operations in the United States are applying a slightly modified form of the pure Japanese type with some success. While they do not provide company housing or large bonuses as in Japan, they attempt to create the same sort of complete inclusion of the employee into the company. That means that supervisors are taught to be aware of all aspects of an employee's life, that extrawork social life is often connected to other employees, that corporate values are adjusted to reflect employee needs as well as profit needs, and that high job security is protected above all else. The American employees expressed a great deal of liking for this "atmosphere" or "climate," with the managerial staff in particular noting the difference from their previous employers.

The study gave evidence that, while Americans probably do not ever want to return to old-style paternalism, they seem to favor a work organization that provides affiliative ties, stability, and job security. The Japanese-American mixed form suggested the model that may simultaneously permit individual freedom and primary group membership.

In the course of this research, it became apparent that there are some American companies that, by reputation, have many of the characteristics of this mixed model. Best known of these are Kodak, Cummins Engine Company, IBM, Levi Strauss, National Cash Register, Procter and Gamble, Utah International, and Minnesota Mining and Manufacturing (3M). In each case, the historical rates of turnover are low, loyalty and morale are reputed to be very high, and identification with the company is reputed to be strong. In addition, it is notable that each of these companies has been among the most successful of American companies for many decades, a record that strongly suggests that something about the form of organization, rather than solely a particular product or market position, has kept the organization vital and strong. It is also widely believed that these companies have, in a sense, been co-opted by their employees. They do not express goals of short-term profitability; rather they pay some costs in order to maintain stability of employment through difficult times. In a real sense, these work organizations may have created the alternative to village life to which Elton Mayo referred.

Compare persons associated with this mixed model to the "ideal type" of bureaucrat whom Weber (1947) and Merton (1957) had in mind when they described the persons involved in the limited, contractual, only partially inclusive relationships that characterize traditional American organizations. In a sense, the scheme being proposed is an organizational analogue of Tönnies' *Gemeinschaft and Gesellschaft* (1957). From this perspective, one can see that just as societies suffer from poor mental health as a result of size, density, heterogeneity, and mobility, which lead to contractualism and segmentalism in life, work organizations can also become segmented and contractual as they grow. This is exactly what Weber (1947) expected. In fact, he advocated the development of a contractual Gesellschaft in work organizations to shield the meritocracy from outside ascriptive values and ties (see Udy, 1959a). In a stable society, individuals can develop ties outside of work to complement the impersonal nature of participation in a contractual organization. In a mobile and changing society, on the other hand, societal values and outside ties are weaker and pose less threat to the efficiency of the organization. Furthermore, more individuals are less likely to have developed personal ties outside of work that satisfactorily complement the impersonal interactions engaged in at work. Thus, organizations whose goals and philosophy are in tune with today's very general societal values can survive and even thrive by being more "personal."

Thus, the organizational form that best suits the social environment may be one that includes either much or little extrawork interaction. In California and in Arizona, where most people have few social "roots," work organizations may often take on broad social functions. In New York or Boston, where many people are of the second or third generation living in the same community, work organizations can be expected to be much more contractual and segmented in nature. First let us specify more clearly the types of work organization, and then we will be able to see the relationship between type of organization and type of social environment and their joint effect on the integration of society.

Three Ideal Types

In the following pages, we describe three ideal types of work organization, argue that each type is an integrated system, and contend that each type will yield either positive or negative outcomes for the society depending on certain environmental conditions.

The three types are A, J, and Z. Type A represents the Western organization, especially the North American and West European forms. Type J represents the Japanese and mainland Chinese forms, and Type Z is emerging from a type that is particularly suited to the United States of America today. Each of these types represents the distillation of interviews with a number of managers from all kinds of American and Japanese companies, from a pilot study conducted in a Type Z company, and from the preliminary results of a survey research project comparing two companies (see Ouchi and Johnson, 1977). Each is intended as an ideal or pure type; that is, as a representation of qualities that are present to some degree in all real organizations, which are believed to be systematically related to each other but which probably do not exist in pure form completely in any one real organization.

Each ideal type contains seven dimensions. Length of employment refers to the average number of years served within the corporation, considering all employees. This is important in two respects: First, if mean number of years of tenure is high, then employees will be more familiar with the workings of the organization and more likely to have developed friendships among their coworkers; second, if the new employee anticipates a long career within one organization, he or she will be willing to incur greater personal costs in order to become integrated into the culture of the organization.

The mode of decision making refers to the typical ways of dealing with nonroutine problems. Individual decision making is a mode in which the manager may or may not solicit information

Table 1. Characteristics of Two Familiar Organizational Ideal Types: A and J.

Type A (American)	*Type J (Japanese)*
Short-term employment	Lifetime employment
Individual decision making	Consensual decision making
Individual responsibility	Collective responsibility
Rapid evaluation and promotion	Slow evaluation and promotion
Explicit, formalized control	Implicit, informal control
Specialized career path	Nonspecialized career path
Segmented concern	Holistic concern

or opinion from others, but in which he or she expects and is expected by others to arrive at a decision without obligation to consider the views of others. In consensual decision making, the manager will not decide until others who will be affected have had
sufficient time to offer their views, feel they have been fairly heard,
and are willing to support the decision even though they may not
feel that it is the best one (see Schein, 1969, chaps. 4–8, for a discussion of these modes of decision making).

Responsibility is not easily distinguished from decision-
making style in all cases, but it represents an important, independent dimension. Individual responsibility as a value is a necessary
precondition for the conferring of rewards on individuals in a
meritocracy. It is possible that a manager could engage in consensual decision making while clearly retaining individual responsibility for the decision: Indeed, we argue that Type Z organization
exhibits just this combination. In the Type J organization, we observe that responsibility for overseeing projects and for accepting
rewards or punishments is born collectively and jointly by all members of a subunit. American companies in Japan that have attempted to introduce the notion of individual responsibility among
managers and among blue-collar workers have met strong resistance from their employees. In the United States, however, individual responsibility is such a central part of the national culture
that no organization can replace it with the collective value of the
J type.

The speed with which evaluation and promotion of individuals takes place is self-explanatory, but its effects are subtle. If promotion is slow, managers have time to become acquainted with the
people and the customs that surround their jobs. They will be
shaped by and ultimately assimilated into the corporate culture.
For better or worse, the maverick will not be promoted until he
has learned to abide by these local customs. It follows that if the
organization has had a history of rapid promotion for many years,
it will not have as unified a culture as will an organization with
slower rates of upward mobility.

In addition to the effects on cultural transmission, the speed
of evaluation has significant effects on the character of interpersonal relationships. In an achievement-oriented organization, eval-

uations of performance must be free of dimensions such as friendship or kinship, which are not related to achievement. The only solution open to an evaluator is an impersonal relationship, since personal feelings cannot influence the evaluation if there are no personal feelings. If evaluations occur rapidly—for example, once each six months—the subject of the evaluation will typically be known only to the direct supervisor, who will be charged with the responsibility of rendering the evaluation. The supervisor is thus blocked from forming personal, friendship ties with the subordinate. If major evaluations occur only once every five or ten years (as is common in Japanese firms), however, then the evaluation is no longer explicitly rendered by one superior but rather emerges through a nonexplicit process of agreement between the many superiors who know the subordinate. Because he is one among many judges, the direct superior is freed from the need to preserve an "objective" attitude toward the subordinate and thus can take a personal interest in him or her. Under rapid evaluation, therefore, the formation of personal ties is much less likely to occur than under slow evaluation.

The dimension of control is represented in the ideal type in an oversimplified manner. In a sense, the whole ideal type represents a form of social control, and each of the three ideal types achieves this social control in a different manner. However, we can identify in Type A organizations the use of explicit standards, rules, regulations, and measures of performance as the primary technique of ensuring that actual performance meets desired performance. In the Type Z, by contrast, expectations of behavior or of output are not explicitly stated but rather are to be deduced from a more general understanding of the corporate philosophy. For example, during one of the authors' visits to a Japanese bank in California, both the Japanese president and the American vice-presidents of the bank accused each other of being unable to formulate objectives. The Americans meant that the Japanese president could not or would not give them explicit, quantified targets to attain over the next three or six months, while the Japanese meant that the Americans could not see that once they understood the company's philosophy, they would be able to deduce for themselves the proper objective for any conceivable situation.

The degree to which a career path is typically specialized according to function or not differs greatly between organizational types. In the A organization, an upwardly mobile manager will typically remain within a functional specialty, going from bookkeeper to clerical supervisor to assistant department head of accounting to head of the accounting department, for example. In the J organization, the typical career path is not specialized by function but may go from bookkeeper to supervisor of the planning department. A specialized career path yields professionalization, decreases organizational loyalty, and facilitates movement of the individual from one company to another. A nonspecialized career path yields localism, increases organizational loyalty, and impedes interfirm mobility. Career specialization also increases problems of coordination between individuals and subunits, while nonspecialization eases the coordination problem. On the other hand, career specialization yields the scale economies of task specialization and expertise, whereas nonspecialized career paths often sacrifice these benefits. Note that the A and J organizations may be the same in formal structure; they may have equal task specialization, for example, but individuals will move through those specialties in quite different patterns. Because differentiation is high structurally but low individually, problems of integration are reduced, with only a moderate sacrifice in expertise.

Concern refers to the holism with which employees view each other and especially to the concern with which the superior views the subordinate. In the A organization, the supervisor regards the subordinate in a purely task-oriented manner and may consider it improper to inquire into the personal life of the subordinate. In comparison to the segmented view of people, the manager in the J organization considers it part of his or her role to be fully informed of the personal circumstances of each subordinate.

By now, it has hopefully begun to be apparent that each of the ideal types represents a set of interconnected parts, each of which is dependent on at least one other part. The systemic nature of each type is best understood by putting each in an environmental context. The A type has developed in a society that is characterized by high rates of mobility of individuals and in a culture that supports norms of independence, self-reliance, and individual responsibility. A work organization in such a setting must contend with high rates of interfirm mobility and a short average tenure of employment. (See Cole, 1973, for a comparison of interfirm mobility rates in the United States and Japan). To the extent possible, an organization in this setting will reduce interdependence between individuals so as to avoid the start-up costs of replacing one part of a team. Individual decision making and individual responsibility both provide an adaptive response to rapid change of personnel. If interfirm mobility is high, it also becomes impossible to integrate new members into the organization on a large number of dimensions. It is much simpler to attend to only the one or two necessary task dimensions of the new member and to integrate only those. Thus a segmented concern will evolve, because a concern for the whole person presents an impossible problem to an organization with high turnover. As a result, however, the employee has only limited, contractual ties to the organization; has not internalized the values of the organization; and must be dealt with in a compliant relationship, one in which control is explicit and formalized. In addition, the organization has a relatively short time in which to realize productive benefits from the necessary investment in the individual (the costs of search and of whatever training is necessary), and it can best realize these benefits by having that person follow a highly specialized career path in which necessary learning can occur rapidly and scale economies are soon achieved. Finally, rapid turnover requires replacement of managers and thus rapid promotion of those at lower levels. Promotion must be preceded by evaluation, to preserve the impression if not the fact of a meritocracy, and thus evaluation also will occur rapidly.

Now let us consider the ideal Type J. These organizations have evolved in a society in which individual mobility has historically been low and in a culture that has supported norms of collectivism. Through an historical accident that preserved a feudal society in Japan into the nineteenth century and then, after the Meiji restoration, rushed Japan into full-blown industrialism (Nakane, 1973), feudal loyalties were transferred to major industrial institutions, with both owners and employees taking the appropriate historical roles of lord and vassal. Employees are expected to be in the same firm for a lifetime; thus control can be implicit and internalized rather than explicit and compliant (as in the A type). Indeed, this form of control will evolve because it is more reliable and because it can account for a wide variety of task- and person-oriented actions, whereas no explicit system of rules and regulations could be sufficiently comprehensive to encompass the range of behavior that occurs in a stable culture. These employees need not follow specialized career paths, because the organization can invest in them for a long period of time and be assured of repayment in later years. Thus they follow nonspecialized career paths, which has the effect of making them experts in the organization rather than experts in some function. They are no longer interchangeable with other organizations, since their particular set of skills and values is unique to one firm; but that is not a cost to them or to the firm. Rather, their loyalty to the firm has increased and so the firm need not monitor them closely, thus saving managerial overhead. Furthermore, problems of coordination are greatly reduced, since employees have both the information and the inclination to enable them to accommodate each other in jointly taking action. Since these individuals are to spend a lifetime together, they have an interest in maintaining harmonious relationships and thus to engage in consensual decision making. The larger culture strongly supports norms of collectivism, which are mirrored in the organization. No individual can properly take credit or blame for actions, since organizational action by its very nature is a joint product of many individuals. Given joint responsibility, rapid evaluation would be very difficult, since the task would be like that of performing a multivariate analysis with a sample of one observation. Since turnover and thus promotion occur slowly, however, evaluation need not proceed quickly, so that many observations of the individual are accumulated over a period of years before the first major evaluation is made. This slow evaluation, by taking the pressure off of a single superior, thus frees him or her to take a holistic concern for the employee.

The relationship between elements of the ideal types are many and complex. They are not yet completely specified; that is one task of our present research, and that task will be aided through empirical analysis of the relationship between the elements. Clearly, however, the major driving force behind development of the ideal types is the rate of interfirm mobility, which is closely related to the cultural values that aid or inhibit mobility (for example, mobility is more easily accepted under norms of individualism than under norms of collectivism). In fact, it can be argued that the A type is an adaptive response to high rates of social mobility while the J type is a response to low rates of social mobility, both forms fitting naturally with their environments. In a sense, the work organization in this view represents simply one of many ways in which members of a society are integrated. Thus the work organization will be both influenced by and will itself influence the structure of its surrounding society.

Having concluded that each of the ideal types represents a natural adaptation to a particular environment, we must now explain how the J type has apparently succeeded in the United States (Johnson and Ouchi, 1974). The United States provided the social environment in which the A type evolved. We are highly urbanized, we move about, we lead segmented lives, and thus we have created a situation in which a work organization must be able to rely on people who are strangers to each other and still get coordinated effort out of them. The answer was the A type, one that is contractual, formalized, and impersonal. Then how can a very different type, the J, flourish in this same social environment?

In order to answer this question, we have spent the past two years in interviewing managers from a large number of companies and collecting survey data (see Ouchi and Johnson, 1977). In particular, the interviews focused on those American companies that by reputation, have many of the characteristics of the Type J. Out of these interviews has come a conception of a third ideal type, Type Z, which initially appeared to be the J but differs from it in some essential characteristics:

• Long-term employment
• Consensual decision making
• Individual responsibility
• Slow evaluation and promotion
• Implicit, informal control with explicit, formalized measures
• Moderately specialized career path
• Holistic concern, including family

The ideal Type Z combines a basic cultural commitment to individualistic values with a highly collective, nonindividual pattern of interaction. It simultaneously satisfies old norms of independence and present needs for affiliation. Employment is effectively for a lifetime although not officially so, and turnover is low. Decision making is consensual, and in these companies there is often a highly self-conscious attempt to preserve the consensual mode. However, it is still the individual who is ultimately the decision maker and responsibility remains individual. This procedure clearly puts strains on the individual, who is held responsible for decisions singly but must arrive at them collectively. These strains are mitigated by the fact that evaluation and promotion take place slowly and that the basic control is implicit and subtle. Thus the complexities of collective decision making are taken into account in rendering personal evaluations, but there will be explicit measures of performance as in the Type A. In the Z organization, it is common to hear it said that, although there are lots of formal accounting measures of performance, the real evaluation is subjective and highly personal. No one gets rapidly promoted nor punished in a Z organization solely because their performance scores are good or bad. In an A organization, by contrast, people's careers often succeed or fail solely on the explicit performance measures, as must be the case in any purely formalized system. Career paths tend to be moderately specialized but are quite nonspecialized by comparison with the Type A organization. Again, the slowness of evaluation and the stability of membership promote holistic concern for people, particularly from superior to subordinate. In the Z organization, this holism includes the employee and his or her family in an active manner. That means that family members regularly interact with other organization members and their families and feel an identification with the organization.

The Function of Type Z Organization in Contemporary Society

It is evident that the ideal Type Z combines characteristics of both the A and J types in a unique pattern, but what is the meaning of this ideal type? More directly, why is the Z type useful in thinking about American organizations if the A type is the natural adaptation to this society and culture? If a second ideal type can be accommodated, it must be that the social conditions have changed.

In this case, the critical aspect of the environment is its ability to provide stable affiliations for individuals. It has been argued above that the traditional sources of affiliation in the American society have been the family, the church, the neighborhood, the voluntary association, and the long-term friendship. It has further been argued that urbanization and geographical mobility have weakened these sources of affiliation. We can now construct a table to represent the combination of societal and organizational sources of affiliation.

Note that Table 2 includes only two of the ideal types, A and Z. The third ideal type, J, represents the pure adaptation to a Japanese society and therefore is not useful as a representation of American organizations. The central point made by this table is as follows: Throughout most of its history, this nation has been high in sources of affiliation outside of the work place. Under this condition, Type A organization evolved, thus creating a stable, integrated state in which most people devoted most of their energies to affiliative networks away from the work place and were only partially included in the work organization. Had the work organization been Type Z, each employee would have been torn between two mistresses and in an overloaded state (Cell 1). In the past few decades, however, much of our society has moved from the "high" to the "low" affiliation state (see Kasarda and Janowitz, 1974; Short, 1971; Warren, 1972). High mobility has broken the traditional patterns of interaction, but the values that supported

Table 2. Organization and Society.

		High	Low
Affiliation in the Organization	High (Type Z)		2. Integrated
	Low (Type A)	3. Integrated	4. Anomic

those patterns will change more slowly. Those values support the notion of partial inclusion in work, of individuality, of the Type A organization. Thus, many find themselves largely in the anomic cell (Cell 4), with the society unable to provide affiliation and work organizations not organized to do so. Clearly, to return to a balanced state, it will have to be one in which affiliation comes mostly from the organization, not from the society at large.

Not all people need the same level of affiliation (or for that matter, of achievement or of power), and thus each person will respond differently to being in each of the cells. If we can accept the arguments of Abraham Maslow (1954), however, then we can contend that all people have a need for affiliation, belongingness, or love, and that this need can be satisfied only through the feeling that they are part of a group or company. On the average, then, people who are in Cell 4, the "anomic" cell, will have unfulfilled needs for affiliation, they will experience what we know as "anomie," the sensation that there is no anchor in life, no standards, and thus a feeling of being lost.

We can combine all of these elements in one model (Figure 1) that describes how the organization interacts with its social environment and with the needs of its individual members to produce high or low loyalty for the organization and high or low mental health for the employees.

If it is true that our society or parts of it are moving from high to low affiliation, then people who are employed in a Type Z organization should be better able to deal with stress and should

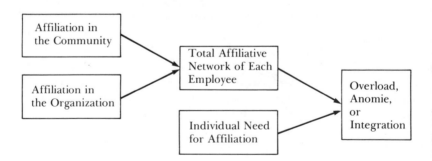

Figure 1. Sources of Primary Affiliation.

be happier than the population at large. Certainly the Type Z organization will be more appropriate for that segment of society that does lack stable and strong affiliative ties. That is not to suggest that the work organization will in any way replace or compete with other national institutions. Quite the opposite: If the company provides a strong basic stability in people's lives, then the family, the church, and the neighborhood can all flourish. It has been argued, for example, that the present high rates of divorce have a great deal to do with the fact that extramarital support groups no longer exist for many people (Ariès, 1962). Throughout the history of the monogamous relationship, it has always been true in the United States, except for the last few decades, that each male was also a member of a stable group of other males whom he came to know intimately and from whom he received support and that every female was also a member of a stable group of other females whom she came to know closely and who supported her. Now, it is not unusual to find a couple in their twenties living in Los Angeles or Denver; he is from Albany, she is from Duluth, and they have lived in Los Angeles for eight months. They live in an apartment community with a rate of turnover so high that deep relationships never develop; they do not belong to a church nor to a club or team; they have no relative nor childhood friends nearby. At the end of the day, he returns home and dumps all of his worries on her, and she returns home and drops all of her problems on him. The burden is too great; the monogamous relationship was never meant to carry such a weight. Seeking relief, they turn to the only escape available, which is divorce, and each finds him or herself then totally alone. Perhaps, in some instances, membership in a work community would provide the support that such people need. During the 1960s, they tried T-groups, encounter groups, communes, and all kinds of artificial groups. Those were not the answer and can never be. The social institutions that can provide stable affiliation must be those which bring people together simultaneously for other, socially legitimated purposes, such as producing goods, earning a living, or some such productive enterprise that justifies continued interaction in our Calvinist world.

　　At this point, some will object that they personally will never support a Type Z approach in their company or university, or that it would never work in their industry. Many of them are right. We have already pointed out that our society contains a range of people and environments; some will always prefer an employer who leaves them alone, who evaluates them purely on objective measures, who recognizes achievement through rapid promotion even over the heads of others. Of course, there will always be organizations for such people and for such tastes, but the trend will be toward the Type Z. In addition, stability of employment is not possible in some industries. Aerospace is one good example. In such an industry, a Type Z organization would be harmful; people would build rich ties with each other and a control system based on personal knowledge, which would be wrenched and destroyed when the contract came to an end and massive layoffs became necessary. Clearly, the Type Z form will not be for everyone.

In a sense, it is by luck that we have available some models of the Type Z organization to study and to learn from. Until recently, the Type A organization was the most successful form in our society. When people had relatives, neighbors, and churches, they didn't need Dr. Spock to tell them why the baby was purple, and they didn't need a company that provided them with a rich network of social contacts. In a few cases, however, companies grew up in small towns, or in places such as California that were populated by emigrants, or in industries that required frequent relocation of employees. In all three of these cases, one side effect was that people had no immediate form of social contact available to them except through their employer. The extreme case is the military base, which seems to look, feel, and smell the same whether it is in Hawaii, Illinois, or New York. In order to make life possible under conditions of high geographical mobility, the military has had to develop a culture that would be immediately familiar and secure no matter where its employees went. In a sense, these organizations, both public and private, had created a social vacuum for their employees and then had to develop internal sources of support to replace what had been taken away. Now, by a quirk of fate, the rest of the country is "catching up" with them as stable sources of support disappear elsewhere. We can look to such models for ideas to show us how to cope with our new society.

In a sense, it may be that all work organizations respond to the forces that have produced the loose coupling in educational organizations that Weick (1976) and J. Meyer and Rowan (Chapter Four) have described. In a society that holds very homogeneous beliefs about what constitutes an education, a school, a teacher, and a student, it may be both undesirable and impossible for an educational institution to possess tight internal connectedness. That is, since everyone, including parents, teachers, and students, knows absolutely how teachers should behave, how students should behave, and what schools should do and since they are sometimes in agreement and sometimes in disagreement on the means as well as the ends, it is not necessary nor possible for a school as a whole to make attempts to exert control. The mechanism of control exists in the social environment of the school.

In like manner, in a society in which all members hold homogeneous beliefs about what workers should do, what bosses should do, and about what the rights of companies are, it is not necessary for the company to exert very much control (nor is it possible), since the mechanism of control exists in the social environment. Indeed, because the company, like the school, imports all of its members from the environment, it is senseless to speak of a boundary between the work organization and the social environment. It is in such circumstances that the Type A organization flourished. With stable communities, strong ethnic churches, and active voluntary associations, a company has no choice but to reflect the values of the larger society and, wherever necessary, to decouple explicit intent from operational act, to remain loosely linked. The members of such an organization are only very loosely linked to each other, since their primary bonds are with groups that are external to the work organization.

If the society or a part of that society (such as southern California) becomes heterogeneous in its beliefs and if it lacks the community institutions that can produce homogeneity of values, however, then the situation is quite different. In this circumstance, the organization must produce its own internal control, since the environment does not supply very much. It is in this setting, in which the social environment is itself loosely coupled, that the work organization can take on the more tightly coupled Type Z form. Here is an apparent paradox: The Type Z organization, which is more diffuse, less precise than the Type A, is characterized by tighter rather than looser bonds between its members. But the paradox is only apparent: It is precisely because members in a Type Z organization share diffuse, overlapping connections between each other that they have no need for the precise, contractual understandings that characterize short-term relationships (see, for example, Light, 1972, pp. 59–61). The cultural underpinnings that bind them together serve to guide behavior and to provide warnings and rewards much more effectively than do the explicit mechanisms of control in the Type A organization.

The work organization is but one of the many institutions that serves to bind together the members of a society. Like any other institution, it both is shaped by and, in turn, shapes its social environment. At different times in the history of this nation and of other nations, each of the principal institutions have taken their turn in supplying relatively more of the glue that holds some or all of the society together. Certainly it has been true in contemporary times that the church was of central importance to ethnic groups at one time, the lending society (Hui or tanomoshi) at another, the school system at still another. Perhaps the current state of affairs is such that for some parts of our society it is the work organization that is best positioned to serve the integrative function in peoples' lives.

6

The Population Ecology of Organizations

Michael T. Hannan
John H. Freeman

Analysis of the effects of environment on organizational structure
has moved to a central place in organizations theory and research
in recent years. This shift has opened a number of exciting possibilities. As yet nothing like the full promise of the shift has been
realized. We believe that the lack of development is due in part to
a failure to bring ecological models to bear on questions that are
preeminently ecological. We argue for a reformulation of the
problem in population ecology terms.

Although there is a wide variety of ecological perspectives,

This chapter was originally published in the *American Journal of Sociology,*
March 1977. The research was supported in part by grants from the National
Science Foundation (GS-32065) and the Spencer Foundation. Helpful comments
were provided by Amos Hawley, François Nielsen, John Meyer, Marshall Meyer,
Jeffrey Pfeffer, and Howard Aldrich.

they all focus on selection. That is, they attribute patterns in nature to the action of selection processes. The bulk of the literature on organizations subscribes to a different view, which we call the *adaptation perspective*.[1] According to the adaptation perspective, subunits of the organization, usually managers or dominant coalitions, scan the relevant environment for opportunities and threats, formulate strategic responses, and adjust organizational structure appropriately.

The adaptation perspective is seen most clearly in the literature on management. Contributors to it usually assume a hierarchy of authority and control that locates decisions concerning the organization as a whole at the top. It follows, then, that organizations are affected by their environments according to the ways in which managers or leaders formulate strategies, make decisions, and implement them. Particularly successful managers are able either to buffer their organizations from environmental disturbances or to arrange smooth adjustments that require minimal disruption of organizational structure.

A similar perspective, often worded differently, dominates the sociological literature on the subject. It plays a central role in Parsons's (1956) functional analysis of organization-environment relations, and it is found in the more strictly Weberian tradition (see Selznick, 1957). It is interesting to note that, while functionalists have been interested in system effects and have based much of the logic of their approach on survival imperatives, they have not dealt with selection phenomena. This is probably a reaction against organization theory that reflects social Darwinism.

Exchange theorists have also embraced the adaptation perspective (Levine and White, 1961). And it is natural that theories emphasizing decision making take the adaptation view (March and Simon, 1958; Cyert and March, 1963). Even Thompson's (1967) celebrated marriage of open-systems and closed-systems thinking embraced the adaptation perspective explicitly (see particularly the second half of Thompson's book).

Clearly, leaders of organizations do formulate strategies and organizations do adapt to environmental contingencies. As a result, at least some of the relationship between structure and environment must reflect adaptive behavior or learning. But there is no reason to presume that the great structural variability among organizations reflects only or even primarily adaptation.

There are a number of obvious limitations on the ability of organizations to adapt. That is, there are a number of processes that generate structural inertia. The stronger the pressures, the lower the organizations' adaptive flexibility and the more likely that the logic of environmental selection is appropriate. As a consequence, the issue of structural inertia is central to the choice between adaptation and selection models.

The possibility that organization structure contains a large inertial component was suggested by Burns and Stalker (1961) and Stinchcombe (1965). But on the whole the subject has been ignored. A number of relevant propositions can be found in the organizations literature, however.

Inertial pressures arise from both internal structural arrangements and environmental constraints. A minimal list of the constraints arising from internal considerations follows.

1. An organization's investment in plant, equipment, and specialized personnel constitutes assets that are not easily transferable to other tasks or functions. The ways in which such sunk costs constrain adaptation options are so obvious that they need not be discussed further.
2. Organizational decision makers also face constraints on the information they receive. Much of what we know about the flow of information through organizational structures tells us that leaders do not obtain anything close to full information on activities within the organization and environmental contingencies facing the subunits.
3. Internal political constraints are even more important. When organizations alter structure, political equilibria are disturbed. As long as the pool of resources is fixed, structural change almost always involves redistribution of resources across subunits. Such redistribution upsets the prevailing system of exchange among subunits (or subunit leaders). So at least some subunits are likely to resist any proposed reorganization. Moreover, the benefits of structural reorganization are likely to be both generalized (designed to benefit the organization as a whole) and

long-run. Any negative political response will tend to generate short-run costs that are high enough that organizational leaders will forego the planned reorganization. (For a more extensive discussion of the ways in which the internal political economy of organizations impedes change or adaptation, see Downs, 1967, and Zald, 1970.)

4. Finally, organizations face constraints generated by their own history. Once standards of procedure and the allocation of tasks and authority have become the subject of normative agreement, the costs of change are greatly increased. Normative agreements constrain adaptation in at least two ways. First, they provide a justification and an organizing principle for those elements that wish to resist reorganization (that is, they can resist in terms of a shared principle). Second, normative agreements preclude the serious consideration of many alternative responses. For example, few research-oriented universities seriously consider adapting to declining enrollments by eliminating the teaching function. To entertain this option would be to challenge central organization norms.[2]

The external pressures toward inertia seem to be at least as strong. They include at least the following factors:

1. Legal and fiscal barriers to entry and exit from markets (broadly defined) are numerous. Discussions of organizational behavior typically emphasize barriers to entry (state licensed monopoly positions, and so on). Barriers to exit are equally interesting. There are an increasing number of instances in which political decisions prevent firms from abandoning certain activities. All such constraints on entry and exit limit the breadth of adaptation possibilities.

2. Internal constraints on the availability of information are paralleled by external constraints. The acquisition of information about relevant environments is costly particularly in turbulent situations where the information is most essential. In addition, the type of specialists employed by the organization constrains both the nature of the information it is likely to obtain (see Gra-

novetter, 1973) and the kind of specialized information it can process and utilize.

3. Legitimacy constraints also emanate from the environment. Any legitimacy an organization has been able to generate constitutes an asset in manipulating the environment. To the extent that adaptation (for example, eliminating undergraduate instruction in public universities) violates the legitimacy claims, it incurs considerable costs. So external legitimacy considerations also tend to limit adaptation.

4. Finally, there is the collective rationality problem. One of the most difficult issues in contemporary economics concerns general equilibria. If one can find an optimal strategy for some individual buyer or seller in a competitive market, it does not necessarily follow that there is a general equilibrium once all players start trading. More generally, it is difficult to establish that a strategy that is rational for a single decision maker will be rational if adopted by a large number of decision makers. A number of solutions to this problem have been proposed in competitive market theory, but we know of no treatment of the problem for organizations generally. Until such a treatment is established, we should not presume that a course of action that is adaptive for a single organization facing some changing environment will be adaptive for many competing organizations adopting a similar strategy.

A number of these inertial pressures can be accommodated within the adaptation framework. That is, one can modify and limit the perspective in order to consider choices within the constrained set of alternatives. But to do so greatly limits the scope of one's investigation. We argue that in order to deal with the various inertial pressures the adaptation perspective must be supplemented with a selection orientation.

We consider first two broad issues that are preliminary to ecological modeling. The first concerns appropriate units of analysis. Typical analyses of the relation of organizations to environments take the point of view of a single organization facing an environment. We argue for an explicit focus on populations of

organizations. The second broad issue concerns the applicability
of population ecology models to the study of human social organization. Our substantive proposal begins with Hawley's (1950,
1968) classic statement on human ecology. We seek to extend Hawley's work in two ways: by using explicit competition models to
specify the process producing isomorphism between organizational
structure and environmental demands and by using niche theory
to extend the problem to dynamic environments. We argue that
Hawley's perspective, modified and extended in these ways, serves
as a useful starting point for population ecology theories of
organizations.

Population Thinking in the Study of
Organization-Environment Relations

Little attention is paid in the organizations literature to issues concerning proper units of analysis (Freeman, 1975). In fact,
choice of unit is treated so casually as to suggest that it is not an
issue. We suspect that the opposite is true—that the choice of unit
involves subtle issues and has far-reaching consequences for research activity. For instance, in the case at hand, it determines
which of several ecological literatures can be brought to bear on
the study of organization-environment relations.

The comparison of unit choice facing the organizational analyst with that facing the bioecologist is instructive. To oversimplify
somewhat, ecological analysis is conducted at three levels: individual, population, and community. Events at one level almost always
have consequences at other levels. Despite this interdependence,
population events cannot be reduced to individual events (since
individuals do not reflect the full genetic variability of the population), and community events cannot be simply reduced to population events. Both the latter employ a population perspective that
is not appropriate at the individual level.

The situation faced by the organizations analyst is more
complex. Instead of three levels of analysis, he faces at least five:
(1) members, (2) subunits, (3) individual organizations, (4) populations of organizations, and (5) communities of (populations of)
organizations. Levels 3 to 5 can be seen as corresponding to the

three levels discussed for general ecology, with the individual organization taking the place of the individual organism. The added complexity arises because organizations are more nearly decomposable into constituent parts than are organisms. Individual members and subunits may move from organization to organization in a manner that has no parallel in nonhuman organization.

Instances of theory and research dealing with the effects of environments on organizations are found at all five levels. For example, Crozier's well-known analysis of the effects of culture on bureaucracy focuses on the cultural materials members bring to organizations (1964). At the other end of the continuum, we find analyses of "organizational fields" (Turk, 1970; Aldrich and Reiss, 1976). But the most common focus is on *the* organization and *its* environment. In fact, this choice is so widespread that there appears to be a tacit understanding that individual organizations are the appropriate units for the study of organization-environment relations.

We argue for a parallel development of theory and research at the population (and, ultimately, the community) level. Because of the differing opinions about levels of analysis, "population" has at least two referents. Conventional treatments of human ecology suggest that the populations relevant to the study of organization-environment relations are those aggregates of members attached to the organization or, perhaps, served by the organization. In this sense, the organization is viewed as analogous to a community: It has collective means of adapting to environmental situations. The unit character of a population so defined depends on shared fate. All members share to some extent in the consequences of organizational success or failure.

We use the term *population* in a second sense: to refer to aggregates of organizations rather than members. Populations of organizations must be alike in some respect; that is, they must have some unit character. Unfortunately, identifying a population of organizations is no simple matter. The ecological approach suggests that one focus on common fate with respect to environmental variations. Since all organizations are distinctive, no two are affected identically by any given exogenous shock. Nevertheless, we can identify classes of organizations that are relatively homogeneous in terms of environmental vulnerability. Notice that the populations of interest may change somewhat from investigation to investigation, depending on the analyst's concern. Populations of organizations referred to are not immutable objects in nature but are abstractions useful for theoretical purposes.

If we are to follow the lead of population biologists, we must identify an analogue to the biologist's notion of species. Various species are defined ultimately in terms of genetic structure. As Monod (1971) indicates, it is useful to think of the genetic content of any species as a blueprint. The blueprint contains the rules for transforming energy into structure. Consequently, all of the adaptive capacity of a species is summarized in the blueprint. If we are to identify a species analogue for organizations, we must search for such blueprints. These will consist of rules or procedures for obtaining and acting on inputs in order to produce an organizational product or response.

The type of blueprint one identifies depends on substantive concerns. For example, Marschak and Radner (1972) employ the term "organizational form"[3] to characterize the key elements of the blueprint as seen within a decision-making framework. For them, the blueprint or form has two functions: an information function that describes the rules used in obtaining, processing, and transmitting information about the states of external environments and an activity function that states the rules used in acting on received information so as to produce an organizational response. To the extent that one can identify classes of organizations that differ with regard to these two functions, one can establish classes or forms of organization.

Since our concerns extend beyond decision making, however, we find Marschak and Radner's definition of forms too limiting. In fact, there is no reason to limit a priori the variety of rules or functions that may define relevant blueprints. So for us an organizational form is a blueprint for organizational action, for transforming inputs into outputs. The blueprint can usually be inferred, albeit in somewhat different ways, by examining any of the following: (1) the formal structure of the organization in the narrow sense—tables of organization, written rules of operation, and so on; (2) the patterns of activity within the organization—what actually gets done by whom; or (3) the normative order—the ways of organizing that are defined as right and proper by both members and relevant sectors of the environment.

To complete the species analogue, we must search for qualitative differences among forms. It seems most likely that we will find such differences in the first and third areas, formal structure and normative order. The latter offers particularly intriguing possibilities. Whenever the history of an organization, its politics, and its social structure are encoded in a normative claim (for example, professionalization and collegial authority), one can use these claims to identify forms and define populations for research.

Having defined the organizational form, we can provide a more precise definition of a population of organizations. Just as the organizational analyst must choose a unit of analysis, so must he choose a system for study. Systems relevant to the study of organization-environment relations are usually defined by geography, by political boundaries, by market or product considerations, and so on. Given a systems definition, a population of organizations consists of all the organizations within a particular boundary that have a common form. That is, the population is the form as it exists or is realized within a specified system.

Both uses of the term *population* (and the ecological theories implied thereby) are likely to prove beneficial to the study of organizational structure. The first, more common, view suggests that organizational structure ought to be viewed as an outcome of a collective adaptive process. According to this view, structure and change ought to depend on the adaptiveness of subunits and on the differential access of subunits to environmental resources. The second view ignores the adaptive activities of elements within the organization except as they constitute organizational structure. It focuses on the organization as an adapting unit. Certainly both perspectives are needed. We are concerned here only with the latter, however.

Finally, we would like to identify the properties of populations most interesting to population ecologists. The main concern in this regard was expressed clearly by Elton (1927, p. 34): "In solving ecological problems we are concerned with *what animals do* in their capacity as whole, living animals, not as dead animals or as a series of parts of animals. We have next to study the circumstances under which they do those things, and, most important of all, the limiting factors which prevent them from doing certain other things. By solving these questions it is possible to discover the reasons for *the distribution and numbers of animals in nature.*" Hutchinson (1959), in the subtitle to his famous essay, "Homage to Santa Rosalia," expressed the main focus even more succinctly: "Why Are There So Many Kinds of Animals?" Taking our lead from these distinguished ecologists, we suggest that a population ecology of organizations must seek to understand the distributions of organizations across environmental conditions and the limitations on organizational structures in different environments and must more generally seek to answer the question, "Why are there so many kinds of organizations?"

Discontinuities in Ecological Analysis

Utilization of models from ecology in the study of organizations poses a number of analytic challenges involving differences between human and nonhuman organizations with regard to their essential ingredients. Consider, first, the nongenetic transmission of information. Biological analyses are greatly simplified by the fact that most useful information concerning adaptation to the environment (which information we call *structure*) is transmitted genetically. Genetic processes are so nearly invariant that extreme continuity in structure is the rule. The small number of imperfections generates structural changes, which, if accepted by the environment, will be transmitted with near invariance. The extreme structural invariance of species greatly simplifies the problem of delimiting and identifying populations. More important, the adaptiveness of structure can be unambiguously identified with net reproduction rates. When a population with given properties increases its net reproduction rate following an environmental change, it follows that the population is being selected for. This is why modern biologists have narrowed the definition of fitness to the net reproductive rate of population.

Human social organization presumably reflects a greater degree of learning or adaptation. As a result, it is more difficult to define fitness in a precise way. Under at least some conditions, organizations may undergo such extreme structural change that they shift from one form to another. As a result, extreme adaptation may give rise to observed changes that mimic selection. This is particularly problematic when the various organizational forms are similar on many dimensions.

We have argued previously (Hannan and Freeman, 1974) for a composite measure of fitness that includes both selection (actual loss of organizations) and mobility among forms (extreme adaptation). Fitness would then be defined as the probability that a given form of organization would persist in a certain environment. We continue to believe that such an approach has value, but we now believe that it is premature to combine adaptation and selection processes. The first order of business is to study selection processes for those situations in which inertial pressures are sufficiently strong that mobility among forms is unlikely.

Furthermore, it is worth noting that the capacity to adapt is itself subject to evolution (that is, to systematic selection). As we argue later, organizations develop the capacity to adapt at the cost of lowered performance levels in stable environments. Whether or not such adaptable organizational forms will survive (that is, resist selection) depends on the nature of the environment and the competitive situation. Therefore, a selection point of view treats high levels of adaptability as particular evolutionary outcomes.

There is a second sense in which human ecology appears to differ from bioecology. Blau and Scott (1962) point out that, unlike the usual biological situation, individual organizations (and populations of organizations) have the potential to expand almost without limit. The expandability of primitive elements is a problem because of our focus on the distribution or organizational forms over environments. A given form (for example, formal bureaucracy) can expand throughout some system, market, or activity, either because one bureaucracy grows or because many bureaucracies are founded. Either process will generate an increase in the prevalence of bureaucratic organizational activity. A literal application of population ecology theory to the problem of organizational change would involve simply counting relative numbers in populations. Such a procedure may miss a phenomenon of central

interest to the organizational analyst. Winter (1964), in discussing
the analytic problem raised here, suggests distinguishing between
survival, which describes the fate of individual organizations, and
viability, which describes the "share of market" of a given organizational form.

    We find at least as much merit in another perspective on the
issue of size. Many theorists have asserted that structural change
attends growth; in other words, a single organization cannot grow
indefinitely and still maintain its original form. For instance, a
mouse could not possibly maintain the same proportion of body
weight to skeletal structure while growing as big as a house. It
would neither look like a mouse nor operate physiologically like
a mouse. Boulding (1953a) and Haire (1959) argue that the same
is true for organizations. Caplow (1957), building on work by Graicunas (1933) and others, argues that the ability of each member
of an organization to carry on face-to-face interactions with each
of the others declines with the number of organizational participants. This creates a shift in the nature of interactions such that
they assume a more impersonal, formal style. Blau and a number
of coauthors have argued for similar causal effects of size on structure (Blau and Scott, 1962, pp. 223–242; Blau and Schoenherr,
1971; Blau, 1972). If it is true that organizational form changes
with size, selection mechanisms may indeed operate with regard
to the size distribution. When big organizations prevail, it may be
useful to view this as a special case of selection, in which the movement from "small form" to "large form" is theoretically indistinguishable from the dissolution ("death") of small organizations and
their replacement by (the "birth" of) large organizations.

    In sum, we have identified a number of challenges. The first
concerns the two sources of change, selection and adaptive learning. We feel that the organizations literature has overemphasized
the latter at the expense of the former. Much more is known about
decision-making practices, forecasting, and the like than about selection in populations of organizations. The second challenge involves the distinction between selection and viability. Whether such
a distinction is necessary depends on the results of research on size
that is currently being pursued by many organization researchers.

The Principle of Isomorphism

In the best-developed statement of the principles of human ecology, Hawley (1968) answers the question of why there are so many kinds of organizations. According to Hawley, the diversity of organizational forms is isomorphic to the diversity of environments. In each distinguishable environmental configuration, one finds, in equilibrium, only that organizational form optimally adapted to the demands of the environment. Each unit experiences constraints that force it to resemble other units with the same set of constraints. Hawley's explanation places heavy emphasis on communication patterns and structural complements of those patterns: "[Organization units] must submit to standard terms of communication and to standard procedures in consequence of which they develop similar internal arrangements within limits imposed by their respective sizes" (1968, p. 334).

While the proposition seems completely sound from an ecological perspective, it does not address a number of interesting considerations. There are at least two respects in which the isomorphism formulation must be modified and extended if it is to provide satisfactory answers to the question posed. The first modification concerns the mechanism or mechanisms responsible for equilibrium. In this respect, the principle of isomorphism must be supplemented by a criterion of selection and a competition theory. The second modification deals with the fact that the principle of isomorphism neither speaks to issues of optimum adaptation to changing environments nor recognizes that populations of organizations often face multiple environments that impose somewhat inconsistent demands. An understanding of the constraints on organizational forms seems to require modeling of multiple, dynamic environments. Of course, we cannot fully extend Hawley's principle here. We attempt only to outline the main issues and suggest particular extensions.

Competition Theory

The first of the needed extensions is a specification of the optimization process responsible for isomorphism. We have already discussed two mechanisms: selection and adaptive learning. Isomorphism can result either because nonoptimal forms are selected out of a community of organizations or because organizational decision makers learn optimal responses and adjust organizational behavior accordingly. We continue to focus on the first of these processes: selection.

Consideration of optimization raises two issues: Who is optimizing, and what is being optimized? It is quite commonly held, as in the theory of the firm, that organizational decision makers optimize profit over sets of organizational actions. From a population ecology perspective, it is the environment that optimizes.[4] Whether or not individual organizations are consciously adapting, the environment selects out optimal combinations of organizations. So, if there is a rationality involved, it is the "rationality" of natural selection. Organizational rationality and environmental rationality may coincide in the instance of firms in competitive markets. In this case, the optimal behavior of each firm is to maximize profit, and the rule used by the environment (market, in this case) is to select out profit maximizers. Friedman (1953) makes use of this observation to propose a justification of the theory of the firm in terms of the principles of evolution. However, Winter (1964) has argued convincingly that the actual situation is much more complicated than this and that it is most unusual for individual rationality and environmental or market rationality to lead to the same optima. When the two rationalities do not agree, we are concerned with the optimizing behavior of the environment.

A focus on selection invites an emphasis on competition. Organizational forms presumably fail to flourish in certain environmental circumstances because other forms successfully compete with them for essential resources. As long as the resources that sustain organizations are finite and populations have unlimited capacity to expand, competition must ensue.

Hawley (1950, pp. 201–203) following Durkheim (1933) among others, places a heavy emphasis on competition as a determinant of patterns of social organization. The distinctive feature of his model is the emphasis on the indirect nature of the process: "The action of all on the common supply gives rise to a reciprocal relation between each unit and all the others, if only from the fact that what one gets reduces by that amount what the others can obtain . . . without this element of indirection, that is, unless units affect one another through affecting a common limited supply, competition does not exist" (Hawley, 1950, p. 202). In Hawley's model, competition processes typically involve four stages: (1) demand for resources exceeds supply, (2) competitors become more similar as standard conditions of competition bring forth a uniform response, (3) selection eliminates the weakest competitors, and (4) deposed competitors differentiate either territorially or functionally, yielding a more complex division of labor.

It is surprising that there is almost no reliance on competitive mechanisms in Hawley's later work. In particular, as we noted above, the rationale given for the isomorphism principle uses an adaptation logic. We propose to balance that treatment by adding an explicit focus on competition as a mechanism producing isomorphism.[5] In so doing, we can bring a rich set of formal models to bear on the problem.

The first step in constructing an ecological model of competition is to state the nature of the population growth process. At a minimum, we wish the model to incorporate the idea that resources available at any moment for each form of organization are finite and fixed. This corresponds with Hawley's notion of limited supply and Stinchcombe's (1965) argument that human communities have limited "capacities for organizing." We also wish to incorporate the view that the rate at which units are added to populations of organizations depends on how much of the fixed capacity has already been exhausted. The greater the unexhausted capacity in an environment, the faster should be the rate of growth of populations of organizations. But the rate at which populations of organizations can expand into unused capacity varies among forms of organization. So there are two distinctive ecological considerations: the capacity of the environment to support forms of organization and the rate at which the populations grow (or decline) when the environmental support changes.

In order to state the model formally, it is helpful to begin with the control function that Hummon, Doreian, and Teuter (1975) use to add dynamic considerations to Blau's theory of size and differentiation. The control model states that the rate of change in the size of any unit (here a population of organizations) varies proportionately with the difference between the existing size, X, and the equilibrium level of size, X^*, permitted in that environment. Then one possible representation would be

$$\frac{dX}{dt} = f(X^* - X) = r(X^* - X) \tag{1}$$

In (1) X^* and r represent the limited supply or environmental capacity and the structural ability of the population of organizations to respond to changes in the environment, respectively.

A particular form of the general growth model in (1) underlies most population ecology work on competition. This is the logistic growth model (for per capital growth):

$$\frac{dX_1}{dt} = r_1 X_1 \left(\frac{k_1 - X_1}{k_1} \right) \tag{2}$$

where X_1 denotes population size, k_1 is the capacity of the environment to support X_1 (this parameter is usually called the *carrying capacity*), and r_1 is the so-called natural rate of increase of the population or the rate at which the population grows when it is far below the carrying capacity.

As we have indicated, both k and r are ecological parameters of fundamental importance. Our research group has begun to compare various forms of organization by estimating the parameters of models such as (2) for each form of organization. We have been successful to date in relating structural features of organizations such as complexity of core activity to variations in r and k (Nielsen and Hannan, 1977; Freeman and Brittain, 1977). This work, together with that of Hummon, Doreian, and Teuter (1975), gives us confidence that the model in (1) and/or (2) gives a good approximation of the growth of populations of organizations.

Up to this point, we have presumed that the limits on growth reflect the finite nature of the environment (for example, community wealth and mix of occupational skills). It is now time to reintroduce competition. According to Hawley, competition enters indirectly when the competitors lower the fixed supply. We can model this by following the lead of bioecologists and extending the logistic growth model. For example, consider a second population of organizations whose size is denoted by X_2. The two populations are said to compete if the addition of units of either decreases the rate of growth of the other. This will be the case when both populations are sustained by the same types of resources. Then the appropriate model is represented in the following system of growth equations (known as the Lotka-Volterra equations for competing populations):

$$\frac{dX_1}{dt} = r_1 X_1 \left(\frac{k_1 - X_1 - \alpha_{12} X_2}{k_1} \right)$$

$$\frac{dX_2}{dt} = r_2 X_2 \left(\frac{k_2 - X_2 - \alpha_{21} X_1}{k_2} \right)$$

(3)

The coefficients of α_{12} and α_{21}, called *competition coefficients*, denote the magnitude of the effect of increases in one population on the growth of the other. In this simple formulation, the only consequence of competition is to lower the carrying capacity of the environment for a population of organizations.

Analysis of (3) produces interesting qualitative results. It is not difficult to show that a stable two-population equilibrium exists for the system in (3) only if

$$\frac{1}{\alpha_{21}} < \frac{k_2}{k_1} < \alpha_{12}$$

(4)

Therefore, very similar populations (that is, populations with competition coefficients near unity) can coexist only under a very precise k_2/k_1 ratio. As a result, when $\alpha_{12} = \alpha_{21} = 1$, no two-population equilibrium can be stable; any exogenous shock will result in the elimination of one of the populations. This result supports the generality of the widely cited "principle of competitive exclusion" (Gause, 1934).[6] According to this principle, no two populations can continuously occupy the same niche. Populations are said to occupy the same niche to the extent that they depend on identical environmental resources. If they are identical, then the addition of an element to X_2 has the same consequences for growth in X_1 as does the addition of an element to X_1; in other words, the competition coefficients are unity. The broad conclusion is that the greater the similarity of two resource-limited competitors, the less feasible is it that a single environment can support both of them in equilibrium.

If two populations of organizations sustained by identical environmental resources differ in some organizational characteristic, that population with the characteristic less fit to environmental contingencies will tend to be eliminated. The stable equilibrium will then contain only one population that can be said to be isomorphic to the environment.

In order to see the implications of the model for organizational diversity, we extend the Lotka-Volterra system to include M competitors:

$$\frac{dX_i}{dt} = r_i X_i (k_i - X_i - \Sigma \alpha_{ij} X_j)/k_i \quad (i = 1, \ldots, M) \qquad (5)$$

The general system (5) has a community equilibrium:

$$k_i = X_i + \Sigma \alpha_{ij} X_j \qquad\qquad (i = 1, \ldots, M) \qquad (6)$$

These equations can be expressed in matrix form:

$$k = A x \qquad (7)$$

where x and k are $(M \times 1)$ column vectors and A is the community matrix:

$$A = \begin{pmatrix} 1 & \alpha_{12} & \cdot\, \cdot & \alpha_{1m} \\ \alpha_{21} & 1 & \cdot & \cdot \\ \cdot & & & \cdot \\ \cdot & & & \cdot \\ \cdot & & & \cdot \\ \alpha_{m1} & \cdot\, \cdot & \cdot\, \cdot & 1 \end{pmatrix}$$

whose elements are the competition coefficients.

The so-called theory of community structure entails the analysis of the equilibrium behavior of the system of equation (7) from the perspective of postulated competition processes.[7] The results, although stated in terms of species diversity, are quite general. In particular, one can show that when growth in population is constrained only by resource availability, the number of distinct resources sets an upper bound on diversity in the system.[8] Even more generally, the upper bound on diversity is equal to the number of distinct resources plus the number of additional constraints on growth (Levin, 1970).

It is difficult to apply either result directly in order to calculate the upper bound on diversity even in the nonhuman context. The chief difficulty is that of identifying distinct constraints. A good deal of empirical work is required if one is to judge how different two constraints must be in order to have distinct consequences for community equilibria. The theorems do, however, imply useful qualitative results. If one can identify environmental changes that add constraints to a system or eliminate them, one can conclude that the upper bound of diversity is increased or decreased.

This broad qualitative result has a number of potential applications to the research problems of interest. For example, the expansion of markets and of state control mechanisms through social systems tends to have the consequence of eliminating or reducing the number of constraints that are idiosyncratic to local environments. Viewed from the perspective of the larger system, the process of expansion of the economic and political center should, then, tend to replace some local constraints with more uniform ones. As long as the local environments were heterogeneous at the outset, expansion of the center ought to reduce the number of constraints on organizations in the whole system.

The theory just discussed implies on the one hand that the change in constraint structure ought to lower organizational diversity through the elimination of some population.[9] One can imagine, on the other hand, that in some local environments, the combination of unaltered local constraints and new larger system constraints might increase the total number of constraints in the local system. In that case, organizational diversity in those local environments should increase. Such an increase would result in the creation or adoption of new organizational forms.

The increasingly important role of the state in regulating economic and social action provides numerous opportunities for analyzing the impact of changes in constraint structures on the diversity of organizational forms. Consider the impact of licensing laws, minimum wage, health, and safety legislation, affirmative action, and other regulations on organizational action. When such regulations are applied to the full range of organizations in broad areas of activity, they undoubtedly alter the size distributions of organizations. Most often they select out the smallest organizations. But it is not difficult to imagine situations in which medium-sized organizations (more precisely, those with some minimum level of complexity) would be more adversely affected. Besides altering size distributions, such regulations undoubtedly affect the diversity of organizational arrangements in other ways. Here one could analyze the impact of state action on the diversity of accounting systems within industries, curricula within universities, departmental structures within hospitals, and so on. In each case, it would be essential to determine whether the newly imposed constraint replaced lower-level constraints, in which case diversity should decline, or whether the constraint cumulated with the existing constraints, in which case organizational diversity would be likely to increase.

To indicate the richness of the simple competition theory we have proposed, we will briefly discuss another sort of empirical test. We noted earlier that research on regulation might concern itself with impacts on distributions of organizations by size. The classical model of organizational size distributions (Simon and Bonini, 1958) proposes the following simple process. A number of organizations begin with the same small size. Some fraction are able to make or borrow some useful technical or organizational innovation that permits them to grow to some larger size. During some specified time period, the process repeats itself with the same fraction making the innovation required to attain a larger size. Such a growth process eventually yields the lognormal distribution that characterizes so many size distributions.

Competition theory suggests a refinement of this classical model. If, as we argued earlier, large changes in organizational size are accompanied by structural changes (changes in form), organizations of very different size in the same area of activity will tend to exhibit different forms. As a consequence of these structural differences, they will tend to depend on different sets of environmental resources (and constraints). That is, within any area of activity, pattern of resource use will tend to be specialized to segments of the size distribution. This being the case, organizations will compete most intensely with similar size organizations. Also, competition between pairs of organizations within an activity will be a decreasing function of the distance separating them on the size gradient. For example, small local banks compete most with other small banks, to a lesser extent with medium-scale regional banks, and hardly at all with international banks. Under these conditions, significant alterations in the size distribution indicate selection for and against certain organizational forms closely associated with regard to size.

Now let us return to the classical model. When large-sized organizations emerge they pose a competitive threat to medium-sized but hardly any threat to small organizations. In fact, the rise of large organizations may increase the survival chances of small ones in a manner not anticipated in the classical model. When the large organizations enter, those in the middle of the size distribution are trapped. Whatever stategy they adopt to fight off the challenge of the larger form makes them more vulnerable in competition with small organizations and vice versa. That is, at least in a stable environment the two ends of the size distribution ought to outcompete the middle. So in a longitudinal analysis of organizational size distributions we would expect to see the number of medium-sized organizations decline on the entry of larger organizations. Also, we would expect the fortunes of small organizations to improve as their competitors are removed from the environment. This reasoning holds generally for competition along a single gradient: Those in the middle will be eliminated in stable environments (MacArthur, 1972, pp. 43–46).

Niche Theory

The principle of isomorphism implies that social organizations in equilibrium will exhibit structural features that are specialized to salient features of the resource environment. As long as the environment is stable and certain, we see no difficulty with this proposition. But does it hold when the environment shifts either predictably or unpredictably among several alternative configurations? Although the issues raised by attempting to answer this question are complex, doing so is crucial to developing adequate models of organizational-environmental relations.

Intuition suggests that isomorphism holds as a good approximation only in stable environments. Faced with unstable environments, organizations ought to develop a generalist structure that is not optimally adapted to any single environmental configuration but is optimal over an entire set of configurations. In other words, we ought to find specialized organizations in stable and certain environments and generalist organizations in unstable and uncertain environments. Whether or not this simple proposition holds for social organizations, only empirical research will tell. However, a variety of population ecology models suggests that it is too simplistic. We cannot hope in one chapter to develop fully the arguments involved. Instead we indicate the main lines of development with reference to one rather evocative perspective developed by Levins (1962, 1968): the theory of niche width.

The concept of "niche," initially borrowed by biologists from early social science, plays a central role in ecological theory. This is not the place for an extended discussion of the multiple uses of the concept (see Whittaker and Levin, 1976). The model that follows uses Hutchinson's (1957) formulation. From this point of view the (realized) niche of a population is defined as that area in constraint space (the space whose dimensions are levels of resources, and so on), in which the population outcompetes all other local populations. The niche, then, consists of all those combinations of resource levels at which the population can survive and reproduce itself.

Each population occupies a distinct niche. For present purposes, it suffices to consider cases where pairs of populations differ with respect to a single environmental dimension, E, and are alike with respect to all others. Then relative competitive positions can be simply summarized as in Figure 1. As we have drawn this figure, one population, A, occupies a very broad niche, whereas the other,

B, has concentrated its fitness, denoted *W,* on a very narrow band of environmental variation. This distinction, which is usually referred to as *generalism versus specialism,* is crucial to biological ecology and to a population ecology of organizations.

In essence, the distinction between specialism and generalism refers to whether a population of organizations flourishes because it maximizes its exploitation of the environment and accepts the risk of having that environment change or because it accepts a lower level of exploitation in return for greater security. Whether or not the equilibrium distribution of organizational forms is dominated by the specialist depends, as we will see, on the shape of the fitness sets and on properties of the environment.

Part of the efficiency resulting from specialism is derived from the lower requirements for excess capacity. Given some uncertainty, most organizations maintain some excess capacity to insure the reliability of performance. In a rapidly changing environment, the definition of excess capacity is likely to change frequently. What is used today may become excess tomorrow, and what is excess today may be crucial tomorrow. Organizations operating in environments where the transition from state to state is less fre-

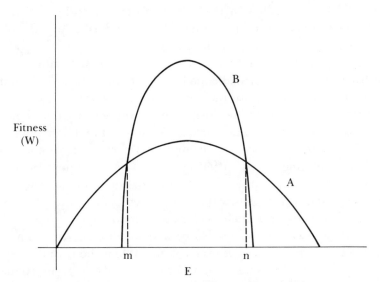

Figure 1. Fitness Functions (Niches) for Specialists and Generalists.

quent will (in equilibrium) have to maintain excess capacity in a given allocational pattern for longer periods of time. Whereas those charged with assessing performance will be tempted to view such allocations as wasteful, they may be essential for survival. Thompson (1967) has argued that organizations allocate resources to units charged with the function of insulating core technology from environmentally induced disruption. So, for example, manufacturing firms may retain or employ legal staffs even when they are not currently facing litigation.

The importance of excess capacity is not completely bound up with the issue of how much excess capacity will be maintained. It also involves the manner in which it is used. Organizations may ensure reliable performance by creating specialized units, as Thompson (1967) suggests, or they may allocate excess capacity to organizational roles, by employing personnel with skills and abilities that exceed the routine requirements of their jobs. This is one of the important reasons for using professionals in organizations. Professionals use more resources not only because they tend to be paid more, but also because organizations must allow them more discretion (including the freedom to respond to outside reference groups). Organizations, in turn, become more flexible by employing professionals. They increase their capacity to deal with a variable environment and the contingencies it produces. For example, hospitals and their patients often employ obstetricians and pediatricians in their delivery rooms, even though the normal delivery of babies can be performed equally well, and perhaps even better, by midwives. The skills of the medical doctor represent excess capacity to ensure reliable performance should delivery not be normal. Usually, the pediatrician examines the infant immediately after birth to see if there is any abnormality requiring immediate action. If the mother is suffering dangerous consequences from giving birth and the child is also in need of attention, the presence of the pediatrician ensures that the obstetrician will not have to choose between them in allocating his attention.

Excess capacity may also be allocated to the development and maintenance of procedural systems. When the certainty of a given environmental state is high, organizational operations should be routine, and coordination can be accomplished by formalized rules and the investment of resources in training incumbents to follow those formalized procedures. If in fact the environment were unchanging ($p = 1$), all participants were procedurally skilled, and the procedures were perfectly tuned, there would be no need for any control structure at all, except to monitor behavior. However, when certainty is low, organizational operations are less routine. Under these circumstances, a greater allocation of resources to develop and maintain procedural systems is counterproductive and optimal organizational forms will allocate resources to less formalized systems capable of more innovative responses (for example, committees and teams). In this case, excess capacity is represented by the increased time it takes such structures to make decisions and by increased coordination costs.

The point here is that populations of organizational forms will be selected for or against depending on the amount of excess capacity they maintain and how they allocate it. It may or may not be rational for any particular organization to adopt one pattern or another. What would seem like waste to anyone assessing performance at one time may be the difference between survival and failure later. Similarly, organizations may survive because high levels of professionalization produce coordination by mutual adjustment despite a somewhat chaotic appearance. Others, in which everyone seems to know precisely what he is doing at all times, may fail. Under a given set of environmental circumstances, the fundamental ecological question is "Which forms thrive, and which forms disappear?"

Generalism may be observed in a population of organizations, then, either in its reliance on a wide variety of resources simultaneously or in its maintenance of excess capacity at any given time. This excess capacity allows such organizations to change in order to take advantage of resources that become more readily available. Corporations that maintain an unusually large proportion of their total assets in fluid form ("slack," in terms of theory of the firm: Penrose, 1959; Cyert and March, 1963) are generalizing. In either case, generalism is costly. Under stable environmental circumstances, generalists will be outcompeted by specialists. And, at any given point in time, a static analysis will reveal excess capacity. An implication—shifting our focus to individual generalists—is that outside agents will often mistake excess capacity for waste.

We can investigate the evolution of niche width if we make the assumption that areas under the fitness curve are equal and that specialists differ from generalists in how they distribute the fixed quantity of fitness over environmental outcomes. Specialists outcompete generalists over the range of outcomes to which they have specialized (because of the fixed level of fitness assumption). As long as the environmental variation remains within that interval (the interval $[m,n]$ in Figure 1), generalists have no adaptive advantage and will be selected against. Alternatively, if the environment is only occasionally within the interval, specialists will fare less well than generalists. These brief comments make clear the importance of environmental variation for the evolution of niche width.

To simplify further, consider an environment that can take on only two states and in every period falls in State 1 with probability p and in State 2 with probability $q = (1 - p)$. Assume further that variations in environmental states are Bernoulli trials (independent from period to period). For this situation, Levins (1962, 1968) has shown that optimal niche width depends on p and the "distance" between the two states of the environment.

To see this, we change focus slightly. Since each organization faces two environments, its fitness depends on fitness in the pair. We can summarize the adaptive potential of each organization by plotting these pairs of values (fitness in State 1 and in State 2) in a new space whose axes are fitness in each of the states, as in Figure 2. In this representation, each point denotes the fitness of a distinct organizational form. The cloud of points is termed the "fitness set." We presume that all of the naturally possible adaptations are represented in the fitness set.

Our interest is in determining which points in the fitness set will be favored by natural selection. Notice first that all points interior to the set are inferior in terms of fitness to at least some point on the boundary of the set. In this sense, the boundary, drawn as a continuous line, represents the optimal possibilities. Since natural selection maximizes fitness, it must choose points on the boundary. This narrows our search to seeking which form(s) on the boundary will be favored.

As Figure 2(b) is drawn, no organizational form does particularly well in both states of the environment—no form has high

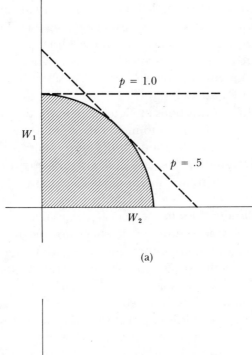

(a)

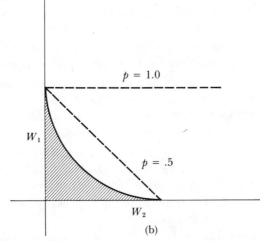

(b)

Figure 2. Optimal Adaptation in Fine-Grained Environment: (a) Convex Fitness Set; (b) Concave Fitness Set.

levels of fitness in both. This will be the case when the two states are "far apart" in the sense that they impose very different adaptive contingencies on organizations. In such cases (see Levins, 1968), the fitness set will be concave. When the "distance" between states is small, there is no reason why certain organizational forms cannot do well in both environments. In such cases, the fitness set will be convex, as in Figure 2(a).

The fitness functions in Figure 2 describe different adaptive situations. The next step is to model the optimization process. To do so, we introduce a further distinction. Ecologists have found it useful to distinguish both spatial and temporal environmental variation according to grain. Environmental variation is said to be *fine-grained* when a typical element (organization) encounters many units or replications. From a temporal perspective, variation is fine-grained when typical durations in states are short relative to the lifetime of organizations. Otherwise, the environment is said to be *coarse-grained.* Demand for products or services is often characterized by fine-grained variation, whereas changes in legal structures are more typically coarse-grained.

The essential difference between the two types of environmental variation is the cost of suboptimal strategies. The problem of ecological adaptation can be considered a game of chance in which the population chooses a strategy (specialism or generalism) and then the environment chooses an outcome (by, say, flipping a coin). If the environment "comes up" in a state favorable to the organizational form, it prospers; otherwise, it declines. However, if the variation is fine-grained (durations are short), each population of organizations experiences a great many trials, and environment is experienced as an average. When variation is coarse-grained, however, the period of decline stemming from a wrong choice may exceed the organizational capacity to sustain itself under unfavorable conditions.

To capture these differences, Levins introduced an adaptive function to represent how natural selection would weight fitness in each state under the different conditions. In discussing fine-grained variation, we suggested that the environment is experienced as an average.[10] The appropriate adaptive function, then, simply weights fitness in the two states (W_1 and W_2) according to frequency of occurrence: $A(W_1,W_2)=pW_1+qW_2$. In order to consider optimal adaptation, we merely superimpose the adaptive function on the fitness set and find points of tangency of adaptive function and fitness functions. Points of tangency are optimal adaptations. The solutions for various cases are represented in Figure 2. If the environment is completely stable (that is, $p = 1$), then specialism is optimal. If the environment is maximally uncertain (that is, $p = .5$), generalism is optimal in the convex case (when the demands of the different environments are not too dissimilar) but not in the concave case. In fact, as the model is developed, specialism always wins out in the concave case.

Consider first the cases in which the environment is stable (that is, $p = 1$). Not surprisingly, specialism is optimal. The results for unstable environments diverge. When the fitness set is convex (that is, the demands of the different environmental states are similar and/or complementary), generalism is optimal. But when the environmental demands differ (and the fitness set is concave), specialism is optimal. This is not as strange a result as it first appears. When the environment changes rapidly among quite different states, the cost of generalism is high. Since the demands in the different states are dissimilar, considerable structural management is required of generalists. But, since the environment changes rapidly, these organizations will spend most of their time and energies adjusting structure. It is apparently better under such conditions to adopt a specialized structure and "ride out" the adverse environments.

The case of coarse-grained environments is somewhat more complex. Our intuitive understanding is that since the duration of an environmental state is long, maladaptation ought to be given greater weight. That is, the costs of maladaptation greatly outweigh any advantage incurred by the correct choice. One adaptive function that gives this result is the log-linear model used by Levins: $A(W_1,W_2) = W_1{}^p W_2{}^q$. The method of finding optimal adaptations is the same. The results are found in Figure 3. Only one case differs from what we found for fine-grained environments: the combination of uncertain and coarse-grained variation with concave fitness sets. We saw earlier that when such variation is fine-grained, it is better to specialize. When the duration of environmental states is long, however, the costs of this strategy are great. Long periods of nonadaptation will threaten the survival of the organization. In addition, the fact that the environment changes less often means that generalists need not spend most of their time and energies altering structure. Thus generalism is the optimal strategy in this case as we see in Figure 3(b).

The combination of coarse-grained environmental variation and concave fitness sets raises a further possibility. The optimal adaptation in the face of environmental uncertainty possesses fairly low levels of fitness in either state. It seems clear that there must be a better solution. Levins discusses this case in depth and concludes that for the biological case with genetic transmission of structure "polymorphism" or genetically maintained population heterogeneity will be selected for. The suggestion is that populations combine types (differing, say, in color, blood type, and so on), some of which are specialized to State 1 and some to State 2. With such a combination, at least a portion of the population will always flourish and maintain the genetic diversity that allows it to continue to flourish when the environment changes state. The set of all such heterogeneous populations (composed of proportions of specialists to each of the two environments) can be represented in the fitness diagrams as a straight line joining the most extreme points with all combinations falling within this line.

Coarse-grained and uncertain variation favors a distinct form of generalism: polymorphism. We do not have to search very far to find an analogous outcome. Organizations may federate in such a way that supraorganizations consisting of heterogeneous collections of specialist organizations pool resources. When the environment is uncertain and coarse-grained and subunits difficult to set up and tear down, the costs of maintaining the unwieldy structure imposed by federation may be more than offset by the fact that at least a portion of the amalgamated organization will do well no matter what the state of the environment. In terms of the model suggested, there are no other situations in which such federated organizations have a competitive advantage. And even in this case the only time during which they have such an advantage is when coarse-grained variation is uncertain.

Such an amalgamated "holding company" pattern may be observed in modern universities. Enrollment and research support wax and wane over time, as do the yield on invested endowment

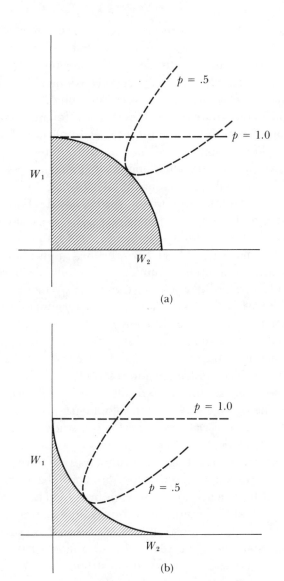

Figure 3. Optimal Adaptation in Coarse-Grained Environments; (a) Convex
Fitness Set; (b) Concave Fitness Set.

securities and the beneficence of legislatures. Some of these resources follow predictable cycles. Others do not. But it is extremely
expensive to build up and dismantle academic units. It is costly not
only in money but also in the energies consumed by political conflict. Consequently, universities are constantly "taxing" subunits
with plentiful environments to subsidize less fortunate subunits. It
is common, for instance, for universities to allocate faculty positions according to some fixed master plan, undersupporting the
rapidly growing departments and maintaining excess faculty in
others. This partial explanation of the unwieldy structures that
encompass liberal arts departments, professional schools, research
laboratories, and so on is at least as persuasive as explanations that
emphasize intellectual interdependence among units.

Much more can be said concerning applications of niche
theory to organization-environment relations. We have focused
on a simple version highlighting the interplay between competition and environmental variation in the determination of optimal
adaptive structure in order to show that the principle of isomorphism needs considerable expansion to deal with multiple environmental outcomes and their associated uncertainty. The literature
in ecology to which we have made reference is growing exponen-
tially at the moment, and new results and models are appearing
monthly. The products of these developments provide students of
organizations with a rich potential for the study of organization-
environment relations.

Consider an example. In his analysis of bureaucratic and
craft administration or production, Stinchcombe (1959) argued
that construction firms do not rely on bureaucratically organized
administrative staffs because of seasonal fluctuations in demand.
Administrative staffs constitute an overhead cost that remains
roughly constant over the year. The advantage of the otherwise
costly (in terms of salaries) craft administration is that coordination
of work is accomplished through a reliance on prior socialization
of craftsmen and upon organization. Since employment levels can
more easily be increased or decreased with demand under a craft
system, administrative costs are more easily altered to meet demand.

The fundamental source of this pattern is the seasonal variation in construction. In ecological terms, the demand environment is coarse-grained. In addition, the two states defined by season

are quite different, resulting in a concave fitness curve. Craft-administered housing construction firms are probably quite inefficient when demand is at its peak and when the kind of housing under construction is standardized. In such situations, we would expect this form of organization to face stiff competition from other firms. For instance, in regions where housing construction is less seasonal, modular housing, mobile homes, and prefabricated housing are more likely to flourish, and we would expect the construction business to be more highly bureaucratized.

Another variation in demand is to be found in the business cycle. While seasonal fluctuations are stable (uncertainty is low), interest rates, labor relations, and materials costs are more difficult to predict. Variations of this sort should favor a generalist mode of adaptation. That is, when environments are coarse-grained, characterized by concave fitness curves, and are uncertain, populations of organizations will be more likely to survive if they hedge their bets by seeking a wider variety of resource bases. For this reason, we think, craft-administered construction organizations are frequently general contractors who not only build houses but engage in other kinds of construction as well (shopping plazas, office buildings, and so on). In comparison, modular housing is cheaper and the units are installed on rented space. Consequently, interest rates are less important. Since organizations producing this kind of housing do not employ craftsmen but use the cheapest and least skilled labor they can obtain, labor relations are less problematical. It may also be that their reliance on different materials (for example, sheet aluminum) contributes to a lower level of uncertainty. In consequence, we would expect this form of organization to be more highly specialized in its adaptation (of course, there are technical factors that also contribute to this as well).

Craft-administered construction firms are set up in such a way that they can adapt rapidly to changes in demand, and they can adapt to different construction problems by varying the mix of skills represented in their work force. Bureaucratically administered construction firms are more specialized, and as a result they are efficient only when demand is high, and very inefficient when it is low. We also believe that they tend to be more specialized with regard to type of construction. Craft-administered organizations sacrifice efficient exploitation of their niche for flexibility. Bureacratic organizations choose the opposite strategy. This formulation is an extension of Stinchcombe's and serves to show that his argument is essentially ecological.

Discussion

Our aim in this paper has been to move toward an application of modern population ecology theory to the study of organization-environment relations. For us, the central question is "Why are there so many kinds of organizations?" Phrasing the question in this way opens the possibility of applying a rich variety of formal models to the analysis of the effects of environmental variations on organizational structure.

We begin with Hawley's classic formulation of human ecology. However, we recognize that ecological theory has progressed enormously since sociologists last systematically applied ideas from bioecology to social organization. Nonetheless, Hawley's (1950) theoretical perspective remains a very useful point of departure. In particular, we concentrate on the principle of isomorphism. This principle asserts that there is a one-to-one correspondence between structural elements of social organization and those units that mediate flows of essential resources into the system. It explains the variations in organizational forms in equilibrium. But any observed isomorphism can arise from purposeful adaptation of organizations to the common constraints they face or because nonisomorphic organizations are selected against. Surely both processes are at work in most social systems. We believe that the organizations literature has emphasized the former to the exclusion of the latter.

We suspect that careful empirical research will reveal that for wide classes of organizations there are very strong inertial pressures on structure arising both from internal arrangements (for example, internal politics) and the environment (for example, public legitimation of organizational activity). To claim otherwise is to ignore the most obvious feature of organizational life. Failing churches do not become retail stores, nor do firms transform themselves into churches. Even within broad areas of organizational action, such as higher education and labor union activity, there appear to be substantial obstacles to fundamental structural change. Research is needed on this issue. But until we see evidence to the contrary we will continue to doubt that the major features of the world of organizations arise through learning or adaptation. Given these doubts, it is important to explore an evolutionary explanation of the principle of isomorphism. That is, we wish to embed the principle of isomorphism within an explicit selection framework.

In order to add selection processes, we propose a competition theory using Lotka-Volterra models. This theory relies on growth models that appear suitable for representing both organizational development and the growth of populations of organizations. Recent work by bioecologists on Lotka-Volterra systems yields propositions that have immediate relevance for the study of organization-environment relations. These results concern the effects of changes in the number and mixture of constraints on systems with regard to the upper bound of the diversity of forms of organization. We propose that such propositions can be tested by examining the impact of varieties of state regulation both on size distributions and on the diversity of organizational forms within broadly defined areas of activity (for example, medical care, higher education, and newspaper publishing).

A more important extension of Hawley's work introduces dynamic considerations. The fundamental issue here concerns the meaning of isomorphism in situations in which the environment to which units are adapted is changing and uncertain. Should "rational" organizations attempt to develop specialized isomorphic structural relations with one of the possible environmental states? Or should they adopt a more plastic strategy and institute more generalized structural features? The isomorphism principle does not speak to these issues.

We suggest that the concrete implication of generalism for organizations is the accumulation and retention of varieties of excess capacity. To retain the flexibility of structure required for adaptation to different environmental outcomes requires that some capacities be held in reserve and not committed to action. Generalists will always be outperformed by specialists who, with the same levels of resources, happen to have hit on their optimal environment. Consequently, in any cross section the generalists will appear inefficient, because excess capacity will often be judged waste. Nonetheless, organizational slack is a pervasive feature of many types of organizations. The question then arises "What types of environments favor generalists?" Answering this question comprehensively takes one a long way toward understanding the dynamic of organization-environment relations.

We begin addressing this question in the suggestive framework of Levins's (1962, 1968) fitness-set theory. This is one of a class of recent theories that relates the nature of environmental uncertainty to optimal levels of structural specialism. Levins argues that along with uncertainty one must consider the grain of the environment or the lumpiness of environmental outcomes. The theory indicates that specialism is always favored in stable or certain environments. This is no surprise. But contrary to the view widely held in the organizations literature, the theory also indicates that generalism is not always optimal in uncertain environments. When the environment shifts uncertainly among states that place very different demands on the organization and when the duration of environmental states is short relative to the life of the organization (variation is fine-grained), populations of organizations that specialize will be favored over those that generalize. This is because organizations that attempt to adapt to each environmental outcome will spend most of their time adjusting structure and very little time in organizational action directed at other ends.

Stated in these terms, the proposition appears obvious. However, when one reads the literature on organization-environment relations, one finds that it was not so obvious. Most important, the proposition follows from a simple explicit model that has the capacity to unify a wide variety of propositions relating environmental variations to organizational structure.

We have identified some of the leading conceptual and methodological obstacles to applying population ecology models to the study of organization-environment relations. We pointed to differences between human and nonhuman social organization in terms of mechanisms of structural invariance and structural change, associated problems of delimiting populations of organizations, and difficulties in defining fitness for populations of expandable units. In each case, we have merely sketched the issues and proposed short-run simplifications that would facilitate the application of existing models. Clearly, each issue deserves careful scrutiny.

At the moment, we are frustrated at least as much by the lack of empirical information on rates of selection in populations of organizations as by the unresolved issues just mentioned. Census data are presented in a manner that renders the calculation of failure rates impossible, and little longitudinal research on populations of organizations has been reported. We do, however, have some information on rates of selection. We know, for example, that failure rates for small businesses are high. By recent estimates, over 8 percent of small business firms in the United States fail each year (Hollander, 1967; Bolton, 1971; see also Churchill, 1955).

In part, this high failure rate reflects what Stinchcombe (1965) called the *liability of newness*. Many new organizations attempt to enter niches that have already been filled by organizations that have amassed social, economic, and political resources that make them difficult to dislodge. It is important to determine whether there is any selective disadvantage of smallness over newness.

We doubt that many readers will dispute the contention that failure rates are high for new and/or small organizations. However, much of the sociological literature and virtually all of the critical literature on large organizations tacitly accepts the view that such organizations are not subject to strong selection pressures. While we do not yet have the empirical data to judge this hypothesis, we can make several comments. First, we do not dispute that the largest organizations individually and collectively exercise strong dominance over most of the organizations that constitute their environments. But it does not follow from the observation that such organizations are strong in any one period that they will be strong in every period. Thus, it is interesting to know how firmly embedded are the largest and most powerful organizations. Consider the so-called *Fortune* 500, the largest publicly owned industrial firms in the United States. We contrasted the lists for 1955 and 1975 (adjusting for pure name changes). Of those on the list in 1955, only 268 (53.6 percent) were still listed in 1975. One hundred twenty-two had disappeared through merger, 109 had slipped off the "500," and one (a firm specializing in Cuban sugar!) had been liquidated. The number whose relative sales growth caused them to be dropped from the list is quite impressive in that the large number of mergers had opened many slots on the list. So we see that, whereas actual liquidation was rare for the largest industrial firms in the United States over a twenty-year period, there was a good deal of volatility with regard to position in this pseudodominance structure because of both mergers and slipping sales.[11]

Second, the choice of time perspective is important. Even the largest and most powerful organizations fail to survive over long periods. For example, of the thousands of firms in business in the United States during the Revolution, only thirteen survive as autonomous firms and seven as recognizable divisions of firms ("America's Oldest Companies," 1976). Presumably one needs a longer time perspective to study the population ecology of the largest and most dominant organizations.

Third, studying small organizations is not such a bad idea. The sociological literature has concentrated on the largest organizations for obvious design reasons. But, if inertial pressures on certain aspects of structure are strong enough, intense selection among small organizations may greatly constrain the variety observable among large organizations. At least some elements of structure change with size (as we argued in the third section of this chapter) and the pressure toward inertia should not be overemphasized. Nonetheless, we see much value in studies of the organizational life cycle that would inform us as to which aspects of structure get locked in during which phases of the cycle. For example, we conjecture that a critical period is that during which the organization grows beyond the control of a single owner/manager. At this time, the manner in which authority is delegated, if at all, seems likely to have a lasting impact on organizational structure. This is the period during which an organization becomes less an extension of one or a few dominant individuals and more an organization per se, with a life of its own. If the selection pressures at this point are as intense as anecdotal evidence suggests they are, selection models will prove very useful in accounting for the varieties of forms among the whole range of organizations.

The optimism of the previous paragraph should be tempered by the realization that when one examines the largest and most dominant organizations, one is usually considering only a small number of organizations. The smaller the number, the less useful are models that depend on the type of random mechanisms that underlie population ecology models.

Fourth, we must consider what one anonymous reader, caught up in the spirit of our argument, called the *antieugenic* actions of the state in saving firms such as Lockheed from failure. This is a dramatic instance of the way in which large dominant organizations can create linkages with other large and powerful ones so as to reduce selection pressures. If such moves are effective, they alter the pattern of selection. In our view, the selection pressure is bumped up to a higher level. So, instead of individual organizations failing, entire networks fail. The general consequence of a large number of linkages of this sort is an increase in the instability of the entire system (Simon, 1962, 1973; May, 1973), and therefore we should see boom and bust cycles of organizational outcomes. Selection models retain relevance, then, even when the systems of organizations are tightly coupled (see Hannan, 1976).

Finally, some readers of earlier drafts have (some approvingly, some disapprovingly) treated our arguments as metaphoric. This is not what we intend. In a fundamental sense, all theoretical activity involves metaphoric activity (although admittedly the term *analogue* comes closer than does *metaphor*). The use of metaphors or analogues enters into the formulation of "if . . . then" statements. For example, certain molecular genetic models draw an analogy between DNA surfaces and crystal structures. The latter have simple, well-behaved geometric structures amenable to strong topological (mathematical) analysis. No one argues that DNA proteins are crystals; but, to the extent that their surfaces have certain crystal-like properties, the mathematical model used to analyze crystals will shed light on the genetic structure. This is, as we understand it, the general strategy of model building.

We have, for example, used results that rely on the application of certain logistic differential equations, the Lotka-Volterra equations. No known population (of animals, or of organizations) grows in exactly the manner specified by this mathematic model (and this fact has caused numerous naturalists to argue that the model is biologically meaningless). What the equations do is to model the growth path of populations that exist on finite resources in a closed system (where population growth in the absence of competition is logistic and the presence of competing populations lowers carrying capacities in that system). To the extent that the interactions of populations of *Paramecium aureilia* and *P. caudatum* (Gause's experiment) meet the conditions of the model, the model explains certain key features of population dynamics and the relationship of environmental variations to structure. To the extent that the interactions of populations of rational-legal bureaucracies and populations of patrimonial bureaucracies also meet the conditions of the model, the model explains the same important phenomena. Neither the protozoa nor the bureaucracies behave exactly as the model stipulates. The model is an abstraction that will lead to insight whenever the stated conditions are approximated.

Throughout, we make a strong continuity-of-nature hypothesis. We propose that, whenever the stated conditions hold, the models lead to valuable insights regardless of whether the populations under study are composed of protozoans or organizations. We do not argue "metaphorically." That is, we do *not* argue that an empirical regularity is found to hold for certain protozoans; because we hypothesize that populations of organizations are like populations of protozoans in essential ways, we propose that the generalizations derived from the latter will hold for organizations as well. This is the kind of reasoning by which biological propositions have most often entered sociological arguments (for example, the famous—or infamous—organismic analogy advanced by Spencer).

Instead of applying biological laws to human social organization, we advocate the application of population ecology theories. As we have indicated at a number of points, these theories are quite general and must be modified for any concrete application (sociological *or* biological). Our purpose has been twofold. First, we sketched some of the alterations in perspective required if population ecology theories are to be applied to the study of organizations. Second, we wished to stimulate a reopening of the lines of communication between sociology and ecology. It is ironic that Hawley's (1944, p. 399) diagnosis of some thirty years ago remains apt today: "Probably most of the difficulties which beset human ecology may be traced to the isolation of the subject from the mainstream of ecological thought."

Notes

1. There is a subtle relationship between selection and adaptation. Adaptive learning for individuals usually consists of selection among behavioral responses. Adaptation for a population involves selection among types of members. More generally, processes involving selection can usually be recast at a higher level of analysis as adaptation processes. However, once the unit of analysis is chosen there is no ambiguity in distinguishing selection from adaptation. Organizations often adapt to environmental conditions in concert, and this suggests a systems effect. Although few theorists would deny the existence of such systems effects, most do not make them a subject of central concern. It is important to notice that, from the point of view embraced by sociologists whose interests focus on the broader social system, selection in favor of organizations with one set of properties to the disfavor of those with others is often an adaptive process. Societies and communities that consist in part of formal organizations adapt partly through processes that adjust the mixture of various kinds of organizations found within them. Whereas a complete theory of organization and environment would have to consider both adaptation and selection, recognizing that they are complementary processes, our purpose here is to show what can be learned from studying selection alone (see Aldrich and Pfeffer, 1976, for a synthetic review of the literature focusing on these different perspectives).

2. Meyer's (1970) discussion of an organization's charter adds further support to the argument that normative agreements arrived at early in an organization's history constrain greatly the organization's range of adaptation to environmental constraints.

3. The term "organizational form" is used widely in the sociological literature (see Stinchcombe, 1965).

4. In biological applications, one assumes that power (in the physical sense) is optimized by natural selection in accordance with the so-called Darwin-Lotka law. For the case of human social organization, one might argue that selection optimizes the utilization of a specific set of resources including but not restricted to the power and the time of members.

5. We include only the first and third of Hawley's stages in our model of competition. We prefer to treat uniformity of response and community diversity as consequences of combinations of certain competitive processes and environmental features.

6. This so-called principle has mostly suggestive value (see MacArthur, 1972, pp. 43–46, for a penetrating critique of attempts to derive quantitative implications from Gause's principle; most of these criticisms do not apply to the qualitative inferences we consider).

7. We restrict attention to the case in which all entries of A are nonnegative. Negative entries are appropriate for predator/prey (or more generally, host/parasite) relations. The typical result for this case is cyclical population growth.

8. A more precise statement of the theorem is that no stable equilibrium exists for a system of M competitors and $N < M$ resources (MacArthur and Levins, 1964).

9. For a more comprehensive statement of this argument with reference to ethnic organization, see Hannan (1975).

10. That selection depends on average outcomes is only one hypothesis. Templeton and Rothman (1974) argue that selection depends not on average outcomes but on some minimum level of fitness. Whether average outcomes or some other criterion guides selection in populations of organizations is open to question. We follow Levins, in order to keep the exposition simple.

11. From at least some perspectives, mergers can be viewed as changes in form. This will almost certainly be the case when the organizations merged have very different structures. These data also indicate a strong selective advantage for a conglomerate form of industrial organization.

Part Two

~~~~~~~~~~~~~~~~~~~~~~~~~~

Empirical Research

~~~~~~~~~~~~~~~~~~~~~~~~~~

This part of the book contains six empirical studies. All are comparative. John Freeman and I analyze some political dimensions of the allocation of positions in school districts when enrollments are growing and declining. The data come from some three hundred California public school districts. Marshall Meyer studies the manner in which leadership stability in roughly two hundred public finance agencies affects the relationship between environmental demand for services and organizational size and structure. John Meyer and his associates explore the socially constructed reality of school district and school organization using data from twenty-five San Francisco Bay area school districts. William Ouchi studies the patterns of control used at different levels of hierarchy in 215 departments of two Chicago department stores. W. Richard Scott and his associates analyze carefully collected and validated patient histories to explore the effects of hospital structure on patient outcomes in seventeen hospitals located throughout the United States. Finally, Jeffrey Pfeffer and his associates study the manner in which uncertainty—in this case, lack of agreement about scientific procedure—affects the use of particularistic information in the resource allocation process. They analyze four social science programs of the National Science Foundation (NSF).

The set of studies taken together includes a good variety of

173

organizations: schools and school districts, public bureaus, department stores, hospitals, and basic research-funding agencies. This diversity of focus adds considerable force to the pattern of findings that emerges. However, it is important to note that none of the studies deals with a diverse set of types of organizations. Rather, each group of investigators chose to study multiple instances of the same type of organization. This design strategy has both advantages and disadvantages worth some comment.

The prime advantage of the small-bore strategy is clarity and precision of comparison. Clearly, the comparison of structural arrangements and outcomes is simplest when one considers a set of organizations in the same business using essentially the same technology. If one studies only hospitals, for example, one may make more subtle distinctions among types of structural arrangements than if the conceptualization and measurement schemes must apply also to department stores and schools. In short, use of the small-bore strategy permits optimal comparisons of structures.

The prime disadvantage of this analytic strategy is the loss of much structural variation. Variations in structural arrangements among schools or bureaus is certainly less than the variation between them. And the small-bore strategy misses all the between-type variation. There is nothing wrong with this as long as both researcher and reader keep the limitation in mind. Do not, for example, conclude on the basis of the work reported here that technology is not an important determinant of structure and outcome. Our designs have eliminated almost all technological variation. The same is true with respect to many types of environmental variation, although the studies differ on this. Some of us study only Chicago or California. None of us includes organizations outside the United States in his sample. I repeat that these limitations do not compromise the findings of the studies. They merely set limits on the scope of applicability of the findings.

In other aspects of design and analysis, the studies are more heterogeneous. Two of the papers report analyses of archival data (Hannan and Freeman; Pfeffer and others); the rest analyze data collected specifically for the research. Three of the analyses are longitudinal (panel analyses); the other three are cross sectional. Perhaps the message here is that there is no one way to conduct quantitative analysis of the causes and consequences of organizational structure. Obviously, we take our measurements of structural variation wherever we find them.

Finally, what about the bearing of these studies on the theoretical work reported in Part One? Given our title, the reader may find it surprising that only two chapters, Seven and Eight, actually analyze the impacts of external environments on organizations. Did we merely delude ourselves into thinking that these chapters bear on organization-environment relations? I must leave that judgment to the reader. Let me, however, suggest an intimate connection between the empirical and theoretical work. The connection is mostly historical. In all but two cases (the chapters by Freeman and myself and by Scott and others), the empirical work preceded the theoretical work. The group came together largely to discuss this work and its implications. Our discussions of the work reported in Part Two led to many of the theoretical arguments of Part One. In a sense, these studies are the empirical data on which some of the theories are based.

Let me be more concrete about the connections between the empirical and theoretical work. The chapters of Part Two all suggest strong limitations on a rationalist organizational design perspective. Four of the chapters report findings that fly in the face of the belief that organizations are simple and malleable tools to achieve limited goals. The chapters by M. Meyer and by Freeman and myself display evidence that public organizations, under at least some conditions, avoid responding to variations in environmental demand for their services. Meyer finds that bureaus with stable leadership effectively resist environmental demands. They also suspend, at least temporarily, the seemingly rational connections among dimensions of structure that characterize those bureaus that have changed leadership positions. The Hannan-Freeman analysis presents evidence that competition for personnel slots is more intense when environmental demand declines; also the speed of system response to changes in demand is slower in decline. John Meyer and his associates find that school and school district organizational arrangements are either temporary and frequently altered or nonexistent. Various informed respondents do not agree as much as these researchers had expected when questioned about the existence of various rules and procedures. Pfeffer and his associates find that programs in the NSF use particularistic information in making grant allocations to social scientists. No rational organizational designer would intend any of these four scenarios.

One of the remaining chapters, that by Ouchi, suggests strong limits on the organizational design perspective. Behavior control works well; it is, however, difficult to transmit behavior evaluations through an organizational hierarchy. Consequently, those at the top of a hierarchy prefer output evaluations that are comparable across subunits, even though output control is less efficient in any subunit. It is clearly difficult, if not impossible, to design a control system that is both efficient and meets the expressed desires of the top controllers for comparable evaluations of subunits.

The analysis of hospital structure effects on patient surgical outcomes tells a story much more in line with the more rationalist perspective. Hospital structure makes more difference than surgeon characteristics.* Moreover, strength of colleague control over surgeons by the surgical staff as opposed to bureaucratic control appears to be the most important structural determinant of good outcomes. So we have an instance in which professional control actually works to foster the interests of the organization as a whole: quality patient care.

Michael T. Hannan

---

*This finding is almost exactly opposite in its implications from that reported in the other chapter of which Scott is an author (J. Meyer and others). The school study finds no structure at the higher levels; the hospital study finds that the causal effect of the larger structure is more important than that of the very local structure, the surgical team.

7

Internal Politics
of Growth and Decline

Michael T. Hannan
John H. Freeman

The empirical literature on organizations has in recent years been preoccupied with the problem of size and structure, particularly with the more narrow administrative intensity problem (for reviews of this literature, see Freeman, 1973; Scott, 1975; Kimberly, 1976). Almost without exception, the early work that explored the forces that shape the size of administrative components in organizations took a decidedly rationalist perspective. Blau, who did more than anyone else to advance the study of organizational internal demography, set the tone. Administrators were assumed to deal with problems of coordination of divided labor. Rational organizations hire (and fire) administrators according to variations in coordi-

This work was supported by National Institute of Education research grant NIE-G-76-0082. A portion of the empirical analysis was conducted under a contract by Assistant Secretary for Planning and Evaluation, HEW to Abt Associates (contract HEW-100-76-0177). Glenn Carroll, Barbara Warsavage, and François Nielsen provided expert programming and other technical services. Nancy Brandon Tuma made helpful comments on an earlier draft.

nation needs. The main variations in the need for coordination were assumed to vary with the size of the organization. Thus Blau and many others analyzed the relationship between size and the proportion of workers in the administrative category. This work produced some valuable insights but also raised serious methodological and theoretical questions. The methodological questions have to do with problems of definitional dependency (see Freemen and Kronenfeld, 1974) and model specification (which issues became clear when cross-sectional designs were replaced by longitudinal designs; see M. Meyer, 1971; Freeman and Hannan, 1975). The theoretical issues concern system closure and organizational politics. Conventional models of administrative intensity presume that organizations behave as closed systems such that the size of various personnel components adjust only to internal exigencies. Moreover, the adjustment is mechanical and rational; it does not involve struggles among personnel components over scarce organizational resources, namely positions. Much of the thrust of this book involves reversing positions on these two issues.

The work reported in this chapter is an attempt to inject organizational politics and environmental dependence into models of organizational demography. It is an extension of our earlier work (Freeman and Hannan, 1975), which was one of the first empirical studies to depart from the rational tradition on organizational demography. After briefly reviewing the earlier work, we propose a dynamic model for the growth and decline of personnel components in organizations characterized by conflicts over positions. Then we estimate the model for California school districts. Our results support the contention that growth and decline processes differ. However, the new model reveals that the processes are complex and that not all of our previous arguments hold up well.

The Original Model

Our earlier work employed a model that mixed organizational politics and administrative rationality. We reasoned as follows. Each district was assumed to face community norms that limited changes in pupil-teacher ratios, a norm of constant class size.

So, as the number of students in a district changes, the number of teachers employed ought to change proportionately. Moreover, this process should work the same way in growth and decline. Regarding the other personnel categories (administrators, pupil service employees, and classified employees), we reasoned differently. As long as the number of students was growing, administrative rationality would dictate that the sizes of each of these components would be adjusted to changes in the number of teachers. To be concrete, the growth model was

$$\frac{dT}{dt} = a + bT + cE \tag{1}$$

$$\frac{dX_j}{dt} = d + eX_j + fT \tag{2}$$

where E denotes size of enrollments, T the number of teachers, and X_j is the size of the jth nonteaching personnel category.

We argued for the same type of model in decline. However, we hypothesized that organizational politics would lead the parameters of the second equation (but not the first) to differ from those that hold in growth. In particular, we proposed that declining districts would maintain higher levels of nonteaching personnel than would be the case for otherwise similar growing districts.

Notice that organizational politics entered this model only in the postulated difference between growth and decline. While we feel that this simple model served a very useful purpose in introducing political considerations into formal empirical analysis of organizational demography, we now conclude that we did not go far enough. Surely both the growth process and the decline process are more political than this model indicates. The growth or decline of any personnel component is surely affected by the sizes of other components. For example, the earlier model did not relate the growth or decline in the number of teachers to the number of administrators. But, insofar as the various categories are competing for a limited budget, this sort of dependence seems likely. One of our major goals in this chapter is to extend the earlier model to incorporate more general organizational politics.

A Competition Model

Following the strategy outlined in Chapter Six, we break the modeling effort into two parts. The first deals with the factors that affect the equilibrium levels of personnel component sizes. So, for example, we will investigate the way in which the carrying capacity for administrators in a district is affected by various internal and external conditions. The second issue focuses on dynamics, the time path of changes from some starting point toward the carrying capacity. Here we will focus, for example, on the responsiveness or speed of response of administrators to some change in their carrying capacity.

Consider first the question of carrying capacities. Recall that a carrying capacity is defined as the upper limit of the size of the population that can be sustained in a particular system. In the most general terms, we expect that the carrying capacity for any personnel component is determined by three classes of variables: *exogenous environmental variations* (such as enrollments and finances), *internal competitive relations* (such as organizational politics), and *history* (such as inertial social, political, and cultural characteristics of the local environment). So the size of any particular category is determined by the availability of environmental resources on which it depends, on the sizes of the competing components and the intensity of competition, and on stable characteristics of the organization and its environment that favor this particular category. We can summarize these assertions as follows. Let $X^*_{ij}(t)$ denote the carrying capacity of the ith local environment for the jth personnel category; let $X_{ij}(t)$ denote the current size of the category; $Z_{ij}(t)$ summarizes the variable environmental conditions and M_{ij} the constant conditions (history). Then the model states:

$$X^*_{ij} = f_j\,(X_{i1}(t), \ldots, X_{i,j-1}(t), X_{i,j+1}(t), \ldots, X_{ij}(t), Z_{ij}(t), \mu_{ij}) \quad (3)$$

$$(i = 1, \ldots, I; j = 1, \ldots, J)$$

To keep the model tractable, we choose a simple form for the dependence of the carrying capacities on the three classes of variables. We assume that the dependence is linear and that the dependence parameters are constant over local environments. Thus

$$X_{ij}^* = \alpha_j + \sum_{k \neq j} \beta_{jk} X_{ik}(t) + \gamma_j Z_{ij}(t) + \mu_{ij} \qquad (4)$$

The parameters of (4) are usually referred to by bioecologists as the *parameters of the niche* of the entity in question. The coefficients of the other components, the X_{ik}, are of special theoretical importance. They are in fact what we called *competition coefficients* in Chapter Six. They indicate the impact of a unit of one component on the carrying capacity of the other. They can, of course, be positive, negative, or zero. When both β_{kj} and β_{jk} are negative, the two components are said to interact *competitively*. When β_{kj} is negative but β_{jk} is zero, we will speak of j's *interference* with k. In the case where both are positive, the relationship is termed *symbiotic*. When β_{kj} is positive but β_{jk} is zero, we will refer to j's *facilitation* of k. Finally, when one is positive and the other is negative, the relationship is one of *predation*. We will follow the usual ecological practice of referring to the β_{kj} as *competition coefficients* where this does not give rise to ambiguities.

Next we consider the dynamic structure. In our earlier work, we argued for a partial adjustment model where the speed of adjustment may differ by category and in growth and decline. We continue to use the simplest continuous-time partial adjustment model: a linear model (for further discussion of such models, see Hummon, Doreian, and Teuter, 1975; Nielsen and Hannan, 1977; Doreian and Hummon, 1977):

$$X_{ij}(t + \Delta t) - X_{ij}(t) = r_j \Delta t \left[X_{ij}^*(t) - X_{ij}(t) \right]$$

or, taken to the limit

$$\frac{dX_{ij}}{dt} = r_j \left[X_{ij}^* - X_{ij} \right] \quad (j = 1, \ldots, J) \qquad (5)$$

The parameter r_j is also of considerable theoretical importance. It indicates the level of responsiveness of a personnel category to changes in its carrying capacity (or, more precisely, to gaps between current levels and the carrying capacity). When there is no structural inertia, $r_j = 1$, the component adjusts completely in the interval Δt. At the other extreme, as r_j approaches zero, the component does not adjust at all. Clearly, the responsiveness parameter r_j indicates the fraction of the required adjustment that is made in the time unit we specify. We choose to parameterize the model in yearly time units. Thus r_j will be the fraction of the gap that is made up each year. We are interested in contrasting this parameter across components and for each component between growth and decline.

We complete the model by making the obvious substitution of (4) into (5):

$$\frac{dX_{ij}}{dt} = r_j \left[\alpha_j + \sum_{k \neq j} \beta_{jk} X_{ik} + \gamma_j Z_{ij} + \mu_{ij} - X_{ij} \right]$$

$$= a_j + \sum_{k \neq j} b_{jk} X_{ik} + c_j Z_{ij} + m_{ij} - r_j X_{ij} \qquad (6)$$

$$= a_j + \sum_{k} b_{jk} X_{ik} + c_j Z_{ij} + m_{ij}$$

where

$$a_j = r_j \, \alpha_j$$

$$b_{jk} = \begin{cases} -r_j \text{ when } j = k \\ r_j \, \beta_{jk} \text{ otherwise} \end{cases}$$

$$C_j = r_j \, \gamma_j \qquad (7)$$

$$m_{ij} = r_j \, \mu_{ij}$$

Estimation

The equations in (6) constitute a system of IJ first-order linear differential equations. To proceed toward estimation of the fundamental parameters just discussed, we must rewrite (5) in matrix form. Let

$$\frac{dX}{dt} = \left(\frac{dX_1}{dt}, \ldots, \frac{dX_J}{dt} \right)'$$

Then

$$\frac{dX}{dt} = ai' + BX + CZ + M \qquad (8)$$

where

$$a = (a_1, \ldots, a_J)'; i' = (1, \ldots, 1) \text{ is } (1 \times I);$$

$$B, X, \text{ and } M \text{ are } (J \times I) \text{ and } Z \text{ is } (1 \times I).$$

The system in (8) has solution

$$X(t) = B^{-1} ai' (C^{B\Delta t} - I) + e^{B\Delta t} X(t_0) + e^{Bt} \int_{t_0}^{t_1} e^{Bt_0} CZ' ds \qquad (9)$$
$$+ B^{-1} M (e^{B\Delta t} - I)$$

As in our previous analysis, we assume that the variable environmental factor changes linearly over $\Delta t = t - t_0$. Then (9) reduces to

$$X(t) = B^{-1} ai' (e^{B\Delta t} - I) + e^{B\Delta t} X(t_0) + B^{-1} C (e^{B\Delta t} - I) Z(t_0) \qquad (10)$$
$$+ B^{-1} C \left[\frac{e^{B\Delta t} - I}{\Delta t} - I \right] \Delta Z + B^{-1} M (e^{B\Delta t} - I)$$

This has a form,

$$X(t) = a*i' + B* X(t_0) + C_1^* Z(t_0) + C_2^* \Delta Z + M* \qquad (11)$$

that is amenable to regression analysis.

The equations in (11) are of the form proposed by Coleman (1968)—see also Kaufman (1976)—with the exception of $M*$. The entries in M^* are unobservable variables that summarize the effects of history. As such, they are forced into the disturbance term that is implicitly specified when regression analysis is applied to the integrated form of the continuous time model. So, if we were to proceed in the conventional manner, we would estimate:

$$X (t) = a^*i + B^* X (t_o) + C^*_1 Z (t_o) + C^*_2 \Delta Z + U \quad (12)$$

where

$$U = M^* + E$$

and E is a matrix whose entries are random measurement errors and other sources of error. There is no problem with the regression assumption that disturbances be uncorrelated with regressors in the case of E. However, this essential assumption cannot apply with respect to M^*. The constant factors in each environment affect $X(t_0)$ as well as $X(t)$ so that M^* must be correlated with $X(t_0)$ —for more complete discussion of the problem, see Hannan and Young (1977). Consequently, application of ordinary least squares regression analysis to (12), ignoring history, will produce biased estimates of the fundamental parameters.

With only two waves of observations (at t_0 and t), there is no simple solution to this estimation problem. However, with more waves of observations, a pooled cross section and time series analysis can be estimated in a way that circumvents the problem. The logic and procedures are discussed in Hannan and Young (1977). In particular, we propose to treat the historical factors not as parameters to be estimated but random variables drawn from a single distribution with finite variance. Then we can apply generalized least squares procedures that have been shown to have good small sample properties.

In fact, we do not use any of the generalized least squares estimators discussed in the econometric literature (see Nerlove, 1971). The reason is that we wish to introduce one further complication. In our earlier work, we found evidence of heteroscedasticity: The variance of the disturbances appeared to be correlated with the size of the organization. Evidence of a similar pattern emerged when we applied Nerlove's modified generalized least squares procedure to the pooled data. We corrected for this problem in our earlier work by employing weighted least squares. This suggests that we form an estimator that combines generalized least squares correction for the historical factors and weighted least squares for heteroscedasticity in the random portion of the disturbance. Such a combined estimator has been developed and employed by Nielsen and Hannan (1977). It involves an application of Henderson's (1952, 1963) method of estimating variance components. For details, see Nielsen (1974) and Nielsen and Hannan (1977). We refer to the estimator as weighted generalized least squares (WGLS).

So the first step in empirical analysis is to obtain WGLS estimates of the coefficients of (11). Then given $\hat{a}*$, $\hat{B}*$, $\hat{C}*_1$, and $\hat{C}*_2$, we work backwards to obtain estimates of the fundamental parameters following the eigenvalue method proposed by Coleman (1968, p. 451). We first estimate the internal or endogenous part of the system using the relationship:

$$\hat{B}* = e^{B \Delta t} \tag{13}$$

and the decomposition

$$\hat{B}* = \hat{V}* \, \hat{\Delta} \, \hat{V}*^{-1}$$

where Δ is the diagonal matrix whose entries are eigenvalues of B (equal to those of B*) and V is the matrix whose columns are the associated eigenvectors (see Coleman, 1968, p. 251). Then it follows that

$$\hat{B} = \hat{V}*(\frac{1}{\Delta t} \, \ln \, \hat{\Delta}) \, \hat{V}*^{-1} \tag{14}$$

Once we have estimated B, the other terms in (8) are obtained by straightforward matrix operations. Finally, we use the identities in (7) to recover estimates of the fundamental demographic parameters.

This set of procedures has one disadvantage. The strategy for estimating the fundamental parameters is somewhat indirect. As we noted earlier (Freeman and Hannan, 1975, p. 222), the nonlinear operations required to go from (10) to (8) do not preserve the asymptotic efficiency of our estimators. Nor do we have sampling distributions for the fundamental parameters. Thus all statistical testing must be done on the integrated form (10). Nonetheless, this procedure does yield consistent estimators of fundamental parameters.

Data

The empirical analysis reported hereafter conforms as closely as possible to that done earlier (Freeman and Hannan, 1975). We use yearly counts of enrollments and the sizes of four personnel categories from California school districts. The personnel categories are teachers (T), administrators (A), pupil service employees (P) (for example, librarians and guidance counselors), and classified nonprofessionals (C) (for example, cafeteria workers and secretaries).

In the earlier work, we employed two- and four-year lags. For each lag, we separated the 823 school districts into those whose enrollments grew each year (growers), those whose enrollments declined each year (decliners), and the rest. We analyzed only growers and decliners. Here we use data from the 1971–1975 period and a two-year lag; that is, we estimate effects for the pooled 1971–1973, 1972–1974, and 1973–1975 periods. We now define growers as those districts whose enrollments grew 10 percent or more over the period. Decliners are defined as those districts whose enrollments declined 10 percent or more. This criterion yields 170 growers and 223 decliners.

Table 1 reports the means for all variables for the growers and decliners. The declining districts' initial mean enrollment was about a third larger than that for growers. However, the average class sizes were quite similar initially (23.2 for growers and 23.8 for decliners). The ratio of administrators to teachers was also quite close (.069 and .068 for growers and decliners respectively). By 1975, the mean enrollments had almost reversed. However, average class size had declined considerably for declining districts, and the A/T ratio had gone from .068 to .077. Similarly, the average levels of the other two elements in what we called the "supportive component," P and C, also resisted decline. The means for both P and C actually *increased* over the period of enrollment decline.

Table 1. Means of Selected Variables.

	Growers		Decliners	
	1971	1975	1971	1975
Average daily attendance (E)	3447	4432	4584	3762
Teachers (T)	143	181	191	178
ADA/T	23.2	23.2	23.8	20.8
Administrators (A)	10.0	11.8	13.9	13.1
A/T	.069	.065	.068	.077
Pupil service employees (P)	9.6	12.9	9.6	10.3
Classified employees (C)	78.4	108.7	99.0	110.7
$N =$	170	170	223	223

Looking only at the means, we see that one of our earlier arguments does not fare well: Class size does not appear to remain constant in growth and decline. Our other broad argument is sustained: The supportive component resists decline; it appears to do so more effectively than the "direct component," T.

We turn now to examine whether this pattern holds for a properly specified multivariate, dynamic model. As we have discussed, the first step involves estimating, by WGLS, a series of linear models with lagged dependent variables. The estimated regression coefficients for enrollments and change in enrollments were always significant at the .05 level. However, some of the effects of one component on another were not. When we used these estimates to solve for the parameters of the dynamic model, we obtained several complex roots. We believed that this was due to the unstable estimates of the few insignificant variables. Therefore, we eliminated the insignificant variables, reestimated all equations, and solved for fundamental parameters. This time, all rates were real, and the procedures we outlined earlier went through straightforwardly.

Empirical Results

Our main interest is in contrasting the organizational demography of growth and decline. Our model separates the organizational demography problem into three parts: (1) competition among components for fixed resources; (2) changes in resource levels; and (3) responsiveness to changes in carrying capacities (determined by levels of resources and sizes of competitors). We turn first to a consideration of the results on competition.

Competitive Structure. We allowed the possibility that the upper level on the size of any component, or its carrying capacity, depends on the size of every other component. The patterns of dependencies that emerge in analysis of the data are simpler than that. Table 2 contains the matrices of competition coefficients for

Table 2. Estimated Competition Coefficients (Community Matrices).

	Growers			
	T	A	P	C
T	1.0		.616	.156
A	.071	1.0	−.136	−.004
P	.127		1.0	−.006
C				1.0

	Decliners			
	T	A	P	C
T	1.0	1.90		
A	.076	1.0		
P	.115	−.016	1.0	−.038
C	−.152	5.54	−2.14	1.0

Note: Entries are β_{jk} in (4). Column variables take the role of k and row variables, j. See Table 1 for explanation of categories (T = Teachers).

growing and declining districts. Recall that when β_{kj} is negative, the carrying capacity for component k declines with the size of component j. In this case, component j is said to *interfere* with k. If β_{jk} is also negative, the two are said to *compete*. Positive coefficients, of course, have the opposite interpretation.

A matrix of competition coefficients for a system is often called a *community matrix*. Such a matrix has the advantage of making plain the pattern of dependencies in a system. Look first at the positioning of zero entries in growth and decline. In the matrix for growing districts, one row and one column have the maximum number of zero entries. In fact, these are the only zero entries in the matrix. The row contains the competition coefficients for classified employees (or nonprofessionals) with other components. The growth of this component depends only on external resources; in other words, in growth none of the components either interfere or facilitate the growth of the nonprofessional staff. At the same time, C affects the carrying capacity of every other component. It interferes with both administration and pupil services but increases the carrying capacity for the teaching component.

Administration is almost a mirror image. It does not affect any other component but is affected by every component. Both of the other nonteaching components, P and C, impede the growth of administration.

The pattern of zeroes suggests a hierarchical structure of dependencies. The level of C adjusts independently to the level of resources. Once C's carrying capacity has been determined, the upper levels for T and P are determined (where T and P stand in a symbiotic relationship to each other but have different relations to the autonomous component, C). Finally, the carrying capacity for administration is determined jointly by the levels of all of the other components.

The picture for decline is very different. Now the zero entries are all in the upper right-hand corner of the matrix. Neither T nor A are affected by either of the other components. Both the teaching staff and administration adjust only to each other and to the outside environment. At the second level in the hierarchy of dependencies, P and C adjust to each of the other components.

What does this mean? We read these patterns as indicating that the competitive position of the administration is very different in growth and decline. When enrollments are growing, the administrative staff appears to get only the remainder of the resource pie. However, when enrollments are declining, administration shifts to a more controlling position in the political struggle for re-sources. The administrative and teaching staffs stand in a symbiotic relationship in decline. They appear to jointly manage their de-pendence on the outside environment, unconstrained by the other components. Administration shifts to an active, dominating posi-tion in the organizational politics in decline.

Another aspect of the broad patterns deserves attention. The entries in the community matrix for decliners are consistently larger than is the case for decliners. It is worth formalizing this difference in *intensity of interaction.* A simple measure of intensity of interaction is the mean of the absolute values of all off diagonal terms in the community matrix. For growers, the average intensity is .093; for decliners, the average intensity is .945. This tremen-dous difference is due in part to the very large dependence coef-ficients for C in decline. But even when we ignore the rows and columns involving C there is a substantial difference in intensity between growth and decline. The average intensities, ignoring terms involving C, are .158 for growers and .351 for decliners. Therefore we conclude that *the intensity of competitive interactions among personnel components is greater in decline than in growth.*

This conclusion regarding intensity of interaction among components supports our earlier reasoning about the political na-ture of organizational decline. As we mentioned earlier, our earlier work treated the growth process as administratively rational and only the decline process as political. In the current model, both are political. Now we find that *it is the intensity of the competitive inter-actions, together with the patterns of interactions, that distinguishes growth and decline.*

Finally, we must note the position of the teaching compo-nent in the resource competition process. No component interferes with the growth teaching staff (that is, there are no negative entries in the two rows for T). Rather, a large supportive component in-creases the carrying capacity for teachers (in growth, it is P and C that do so, while in decline it is A). Moreover, teachers on the whole do not lower carrying capacities for other components (the only exception is for C in decline). At any given level of enrollments, the larger the size of the teaching staff, the larger the administra-tive staff and the pupil service staff.

Carrying Capacities. The next step is to examine how carrying capacities for components are determined. Unlike the previous findings, our earlier model made clear predictions concerning carrying capacities (although we used different language). We claimed that the relationship of the size of T to enrollments would be the same in growth and decline. We also argued that the supportive component (A, P, and C—but especially A) would resist decline. That is, we hypothesized that a given enrollment would support more supportive personnel in decline. Of course, we have now altered the model substantially, and it is not clear that the same reasoning holds. Nonetheless, it is informative to address the questions in terms of $\hat{\alpha}_j$, $\hat{\beta}_{jk}$, and $\hat{\gamma}_j$, the parameters of the niche of each component.

Estimates of the niche parameters, the coefficients of the determinants of carrying capacities, are presented in Table 3. Only $\hat{\alpha}_i$ and $\hat{\gamma}_i$ are new since the $\hat{\beta}_{jk}$ are the entries in the community matrices just discussed. While there is some variation in the $\hat{\alpha}$'s, they are all small relative to other differences in the model. Consequently, we focus on the $\hat{\gamma}$'s, the effects of enrollments.

The four components fall into two groups. The carrying capacities for teachers and classified employees depend strongly and *directly* on enrollments. The carrying capacities for the other two components, A and P, react more to factors *internal* to the work organization and only weakly to enrollments. The direct effect of enrollments on A and P are much smaller than would be required to generate directly the levels of A and P reported in Table 1. Thus it appears that we have two components specialized to adapting to

Table 3. Estimated Niche Parameters (Effects on Carrying Capacities).

Growth T = 1.80			+.616P	+.156C	+.0569E
Decline T = .756		+1.90A			+.0388E
Growth A = .050	+.071T		−.136P	−.004C	+.0011E
Decline A = .133	+.076T				+.0003E
Growth P = .870	+.127T		−.006P		
Decline P = .306	+.115T	−.016A		−.038C	+.0011E
Growth C = 4.89					+.0510E
Decline C = 3.40	−.152T	+5.54A	−2.14P		+.0441E

Note: See Table 1 for explanation of categories (T = Teachers).

Table 4. Total Effects of Enrollments (E).

	Growth	Decline
T	3.35 + .0702E	1.18 + .0445E
A	.113 + .0049E	.222 + .0032E
P	1.29 + .0086E	.293 + .0046E
C	4.89 + .0510E	5.08 + .0637E

Note: See Table 1 for explanation of categories (T = Teachers).

direct variations in enrollments. The other two, A and P, are specialized to adapting to flows of resources mediated by T and C.

This clear difference, that characterizes both growth and decline, leads us to rethink our earlier classification scheme. We followed the literature in distinguishing between a production component that does the legitimated work of the organization and a supportive component that services and buffers the direct component. We treated only teachers as direct component staff. Classified employees were treated as supportive staff. But the estimates in Table 3 belie this classification. It appears that both teachers and classified employees are doing the production work in these organizations. We infer this from the fact that the carrying capacities for only these two components depend directly (in a strong way) on the demand for the services of the organization. The mix of workers involved in C (bus drivers, janitors, cafeteria employees, clerks) is relatively heterogeneous. Yet there are many that are directly tied to the volume of students. So we have no difficulty accepting the classification suggested by the results, that C is part of the direct component.

In three of four cases, the direct effect of enrollments is larger in growth (P is the only exception). This is true both for T (where we expected no such difference) and for A (where the ratchet analogue suggests a reverse ordering). But, these direct-effect measures do not tell the whole story. As we have indicated, the effects of enrollments are mediated by T and C. More generally, environmental effects reverberate through the competitive structure. So it is natural to investigate the effects of enrollments on a steady state. To do this, we calculate *total effects* by solving the systems of equations (for growers and decliners) in Table 3 for T^*, A^*, P^*, and C^* as functions only of E.

The total effects of enrollments are presented in Table 4. The simple reasoning about the difference between growth and decline does not fare any better when we consider total effects. It is easier to see this from another calculation. In Table 5, we indicate the predicted equilibrium levels for each component in a school district with 10,000 students (the results for districts of other sizes will not differ much, since the constants are so small). The second and fourth columns of Table 5 record the levels for each component that would be expected from the ratios in the 1975 data (for example, from ratios of T to ADA). The differences between the predictions and the 1975 observations give an indication of how far the districts are from equilibrium. We first discuss the predictions for growth and decline and then consider the issue of distance from equilibrium.

The predicted equilibrium level for teachers in decline is initially the same as that observed in the data, an average class size of approximately 22.5 students. For growing districts, the predicted equilibrium level of T gives an average class size of approximately 14.3. Similar differences hold for A^*. However, the A^*/T^* ratio would not be much changed under these predictions. In fact, the ratio of administrators to teachers is predicted to be slightly higher in decline, .072, than in growth, .069. Similarly, the predicted A^*/P^* ratio is also larger for decline, .70 versus .56.

Only for the classified staff does the model predict higher equilibrium levels in decline. However, the predicted C^* for both growth and decline are very much higher than current levels.

What do we make of these results? It is difficult and perhaps unwarranted to conclude more than that growth and decline pro-

Table 5. Predicted Levels of Personnel Components in Equilibrium (Enrollments = 10,000).

	Growth		Decline	
	Predicted	1975 Observed	Predicted	1975 Observed
Teachers	705	430	446	480
Administrators	49	27	32	35
Public service employees	87	29	46	27
Classified employees	515	245	642	294

cesses differ for these organizations. We hesitate to make more of the findings than this broad conclusion for several reasons. The predicted equilibria for several categories are very far from current observed levels. Thus the prediction is really an extrapolation quite far beyond the data used to estimate model parameters. Under such conditions, the linearity we imposed for simplicity becomes quite important. Departures from linearity (either in the dynamic model or in the behavior over time of the exogenous variable) may produce only slight distortions in predictions to nearby equilibria. When, on the other hand, the predicted equilibria are distant, departures from linearity may give completely misleading results.

There is a second, more substantive, issue. Suppose these results give accurate predictions of the carrying capacities toward which the components are adjusting during the period studied. We find it hard to believe that the environment would not intervene were these tendencies revealed over a sustained period. If, for instance, the number of classified employees or teachers continually grew out of proportion to the size of the organizations, we would expect the communities that finance these organizations would take action to alter the growth process. In short, we doubt that growth on the order predicted here is politically feasible. In work in progress, we are incorporating financial variables and using longer lag periods in an effort to understand more clearly the environmental factors affecting carrying capacities. Meanwhile, we must treat the findings reported here as quite tentative. To repeat, it is unwise to conclude more than that growth differs from decline.

Partial Adjustment. Finally, we consider estimates of the speed with which each component adjusts to changes in its carrying capacities: that is, to changes in environmental conditions and to the sizes of competitors (and facilitators). The relevant parameter was denoted by r in (5). Recall that r indicates the fraction of the gap between current size and current carrying capacity that is reduced in a year. The estimated r's are found in Table 6.

We find that two components, A and C, are almost equally responsive in growth and decline. Administration adjusts about half way each year, while the size of the classified staff adjusts only about a fifth of the way. For the other two categories, T and P,

Table 6. Estimates of r, the Responsiveness Parameter.

	Growth	_Decline_
Teachers	.441	.258
Administrators	.523	.588
Public service employees	.322	.183
Classified employees	.192	.211

adjustment is considerably faster in growth. That is, they respond more quickly to an increase in carrying capacity than to a decrease.

This is not what we had expected. Our expectation was that administrators would respond more quickly in growth and that the response of teachers would not much differ in growth and decline. Nor did we expect that administrations would be more responsive than all the other categories. Now, however, it is clear where we went wrong. Previously, we thought of each personnel component as adjusting to exogenous demand. But we saw earlier that the carrying capacity for administration is not strongly and directly affected by changes in environmental demand. Rather, it responds to the sizes of other personnel components. This is particularly true for decline. And, in growth and decline, A^* is responsive to different conditions. In growth, A^* depends on all the other components: P and C impede A's growth. In decline, A^* depends only on T. Thus the conditions to which the component responds are quite different. In growth, it is in part a response to competition (lowering A^*). In decline, there is no competition. Consequently, there is no reason to expect that r for growth would be greater than r for decline. Our previous reasoning did not take such complexities into account.

It is worth noting that the dynamic behavior of the whole system will differ in growth and decline due to the differences in r for T and P. The difference for T is undoubtedly more important. Recall that environmental demand is mediated largely by T and C. So the fact that T in declining districts responds slowly suggests that _response to decline will be slower throughout the system._

Returning to the issue of the responsiveness of A, in decline, as we have seen, A^* responds only to T (and only very slightly on the environment). The fact that T responds slowly in decline implies that *A also responds slowly to environmental changes in decline.* From this perspective, the ratchet effect we posited previously appears to hold for the dynamics of the response of A to changes in demand for the services of the organization. But the ratchet effect holds because of differences in responsiveness of the size of the teaching staff and because of growth-decline differences in the competitive structure.

Discussion

We find broad differences between growth and decline in all three of the subprocesses studied: (1) Competitive interactions are stronger on average in decline, (2) carrying capacities for most personnel components are lower at a given level of enrollment in decline, and (3) the organizational systems respond more slowly to environmental changes in decline. Any one of these findings would be enough to sustain our earlier contention that the growth and decline processes differ. The fact that all three differ is dramatic evidence. Thus analysis of the revised model reinforces our earlier critique of the wholesale failure in the organizations literature to distinguish growth and decline processes.

By making the model fully political, we have obtained results that are more complex than in our earlier work. The growth-decline difference is now more pervasive since the pivotal teaching component behaves differently in growth and decline. The main analytic consequence of this difference is to vitiate some of our earlier reasoning. In particular, we must discard the argument for a "norm of constant class size" that implies symmetric growth and decline for the teaching component. Abandoning this simplification complicates attempts at contrasting patterns, as there is now no stable baseline.

What remains of our earlier argument about the specific differences between growth and decline? Our general argument was that organizational politics would distort the decline process. The more specific argument was that the supportive component resists decline (while the teaching staff does not) so that ratios of supportive staff to teachers will be higher at the same level of enrollments in decline. We conclude that the results support the broad argument; the politics are different in decline. We see this in two ways. First, the strength of competitive interactions is stronger in decline. The structure of competitive interactions also changes with administration shifting to a more dominating position. These changes, taken together, suggest that adjustments in the sizes of components are made less on the basis of administrative rationality and more on the basis of political struggles among components in decline. Second, the systems respond more slowly to decline. It is clearly in the narrow interests of each component, but not administratively rational, to resist decline. The fact that response is slow in decline suggests that the personnel components are at least partially successful in enacting these interests. In these respects, the organizational politics work in the way we anticipated.

It is more difficult to assess the specific argument concerning relative sizes of supportive and direct components in growth and decline. We classified only administration and pupil services as supportive and teachers and classified employees (on the basis of empirical results) as the direct component. We find that the predicted ratio of administrators to teachers increases slightly in decline. However, the ratio to teachers and classified employees is smaller in decline. For the pupil service category, both ratios are larger in growth. But both A and P respond more slowly than T and C in decline. For P, we see this merely by inspecting r. For A, we must recall that A responds almost solely to T in decline. Thus A's response is some fraction of T's response. So the short-run behavior of the two supportive components may give rise to ratchetlike effects when districts cycle between spells of growth and decline. Otherwise, the long-run equilibria predictions do not support our earlier hypothesis. We must add again the caution that these predicted equilibria are the most delicate of our findings. Departures from linearity in particular may rob these calculations of much value. Therefore, the conclusions regarding equilibrium levels of components should be treated as very tentative.

There are two important premises underlying the changes we have introduced into our model. First, we assume that each personnel component is organized in a self-interested way. Administrators take care of their own, and so do teachers and the rest.

Second, we assume no functional priority among them. Whether teachers are more necessary to the operation of school districts than nonteaching professionals is, of course, arguable. We believe such arguments occur regularly in most school districts. How they come out is a matter that depends on political power more than anything else. So we see these population components very much as we see social classes, ethnic groups, and other social collectivities that compete for scarce resources.

In this respect, our work draws on a variety of sources. From political economy, we draw our emphasis on internal competition for resources, status, and power. The work of Michels ([1915] 1949) is clearly relevant here. In this volume, Chapter Two, by Pfeffer, on micropolitics, is complementary. Similarly, Chapter Four, by Meyer and Rowan, argues that institutionalized rules, rooted in the environment rather than any functional necessity born of an established technology, explain why schools are the way they are. We agree with them, although we see these rules as subject to political negotiation rather than as institutional "givens." Although their perspective is static, explaining why things are as they are rather than how they came to be that way, we probably do little violence to their argument by noting that we and they would probably both agree that it is when environmental shocks are experienced that breakdowns are observed in the precedents and traditions on which normative consensus rests. Finally, these ideas have much in common with those of Cohen, March, and Olsen (1972), March and Olsen (1976), and Weick (1976). We do not assume that school districts have well-known goals. We do assume that they have no well-understood technology and that participation is variably fluid over time and across population components. So, in many respects, we see school districts (and their constituent schools) as organized anarchies. Organizational demography is not the simple outcome of administrative rationality. It is the lack of deterministic standards by which decisions are made, coupled with competition for scarce resources, that contributes the political quality to these organizations. In organizations with clear-cut goals, using well-understood technologies, in which participants and nonparticipants are clearly differentiated, we would expect fewer of the issues driving demographic dynamics to be "up for grabs." And they should come closer to what would be expected under rationalist assumptions.

These observations serve to place this research in perspective. The degree of politicization is variable across the universe of all organizations. Further research in a variety of organizational contexts will be required before we know how much the models advanced in this chapter can tell us about organizational dynamics in general.

The model we have worked with in this chapter implies internal political process but it also suggests external political process as well. When organizations differ in growth and decline, as California school districts clearly do, the aggressiveness with which they seek out resources can be expected to differ. In this continuing line of research, we plan to expand the analysis to take resource constraints into account. But we should note that school districts may adopt entrepreneurial behavior patterns in order to build up the slack they use to keep internal competition in check. Where these resources come from has much to do with the uncertainties and constraints on the organization. Federal money, for instance, often mandates clerical and administrative effort. This is to say that it has bureaucratic strings tied to it. Money raised at the school site level (for example, from PTA activities and building rentals) often has no such bureaucratic strings but does carry with it uncertainty generated by unstable participation of parents and other contributors.

Work currently in progress should place these issues in a sharper light. In the interim, we conclude that the revised model (and estimation procedures used here) yield an improved understanding of the complex ways in which organizational demography responds to variations in environmental demand for services. This research highlights the preeminently political character of organizational demography and suggests the value of further research on the micropolitics of organizational demography.

8

Leadership and Organizational Structure

Marshall W. Meyer

This chapter is about the effects of leadership on the administrative structure of organizations, but it is broader in scope than the title implies. It is necessarily about the organizations that were surveyed in order to gather data for the research—city, county, and state departments of finance headed by the chief financial officers of the jurisdictions. It also touches on one of the central theoretical issues in the sociology of organizations: the debate between so-called open-systems and closed-systems approaches. The three strands of argument are inseparable here. The empirical findings cannot be understood without a description of what finance de-

This chapter was originally published in the *American Journal of Sociology*, November 1975. The research was supported by National Science Foundation grants GS-33509 and SOC73-05688 (formerly GS-39637), which are gratefully acknowledged. I wish to thank the following people for extensive comments on an earlier draft of this chapter: Howard Aldrich, Chris Argyris, M. Craig Brown, Richard Hall, Charles Halaby, Neil Henry, Oscar Grusky, John W. Meyer, Charles Perrow, and James L. Price. Brown's excellent research assistance is also acknowledged.

partments were like in the past, finance officials' beliefs about what their organizations should look like, and the changes in technology and management practices that have forced a different reality on these agencies. The findings suggest that characteristics of leadership positions have a profound impact on organizations, and they call into question the distinction between open and closed systems, of which much has been written. The description of finance departments, however, must precede consideration of the larger issues.

Finance departments are essential to local government administration. Typically, their duties include assessment and collection of taxes, maintenance of the various accounts of local governments, preauditing of disbursements and the actual issuing of checks or warrants, borrowing of funds as well as investment of surplus revenues, and ancillary tasks such as insurance, management of revenue-generating properties, and postauditing of accounts at the end of the fiscal year. Some of the agencies studied here are called *auditors'* or *comptrollers' offices*; these titles are most frequent in the East. The term *department of administration* is increasingly popular: it is used when nonfinancial housekeeping activities are combined with the usual financial responsibilities. But a majority of the agencies surveyed for this study are called *finance departments*.

Even though they are essential, finance agencies are not invulnerable to change. The term *finance department* is itself fairly new. Prior to World War II, fiscal responsibilities were usually divided among departments of revenue, accounts, treasury, and auditing. In the 1950s, the concept of centralized finance administration under a single director of finance emerged. Administration was to be streamlined by having a chief financial officer responsible directly to the head of government. The Municipal Finance Officers Association of the United States and Canada has long advocated centralized administration, and most finance directors share this preference. But in the last few years centralized financial administration has become increasingly difficult to manage. What were in the 1950s fairly similar and routine tasks have become disparate—some still routine and predictable, others fraught with uncertainty and requiring technical skills beyond a knowledge of accounting. Two developments brought about this change. The first is computerization, which raised the issue of who was to control data-processing facilities and thereby the key pressure points in the information flow of local governments. Initially, finance departments retained control of the computer, but they are slowly losing their monopoly as other government agencies recognize the potential of electronic data processing. The second development is new budgeting techniques variously labeled systems analysis, PPBS, cost-benefit analysis, and the like. All of these depart from traditional line-item budgeting because they attempt to link costs to outputs and to identify the least expensive means of providing satisfactory levels of services. They also require the kind of guesswork that is anathema to the traditional accountant: hence, some budget units have been moved out of finance departments.

A general trend exists, then, toward contraction of the responsibilities and administrative structures of finance departments. As this chapter will show, leadership affects this process. Certain leadership conditions minimize the effects of the environment on the size and structure of finance departments so that they remain essentially stable over time. Under other conditions, environmental demand attenuates growth and leads to loss of functionally specialized subunits. Contraction and dedifferentiation of finance departments are accompanied by growth of other agencies serving local governments. Some evidence of this process will be shown toward the end of this chapter.

One more prefatory note is in order. A small set of "new" departments, agencies that have changed both their names and administrative structures since 1966, are excluded from this analysis. Unlike the others, their size and internal structures have grown with environmental demands. These departments are discussed in M. Meyer (1975). They are mentioned here only to indicate that some circumstances reverse the erosion of finance departments.

Leadership in Organizational Theory

The literature on leadership in organizations is large, but the findings are few. No simple relationship of leadership style to the performance of workers has been found (see Campbell and others, 1970; Graen, Dansereau, and Minami, 1972). The link between the two is either moderated by other variables or non-existent. Similarly, the relationship of leadership to overall organizational performance has been found to be tenuous. The effects of business cycles, peculiarities of specific industries, and histories of individual firms account for far more variance in the performance of large businesses than does leadership (Lieberson and O'Connor, 1972). One might conclude that leadership makes no difference to large organizations. But to do so would violate common sense, and, more importantly, it would overlook the connection between leadership and variables describing organizational structure that we do not normally associate with effectiveness or performance. This chapter will show some small but consistent relationships between the stability of leadership and the stability of organizational structures. It will also show that leadership characteristics affect causal relationships among organizational variables.[1] Such relationships are all but absent among organizations with stable, autonomous, and insular leadership. By contrast, where there is turnover in leadership positions, dependence on higher authority, and frequent communication with immediate superiors, causal relationships abound. The function of leadership, I argue, is to mediate between environmental uncertainties and organizational structure. Where organizations are insulated from uncertainties, variables describing organizational structure are stable over time and do not affect one another. Where uncertainties intrude because of leadership conditions, stability declines, but there are orderly causal links among environmental measures, organizational size, and structure.

Sociological theories of organizations have all but ignored the question of leadership. This tendency, I believe, has several sources. One is the theory of bureaucracy, that emphasizes the permanence of the administrative structure of government and its superior competence compared with elected officials. As Max Weber wrote, (1946, pp. 228, 232), "Once it is fully established, bureaucracy is among those social structures which are hardest to destroy. Bureaucracy is *the* means of carrying 'community action' over into rationally ordered 'societal action'. . . . The power position of the fully developed bureaucracy is always overpowering. The 'political master' finds himself in the position of the 'dilettante' who stands opposite the 'expert,' facing the trained official who stands within the management of administration." Leadership is also overlooked in contemporary organizational theory. James D. Thompson (1967), for example, argues that technical requirements and environmental uncertainties shape most behavior in organizations. To be sure, Thompson discusses boundary-spanning activities, particularly those involved when environmental contingencies are diverse and uncertain, but he never identifies such activities with leadership. Together, the two theoretical perspectives form a paradox. One overlooks leadership on the grounds that organizations that are rational, hence bureaucratic, are so efficient compared to other forms of administration that changes in leadership cannot affect their stability. The other overlooks leadership because organizations that are rational, and hence responsive to environmental uncertainties, require considerable boundary-spanning activity, only part of which can be handled by a single leader. Put somewhat differently, bureaucratic theory deemphasizes leadership because nothing changes, and contemporary organization theory deemphasizes leadership because everything is in flux.

Another source of sociologists' reluctance to consider leadership is the discrepancy between the few theories of leadership we have and the kinds of research studies that have been conducted. Selznick (1957), for example, speaks of leadership's responsibility for shaping organizational character, infusing values, and generating a sense of distinctive competence among members. Much research, by contrast, has been concerned with dimensions of leadership style, primarily "initiation of structure" and "consideration" (see, for example, Stogdill and Coons, 1957), which seem far removed from Selznick's discussion of institutionalization. Almost equally removed from Selznick's theoretical ideas are some studies of leadership change, or what is called *managerial succession* (Gouldner, 1954; Grusky, 1961, 1963; Kriesberg, 1962), although Grusky's results have been challenged by Gordon and Becker (1964). Where change does occur, it saps morale, either because of increased bureaucratization (Gouldner, 1954) or because the departure of a leader is taken as evidence of organizational failure (Grusky, 1963). So great is the gap between sociological theorizing and research on leadership that it is tempting to dismiss leadership as a sociological variable altogether.

An alternative is to reformulate theories so that sociologically interesting propositions emerge and can be tested. Let me suggest several possibilities. First, both extreme positions—that organizations are rigid closed systems or that they are fraught with uncertainty—should be disregarded. A more appealing notion is that organizations are sometimes placid and sometimes turbulent.[2] Second, one should ask how leadership affects the relative placidity or turbulence of organizations. The literature on management succession suggests that changes in leadership are accompanied by other changes in organizations: hence, a plausible hypothesis is that leadership turnover creates turbulence or uncertainty in organizations. Third, instead of pursuing relationships between social-psychological characteristics of leaders and organizational properties, research should focus on variables describing the larger network of relationships in which leadership roles are embedded. For example, one might hypothesize that to the extent to which a leader is autonomous rather than dependent on higher authority, he can protect his organization from uncertainties arising in the environment.

In discussing the degree of uncertainty or turbulence within organizations, one must consider the broader question of the "openness" or "closedness" of organizational structures. There has been much discussion of the need for an "open-systems" approach to organizations and recognition of the causal primacy of variables describing the environment (see, for example, Katz and Kahn, 1966; Terreberry, 1968). However, many research studies have overlooked environmental variables, either because they were not measured in the first place or because they were measured but could not be separated from basic organizational attributes such as size (Blau and Schoenherr, 1971, p. 144). Some effects of environmental variables on organizational structure will be examined in this chapter, but only after controlling for several variables describing leadership. The basic premise is this: At least for the organizations studied, whether they are more like "open" or "closed" systems is variable. To the extent to which leadership is vulnerable to external pressures, it also allows environmental uncertainties to intrude on organizational structures. And to the extent to which leadership characteristics are associated with stability, the impact of the environment is diminished.

The Study of Finance Departments

Data describing some 215 city, county, and state departments of finance, comptrollers' offices, auditors' offices, and the like are analyzed in this article. The agencies were surveyed in 1966 and again in 1972. The data describe finance departments at these two points only. Little retrospective information was sought in the surveys. We do not know when changes in organizational structure that occurred between 1966 and 1972 actually took place, and, although we know the tenure of department heads in 1966 and 1972, there is no information on their predecessors. Hence, analysis of organizational changes is limited to the six-year interval between 1966 and 1972. A year-by-year account of the effects of leadership is not possible. Clearly, it is desirable to replicate this analysis over intervals both shorter and longer than six years. Data now being collected will yield three- and nine-year intervals in addition to the six-year span we now have.

As noted earlier, some finance departments lost control over key activities during the interval between the surveys. Of the 215 departments studied, 120 used computers in 1966, and 91 had their own data-processing facilities. Virtually all use computers now, but of the group that was computerized in 1966, only 67 still operated their own equipment in 1972. A similar pattern holds for the budgeting activity. Of the 215 departments, 95 had full responsibility for preparation of the operating budget in 1966, but only 83 had it in 1972. The number of persons employed in finance departments is not shrinking, however. Quite the contrary; their mean size increased from 102.3 to 126.7 full-time employees between 1966 and 1972, mainly because of new accounting requirements imposed by federal categorical grant programs and revenue sharing. And despite the loss of responsibilities, the internal structures of these agencies have not changed much overall.

The average number of major subunits, called *divisions* or *bureaus*, decreased from 5.73 in 1966 to 5.62 in 1972; the mean number of levels of hierarchy increased from 3.85 to 4.08, while the number of minor subunits or sections changed only from 11.71 to 12.40. The pattern of growth has not been uniform for all agencies, however, as we shall see.

The heads and other high-ranking personnel of some 254 finance agencies were interviewed in 1966. In the 1972 survey, 249 departments were meant to have participated, and usable data were obtained from 240.[3] Of the 240 cases, 25 were eliminated from the present analysis for several reasons. In a few instances, we directed interviewers to the wrong informants; in a handful of others, it was not clear just where the interviewer went. Of the 25, 14 were eliminated because they had both changed their names and fundamentally altered their organizational structures; they are the "new" agencies to be analyzed separately. The remaining 215 thus include some departments that either reorganized or changed their names, but not both, during the interval between the two surveys.

The analysis of the data describing the 215 departments will proceed as follows: We shall first examine autocorrelations between the 1966 and 1972 measures of four basic organizational variables: size, the number of divisions, the number of levels of supervision, and the number of subdivisions or sections. These autocorrelations will be our measures of the predictability of organizational structure over time. The 215 departments will be grouped according to variables describing leadership, and the autocorrelations within different groups will be compared. For example, the second column of Table 1 shows autocorrelations of the four variables for 113 departments in which leadership changed between 1966 and 1972, while the third column shows the autocorrelations for 102 departments in which there was stable leadership. We shall also look at turnover of control of computing facilities, again grouping the departments according to variables describing leadership. Results of regressions testing for causal relationships among environmental variables, organization size, and measures of structure will then be examined. Here too, the data will be grouped according to variables describing leadership. Finally, relationships between environmental variables and the size of data-processing and budget units will be reviewed. Needless to say, the effects of environment on the growth of data processing and budgeting are quite different from what they are on whole finance departments.

Leadership and Predictability of Organizational Structure

Some effects of leadership will now be considered. To begin, the impact of leadership turnover on the stability of organizational structures will be examined. I shall then turn to effects of autonomy of leadership positions. The question of whether or not change of control of data processing facilities is a function of leadership conditions will also be explored.

Turnover of Leadership. The most reasonable, indeed obvious, hypothesis with which to begin is that change in leadership is associated with change in organizational arrangements and, correspondingly, stability in leadership positions is a concomitant of organizational stability. To test this proposition, departments were grouped according to the length of time their heads had held their offices in 1972. One group consists of 113 departments whose top executives, having held their jobs for less than six years at the time of the 1972 survey, had come into office after the 1966 data were collected. The remaining 102 departments had the same leadership in 1972 as in 1966. The autocorrelations in Table 1 generally support the hypothesis that turnover is associated with instability, but the differences are not large, and there is one reversal. The autocorrelation of departmental size—the number of full-time employees—increases from .9380 in agencies with a turnover to .9786 where there is stability; the autocorrelation of the number of divisions increases from .5178 to .6246, and for the number of sections there is a similar increase from .6372 to .7434. The autocorrelation of the number of levels of supervision does not follow this pattern; it drops from .6058 to .5747.[4]

Aside from the weakness of the empirical evidence, the hypothesis that stability of leadership is associated with predictability of organizational structure is fraught with other problems. Most

Table 1. Autocorrelations of Structural Variables by Leadership Conditions.

Variables	All Departments (N = 215) (1)	1972 Tenure 0–5 Years (N = 113) (2)	1972 Tenure 6+ Years (N = 102) (3)	1966 Tenure 0–5 Years (N = 122) (4)	1966 Tenure 6+ Years (N = 93) (5)	Head Is Political Appointee (N = 93) (6)	Head Is Elected or Civil Servant (N = 71) (7)	More than 10 Percent of Time with Head of Government (N = 65) (8)	Up to 10 Percent of Time with Head of Government (N = 150) (9)
Size	.9497	.9380	.9786	.8825	.9789	.8551	.9944	.8196	.9694
Divisions	.5765	.5178	.6246	.5032	.6791	.5316	.6152	.5241	.5931
Levels of supervision	.5896	.6058	.5747	.5395	.6703	.5225	.6716	.4655	.6460
Sections	.6713	.6372	.7434	.6320	.7409	.6358	.7726	.4769	.7135

important is that where leadership has changed, some, though not all, of our informants have changed.[5] Apparent instability in organizational structures may reflect different perceptions of similar administrative arrangements. Where leadership has not changed, apparent instability may reflect either ignorance of or unwillingness to accept actual change. A second problem is the causal direction of the association between leadership turnover and organizational stability. I would like to argue that leadership is the causal variable, but there are two other possibilities. One is that leaders quit when their organizations are compelled to change; indeed, one might speculate that leadership is often forced out under the cover of reorganization. Another possibility is that a simultaneous relationship holds between stability of leadership and that of organizational structure. More turbulent organizations may have higher rates of turnover that make them more turbulent, and so forth.

One way of handling both of these problems is to lag the measure of leadership turnover. If changes in leadership engender fluctuations in organizational structure, then leadership at an earlier time should predict organization at a later time as well as or better than leadership turnover occurring at the same time organizational changes are observed. Should the relationship between leadership turnover and structure be simultaneous or should structural changes affect leadership, the differences revealed by the lagged measure of leadership should be small if not altogether degenerate. Furthermore, turnover in leadership before 1966 should not greatly affect changes between 1966 and 1972 in whom we interviewed.[6] The fourth and fifth columns of Table 1 show the autocorrelations of structural variables measured in 1966 and 1972 controlling for the tenure of leadership prior to 1966. The differences in the autocorrelations are somewhat greater than those yielded by controlling for leadership turnover between 1966 and 1972. Where leadership changed before 1966, the autocorrelations of size, the number of divisions, levels of supervision, and sections are .8825, .5032, .5395, and .6320; where there was stability, the autocorrelations are .9789, .6791, .6703, and .7409, respectively. Continuity of leadership during an earlier interval is associated with predictability of organizational structure later on.

These results suggest that leadership is the causal variable, but the other possibilities ought to be examined.

The data do not allow a complete test of the effects of organizational change on leadership turnover rather than the other way around. In part, this is because of the complexity of the problem. Department heads who anticipate reorganization may quit before the actual changes take place; the effect, leadership turnover, may appear before its cause. In part, the design of this research prevents a direct test. I have little information about organizational structure prior to the first wave of interviews; hence, specific changes in structure between 1960 and 1966 are not known. One item that is available, however, concerns whether any major changes in organizational structure occurred in finance agencies during the year preceding the 1966 interviews. About one third of the departments reported such changes. Lacking better data, we will have to rely on this item. Briefly, the tabulations show that departments that experienced structural change between 1965 and 1966 were much more likely than others to have had leadership turnover between 1960 and 1966. Moreover, organizational change before 1966 does not predict leadership turnover between 1966 and 1972. Departments that have had structural change kept their chiefs slightly (but not significantly) longer than others.[7] Disregarding a possible anticipation effect, then, structural change does not appear to be the source of much leadership turnover.

Testing for simultaneity between turnover and structural change is even more difficult but not impossible. While I cannot identify all of the conditions that might cause simultaneous change in both organizational structure and leadership, I do have information on one. The 1972 questionnaire asked whether there had been a major reorganization of local government since 1966. Two effects of governmental reorganization are evident. First, reorganization is significantly associated with leadership turnover. Of the thirty departments that reported reorganization of local government (although not necessarily of the finance agency), twenty-two, or 70 percent, changed leaders between 1966 and 1972, whereas only 49 percent of the others did. Second, although the autocorrelations of variables describing organizational structure are weaker where the structure of government has changed—especially with regard to the number of divisions—the effects of leadership turn-over remain. Indeed, the impact of leadership is greatest where there has been governmental reorganization.[8]

On balance, it appears that organizational change affects leadership turnover very little and that exogenous forces that disturb organizational structure do so mainly through their impact on leadership, although they do have some direct effect. I have no way of controlling for anticipation effects, nor do I have information on all the factors that might render the association between stability of leadership and organizational stability spurious. With these limitations in mind, it seems appropriate to speak of leadership as the causal variable.

Autonomy and Insularity of Leadership. A second hypothesis is that constraints on leadership affect the stability of organizational structures. One possibility is that minimal external influence allows leaders to change organization at will: hence, autonomy of leadership should be associated with unstable structures. More plausible is the notion that autonomous leadership shields organizations from pressures to change administrative arrangements; this prediction is most consistent with the argument that uncertainty is generated by the environment rather than by internal processes in most organizations. An indicator of department heads' dependence on higher authority is the method of appointment. Finance directors who are appointed by their immediate superiors or otherwise politically appointed are considered to be dependent on higher authority; those who are either elected or appointed through civil service procedures are considered autonomous.

The autocorrelations of variables describing organizational structure suggest that there is greater predictability when leadership has autonomy from higher authority than when it is dependent. In the sixth and seventh columns of Table 1, finance agencies are grouped according to the method of selection of department heads. The sixth column includes departments whose heads are political appointees, hence subject to arbitrary dismissal, while the seventh column shows autocorrelations for agencies whose heads are more independent because they are either elected or appointed through civil service procedures. For all four measures of organizational structure, the autocorrelations are higher where department heads are elected officials or civil servants. Where chief financial officers are political appointees, the autocorrelations of size, numbers of divisions, levels of hierarchy, and sections are .8551, .5316, .5225, and .6358, respectively. The autocorrelations increase to .9944, .6152, .6716, and .7726 where department heads are not dependent on the head of government because they have been elected or have civil service protection.

A similar pattern is evident when the insularity of department heads in relation to higher officials is controlled. Presumably, the more time a finance director spends in dealing directly with the head of government, the more the former is influenced by the latter and the more vulnerable to external influence the finance department becomes. In the eighth and ninth columns of Table 1, the proportion of time department heads spend with the head of government is controlled. The eighth column in Table 1 shows autocorrelations of the structural variables for departments whose heads spend more than 10 percent of their time with their nominal superiors; the ninth column shows autocorrelations for the remaining departments, where the head of government takes up to one tenth of the working hours of his chief financial officer. For the former group of departments, the autocorrelations of size, divisions, levels, and sections are .8196, .5241, .4655, and .4769, respectively. For the latter group, they are somewhat higher: .9694, .5931, .6460, and .7135. For both indicators of department heads' higher authority, the results are similar and quite consistent. The less dependence and the less interchange, the greater the predictability of organizational structure.

Control of the Computer. Just as leadership affects the predictability of organizational structure, it also influences the likelihood of change in control of the computing facilities used by the finance department. Of the 120 departments that used computers in 1966 (all but a handful do now), 91 ran their own computers, but only 67 do so now. Since 1966, 32 have given up control of the computer, while 8 have gained it.

Table 2 shows Q-coefficients derived from the cross tabulation of the finance departments' management of their own computers in 1966 and in 1972. The coefficients show that stability of the location of data-processing facilities in local governments, like the administrative structure of finance departments, depends on leadership conditions. To illustrate, the Q-coefficient of predictability of control of the computer is .6575 for all 120 departments but .5190 for agencies whose leaders changed between 1966 and 1972 and .7576 for departments with stable leadership. Where the department head is a political appointee, the Q-coefficient drops to .1667; it is .8445 where the head is either elected or a civil servant. Other variables describing leadership have similar effects on the stability of control of the computer. This adds to the evidence that organizational properties are affected by the rate of turnover of leaders and their relationships to superiors.

Causal Relationships Among Organizational Variables

In this section, I test the hypothesis that, where leadership allows uncertainties to intrude in organizations, causal relationships among organizational variables appear, whereas leadership conditions that minimize uncertainty make causal links vanish. Three sets of variables will be examined. One is measures of environmental demand for the services of finance departments. The demand variables are the total amount of funds a department administers for a city, county, or state; the size of the general or corporate fund that covers common activities such as police and fire protection, debt service, and health and welfare; the number of full-time government employees of the city, county, or state served; and the population of the jurisdiction served by a finance department. The second is organizational size, the number of full-time employees of a finance department. The third consists of measures of organizational structure: the numbers of divisions, levels of supervision, and sections in an agency. I use the terms *causality* and *causal relationship* in the same sense as in an earlier article on organizational size and structure, (M. Meyer, 1972a). A causal relationship is said to exist when the value of a variable at a later time is predicted by another variable measured at an earlier time with the dependent variable at the earlier time controlled. This is the cross-lagged path model outlined by Heise (1970). The reader is referred to Heise and to my earlier article on size and structure for illustrations of the use of the cross-lagged path technique. For

Table 2. Q-Coefficients of Turnover of Operation of Computer by Leadership Conditions (Departments that Used Computers in 1966).

All Departments (N = 120) (1)	1972 Tenure 0–5 Years (N = 61) (2)	1972 Tenure 6+ Years (N = 59) (3)	1966 Tenure 0–5 Years (N = 70) (4)	1966 Tenure 6+ Years (N = 50) (5)	Head Is Political Appointee (N = 50) (6)	Head Is Elected or Civil Servant (N = 43) (7)	More than 10 Percent of Time with Head of Government (N = 27) (8)	Up to 10 Percent of Time with Head of Government (N = 93) (9)
.6575	.5190	.7576	.6092	.7561	.1667	.8445	.4783	.8109

the sake of brevity, full path models are not presented here; results of some 84 regressions are summarized in Tables 3 through 8. The reader should keep in mind that no causal relationship exists when the only significant predictor of a dependent variable is the same item measured at an earlier time. When other variables at an earlier time predict the dependent variable at a later time net of the dependent variable at an earlier time, we speak of causality.[9]

The specific hypotheses to be tested are the following: (1) where leadership conditions tend toward uncertainty, environmental demand affects organizational size; (2) where leadership conditions tend toward uncertainty, environmental demand affects organizational structure; (3) where leadership conditions tend toward uncertainty, organizational size affects structure; and, (4) where leadership conditions tend toward certainty, environment affects neither size nor structure, and size does not influence structure. My description of finance departments suggests that the impact of environment on size and structure should be negative for these agencies, even though it should be positive for most organizations. The effect of size on structure should be positive, as in the earlier article. I deal with these hypotheses seriatim.

Effects of Environment on Size. The results of regressions of 1972 size on 1966 size and the four measures of environmental demand are summarized in Table 3. In the first and second rows, 1972 size is regressed on 1966 size and 1966 total funds administered by the finance department; in the third and fourth rows, 1972 size is regressed on 1966 size and 1966 general fund; and in the remaining rows, the environmental variables are 1966 total government employees and 1965 population, respectively. The columns represent different leadership conditions. For example, the first column shows results of regressions for departments whose heads had been in office for less than six years before 1972, while the second column presents results for agencies where the 1972 tenure of the head was six or more years. Each column shows the zero-order correlation of each independent variable with 1972 size as well as the standardized regression coefficient (B^*). Coefficients less than twice their standard errors are in parentheses.

The odd-numbered columns in Table 3 report regressions for departments where leadership conditions tend toward uncer-

... and 1966 Demand Variables, Controlling for Leadership Conditions.

Variables	1972 Tenure 0–5 Years (1)		1972 Tenure 6+ Years (2)		1966 Tenure 0–5 Years (3)		1966 Tenure 6+ Years (4)	
	Zero Order	B*	Zero Order	B*	Zero Order	B*	Zero Order	B*
1966 size	.9380	1.0293	.9786	.9873	.8825	.9868	.9789	1.0023
1966 total funds administered	.2255	-.2140	.7035	(-.0121)	.3033	-.2032	.4679	(.0457)
1966 size	.9380	1.0160	.9786	.9779	.8825	.9293	.9789	1.1104
1966 general fund	.2776	-.1750	.6765	(.0010)	.3736	(.0993)	.6721	-.1728
1966 size	.9380	1.0204	.9786	.9768	.8825	.9518	.9789	1.0367
1966 total government employees	.5711	-.1215	.7076	(.0025)	.3525	-.1354	.8499	(-.0654)
1966 size	.9380	1.0093	.9786	.9933	.8825	.9760	.9789	.9974
1965 population	.5564	-.1083	.6977	(-.0204)	.3804	-.1670	.7267	(-.0245)

Variables	Head Is Political Appointee (5)		Head Is Elected or Civil Servant (6)		More than 10 Percent Of Time with Head of Government (7)		Up to 10 Percent of Time with Head of Government (8)	
	Zero Order	B*	Zero Order	B*	Zero Order	B*	Zero Order	B*
1966 size	.8552	.9430	.9944	.9982	.8196	.9496	.9694	1.0073
1966 total funds administered	.2147	-.1999	.6976	(-.0053)	.2057	-.2633	.4376	-.0745
1966 size	.8552	.9229	.9944	.9725	.8196	.9416	.9694	.9838
1966 general fund	.2617	-.1514	.7094	(.0314)	.2033	-.2522	.5894	(-.0231)
1966 size	.8552	.9268	.9944	.9578	.8196	.9583	.9694	.9865
1966 total government employees	.2442	-.1630	.8988	(.0409)	.2457	-.2618	.7535	(.0218)
1966 size	.8552	.9204	.9944	.9720	.8196	1.0330	.9694	.9751
1965 population	.2611	-.1471	.9161	(.0245)	.2138	-.3747	.6747	(-.0082)

Note: Coefficients in parentheses are not statistically significant.

tainty—1972 tenure of department head less than six years, 1966 tenure less than six years, political appointment of department head, and more than 10 percent of department head's time spent with the head of government. In these columns, the measures of environmental demand have almost consistent negative effects on 1972 size of finance departments. (One of the sixteen coefficients is not significant.) By contrast, in the even-numbered columns, where leadership conditions would tend to limit the impact of external uncertainties because of long tenure of the department head, election or civil service appointment, and insularity from the head of government, the coefficients of the environmental variables are almost consistently zero. (Two of the sixteen are significant.) Environmental demand appears to have a negative effect on the size of finance departments where leadership introduces uncertainty or unpredictability but no effect at all under other leadership conditions. Leadership thus mediates or filters the effect of environment on organizational size.

Effects of Environment on Structure. The effects of environmental demand on organizational structure are not so clear-cut as they are on size. To begin, there are some null findings. Neither the total funds administered by a department, the size of the general fund, total government employment, nor the population served predicts the number of levels of supervision in a finance agency under any conditions. The vertical structure of bureaucracies is apparently unresponsive to environmental fluctuations. Whether an organization has an elaborated or a truncated hierarchy is determined by internal administrative needs. In addition, when the tenure of leadership in 1972 is controlled, there are very few significant effects of the demand variables on organizational structure, and the few that appear are inconsistent. Similarly, controlling for the amount of time department heads spend with the head of government yields only sparse and inconsistent effects of demand on structure. The null effects that appear when finance agencies are grouped according to the tenure of the department head in 1972 reflect very long lags between changes in leadership and their impact on organizational structure. The null effects that appear when time spent with the head of government is controlled may be due to poor measurement—it is an estimate—but are otherwise not easily explained.

Two measures of organizational structure that do respond to environmental pressures are the number of divisions and the number of sections or subunits within divisions. The effects of environment on the number of divisions, controlling for leadership conditions, are shown in Table 4; Table 5 shows relationships of the environmental measures of demand on the count of sections. The findings can be summarized as follows: Even when 1966 size is included in the regressions (the effects of size will be discussed later), environmental demand *contracts* the horizontal structure of finance departments where leadership conditions contribute to uncertainty, but environment has no effect where leadership tends toward certainty. In Table 4, the four demand variables have negative effects on 1972 divisions when the 1966 tenure of leadership was less than six years and the department head is politically appointed. (Two of the eight coefficients are not significant, however.) In six out of eight instances, environment has no effect on the number of divisions where leadership had six or more years' tenure prior to 1966 and where it is either elected or appointed through civil service procedures. And the two significant coefficients that appear under these leadership conditions are positive. The safest conclusion seems to be that environmental demand decreases the number of divisions in finance departments where leadership has been unstable in the past or is politically appointed, but that under other conditions demand has no effects on the number of subunits reporting to the head of the department.

A similar pattern appears in Table 5, where the number of sections is regressed on 1966 size, 1966 sections, and the four demand variables. Where leadership creates uncertainty, demand variables are negatively related to the number of sections, although one of the eight coefficients is not significant. Where leadership has long tenure and is autonomous of higher authority, six of the eight coefficients of the environmental measures are not significantly different from zero, one is positive, and one is negative. The same leadership conditions that allow the environment to erode the number of divisions also allow contraction of subunits within

Table 4. Regressions of 1972 Divisions on 1966 Size, 1966 Divisions, and 1966 Demand Variables, Controlling for Leadership Conditions.

Variables	1966 Tenure 0–5 Years (1)		1966 Tenure 6 + Years (2)		Head Is Political Appointee (3)		Head Is Elected or Civil Servant (4)	
	Zero Order	B*	Zero Order	B*	Zero Order	B*	Zero Order	B*
1966 size	.3318	.2172	.3695	(.0302)	.3977	.3001	.3122	(–.1428)
1966 divisions	.5032	.4253	.6791	.6347	.5316	.4146	.6152	.5387
1966 total funds administered	–.0329	(–.1229)	.3003	(.1213)	–.0226	(–.1793)	.4523	.3500
1966 size	.3318	.3113	.3695	(–.1886)	.3977	.3420	.3122	(.1255)
1966 divisions	.5032	.4921	.6791	.5064	.5316	.4232	.6152	.6126
1966 general fund	–.5032	–.3685	.5910	.4428	–.0683	–.2780	.4045	(–.0724)
1966 size	.3318	.3220	.3695	(.0972)	.3977	.3442	.3122	(.3803)
1966 divisions	.5032	.4356	.6791	.6387	.5316	.4044	.6152	.5873
1966 total government employees	–.0843	–.3360	.2617	(–.0076)	–.0896	–.2698	.2232	(–.3299)
1966 size	.3318	.2861	.3695	(.1256)	.3977	.3188	.3122	(.1891)
1966 divisions	.5032	.4345	.6791	.6362	.5316	.4140	.6152	.5834
1965 population	.0095	–.2422	.2179	(–.0450)	–.0438	–.2194	.2771	(–.1121)

Note: Coefficients in parentheses are not statistically significant.

Table 5. Regressions of 1972 Sections on 1966 Size, 1966 Sections, and 1966 Demand Variables, Controlling for Leadership Conditions.

Variables	1966 Tenure 0–5 Years (1)		1966 Tenure 6+ Years (2)		Head Is Political Appointee (3)		Head Is Elected or Civil Servant (4)	
	Zero Order	B*	Zero Order	B*	Zero Order	B*	Zero Order	B*
1966 size	.7019	.6165	.6220	(.1101)	.7184	.6110	.3122	(−.1428)
1966 sections	.6320	.3418	.7409	.6485	.6358	.2983	.6152	.5387
1966 total funds administered	.1901	−.2713	.3623	(.0151)	.1439	−.2569	.4523	.3500
1966 size	.7019	.5774	.6220	.2580	.7184	.5707	.3122	(.1255)
1966 sections	.6320	.3802	.7409	.8484	.6358	.3988	.6152	.6126
1966 general fund	.2349	−.2497	.4809	−.3884	.1514	−.3283	.4045	(−.0724)
1966 size	.7019	.6124	.6220	(.2900)	.7184	.5999	.3122	(.3804)
1966 sections	.6320	.3722	.7409	.6193	.6358	.3277	.6152	.5873
1966 total government employees	.1867	−.3027	.4667	(−.1692)	.1399	−.2811	.2232	(−.3299)
1966 size	.7019	.5839	.6220	(.1657)	.7184	.5850	.3122	(.1819)
1966 sections	.6320	.3495	.7409	.6435	.6358	.2710	.6152	.5834
1965 population	.3060	−.1993	.4130	(−.0583)	.2299	(−.1506)	.2772	(−.1121)

Note: Coefficients in parentheses are not statistically significant.

divisions, and conditions that protect the number of divisions also maintain the horizontal structure of finance departments at the third level of hierarchy. All other things being equal, including size, environmental demand leads to loss of functionally specialized subunits from finance departments, just as demand impedes growth. Leadership mediates the effects of environment on organizational size and structure: continuity and autonomy of leadership shield finance departments from environmental pressures, whereas turnover and dependence allow outside forces to take their toll.

Effects of Size on Structure. Here I wish to show that the causal relationship between organizational size and measures of structure that was documented in an earlier article (M. Meyer, 1972a) is contingent on leadership characteristics. The reader is directed again to Tables 4 and 5 as well as to Table 6. In Table 4, we are now interested in the coefficients of 1966 size net of 1966 divisions and the environmental variables. Similarly, in Table 5 we are interested in 1966 size net of 1966 sections and environment. The effects of 1966 size on 1972 divisions when other variables are controlled are unambiguous. Under leadership conditions tending toward instability—short tenure of department head and dependence on higher authority—the causal impact of size is evident. All eight coefficients are positive and significant. Where leadership aids stability—where the department head has six or more years' tenure and where he is either elected or a civil servant—no significant effects of size on the number of divisions appear in Table 4. Much the same pattern is in evidence in Table 5, where 1972 sections are regressed on other variables. Where department heads had held office less than six years prior to 1966 and where they are politically appointed, all eight coefficients of size are positive and significant. Where they had lengthy tenure and were autonomous of higher authority, seven of the eight coefficients of 1966 size are not significantly different from zero.

Regressions of 1972 levels of supervision on 1966 levels and 1966 size are shown in Table 6. Variables describing environmental demand, it will be recalled, had no effect on the hierarchical structure of finance departments; hence, they are not included in the regressions. As before, size has a significant effect on organizational structure only where there is turnover in leadership positions and where dependence on or vulnerability to superior officials reduces department heads' autonomy. Where there is no turnover and where department heads have the security of a civil service appointment or an elected office, the causal link between size and the number of levels of hierarchy vanishes.

Recapitulation. The hypothesis that leadership conditions affect causal relationships among organizational variables is for the most part confirmed. Effects of environment on size and structure and effects of size on structure are contingent on leadership allowing external uncertainties to intrude on organizations. Two comments are in order. First, these findings suggest that one should be cautious in elaborating mechanistic theories of relationships among abstract categories describing organizations. Operative causality is in fact change, and change in organizations can be resisted by firmly entrenched leadership. Change is also promoted, sometimes by replacing leadership, sometimes by making leaders more directly responsible for their organizations' activities. Organizational change is the consequence, whether intended or unintended, of choices made by people; it does not occur either automatically or necessarily. This reality is not captured by mechanistic theories. Second, the leadership conditions associated with high predictability or stability of organizational variables are also characterized by the absence of causal relationships. Contrariwise, conditions associated with instability or unpredictability are also those where causal relationships abound. These correspondences suggest that the most fundamental difference between organizations is whether they are stable or changing, not whether they are "open" or "closed" to the environment.

Closing the Circle

Early in this chapter it was noted that contraction and dedifferentiation of finance departments are accompanied by expansion of other agencies. Before summarizing the findings, I wish to present data indicating that this latter process indeed takes place. The interviews with finance department officials were supplemented with questionnaires administered to heads of units re-

Table 6. Regressions of 1972 Levels of Supervision on 1966 Size and 1966 Levels of Supervision, Controlling for Leadership Conditions.

Variables	1966 Tenure 0–5 Years (1)		1966 Tenure 6+ Years (2)		Head Is Political Appointee (3)		Head Is Elected or Civil Servant (4)	
	Zero Order	B*	Zero Order	B*	Zero Order	B*	Zero Order	B*
1966 size	.5646	.3969	.4646	(.1595)	.5264	.3321	.4924	(.2460)
1966 levels	.5395	.3485	.6703	.5875	.5859	.3225	.6716	.5641

Note: Coefficients in parentheses are not statistically significant.

sponsible for data processing and for budgeting regardless of whether or not these units were part of the finance department. Interviews with heads of 146 data-processing units organized in 1966 or before were completed. Eighty-nine of the units are divisions or bureaus of finance departments; 57 are either departments in their own right or divisions of other departments. Ninety-five interviews with heads of budget units formed in 1966 or before were also completed. Forty-seven of these units are within finance departments, and the others are elsewhere.[10]

Whereas environmental demands impede the growth of finance departments, we would expect data-processing units to increase their size over time in response to external pressures. A further expectation is that the impact of demand on growth should be greatest for data-processing units located outside the finance department. The data describing units that do computing work for finance departments bear out these expectations very nicely. In Table 7, 1972 size of data-processing units is regressed on their 1966 size and the four measures of environmental demand, controlling for the location of data processing. The regressions can be summarized simply: The size of data-processing units within finance departments is unaffected by the environment, but data-

Table 7. Regressions of 1972 Size of Data-Processing (DP) Unit on 1966 Size of Data-Processing Unit and 1966 Demand Variables, Controlling for Location of Data Processing.

Variables	DP Unit in Finance Department (N = 89) (1)		DP Unit Outside Finance Department (N = 57) (2)	
	Zero Order	B*	Zero Order	B*
1966 size of DP unit	.6984	.7004	.9006	.9041
1966 total funds administered	.1614	(−.0081)	.0899	.1176
1966 size of DP unit	.6984	.7118	.9006	.8759
1966 general fund	.1783	(−.0430)	.2948	.1377
1966 size of DP unit	.6984	.7156	.9006	.8661
1966 total government employees	.2490	(−.0421)	.3569	.1337
1966 size of DP unit	.6984	.6910	.9006	.8633
1965 population	.1899	(.0325)	.3764	.1314

Note: Coefficients in parentheses are not statistically significant.

processing units ouside finance departments *grow* in response to environmental demands. For example, the coefficient linking 1965 population with 1972 size of data-processing unit net of its 1966 size is not different from zero for units in the finance department but is .1314 where data processing does not report to the director of finance. The same effects appear for the other measures of environmental demand.

The pattern of growth in budget units is similar to that in data processing ones. Briefly, Table 8 shows that for budget units located within finance departments, the four measures of environmental demand do not affect 1972 size significantly, net of 1966 size. (Fairly sizable coefficients are not significant for these units because 1966 size and the environmental variables are nearly collinear. In any case, the coefficients are all negative.) Budget units unattached to finance departments appear to grow in response to environmental demand, however. For these departments, total funds administered, size of the general fund, and government employment are positively related to 1972 size. Only 1965 population does not significantly affect 1972 size.

Table 8. Regressions of 1972 Size of Budget Unit on 1966 Size of Budget Unit and 1966 Demand Variables, Controlling for Location of Budget Unit.

Variables	Budget Unit in Finance Department (N = 47) (1)		Budget Unit Outside Finance Department (N = 48) (2)	
	Zero Order	B*	Zero Order	B*
1966 size of budget unit	.8996	1.1251	.9635	.9487
1966 total funds administered	.7691	(−.2491)	.2690	.1980
1966 size of budget unit	.8996	1.1114	.9635	.9395
1966 general fund	.8053	(−.2278)	.3008	.1494
1966 size of budget unit	.8996	1.0034	.9635	.8587
1966 total government employees	.8208	(−.1117)	.8219	.1302
1966 size of budget unit	.8996	.8353	.9635	.9198
1965 population	.8337	(−.0703)	.6596	(.0681)

Note: Coefficients in parentheses are not statistically significant.

Unfortunately, there are no data about leadership of data-processing and budget units with which to test other propositions developed in this article. One would want to know whether the rate of growth of units outside the finance department is greatest where leadership is unstable, dependent on higher authority, and in close contact with supervisors. My findings do suggest, however, that finance officials' worries about "the status of the profession," as they are sometimes expressed, are justified. Environmental conditions that impede growth and contract the structures of finance departments promote expansion of other agencies of local governments. For the larger cities, counties, and states, the centralized model of finance administration has lost viability, if the experience of the recent past predicts the future.

Summary and Conclusions

Clearly, I have just begun to scratch the surface. Three variables describing leadership—turnover, dependence on higher authority, and insularity—predict fundamental differences in organizations. Where leadership is stable, autonomous of higher authority, and insulated from it, organizational structures have high predictability over time. More important, where leadership is stable and autonomous, causal relationships among organizational variables are remarkably absent. Variables describing the environment affect neither the size nor the structures of finance agencies, and causal relationships between organizational size and structure are attenuated. By contrast, where leadership has changed in the past and where it is dependent on higher authority and in close contact with superiors, organizational structures have less stability. Environmental variables indicating demand for the work of finance departments have significant effects on size, and they influence measures of horizontal differentiation when leadership has changed and is dependent. Only the number of supervisory levels is unaffected by demand characteristics. Finally, causal relationships between size and measures of structure abound when leadership conditions introduce uncertainty into organizations. That variables describing leadership positions, not individual leaders, predict fundamental differences in organizations suggests several things.

First, more detailed information on leadership than was sought in these surveys of finance departments might reveal even greater differences among organizations. For example, it would be useful to have information about the social groups from which leaders are recruited and the ways in which informal networks intersect with organizational structures. A rich tradition in political sociology treats leadership as representative of constituencies (see, for example, Dahl, 1961). There is no reason why studies of public bureaucracies or even, for that matter, large business firms should overlook characteristics of the groups from which leaders are drawn. Organizational structures may reflect other types of social structures more than theories of bureaucracy have led us to believe. Second, the results of this research, together with the null or inconsistent findings in the social-psychological literature, suggest that the focus should be on leadership *positions* rather than on the people who happen to be leaders. Whether a leader shows consideration to subordinates may be far less important than his autonomy in hiring and rewarding employees and in setting the policy goals of his organization. Until many of the influences affecting leadership positions have been identified and controlled statistically, it would be premature to expect to find consistent effects of characteristics of individual leaders. Third, attempts to evaluate the effectiveness of organizations will have to consider leadership characteristics if the kinds of basic differences in causal patterns revealed here bear any relationship to performance. Again, a focus on individual leaders is not likely to be fruitful, as Lieberson and O'Connor (1972) have shown. Rather, characteristics of the social networks—both organizational and extraorganizational—in which leadership roles are embedded will have to be examined.

Another implication of these findings is that the polarity between open-systems and closed-systems approaches to organizations in the theoretical literature may be misleading. Proponents of the open-systems perspective argue that organizational attributes are largely determined by characteristics of the environment. The closed-systems approach treats organizational variables as interdependent and the environment as a residual category. My findings suggest, however, that, where organizations are affected by environmental contingencies, orderly causal relationships between variables describing size and structure appear. But where the environment has no impact organizational variables do not affect one another either. A more complex model of organizational processes than the open-system/closed-system dichotomy is indicated. Environmental pressures impinge on all organizations, but their impact is mediated by characteristics of leadership positions. To the extent to which leaders are vulnerable to external pressures, changes in the environment lead to changes in organizations that are followed by other organizational changes. A chain of causal relationships is evident. Invulnerable leadership, in contrast, blocks outside pressures, with the result that causal links vanish. Stability of organizational variables over time is contingent on the capacity of leaders to stave off environmental demands. In public administration, the formal authority structure as well as the prestige or "clout" of an official determines tenure in office and capacity to resist superiors' wishes. In business, growth and profitability may similarly insulate organizations. Contingencies of this sort must be built into organization theory. Perhaps it would be best for researchers to retreat from the position that organizations are either open or closed and ask, open-mindedly, when organizations are affected by their environments and when they do not respond. Answers to this dual question have obvious policy implications that need not be elaborated here.

A cautionary note is in order too. Finance departments are not representative of all organizations. They are administrative bureaucracies, not small businesses, manufacturers, or service organizations such as hospitals and schools. They have more permanence and stability than other types of organizations, partly because almost all uncertainties arising in the environment are filtered through leadership positions. Leadership may not be so effective a filter of uncertainty for organizations operating in more dynamic and turbulent environments; hence, the effects of leadership on organizational structure may be quite different in other types of organizations. It is an old saw, but further research is needed. My hunch is that most of the findings reported here hold for bureaucracies and other nonprofit organizations removed from vicissitudes of the marketplace. But the hunch should be tested.

Appendix

Table A1. Tabulations Concerning 1965–66 Structural Change.

	1966 Tenure of Department Head	
	0–5 Years	6+ Years
1965–66 structural change:		
Yes	45%	19%
No	55	81
	100%	100%
	(120)	(93)
	1965–66 Structural Change	
1972 tenure of department head:		
0–5 years	49%	55%
6+ years	51	45
	100%	100%
	(72)	(141)

Table A2. Autocorrelations of Structural Variables by Governmental Reorganization and 1966 Tenure of Department Head.

	Government Reorganization			
	Yes		No	
	1966 Tenure of Department Head			
	0–5 Years	6+ Years	0–5 Years	6+ Years
Size	.7179	.9838	.9492	.9785
Divisions	.0715	.4200	.5263	.7016
Levels	.3190	.6310	.5659	.6375
Sections	.5134	.7534	.5886	.7356

Notes

1. By *leadership*, I mean characteristics of top positions in finance departments, not the numerous acts of leading that leaders are called on to perform. Perhaps *headship* would be more appropriate, but I am following Lieberson and O'Connor's (1972) use of the term *leadership*.

2. My perspective is slightly different from that of Thompson (1967), who argues that different parts of organizations face different degrees of uncertainty, least in the technical core and most at the boundaries. The argument here is that uncertainty in organizations varies over time and from organization to organization owing to characteristics of leaders.

3. The field department of the National Opinion Research Center (NORC) completed 97 percent of the assigned interviews, and their persistence in the face of occasional adversity (including one sheriff's deputy blocking the door) is gratefully acknowledged. The data-processing department of NORC did a superb job of translating the interviews into usable data; the efforts of the coding and programming staffs contributed materially to the quality of the 1972 data.

4. Not all of these differences in autocorrelations are statistically significant. The test for significance of differences between correlations is described by Blalock (1972, pp. 405–407). Should the reader doubt the importance of these differences, he is asked to suspend his disbelief for a while.

5. Department heads, some of their deputies, and all division heads were interviewed; information on levels of supervision and the number of sections was provided by the latter.

6. Here are the exact figures: Of 93 departments with stable leadership between 1960 and 1966, only 39 kept the same leadership through 1972. But of 122 that had changed leaders in the five years before 1966, 63 had stable leadership between 1966 and 1972. In other words, turnover in leadership positions is not consistently high for some finance departments and consistently low for others. Quite the opposite: Stability in one period is followed by succession in the next, and vice versa.

7. See Appendix for the tabulations.

8. See Appendix for the autocorrelations with governmental reorganization controlled.

9. In Tables 3 to 8, we are concerned with the significance of path coefficients, not with whether they are significantly different under different leadership conditions. This is for two reasons. First, the hypothesis is that causal relationships among organizational variables hold (that is, are significantly different from zero) under some leadership conditions but are absent (that is, not significantly different from zero) under other conditions. Second, the magnitudes of paths and hence the differences between them may not be meaningful with data from only two measurements. In cross-lagged models, small effects accumulate over time so that, to a point, the greater the interval between measurements compared with the actual interval between cause and effect, the greater the exaggeration of causal paths. And estimates of causal paths are diminished to the extent that the measurement interval is shorter than the actual lag. Consider the model shown in Figure 1. If the stability coefficients (that is, $P_{x_1 x_0}$, $P_{r_2 x_1}$, $P_{y_1 y_0}$, and so on) and the exogenous correlation are fairly high as they are in our data, and if the cross paths ($P_{y_1 x_0}$, and so on) are small

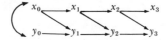

but consistent, the estimate of the cross path between x and y based on data collected at times zero and three only will be substantially larger than the true causal paths. For example, if the stabilities and the exogenous correlation are all .8 and the cross paths are .2 in the model, then $P_{y_3 x_0}$ will be .384. Of course, should the cross paths be randomly distributed with a mean of zero, the longer the measurement interval compared with actual causal lags, the closer to zero the estimate of the causal relationship of x to y will be. One substantive implication ought to be pursued briefly.

It might be argued that causal lags among organizational variables are a function of the tenure of leadership: The longer the tenure of leaders, the longer the lag. Our data from two points in time cannot prove this, but they are not inconsistent with the hypothesis. Data from a third and perhaps a fourth wave will be needed to test it.

10. Data-processing units are almost always called data-processing systems, or some like term. Units in charge of budgeting are more heterogeneous. Some are planning and development offices, some are executive agencies not unlike the office of management and budget in the federal bureaucracy, and others are divisions of finance or administration departments called simply "budget."

9

$\sim\sim\sim\sim\sim\sim\sim\sim\sim\sim\sim\sim\sim$

Instructional Dissensus and Institutional Consensus in Schools

$\sim\sim\sim\sim\sim\sim\sim\sim\sim\sim\sim\sim\sim$

John W. Meyer
W. Richard Scott
Sally Cole
Jo-Ann K. Intili

In what respects are schools and districts coordinated organizations, and in what respects are they not? In this chapter, we examine the degree of coordination within districts and schools by showing the extent to which these organizations exhibit internal consensus among subordinates and agreement between subordinates and superiors on their instructional policies and practices. In

An earlier version of this paper appeared in Elizabeth G. Cohen, Terrence E. Deal, John W. Meyer, and W. Richard Scott, "Organization and Instruction in Elementary Schools: First Results, 1973" (Stanford Center for Research and Development in Teaching, Technical Report No. 50, October 1976). The research reported herein was conducted at the center, which is supported in part by the this manner, we attempt to determine how much the educational activities and programs of schools are coordinated within district organizations and how much the educational activities of classrooms are coordinated within schools.

Let us outline the possibilities. With respect to their instructional programs, schools and districts could be (1) functionally differentiated, coordinated organizations, (2) segmental, coordinated organizations, or (3) segmental, decentralized organizations. At the outset of this research, we had expected to find schools of all three types with one or another dominant. More important, these three types seemed to exhaust the possibilities. However, the data collected from surveys of superintendents, principals and teachers in a sample of districts and schools in the San Francisco Bay area seemed inconsistent with each of these types.

This paper reports our original conceptual models of school organization, the data gathered to evaluate these conceptions, and an attempt to develop a new model of school organization more consistent with the evidence. A fuller description of the new model appears as Chapter Four in this book.

Three Conventional Models of School Organization

We define here three conventional models of organizations by which schools are sometimes interpreted; each faces considerable difficulty in confronting the organizational realities of schooling.

Schools as Functionally Differentiated and Coordinated Organizations. In the first model, that of schools as functionally differentiated and coordinated organizations, the components of districts (that is, schools) and of schools (that is, classrooms) would be highly specialized in their educational programs and interdependent with one another. Schools or classrooms would specialize in

National Institute of Education (NIE), U.S. Department of Health, Education, and Welfare (Contract No. NE-C-00-3-0062). The opinions expressed do not necessarily reflect the position, policy, or endorsement of the NIE.

We acknowledge, with thanks, the assistance and helpful comments of Elizabeth G. Cohen, Terrence E. Deal, Margaret Davis, and Ann Stackhouse, as well as the cooperation received from school officials and teachers in the San Francisco Bay area.

the types of students they would service or the types of subject areas taught. Further, as districts or schools expanded, they would add subunits that were increasingly highly specialized. Considerable administrative machinery would be required to coordinate the various programs, to see that the right students found their way to the right programs, and to oversee transfers. For the system to function smoothly, consensus on the operating rules and procedures would need to be high.

Even a cursory inspection of schools clearly suggests that this picture is largely inappropriate. Although larger schools and districts may exhibit a little more specialization and although a few may create—for whatever reasons—a certain amount of coordination, as districts grow they typically add more schools much like the ones they already have; and big schools are much like smaller ones, but with more classrooms. Specialization, interdependence, and coordination of instructional activities are minimal. Schools and districts are not made up of specialized, functionally interdependent components but of relatively distinct and functional similar ones.

Schools as Segmental and Coordinated Organizations. Schools and districts could, like fast food chains, be made up of almost identical subunits, all subject to the same policies and procedures. The classrooms in each school and the schools in each district would be alike—doing essentially the same work and controlled by the same central authority and the same policies. They would be similar units with little functional interdependence.

This picture of schools and districts as *segmental* organizations clearly makes some sense. The question is, how similar are the segments—classrooms within schools and schools within districts? Before examining the data bearing on this question, consider the various forces that might foster consistency. The following four types of forces may be distinguished.

First, if each school or district adopted particular, binding technologies of work, consistent patterns of work and structure in each subunit might follow (Perrow, 1970). We mean by technology not "hardware" but whatever curricular materials and instructional practices are used in teaching (Baker, 1973; Lortie, 1973). Technologies that are highly developed and consistently efficacious in producing desired outcomes are likely to be widely adopted, and they are likely to impose consistent patterns on the activities of performers and on related work arrangements.

Second, if each school or district adopted an educational ideology, a consistent pattern might be imposed on the activities and structures of its subunits. Ideologies—elaborated belief systems relating to the proper role or functioning of a system—can provide normative support for particular work arrangements even in the absence of clear evidence that structures are producing the intended effects (see Perrow, 1965). Were a school district to embrace a well-developed educational ideology, consistent patterns of organization might be expected to appear in the schools within it.

Third, if each school or district had a central locus of organizational authority with the right to decide educational policies and to specify procedures for implementing them, high consistency would be expected within schools and districts.

Finally, if each school or district were confronted by district environmental pressures that selected out given structural patterns for survival, some consistency would appear within districts or within schools confronting the same environment.

None of these conditions seems to exist for elementary schools in the United States at the present time. The technology of teaching is notoriously unclear. Educational ideologies certainly exist, but none seems powerful or pervasive enough to dominate public school education. It does not appear that authority to deal with important instructional matters exists in any centralized organizational location, whether school or district. This circumstance may vary from one country to another, however. In many countries, a great deal of educational authority is vested in a ministry of education—France is often cited as an example. Some observations of Israeli education also seem to show this type of pattern, as does the English school system, where a great deal of authority is vested in the headmaster or head teacher. Finally, while environmental pressures may be great in the sense that finances or some idiosyncratic issues may be highly salient, they do not seem to determine particular classroom or school organizational patterns. Thus schools are segmental and likely to be decentralized.

Schools as Segmental Decentralized Organizations. The segmentation and decentralization of school districts would permit each school—and even each classroom within each school—to go its own way. In the absence of shared technologies, widely embraced ideologies, centralized and legitimated educational authorities, and determinant environmental pressures, we would expect to find little consistency. Basic educational decisions would be delegated to individual schools and ultimately to individual teachers in classrooms. This is the descriptive hypothesis with which we began our empirical study of classroom and school organization. A related hypothesis examining complexity of instructional programs in relation to complexity of classroom and school organization was also tested in a longitudinal survey design (Cohen and others, 1977). However, the results reported here are based on data gathered at one point in time.

Research Design

Here we briefly outline the research design of the larger study from which our data are taken.

The Sample and Data Sources. To examine these models of school organization, data were collected in 1973 from a sample of schools in the San Francisco Bay area as the first wave of a study conducted by the Environment for Teaching Program of the Stanford Center for Research and Development in Teaching (Cohen and others, 1976). School districts located in six San Francisco Bay area counties were stratified into four size categories: large (25 or more elementary schools), medium-to-large (15 to 24 elementary schools), medium (7 to 14 elementary schools), and small (1 to 6 elementary schools). A varying proportion of districts were randomly selected from each size category; for example, all of the large districts were selected, but only 19 percent of the small districts were included. Within districts, elementary schools were also randomly selected with the proportion of the schools included varying inversely with size. Data were gathered from 34 school districts and from 188 elementary schools.

The San Francisco Bay area is not presumed to be representative in its educational systems of other parts of the country. However, the selection process described did yield a diverse set of schools. Organizationally, schools ranged from having self-contained classrooms with relatively isolated, independent teachers to open-space facilities and highly interdependent teaching teams. Instructionally, schools varied from those in which entire classes were using identical materials to those in which individual students followed individually tailored learning programs. The environmental setting of sample schools ranged from urban locations with high proportions of lower-income minority students, to suburban locations serving predominantly upper-income white students, to rural areas.

The major source of data on the organizational and instructional patterns within schools was a combination questionnaire-interview with the principal at each school. Principals served primarily as expert informants describing the educational programs carried on within their school. Because teaching patterns and instructional materials are known to vary by subject area, questions focused attention on the teaching of reading in grades 1 through 3, the most important subject area in early primary education. Principals were asked to describe the staffing arrangements within their schools and curricular materials that characterized the teaching of reading in most classrooms in grades 1 through 3 within each school. They were also asked general questions about school and district organization and policies.

A similar combination questionnaire and interview was employed to obtain information on district structure and policy from the school superintendent within each district surveyed. In addition, in a subsample of sixteen schools, data were also gathered by questionnaire from classroom teachers in grades 1 through 3. Questions asked of teachers paralleled in content those asked of principals, although individual teachers were asked to describe their specific teaching situations and instructional programs.

The instruments used in the study underwent extensive field testing prior to their use. They are listed and described briefly hereafter. At each level, comparable items were included both for purposes of validity and to permit the type of interlevel comparisons reported in this chapter.

District Level

| Superintendent Questionnaire | Basic data about district finances and personnel, and other descriptive information |
| Focused interview | Superintendent's perceptions of district organizational and instructional patterns |

School Level

| Principal Questionnaire | Information about school finances and personnel and other descriptive information |
| Focused Interview | Principal's perceptions of various organizational and instructional patterns and processes in the school |

Classroom Level

| Teacher Questionnaire | Teacher's perceptions of the organization at the school and classroom level, and descriptions of specific classroom practices |

Major Questions Addressed. The following analyses approach four specific questions:

1. Do principals and superintendents agree in their description of policies and practices?
2. Regardless of their agreement with the superintendent, do principals in the same district report similar policies and circumstances?
3. Do teachers and principals agree in their description of policies and practices?
4. Regardless of their agreement with the principal, do teachers in the same school report similar policies and circumstances?

The answers to these four questions tend to be no. We will conclude that the evidence supports the view that the organizational structure of the school system is not only highly segmented and decentralized, but that it is internally inconsistent—or "decoupled" —as well. We will spell this argument out by developing a model distinct from those with which we started.

Two possible objections to this conclusion should be dealt with at the outset. First, it is possible that heterogeneity of school and classroom structure is evidence not for decentralized segmentation but for coordinated and planned diversity. While this situation is currently advocated by some educators, nothing in the data suggests that the diversity that exists is centrally planned or managed. Superintendents responded to a question concerning the relative value they would place on having schools in their district use the same or different reading programs. Sixteen of those responding indicated that they placed high value on heterogeneity; nine placed some value on it; and four placed high value on homogeneity. Educators do seem to value diversity, but a diversity that is neither planned for nor coordinated. Responding to a question regarding where decisions are made, twenty-seven superintendents reported that decisions on such issues as staff reorganization, choice of reading program, and pupil grouping were made at the school level, and twenty-nine said they preferred it that way. Thus, although heterogeneity may be the ideology of some educators, in our view this frequently meant autonomy rather than institutionalized coordination of diversity. Further, the analyses suggest that the heterogeneity that actually exists may not be perceived—let alone planned—by organizational superiors.

A second possible objection is that the lack of consensus and consistency reported here may reflect, not real differences between teachers, principals, and superintendents, but simple unreliability in the data. Random unreliability could account for many of the findings. In one respect, we do not accept this alternative interpretation: The respondents were not asked to discuss subtle aspects of their individual attitudes or values. They were treated as informants on day-to-day organizational matters, and the questions were usually formulated in language they themselves might use. If in fact they interpreted these questions very differently from each other, the unreliability involved may be built into the structure of the school system itself—its rules, policies, and definition of its own activities. Reaching a similar conclusion, Gross and Herriott (1965), in a study of principal leadership in public schools, report that although the unreliability of respondents is usually assumed to be the cause of variance within a class of respondents, they believe that variance among teachers' descriptions of their principals' behavior results from genuine variation in the principals' performances.

Results: Districts and Schools

We now present our findings on the vertical integration of the educational systems we studied. The data show how the degree to which various levels of the organization—districts, schools, and classrooms—are closely coordinated on instructional matters.

Agreement Between Superintendents and Principals. In this section, we report the degree of agreement between superintendents and principals in the same district on a series of issues. We do this by showing the correlation between the superintendent's response and the mean response of the principals in that superintendent's district (four districts have only one principal, whose response is used directly). This procedure partly overstates the level of agreement. As will be shown, principals disagree a great deal within districts. When the superintendent's answers are related to those of his or her individual principals, this lack of internal consensus lowers the correlation. However, this section addresses, not the reliability of the answers of one of the parties, but the agreement between parties, and for this purpose the mean principal response is the appropriate analogue to the superintendent's response.

One of the most direct means of unifying the programs and structures of schools within a district is evaluation. The right to evaluate schools, and to hire, evaluate, transfer, and fire principals is vested in the district office (and the school board). How clearcut are these controls and their effects? The superintendents were asked how frequently they evaluated the elementary schools in their districts. The principals were asked how frequently their schools were evaluated by the districts. For thirty of our thirty-four districts, both parties' answers to this question are available. The correlation between their answers was .45, which implies that only about 20 percent of the variation among principals' answers could be accounted for by the superintendents' answers. The two parties, in other words, have little agreement about the most obvious aspect of the evaluation process. Moreover, this was one of the *highest* correlations to be found in the data.

Both parties were asked how many types of information were gathered on schools by the district office for evaluation purposes. In only eighteen cases is information from both available, which itself indicates very low organizational clarity. The correlation between the two parties' answers across these cases was an insignificant .17. Both principals and superintendents were asked whether changes in the procedures for evaluating teachers were required by the Stull Act, passed by the California legislature in 1972. Many principals and superintendents said they had changed their procedures, but the correlation between the two sets of answers was only .51 (thirty-four cases).

Principals and superintendents were also asked parallel questions about the existence of district policies in certain areas. Two of these areas were quite specific: "To what extent does the district have formalized policies about (1) pupil grouping and (2) team teaching?" Respondents were not asked what these policies were but simply whether the district had explicit policies in these areas. The answers showed a good deal of variation among districts, and little consistency between principals and superintendents. For pupil grouping, $r = .40$ (twenty-nine cases); for team teaching, $r = .53$ (thirty cases). A more general question was also included: "Does the district have formal policies in regard to the elementary school curriculum?" Less agreement might be expected on such a general item, but the level actually found was extremely low ($r = .14$, thirty cases) and in fact indicated a statistically insignificant correlation between the answers of principals and superintendents to the same item. The meaning of the correlation seems reasonably clear.

In short, there is no evidence for substantial consensus between principals and superintendents on any of a series of policy and procedure issues.[1] We do not interpret the lack of consensus as reflecting a high level of conflict. Rather, these data reflect low levels of central coordination and/or homogeneity in school districts. Districts exercise very limited controls over the schools within them on matters closely related to instruction, and such controls as they create are undoubtedly applied unevenly.

Consensus Among Principals. The question can be considered in a broader way: Regardless of their agreement with the superintendent, to what extent do the principals in a district report similar organizational worlds? How much variation in the answers of the principals in the sample is to be accounted for by working in a given district? Of course, if district location does account for much of the variation, many explanations beyond organizational consistency are possible. Perhaps, for instance, principals in a given district face the same environmental pressures, which lead them to report similar organization. But this procedure at least shows the extent to which *any* factors, including organizational ones, generate homogeneity within districts.

A series of one-way analyses of variance using data from principals were performed. For each variable (a school characteristic), we report an F-ratio that defines the statistical significance of the *between-district variation* in the principals' answers compared with that to be expected on the basis of the *total variation* (see Table 1). Given the present large sample, if the between-district variation is insignificant or marginally significant, this is very strong evidence that school districts are segmental, decentralized organizations—with each school more or less going its own way.

Table 1 also shows the eta-squared value—a measure of the *proportion of variance* in principals' answers that can be accounted for by the district in which the principal works. This measure of association can vary between 0 and 1: A value of 1 would indicate that all the variation among principals is accounted for by district membership, while a value of 0 would suggest that none is. A value of 0, however, is unlikely. Even if principals' answers were randomly distributed among districts, some variations among districts would occur and would appear to account for part of the variation in principals' answers. Given these data, a random distribution of principals among districts would produce an eta-squared value of about .15. The question, therefore, is to see how far above this level the values of the observed coefficients are.

Table 1. Analysis of Variance for Principals' Responses.

Variable	Source[a]		F-Ratio[b]	Eta-Squared[c]
General school characteristics				
School size	ES		3.39	.36
Percentage of nonwhite students	ES		14.26	.70
Percentage of teachers with tenure	PQ	6	2.48	.30
Principal's tenure in district	PQ	8	2.78	.32
Number of open-space pods	PI	7	2.14	.26
Percentage of teachers teaching jointly	PI	1	1.53	.20
Centralization and the distribution of influence				
Decision-making level: personnel	PI	11a	2.05	.25
Decision-making level: major curriculum changes	PI	11b	1.29	.18
Decision-making level: reading materials, grades 1–3	PI	28	.99	.14
Formalization of district policies on team grouping	PI	14	1.63	.21
Formalization of district policies on pupil grouping	PI	15	3.00	.33
Total district influence on decisions	PI	11	4.62	.44
Total principal influence on decisions	PI	11	.89	.13
Total faculty decision participation	PI	10	1.29	.18
Total teacher decision participation	PI	10	1.79	.23
Total community decision participation	PI	10	2.62	.30
Teachers' organization influence: curriculum	PI	20a	2.89	.30
Frequency of faculty meetings	PQ	10	4.32	.42
Evaluation patterns				
Frequency of district overall evaluation of school	PI	64	3.66	.38
Frequency of reading teacher evaluation, grades 1–3	PI	58	1.27	.17
Curriculum (grades 1–3 only)				
Amount of choice provided by reading materials	PI	43	3.23	.35
Variation in pacing (within school) in reading instruction	PI	31	1.71	.23
Variation in reading materials and methods	PI	29	1.68	.22
Special training for reading materials	PI	46	.70	.10

Financial matters

Total specific district funds for reading given to school	PQ 14	1.70	.22
Number of specific district fundings of school programs	PQ 14	3.26	.35
Number of new positions created with special funds	PQ 16	.69	.11

Staffing

Number of paid aides	PQ 4	2.66	.31
Number of adult volunteers	PQ 5	1.47	.20
Number of special teachers (FTE) based in school	PQ 1	.94	.14
Number of special teachers (FTE) based in district	PQ 1	2.58	.33
Number of specialists (FTE) funded by school	PQ 1	1.04	.15
Number of specialists (FTE) funded by district	PQ 1	1.92	.26

Note: The results are for about 150 principals in twenty-five districts. Districts with only one or two schools in the sample were eliminated from the analysis.

[a]PQ indicates the Principal Questionnaire; PI indicates the Principal Interview; ES indicates a state document (External Source). Question numbers refer to the specific items used. Questionnaires are available in Cohen and others (1976).

[b]An F-ratio value of 1.91 is significant at the .01 level.

[c]A value of eta-squared of about .15 is to be expected by chance.

Two results shown in Table 1 are striking. First, on only seventeen of the thirty-three variables, or about half, did variation among districts significantly account for variation among principals' responses. (The proportion in all such data that we have examined would be even lower.) Second, even when the between-district variation was statistically significant, it almost always accounted for a minor proportion of the variance in principal answers. Only three of all the eta-squared values indicate that 40 percent or more of the variance was related to district variation —in analyses in which 15 percent of the variance is accounted for by chance. The principals in each district are reporting different structures that seem to vary more within districts than between them.

Let us consider some of the findings in greater detail. Several of the variables that do show significant between-district variation seem to reflect environmental, rather than organizational, patterns. There was more homogeneity within districts on the proportion of a school's students who were nonwhite than on any other variable we examined—evidence that school district boundaries capture a good deal of de facto racial segregation.[2] School size, on which there was also some homogeneity, is shown by other analyses to be related to the urban context of a district. Principals in the same district tended to give similar responses to questions about open space, but this reflects an economic fact (that, in the San Francisco Bay area, suburban districts have more often built new, open-space schools) rather than an organizational one. The lack of agreement on the presence of teaching teams—the educational rationale for the construction of open-space facilities— shows clearly that the open-space finding does not reflect an educational policy commitment of school districts.

District funds vary a great deal, and those variables directly related to the district's capacity to *buy* staff and materials show higher levels of agreement. Thus, tenured teachers and experienced principals are likely to be concentrated in districts with more funds and better pay. Wealthy districts also can pay for more reading materials, as well as for aides, special teachers, and specialists. It is noteworthy that special teacher positions funded at the district level show more consensus within districts than those funded at the school level.

In only a few areas do district *policy* variations show up. Districts apparently vary in the frequency of faculty meetings they prescribe; in their rules about grouping pupils, which has lately been the subject of tension in some racially mixed communities; in their frequency of evaluating schools; and in their willingness, or perhaps ability, to fund special school programs. Districts may also vary in the amount of influence exerted on policy decisions by teachers' organizations and community groups.

School characteristics such as degree of group influence on curriculum and staffing do not exhibit significant differences among districts. Nor do principals' reports on the participation of various groups in school and district decisions, although districts vary in the extent to which major curricular decisions were influenced by teachers. Most items show small or insignificant variations among districts. In a few cases, variations in specific district rules, such as hiring and pupil assignment, show up in the data.

Despite the fact that consensus within districts is generally low, districts do seem to vary in their participation in and influence on decisions, as reported by principals. This variable shows a higher level of consensus (44 percent of the variation is accounted for by district) than any other such variable in the data. This finding suggests two questions: "What factors affect district power over schools? And do districts that have higher levels of power use it to create higher levels of consensus among principals within the district?"

Strong Districts. In an effort to see which district characteristics led principals to report higher levels of district influence on their decision making, we carried out a series of regression analyses. These analyses attempt to explain variations in principals' perceptions of the influence of the district. From a battery of items asking principals about the influence of various parties on a series of school decisions, an index was created. Principals' scores on this index were analyzed, rather than aggregating these scores by district, although the results would not differ greatly.

Table 2 shows the simultaneous effects of district characteristics that exhibited interpretable, significant effects on principals' perceptions of district influence. Several other variables are included that did not show such effects.

The results in Table 2 defy any simple description of the school as an organization. Consider the measures of district resources. As expected, districts that had more special administrators —a category of administrators previously reported as linking districts and schools (see Deal, Meyer, and Scott, 1975)—were more likely to be located in districts that principals reported to be more influential. But a more obvious resource measure—district funds, higher levels of which must certainly be related to district discretionary power—showed a *negative* effect on reported district influence. Next, consider two measures of district authority. If a superintendent had been in the district longer, the district was reported to be more influential. This makes some sense: Superintendents who have held administrative positions in the district for longer periods probably *do* have more power. But the frequency with which the district evaluates the school—a more direct link—shows a *negative* effect. Does this mean that more formal

Table 2. Multiple-Regression Analysis of Principal Reports of
Total District Influence on School Decisions.

Variable	Source[a]	Beta	F-ratio (4.2 = .05 level)
District context			
Percentage of nonwhite students	ES	.26	3.7
Urbanness (dummy variable: central cities coded high)	ES	−.33	4.6
District resources			
Size of district special administration	SQ 5	.46	5.7
Total district current expenditure per student	ES	−.22	3.9
District authority			
Superintendent's tenure in district	SI 2	.35	19.6
Frequency of school evaluation	SI 11	−.21	7.3

Note: These results are based on 148 cases for which all variables were reported.

[a]SI indicates Superintendent Interview; SQ indicates Superintendent Questionnaire; ES refers to state documents (External Source). Questionnaires are available in Cohen and others (1976).

evaluation is associated with less control? In this connection, note the variable we have called "urbanness," which also has an apparently negative effect on district power. It may be that larger, more "bureaucratized" districts develop sets of rules and procedures that actually limit discretionary district power over schools. The only variable of this kind that showed a positive effect on district power was the proportion of nonwhite students. It may be that districts with many nonwhites are going through changes that lead them to exercise more direct controls over schools.

In any case, the data show few indications that the factors that affect a district's capacity to influence its schools are organizational in character. Other variables we have considered support this conclusion. For instance, two variables were expected to express the district-school link directly: (1) the frequency with which principals were evaluated by the district and (2) the reported number of written directives sent by the district to the school. *Neither* variable showed a significant effect. Here again are two bureaucratic links that apparently have little impact on school decisions.

District-School Consensus in Influential Districts. Do districts that are reported to have more influence create more district-school consensus? The preceding analysis suggests that reported district power is not a highly organized, bureaucratic phenomenon and that it is not likely to work in ways that create standardization among principals. We turn again to the data on superintendent and principal agreement to determine whether agreement is higher among principals who saw the district as more influential. The data offer no support for this hypothesis. In fact, most of the correlations are higher (although not significantly higher) among principals who reported *low* district influence. This was true, for instance, for all three of the indicators of formalized district policies: team teaching, curriculum, and pupil grouping.

How are we to make sense of these findings? The principals' reports of overall district influence can be dismissed as meaningless, but doing so disregards the answers of the best available informants to a rather straightforward set of questions. It makes more sense to assume that district influence, in the main, is exercised through channels that are not standardized and codified and is not built into the nominal system of formal evaluation. The district is a highly decentralized organization—its influence on educational matters is exercised idiosyncratically. People in the district offices—Table 2 calls attention to special administrators—have a number of specific themes and programs in which they are interested and can offer special help. When the opportunity arises, they aid (or perhaps restrict) a given school in creating or altering a program, operating more through personal contacts than through regularized and standardized channels. They do not act to create, district-wide, a reading program, preferred set of materials, or preferred set of methods but rather offer suggestions and help on a particularistic basis in an effort to fit a particular local situation.

The comments of experienced educational administrators who insist that their appropriate role is that of a "change agent" who "works with people" rather than that of an administrator who applies a set of rules should perhaps be taken more seriously. Such a role implies that administrators have little substantive educational authority to *direct* educational programs. If they are to be effective at all, they must be so through specific interpersonal skills rather than through administrative or even professional authority. In a decentralized, segmental educational system, fundamental educational decisions are under the jurisdiction of teachers and, perhaps, principals. The district is there to help, advise, or set limits on the autonomy of schools, but not to administer a standardized educational program.

Results: Schools and Classrooms

In this section we examine the linkages between the school as an organization and the classrooms within it.

Agreement Between Principals and Teachers. We turn now from a consideration of the relation of principals with their districts to analyze the relation of teachers with their schools. To a large extent, the same intellectual images apply—teachers may be as autonomous within schools, in central educational matters, as schools are within districts. However, for several reasons a higher level of coordination might be expected within the school than within the district. The teachers are all located on the same physical site and interact with each other and the principal with some frequency; they tend to face the same environmental context both in the outside community and in the physical layout of the school. In addition, it appears that principals, more than district officials, have a certain amount of legitimated educational authority, and may therefore produce a more integrated program.

Using as data the responses of 232 teachers and sixteen principals from sixteen schools, we examine first the level of agreement between the principal and the average response of teachers in the same school to similar questions. To aggregate the responses of teachers in this manner produces higher correlations than would be found between individual teachers and their principal because, as is shown at length in the next section, there is great variation among teachers within schools. However, the present analyses are concerned with the overall agreement between two organizational positions: principal and teacher.

The pattern of results follows that of the principal-district analysis, although some of the correlations are higher. (With sixteen cases, a correlation of .42 is significant at the .05 level.) It should be noted that the results of this analysis are less stable because they are based on a much smaller number of cases (sixteen schools, as compared to thirty-four districts). Although there would be more cases and hence more stability were the analysis to be based on individual teachers, this approach would mix principal-teacher disagreement with teacher-teacher disagreement.

The results can be readily summarized as follows. There is a fair amount of agreement about the characteristics of the environment. The correlation between the average response of teachers and the response of their principal to a question about the economic level of the pupils' families was .50. This figure is not high, compared with our expectations for agreement on this type of item, but it is one of the highest values observed in our measures of agreement.

Issues involving money reveal greater agreement between teachers and principal, presumably because the principal tends to find out what teachers are doing through budget-related processes. Both teachers and principals were asked how many paid teacher aides were present in a typical instructional period in grades 1 through 3. The correlation was .93. In contrast, their agreement on the number of adult volunteers typically present for reading instruction in grades 1 through 3 was only .21. The difference may be that adult volunteers are, of course, unpaid, and their presence is (1) less likely to be standardized across the school and (2) less likely to be of intimate concern to the principal.

The same theme comes up throughout the data in connection with educational materials. Principals know a good deal more about materials used in their schools than about teaching methods or forms of classroom organization, presumably because materials are purchased from the school budget and are typically obtained through requests to the district office, channeled through the principal's office. Thus, for example, the agreement between teachers and principals on the extent to which pupils used different materials in a typical reading instruction period was .63. In contrast, agreement on classroom organization on a question asking how often reading-group membership changed over time was only .09. And agreement on teaching methods on a question asking who generally decided what methods to use in teaching reading was only .09.

As a more general measure, several of the principals' answers to questions about reading materials were combined into an index of materials differentiation (discussed in detail in Cohen and others, 1977). The object of the index was to measure the extent to which the available reading materials offered complex alternatives to teachers and students. The teachers were asked a somewhat similar set of questions about their own materials. The two sets of answers are correlated .41, again suggesting at least some correspondence between the two parties on a matter in which funds are involved.

Apart from items related to environment and funds, agreement between principals and teachers was very low. The principals' reports on overall parent participation in decision making was correlated only .20 and −.20 with two items asking teachers about parent influence on lesson content and discipline. Teacher reports of the principal's helpfulness with generating new teaching ideas were correlated with principal reports of influence on curriculum (.50) and on teaching methods (.29). And, as with the district-school data, agreement on the evaluation system within schools was low (.21).

In considering principal and teacher reports of influence on decision making within the school, low levels of agreement again appear. Agreement on the principal's influence on pupil assignment and handling of serious discipline problems was only .28 and −.08. Agreement on the teachers' influence on pupil assignment was higher (.67), but for discipline it was only .13.

Overall, these findings are quite similar to those relating the answers of principals to the answers of superintendents. The general level of agreement between principals and teachers on educational matters is low, although higher than principal-superintendent agreement. Again, it would be a mistake to regard these data as suggesting a high level of conflict—we have no evidence for this interpretation. Rather, the findings are consistent with the suggestion that principals and teachers are separated by jurisdictional boundaries. They agree in general on their roles, but they seem to have little agreement on specifics within each school. They also apparently agree that what each one does within his or her jurisdiction is by and large not the other's business. And, they apparently agree that their jurisdictions do not overlap very much.

Consensus Among Teachers. Leaving aside their agreement with the principal, do teachers in the same school report the same organizational world? In order to investigate this issue, a series of one-way analyses of variance were performed to see if variation among schools (N = 16) accounted for a statistically significant proportion of the overall variance among the 232 teachers and also to see what proportion of the variance could thus be accounted for. To deal with the first issue, the F-ratio associated with between-school variation is reported. To deal with the second issue, we report values of eta-squared. Again, the reader should bear in mind that this is a biased measure of the variance accounted for by the school, since even if the teachers' answers were randomly distributed among schools, a typical eta-squared value of .08 would be produced.

The results shown in Table 3 conform to the familiar pattern. Between-school variation (or within-school consensus) is greater, in general, than the comparable measures at the district level shown in Table 1, but in most respects it is quite low. In only

Table 3. Analysis of Variance for Teachers' Responses
(N = 232 teachers, sixteen schools).

Variable	Source[a]	F-Ratio[b]	Eta-Squared[c]
General school or classroom characteristic			
Teach in an open space classroom	TQ 6	23.18	.66
Number of aides in a typical reading class	TQ 59	13.88	.50
Number of volunteers in a typical class	TQ 59	6.04	.30
Family economic level of pupils	TQ 72	5.93	.29
Interdependence within school			
Frequency of cross-grouping pupils in math	TQ 10	9.17	.40
Frequency of cross-grouping pupils in reading	TQ 10	5.84	.30
Frequency of cross-grouping pupils in social studies	TQ 10	2.84	.17
Member of a teaching team	TQ 16	12.83	.47
Degree of teaching collaboration	TQ 15	10.07	.42
Team meeting frequency	TQ 23	2.73	.29

Curriculum and methods

Most frequently use whole-class method: math	TQ 12	3.65	.31
Most frequently use whole-class method: reading	TQ 12	3.01	.32
Most frequently use whole-class method: social studies	TQ 12	.99	.07
Frequency of ability grouping in math	TQ 13	1.22	.09
Frequency of ability grouping in reading	TQ 13	2.02	.14
Frequency of ability grouping in social studies	TQ 13	1.73	.15
Amount of variation in math materials	TQ 34	5.03	.27
Amount of variation in reading materials	TQ 34	6.65	.32
Amount of variation in social studies materials	TQ 34	3.37	.21
Frequency students choose materials: math	TQ 35	1.19	.08
Frequency students choose materials: reading	TQ 35	1.94	.12
Frequency students choose materials: social studies	TQ 35	2.07	.13

Influence and evaluation

Influence of district policies: discipline problems	TQ 46	1.57	.19
Influence of district policies: lesson content	TQ 44	2.12	.26
Principal's influence on lesson content	TQ 44	2.43	.16
Principal's influence: pupil assignment	TQ 49	3.25	.19
Faculty's influence: pupil assignment	TQ 49	4.26	.24
Teacher's influence: pupil assignment	TQ 49	4.84	.27
School policy influence: student conduct	TQ 50	2.27	.15
School policy influence: curriculum	TQ 51	2.85	.18
School policy influence: evaluation of students	TQ 52	.73	.05
Parent influence: lesson content	TQ 44	2.29	.15
Principal's evaluation frequency: teaching subject matter	TQ 62	2.39	.15
Principal's evaluation frequency: class control	TQ 62	1.96	.12
Principal's evaluation frequency: record keeping	TQ 62	2.13	.13

[a]TQ indicates Teachers Questionnaire. For specific items, see Cohen and others (1976).

[b]The numbers of teachers answering the questions varied, from 180 to the maximum of 232, because some questions were inappropriate for particular groups of teachers. Consequently, the level of statistical significance indicated by a given F-ratio varies slightly. We use a conservative definition in Table 3: an F-ratio of 1.98 is significant at the .05 level for any of the analyses reported here. In some instances with more cases, an F-ratio of only 1.74 would be significant at the same level.

[c]A value of eta-squared of about .08 is to be expected by chance.

one instance is the proportion of variance among teachers accounted for by their school as high as .50. More often, the value is extremely low.

The specific interpretations that can be made generally conform to our earlier findings. Agreement about environmental features was fairly high. Of the variation in teacher reports of open-space classrooms, 67 percent was accounted for by school membership. Of the variance in reported pupil family economic level, 29 percent was shared within schools.

Variables that reflect funding differences among schools showed fairly high agreement. There was some agreement on the amount of variation in materials for math, reading, and social studies, presumably because richer districts or schools can buy more. Similarly, there was considerable agreement among teachers on the presence of aides for reading—more agreement than on the presence of unpaid volunteers.

For the first time, the data show clear examples of explicit interdependence within schools. The teachers, to some extent, agreed on whether they were team members, how much teacher collaboration there was, how frequently teams met, and how frequently they cross-grouped students. Some agreement was also evident on whether the whole-class method of instruction was used in math and reading. This finding may reflect school policies but may also reflect the fact that some of these schools are open space, while others are not. The whole-class method is less commonly employed in open-space schools and is in some respects ill suited to them.

On most organizational and educational matters, there was little agreement. Even given some agreement on variation in materials, there was little agreement within schools on whether pupils chose their materials. There was also little agreement on the practice of ability grouping. And agreement on the whole battery of measures of influence and power within the school was very weak, considering that the teachers are here reporting, not their individual practices, but school-wide patterns, as they see them. In most of these instances, agreement is statistically significant (in part because of the large number of teachers and the small number of schools), but it is substantively unimpressive. Finally, agreement on

patterns of teacher evaluation—putatively a main method of control—was almost nonexistent within schools.

The results of these analyses conform to the earlier findings
about agreement among principals. Agreement was highest in response to obvious environmental circumstances or funding arrangements. Although teachers did agree in describing a few areas
involving interdependence, by and large each teacher seemed to
experience the organization from the viewpoint of an autonomous
agent.

Consensus Among Interdependent Teachers. Do interdependent
teachers show more consensus? The finding that teachers tend to
agree in describing areas of obvious interdependence suggests an
additional hypothesis. Perhaps teachers who work interdepen-
dently show more within-school agreement than other teachers.
Interdependent teachers are more involved in the school organization, as opposed to the isolated world of the classroom, and
might routinely be able to describe consensually some processes
that are irrelevant to other teachers. As a simple measure of
interdependence, the teachers were divided into two groups depending on whether they reported being a member of a team.
Eighty-five teachers in thirteen schools reported being on teams,
and 110 in thirteen schools said they were not. The analyses of
variance reported earlier were repeated separately for the two
groups, to see whether more variation was accounted for by school
membership among teamed teachers than among unteamed
teachers.

The results offer some encouragement. On a number of
items, teamed teachers showed higher levels of consensus. They
agreed more than independent teachers on the degree of school
influence on discipline patterns (eta-squared was .37, as compared
with .07) and curriculum (.30, .09); on the degree of influence of
the principal (.31, .21) and the community (.36, .24); on the sharing
of materials (.53, .25); and on the cross grouping of pupils for
reading (.45, .15). On most other items, however, differences were
smaller or nonexistent. By and large, these analyses suggest that
higher levels of teacher interdependence generate somewhat more
agreement on organizational rules. When schools are classified by
the frequency with which the principal reported that teachers en-

gaged in joint teaching, however, these effects did not occur: Schools reported as collaborative showed little more teacher agreement than noncollaborative schools.

We also entertained the hypotheses that more agreement within schools might be found if the school organization was stronger in either of two respects: (1) the principal reported himself to be influential in many aspects of school life or (2) the principal reported high levels of participation in school decisions by both himself and the teachers. Schools high on these variables, it seemed, might have more explicit and better enforced rules with which every teacher would be familiar. Consequently, the analyses of variance were repeated separately for schools classified as low and high on these variables. Few consistent differences were found when schools were distinguished according to "principal power." When schools were distinguished by levels of teacher participation in school decisions, those with more teacher participation showed some tendency to have more policy agreement among the teachers, although the differences were not large.

The results of these exploratory analyses suggest that it may be profitable to look further for higher levels of organizational coherence among schools that have more teacher participation and more teacher interdependence. However, even the most positive of these results do not show high levels of agreement among teachers in describing the facts of organizational life. Even the most interdependent schools rarely show levels of agreement in which between-school variance accounts for as much as 40 percent of the variation among teachers' responses to our questionnaire.

Conclusions

We can summarize the findings very simply. First, there may or may not be a good deal of agreement in the whole educational system between principals and superintendents in describing typical district organizational and educational policies. But within this larger frame, agreement between principals and superintendents in the same district is quite limited. Second, and similarly, the particular level of agreement distinctive to principals in the same district, in describing district rules or educational policies, is *very low*.

Moreover, the more influential district offices do not exercise their influence through regular bureaucratic channels and do not impose greater uniformity on their schools. Third, whatever generalized agreements there are in the whole educational system between teachers and principals in describing school and district policies, the level of specific agreements distinctive to teachers and principals in particular schools is usually rather limited (although higher than that between principals and superintendents). Fourth, and similarly, the teachers within a given school exhibit relatively little agreement in describing school and classroom policies (although more than principals within districts). Agreement is somewhat higher in reporting on the environment, matters concerned with funding, and areas of obvious interdependence. Also, teachers who are more interdependent agree somewhat more than independent teachers in describing school policies and practices.

These findings are surprising because they concern reports about organizational rules and practices, not individual attitudes. The school system as an organization appears to have very weak links, especially so far as rules and practices relating to instruction are concerned.

What do these findings mean? They clearly indicate that schools are not *functionally differentiated, coordinated organizations, or even segmental, coordinated organizations,* with respect to the structuring of instructional work. These models of organization clearly presume the presence of specific, explicit, and consensual arrangements for coordinating work. One could argue that all schools and districts face such similar environmental and technological problems that there is homogeneity within the whole system—in which case variance of our various measures would be low, and there would be agreement in the whole system. But the measures do show considerable variation, and it is clear that schools and districts do vary in environments and in instructional technologies. So the absence of agreement within school and district units on coordinative rules and practices lends little support to these models of educational organization.

The findings also indicate that schools and districts are not simply *segmental decentralized organizations,* either. In such a situation, there would be considerable homogeneity and agreement in reporting the absence of central school and district rules and policies. We find, rather, that various participants in these systems do report varying levels of central rules and policies but *do not agree* in reporting their presence or absence in particular schools or districts.

We are left with the idea that schools and districts are *institutionalized organizations* and are *loosely coupled* so far as technical educational work is concerned. We need to explain what this means and how it occurs. First of all, the idea that schools are loosely coupled (March and Olsen, 1976; Weick, 1976) organizations so far as technical work is concerned is strongly supported in the data. There is little agreement or consensus distinctive to particular schools and districts on a wide range of matters having to do with educational or instructional policy. These findings fit with other data and conceptual discussions (Bidwell, 1965; Dreeben, 1973; Gross and Herriott, 1965; Lortie, 1973; Weick, 1976; see also Chapter Four of this book.) Instructional work tends to go on beyond the purview of the formal organizational structure of the school and district. Policies exist at one level without implementation at other levels.

The theoretical question is how such organizations—with weak controls and with dissensus about their central activities— survive and achieve stability. One possibility is that they do not— that schools and districts are riddled with conflict and dissatisfaction and are highly unstable organizational forms. The answer is clearly wrong (see J. Meyer and Rowan, 1977, for a discussion): Data from our own study show high levels of participant satisfaction and low levels of internal conflict. Data from other surveys show high levels of client (parent, child, and community) satisfaction with schools (see, for instance, Acland, 1975). And it is common knowledge that school and district organizations have high levels of stability and longevity and obtain high and rather stable levels of resources from their environments. A given public school, for instance, obviously has a much greater likelihood of survival than a typical small business with the same budget.

The solution we propose to the problem of the success and

stability of educational organizations is that they are highly *insti-tutionalized,* as a structural form, in society. Elaborate understand-ings define schools as essential—and equally elaborate rules ac-credit particular schools. The status of teacher is defined, prescribed, and credentialed. Student participation is built into the educational requirements of state law and employment practice. Principal and district-level roles are defined in, made necessary by, and funded from the wider social context of community opinion and state law. How do these broader understandings and rules—many of them taking the form of legal prescriptions—affect the structure and functioning of individual school organizations? By determining the conditions of their survival. If a school maintains general structural conformity to the societal rules and understand-ings defining educational systems, it is likely to survive and pros-per. If it does not, support—both fiscal and moral—will be with-drawn. Thus it comes about that *school and district organizational structure have primary importance as internal reflections of institutional-ized rules of the wider state and society.* The process that holds edu-cational organizations together and gives them meaning and value is not the success of the system in achieving internal coordination but rather their structural conformity to prevailing institutional rules.

Consider what consequences this arrangement has for par-ticular schools and districts. The formal structure of the system —the reflection of the wider rules of education—is not loosely, but very tightly coupled. Our findings do not reflect this because we did not think to ask our respondents questions about the structural matters on which agreement is so high as to be taken for granted. Among principals within districts and between principals and su-perintendents, there would be very high agreement on:

- The fact that each school must have a principal and some cre-dentialed teachers
- Who is the principal of each school
- The number of grades taught in a given school
- The number of schools in the district
- The pay of a teacher or principal of given experience and credentials

- The approximate number of pupils assigned to each teacher
- The list of substantive topics of instruction that make up the curriculum for students in a given grade.

The list could go on and on. The formal structure of educational organization is in important ways taken for granted, derived from—not the coordinative exigencies of instruction—but the rules of the wider system. The district system reflects these rules and applies the taken-for-granted structure to the definition of each school and the allocation of pupils, teachers, principal, and formally defined curricular topics to it.

In the school, similarly, there would be great agreement on questions we did not ask:

- Who are the teachers in the school?
- Which teacher is assigned to each room and grade?
- Who is and is not a student, and to which grade and teacher is each student assigned?
- Who is the principal?

In maintaining the institutionally prescribed structure, schools and districts are tightly coupled: They keep track of students and teachers (and the credentials of each), and principals, buildings and funds. They derive their legitimacy (for instance, accreditation) from these structural elements. These are the elements that define a school as valid and maintain its continued flow of support. And on these elements the level of consensus is so high—and so much taken for granted—that we as researchers did not think to inquire.

But what of instruction and educational policy? These matters—which all participants understand are central to the larger purposes of the system—are *organizationally* peripheral. If the valid structure is maintained, conduct of instruction can be left to the individual decisions and informal negotiations of the properly certified members of the organization. The widely shared understandings about the nature of education create a context within which enough agreement exists to allow the conduct of instructional business to proceed reasonably smoothly. "Everyone knows" that third-graders study—and are taught by teachers—subjects such as math and reading. These are activities all parties know must go on, and, even though nobody in the superintendent's office or principal's office directly enforces or inspects them, they go on anyway.

These arguments suggest two implications for our data on educational policy and instruction. First, in important ways, these data and inferences describe a real situation: So long as the institutionally valid structure of district and school is maintained, a great deal of flexibility and variety in actual technical educational work is possible with little disruption. And allowing such uninspected variability to occur may even help the organization to retain the clarity and validity of its public formal organization (see Chapter Four of this book). But, second, the analyses we have reported may in some measure be misleading. Perhaps there is much greater consensus on substantive educational matters in the system than the data suggest. There is little consensus *distinctive to particular schools and districts* in the data. But we have not shown that there is great dissensus on educational matters in the whole system of schools and districts. The present arguments suggest that the real source of consensus unifying the educational system is the larger network of societal agreements defining education. The real unit of analysis, then, is not the particular school or district organization but the whole institutional matrix in which they are embedded. Perhaps there is enough consensus within this whole system on how teaching and learning are to occur that the particular rules and policies created organizationally in schools and districts are simply marginal organizational footnotes to wider understandings.

To see if this is true, we would have to show that the whole sample of superintendents, principals, and teachers really agree on many central issues—not only of organizational structure, about which they were not asked, but also about actual instructional practices. The present measures show variance, but perhaps much less variance than would be required to show genuine institutional inconsistencies. What comparisons would suggest, on the measures described in this chapter, that this was the case? We would have to show that the variance in these samples on matters of instruction and policy is very small compared with that to be found between different institutional educational contexts. This would suggest that the whole San Francisco Bay area is an educational community showing a great deal of consensus compared with the variability to be found across societies and states. The present data are, of course, not adequate for this purpose. But it is clear that, if education is an institutionally (not organizationally) defined set of activities, then variations across institutional contexts will be more meaningful than variations across organizational units.

Two possibilities, then, are left. First, perhaps the social consensus on the requisite structural forms of the educational system leaves actual instruction free to vary widely within it. Or, second, perhaps a good deal of institutional consensus regulates the daily activities of educational work too—consensus we did not find because of the provincial character of our data bases.

Notes

1. The correlations tend to be slightly higher when only principals who have held their positions for more than two years are considered. Principals with more experience in their school agree slightly more with the superintendent's answers—but only slightly.

2. The data on ethnicity were obtained from sources outside the school.

10

Coupled Versus Uncoupled Control in Organizational Hierarchies

William G. Ouchi

The transmission of control through a hierarchy has long been a central issue in the study of organizations. It is the nexus around which revolve questions of control, of loose coupling, and of evaluation. Indeed, if organizations have no ability to transmit policy guidelines through many levels of hierarchy, then they are incapable of organized action.

The traditional approach to the question of transmission of

This research was supported by a grant from the National Science Foundation, Sociology Section. The author is grateful to his colleagues, Eugene J. Webb and John W. Meyer, for their suggestions. This paper is based on "The Transmission of Control Through Organizational Hierarchy," *Academy of Management Journal,* in press.

control through a hierarchy has stressed both the normative position that accurate transmission is necessary and desirable as well as the descriptive assertion that most large organizations are quite ineffective in this regard. This point has been made repeatedly, by Downs (1956), Patchen (1963), Tullock (1965), Williamson (1971), Hopwood (1972), and Evans (1975). In each case, the authors describe the need for a multitiered organization to be able to accurately communicate organizational objectives from top to bottom and then be able effectively to monitor actions and results in order to determine whether the desired results have been obtained and, if not, to order corrective action. This is the essence of the process of organizational control.

Using this traditional conceptualization of the process of organizational control, Dornbusch and Scott (1975) were surprised to discover no evidence of effective evaluation or control in school systems. Although it is manifest that school systems have survived the test of time and that they are successful as organizations, they apparently do so completely unaided by the control mechanisms specified by organizational researchers. This discovery led to a variety of speculations, including those of Weick (1976) and by Meyer and Rowan (Chapter Four), concerning the ability of organizations to exist in a "loosely coupled" state. It may be true that, for a large class of organizations, a loose coupling of explicit intent to action or of superstructure to substructures is more desirable than is the tight coupling advocated by earlier researchers. Indeed, if one thinks of organizational hierarchy as consisting not of a hierarchy of authority but rather as consisting of a hierarchically ordered set of units nested within larger units (Simon, 1962), then the idea of loose coupling seems quite plausible. To the extent that each subunit has a cohesiveness or a unity of its own, each is more stable than it would be if each of its members had no such connections and were linked only in a sort of pooled interdependence (Thompson, 1967) through their membership in the larger organization. However, while the existence of nested subunits brings greater stability to the entity as a whole, it inevitably means that there are some differences in objectives, in style, and in structure between subunits (Simon, 1962; Lawrence and Lorsch, 1967), differences that impede the kind of perfect communication and cooperation that constitute the traditional model of organizational control. At the extreme of this loose-linking idea, Aldrich (1971) has asserted that most organizations ought to be loosely coupled internally, in part because tight coupling between subunits implies that any change or reaction to the environment on the part of one subunit will necessarily (under conditions of tight coupling) be transmitted throughout the organization, leaving it in a state of perpetual chaos.

Thus it has been reasonably argued that a complex organization, if it is to achieve production objectives, must have some accuracy of control transmission, but it has also been convincingly argued that accurate transmission of control through a hierarchy is disruptive to both the stability and the objectives of specialized subunits within the organization. Thus Evans (1975) suggests that the problem of control loss in a traditional hierarchy becomes overwhelming if there are more than three levels, while Franklin (1975) demonstrates that organizations are quite loosely linked with respect to managerial style. Finally, it is observably true that many organizations exist that contain five, seven, and more levels of hierarchy. Indeed, contemporary work organizations frequently exceed the size of the largest ancient cities, and their complexity can be very great. It must be true, therefore, that complex organizations somehow achieve simultaneously the transmission that is necessary for effective collective action while maintaining sufficiently loose internal coupling to permit stability and variety in their subunits. It is the objective of this chapter to describe two alternative mechanisms of control that exist in most work organizations, one that permits accurate transmission between levels and another that allows for local variation.

If we accept the rather simple notion that control in organizations can be described as a process of monitoring, evaluating, and providing feedback, then we can ask what it is that is monitored and evaluated. In organizational evaluation, there are only two kinds of phenomena that can be monitored or counted: These are behavior and outputs that result from behavior as observed by March and Simon (1958). No one would disagree with the assertion that it is possible for a manager to observe his or her subordinates and count the number of times that they engage in any particular behavior.

Alternatively, the supervisor in some cases may be able to measure performance less obtrusively by monitoring the aftereffects of behavior, which are the outputs of the productive process. Some managers may choose instead to measure inputs, but we will regard that common practice as falling outside the domain of control, since there is no necessary relationship between inputs and goal achievement except at the extreme, where zero inputs will ordinarily guarantee lack of goal attainment.

Now, given that the supervisor is able to monitor either behavior or the aftereffects of behavior, we can ask whether evaluation is possible. Briefly, the measures of behavior may be used for evaluation only if the technology is sufficiently well understood that "proper" or "good" behavior is recognizable. If the appropriate behavior is unknown, then the observations of actual behavior are of no use for control purposes. As for the leavings of behavior, these can be evaluated only if they are valid representations of goal attainment. If these observable outputs are representative of the desired objectives, then output control is possible (Ouchi, 1977).

Thus, conditional on the state of the organization's technology and its ability to measure desired end states, we can speak of behavior control and output control as the two alternative methods. Ordinarily, behavior control will be more subtle, more flexible, and richer. It will be able to capture a large range of desired activities and to do so with the flexibility to take account of local differences. Because of this very flexibility, however, and because of the subjective quality of the assessments, behavior control will have poor transmittal qualities through organizational levels. We cannot expect the president to be aware of the subtleties of behavior that are valued in each organizational subunit, with the result that behavior control will serve very well as a local control mechanism but very poorly as an organization-wide control mechanism (Ouchi and Maguire, 1975).

Output control is typically quantifiable and therefore at least apparently comparable across levels and across functions. However, it will ordinarily be impossible to capture all of the complexity of what a department should be doing in one or a few such measures. As a result, output control will be relatively successful at satisfying the organizational need for some commensurable measures of performance, imprecise though they may be, but it will be poor at satisfying local needs for detailed performance information.

Let us note that, whether the control process is based on behavior or on output, it is always behavior that is the ultimate object of feedback and of change. Hopwood (1972) notes that accounting data, which are ordinarily measures of output, have a profound effect on the behavior of managers when these data are knowingly used for performance evaluation. In a sense, then, all control is behavior control. In the language of Thibaut and Kelley (1959), unless fate control can be converted to behavior control, no change will occur.

Returning to the classical problem of control loss in hierarchies, we can now argue that some, but not all, forms of control ought to be accurately transmitted through hierarchies. The control and evaluation needs of the organization can be met by output control, while the local needs of subunits for variation can be met by behavior control. Thus, the organization will experience sometimes conflicting pressures to respond to those output measures that satisfy needs for external evaluation while simultaneously meeting local demands for behavioral surveillance that is suited to the conditions of the immediate department (Hopwood, 1972, and Gouldner, 1954, illustrate the point well). If this is an accurate depiction of the control process in organizations, then we should find a much more consistent transmission of output control than of behavior control in organizations. That is, subordinates should be quite similar to their superiors in the degree of emphasis they place on output control but should show little similarity in their emphasis on close behavior control. A superior who wishes to place great (or little) emphasis on measures of output can thus transmit that wish accurately through the organization, while a similar desire to emphasize close (or distant) monitoring of behavior cannot be communicated with the same accuracy.

This study draws on a set of data collected through questionnaires during 1972. Two department store companies in the midwestern United States provided a total of five sites, including the central administrative offices and branch stores. From these, a sample of 215 departments was drawn, representing both sales and sales support functions. Questionnaires were administered to each employee in every department in the sample, yielding 2,363 usable questionnaires, a response rate of 83 percent. These were then aggregated into the original 215 departments, so that each case includes data from the department manager, the mean of scores of assistant department managers, if any, and the mean of scores from first-line employees. Data on employees above the level of department manager are not reported in this chapter.

Retail department stores differ from other organizations in many ways. One major difference is that measures of output are easily obtainable for the sales function of department stores. These measures usually consist of a gross measure of sales volume, and they sometimes also are adjusted for returns and exchanges. Even this more complex output measure, however, fails to capture many of the other areas in which performance is considered important, such as stockwork, training new salespeople (a large task, since turnover is high in most retail stores), and coordinating delivery dates.

Even in departments other than sales, output measures are commonly used. Some stores, for example, keep records of the number and dimensions of each parcel processed through the wrapping and packing department. Others measure the performance of the receiving and marking function by keeping track of the number of hours from the time that a shipping container is received at the warehouse until the goods are on the shelves and racks in the stores. In general, however, the use of output measures in sales support areas is less common than in sales departments.

While output control is perhaps more common in department stores than in other kinds of organizations, behavior control is also widely used. The study reported by Ouchi (1975) used a modified echo technique to identify eleven principal performance goals that most department stores apply to sales personnel. Of these, only one or two are represented in the sales volume measure. The others must be evaluated through the supervisory skills of the department manager applying behavior control as he or she watches, corrects, and guides the first-level employees. Thus both forms of control are commonly used in retail department stores, whereas other kinds of organizations may tend to rely more heavily on behavior control alone.

The hypothesis to be tested is simply that output control will be transmitted more accurately through the hierarchy than will behavior control. The test is a weak one, because it does not measure agreement between levels on the substance of the goals and the exact levels of performance that are considered satisfactory and unsatisfactory. Instead, the measures used here reflect the agreement between levels on how much emphasis is placed on output and how much emphasis is placed on behavior.

The principal measures are of "behavior control given"; "behavior control received"; "output control given"; and "output control received." For department managers and assistant department managers, all four measures were obtained. For first-level employees, who have no subordinates to whom control can be given, only the measures of behavior control received and of output control received were obtained.

These four measures were obtained from the following questionnaire items:

1. *Output control given.* An index coded into values 1, 2, and 3 from the following item: "When you are evaluating the people who report directly to you for raises or promotions, how much weight do you give to their output records?" (1 = output records are not considered at all in the decision; 7 = decision is based entirely on output records.) More than one half of the department managers and assistant department managers reported having no records of output. Those were coded as 1, original values of 2 to 4 were coded as 2 and 5 to 7 coded as 3. A comparison of correlations between the original and recoded variables is presented in Appendix 3. The path analysis reported hereafter was also run with both sets of variables; the findings in each case were the same.

2. *Behavior control given.* "How often do you see each of the people who reports directly to you?" (1 = I see each person less than once a week; 7 = they are almost never out of my sight.)

3. *Output control received.* An index coded into values 1, 2, and 3 from the following item: "In some departments, records are kept

for each employee that show his or her output—for example, sales volume, selling cost, or number of parcels handled. Does your immediate superior keep such records of your individual output?" (If yes, then answer the following question.) "When you are being evaluated for a raise or promotion, how much weight does your supervisor give to the records of your output?" (1 = output records are not considered at all in the decision; 7 = decision is based entirely on output records.)

4. *Behavior control received.* "How often does your immediate supervisor check to see what you are doing on the job?" (1 = checks once a week or less; 8 = can see me almost all the time.) Behavior control given asks how often you "see" your subordinates, while behavior control received asks how often your supervisor "checks" on you. These different wordings were used for the following reason: The most direct measure of the underlying construct is represented by asking how often your supervisor "checks" on you, and that form was used for control received. A pretest of the item suggested, however, that the word *checking* on someone carried negative connotations when applied to the giving of control and that supervisors were underreporting their behavior. For that reason, the less threatening form, asking how often you "see" your subordinates, was substituted for measuring control given.

The other operational measures are reported in Appendix 1, along with their means and standard deviations. The matrix of zero-order correlation coefficients is reported in Appendix 2.

Of the 215 departments, only 36 had one or more assistant department managers; the others had no one in this position, thus having only two levels of hierarchy. A person who identified himself as an assistant manager in rank but who had no superior within the department was treated as the manager of that department. All departments had at least one subordinate and had only one department manager. Data for the 36 departments with three levels of hierarchy will be reported separately from data for all 215 departments. Now let us consider the results.

The transmission hypothesis was tested by comparing two sets of correlations for each form of control. The first was to test for emulation effects, that is, to inspect the correlation between behavior control received and behavior control given, and the correlation between output control received and output control given, within each of the two supervisory ranks. The hypothesis was that these correlations would be greater for output control than for behavior control, suggesting that subordinates more closely copy their superiors in output control than in behavior control.

The second set of correlations, to test for interlevel transmission, is between (1) behavior control given by a higher level and behavior control received by a lower level and (2) the correlations between output control given by a higher level and output control received by a lower level. The prediction was that these correlations would be higher for output control than for behavior control. This suggests that output control is transmitted between levels more accurately than is behavior control. The results are combined in Figure 1, which demonstrates the striking difference in transmission between the two forms of control.

In Figure 1, it seems as though everything is correlated with everything else within the set of output measures, while few significant correlations appear within the set of behavior control measures. This pattern is true both of the three-level and of the two-level departments. The initial explanation that suggests itself is that output control is either emphasized or deemphasized as a matter of company policy, while behavior control is arrived at through local decisions taken by department managers. The data fail to support that hypothesis, however, with the correlations between the dummy variable for "company" and the measures of output control ranging from $r = .06$ to $r = .29$ (see Appendix 2). In fact, the average correlations between the company variable and the measures of behavior control are much larger. A further breakdown of the data into organizational subunits within companies also failed to produce any difference in the relationships.

This led to a path analysis, the results of which are presented in Figure 2. Figure 2 shows all significant paths for the output control variables. None of the paths between behavior control variables reached that level, so the same paths are shown for purposes of comparison.

Figure 2 shows that the expected effects take place. That is, output control is accurately emulated within each supervisory level

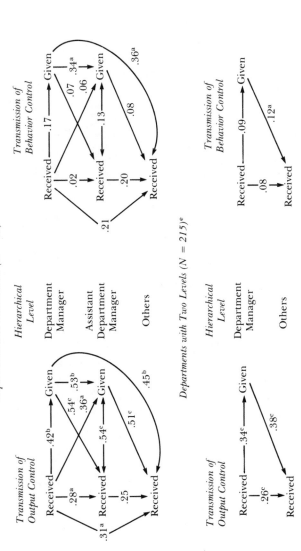

Figure 1. The Transmission of Control: Zero-Order Effects (**Zero-Order Correlation Coefficients**).

[a]p = .05.
[b]p = .01.
[c]p = .001.
[d]Of these thirty-six departments, twenty-one are from Company A and fifteen from Company B.

[e]These data include departments that have three levels, with the middle level excluded from this particular analysis. Results for only those departments that do not have assistant managers (N = 179) do not differ from these.

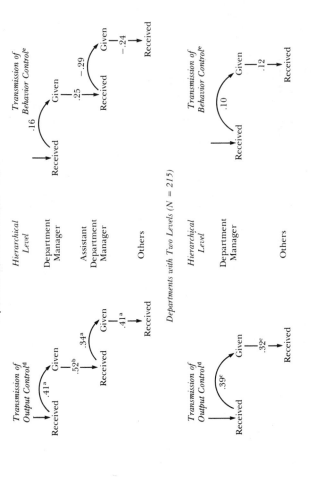

Departments with Three Levels (N = 36)

Departments with Two Levels (N = 215)

Note: The path coefficients are standardized regression coefficients.

[a]$p < .05$.
[b]$p < .01$.
[c]$p < .001$.

[d]These path diagrams show only paths that are at least two times their standard error.

[e]In these path diagrams, none of the paths are at least two times their standard error, so the predicted paths are shown to provide a comparison with the other diagrams.

Figure 2. Transmission of Control: Path Coefficients.

and is accurately transmitted between levels, while there is little emulation or transmission of behavior control. There is no evidence here that a general policy orientation accounts for the transmission of output control, for such an orientation would yield significant path coefficients between the three measures of control received and between the two measures of control given. Rather, the zero-order association between the receipt of output control by managers and by assistant managers is accounted for by the fact that managers transmit their control style to their assistant managers. After that transmission effect is accounted for, there is no remaining significant similarity between output control received by the two levels of managers.

In the case of output control given, however, there is some remaining similarity (although not significant) between the supervisory ranks even after the transmission effect is removed ($b = .29$). This similarity may be accounted for by the fact that assistant department managers, on the whole, are upwardly mobile and feel that they are "in training" to become department managers. They are thus subject to anticipatory socialization, and these data suggest that there is a general policy orientation that is shared both by department managers and by their assistants. Even with the transmission effect removed, therefore, there is some remaining similarity between the output control orientation held by the two levels of managers.

It is also interesting that there is some antitransmission of behavior control. The more behavior control an assistant manager receives, the less he or she will pass on to their subordinates. This may be due to the assistant manager's following the "golden rule" and doing unto their subordinates as they wish their superior would do unto them. Those whose superiors exercise very close behavior control may be highly sensitive to the form of control, dislike it, and take care not to use that form of control on their subordinates. Conversely, those whose supervisors exert very little behavior control may feel neglected and respond by watching more closely over their own subordinates.

The much larger number of cases in the analysis of two-level departments, 215 departments versus only 36 departments with three levels, produces the same findings. Here it is clear that both emulation and transmission take place with respect to output control, but neither effect exists for behavior control.

A number of further investigations were conducted, the most important of which are reported here. First, a discriminant validation was performed by combining output control given with behavior control received and combining behavior control given with output control received. The test should demonstrate no difference between these two mixed transmission processes. The results revealed no difference between the mixed processes in either two-level or three-level departments. None of the correlations in this test reached significance.

The next test was to examine more closely the meaning of the operational measure of behavior control given. The questionnaire item asks, "How often do you see each of the people who reports directly to you?" It is entirely possible that this question was interpreted by supervisors as referring to the frequency with which they could physically see subordinates, rather than to the frequency of checking on or otherwise controlling them. In that case, the lack of correlation between that variable and the measure of behavior control received, which refers more directly to frequency of checking to see how the respondent is doing on the job, would not be surprising, since the two would be measuring quite different things.

In order to check, an additional variable, "information from observing," was introduced. This variable (see Appendix 1) measures the supervisor's perception of how much information he can gain from watching his subordinates. Clearly, if he feels that observation is of no use, then he cannot rationally apply behavior control. If this variable, when substituted for behavior control given in Figure 2, produced results similar to those for output control in that table, then the original results must be discarded. Information from observing is correlated with behavior control given, $r = .28$ $(p < .001)$ for department managers and $r = .35$ $(p < .05)$ for assistant managers. However, making the substitution produced a transmission pattern that is indistinguishable from the pattern for behavior control in Figure 2. This third test also fails to invalidate the results of Figure 2.

If the results in Figure 2 can be generally accepted as valid, then a number of other interesting questions arise. First is the question of whether the transmission of control pattern differs between the two companies, between the sales and sales support departments, or between high- and low-performing departments.

Between the two companies in the sample, there is no difference in the patterns of transmission. Both companies display a relatively consistent transmission of output control, and both show virtually no transmission of behavior control. Between the sales and the sales support departments, there are some consistent differences, in the direction first suggested by Ouchi and Maguire (1975). The transmission is somewhat more accurate (the correlations are higher by about .10) for both output control and for behavior control in the sales support departments. While the interpretation of this finding must be speculative, it suggests that in sales departments, where a hard measure of performance is ordinarily used, subordinates pay less attention to the control schemes of supervisors. They are less likely to accurately receive what their supervisor is sending, and they are less likely to emulate their supervisor in their own control attempts. This may be the freedom that accompanies a relatively unambiguous measure of performance. The professor in a research university is in a similar position. If he knows that the volume of his publications and the frequency with which they are cited determines his standing, then he will pay little or no attention to other control devices that the administration may be attempting to employ.

Perhaps more interesting is the similarity in transmission patterns between high-performing departments and low-performing departments. The results of this analysis are in Figure 3.

The departments were separated into high- or low-performing categories according to a self-reported measure of departmental performance (see Appendix 1). The rating used here was the department manager's rating of departmental performance, which is highly correlated with the assistant manager's rating ($r = .66$, $p < .001$) and less highly correlated with the ranking given by others ($r = .23$, $p < .001$). This measure of performance, like all self-report performance measures, is associated with job satisfaction ($r = .17$, $p < .01$), but the correlation is not close to unity.

The lack of difference in transmission patterns between

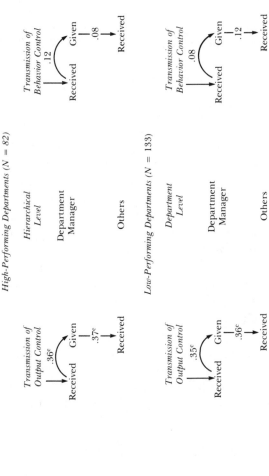

Figure 3. Transmission of Control in High- Versus Low-Performing Departments, Departments with Two Levels (*N* = 215) (Zero-Order Correlation Coefficients).

Note: Departments were separated into high or low performance categories according to a self-reported measure of departmental performance. The rating used here was the department manager's rating, which is significantly correlated with the ratings of assistant managers and of others. Like other self-report measures, this one is associated with job satisfaction (*r* = .17, *p* < .001).

These data include the departments that have three levels, although the middle level was excluded from this particular analysis. Results for only those departments that do not have assistant managers (*N* = 179) do not differ from these.

[a] *p* < .05.
[b] *p* < .01.
[c] *p* < .001.

high- and low-performing departments is surprising since common sense suggests that high-performing departments should have better consistency of control than low performers. The only observation that can be made in addition to that is that the significant interlevel effect for behavior control in Figure 1 seems to be due mostly to the low-performing departments. That observation is at least not refuted by the skimpy data on the three-level departments. After division on level of performance, there are only thirteen such high-performing departments and twenty-two low performers with three levels.

The data on the three-level departments suggest that behavior control is transmitted with significantly greater consistency in low-performing departments than in high-performing ones. The implications are tantalizing, but the data are insufficient to warrant further investigation or speculation.

Thus, we are left with two questions remaining. First, if behavior control is not determined by transmission through levels of a hierarchy, what does influence it? Can we identify some factors that will reveal the sources of behavior control and suggest why it is that interlevel linkage transmission is so loose? Second, how can it be that high- and low-performing departments do not differ in control? In particular, how can high-performing departments have the same lack of transmission of behavior control that characterizes the low performers? Is that interlevel transmission or tight linking of behavior control not necessarily desirable?

In order to get at these questions, which were raised by the transmission analysis, behavior control given by department managers was regressed on a set of variables that are of two kinds. First are variables that reflect the possibility that behavior control given is tailored to the specific control needs of a department; for example, the usefulness of observational monitoring ("information from observing"), the familiarity of the manager with the particular techniques used by his or her subordinates ("manager's expertise"), and the level of interdependence with other departments ("interdependence"), which might call for closer behavior control. Second were variables that reflect the freedom or autonomy of the manager to apply as much or as little behavior control as he or she wants to; for example, routineness of the manager's job ("percent routine"), which leaves more time for close monitoring; the manager's general freedom to try out innovations ("autonomy"); evidence of emulation (behavior control received), and a dummy variable to reflect possible company-wide common practice ("company"). These are the kinds of variables that reflect the local differences between subunits that may necessitate loose coupling. Perhaps "accurate transmission" is the wrong term for describing consistency of behavior control; perhaps it is not surprising that high and low performers fail to differ on this dimension. The results of this analysis are presented in Table 1.

The variables in Table 1 are essentially those discussed in Ouchi and Maguire (1975), except that two are renamed, one has been excluded, and one has been added. "Information from observing" was called "technical knowledge" in the earlier study, and "manager's expertise" was called "supervisor's expertise." "Hierarchical level" has been excluded, since this analysis occurs only at one level of the hierarchy, the department manager, and "autonomy" has been added. Description of the variables are in Appendix 1.

The findings are consistent with the unaggregated data reported in the earlier study. Department managers place greater emphasis on behavior control when they feel that it yields more information about performance, when their own task is more routine and therefore gives them more time for surveillance, when they are more knowledgeable about their subordinates' tasks (as reported by others), when they enjoy greater autonomy in initiating, when their tasks are more interdependent, and when they are in Company A as opposed to Company B. As expected, behavior control received has no effect on behavior control given.

High-performing departments differ from low-performing departments in what determines the use of behavior control by managers. In particular, in high-performing departments only, task interdependence and manager's expertise influence the giving of behavior control. In both high- and low-performing departments, the information from observing and company membership influence the giving of behavior control.

Thus high performers are distinguished by the fact that the use of behavior control is influenced by task interdependence,

Table 1. Regression on Behavior Control Given by Department Managers (Standardized Regression Coefficients).

Sample	Information from Observing	Percent Routine	Manager's Expertise	Behavior Control Received	Autonomy	Interdependence	Company	Multiple R^2
All departments (N = 207)	.16[b]	.14[b]	.14[b]	.01	.12[a]	.11[a]	.22[b]	.21
High performing departments (N = 80)	.18[a]	.06	.17[a]	.07	−.05	.21[a]	.27[b]	.26
Low performing departments (N = 127)	.15[a]	.17[a]	.12	−.02	.22[b]	.05	.20[b]	.21

[a]At least one and one-half times its standard error.
[b]At least two times its standard error.

which can be reasonably assumed to affect the need for control, and it is influenced by the expertise of the manager, with more knowledgeable managers applying more behavior control while less knowledgeable managers in high-performing departments apparently leave well enough alone and apply little behavior control. In low-performing departments, however, those considerations are unimportant, and the use of behavior control is tied to the manager's free time and his freedom from control from above. In such low performers, the manager with more time on his hands and greater autonomy will apply more behavior control, a condition that suggests the creation of feudal despots within the organization.

These factors together account for one fifth to one fourth of the variance in behavior control given by department managers. That is clearly not the majority of the variance, but the character of the variables is important to this argument. The factors that influence the giving of behavior control are closely tied to the characteristics of the tasks of superior and of subordinate. Inasmuch as tasks differ across levels of hierarchy, it would be difficult for a top manager to create behavior control procedures from his experience that could be applied down through the organization. In addition, there is a strong "company effect," which suggests an effect of company size (see Appendix 1, Item 10), as well as a norm of great or little behavior control in each firm. This effect is not transmitted through the hierarchy, except insofar as anticipatory socialization may be a hierarchical effect.

Regressions were also run with behavior control received as the dependent variable. These were run for all three levels of the hierarchy and by store, by sales and sales support, and by high- and low-performing departments. The results are similar to those for behavior control given, except that only one half as much of the variance in the dependent variable is explained. In every case, company membership has a large effect, although it is most pronounced for others (β = .25), then for department managers (β = .20), with the least effect on assistant managers (β = .10).

High- and low-performing departments are distinguished mostly by the fact that "manager's expertise" has a significant effect in high-performing departments and no effect in the low performers. Conversely, "percent routine" has a significant effect on behavior control received in low-performing departments, but no effect in the high performers.

Thus it appears that, because behavior control is tailored to the task needs of each department, it is not easily transmitted through an organizational hierarchy, nor should it be. A high emphasis on behavior control may be appropriate for one level but inappropriate for the level below. Thus, it is not surprising that high- and low-performing departments do not differ in the transmission of behavior control, although they do differ in the pattern of variables that determines the emphasis on behavior control.

Control in hierarchies is a many-faceted phenomenon, one that we have only begun to probe. That control passed only from one level to another rather than from a central point to all levels will suffer a great deal of loss is unquestionably true. Those who have advanced the arguments surrounding control loss in hierarchies pose a problem that organizations have obviously solved, however, since they often have as many as five or six levels. The dual hierarchy proposed by Evans (1975) is certainly one mechanism for minimizing control loss, but it is a sufficient protection only if one assumes levels of interlevel control that reach .9. As Franklin (1975) has suggested, such high levels of consistency in climate or managerial style between levels are unrealistic. On the other hand, if Franklin's more modest interlevel correlations are common, then we are back to the problem of an intolerable control loss, which large organizations manage to tolerate.

Switching from the traditional control-loss paradigm to the loose-coupling point of view, the evidence can be interpreted quite differently. The evidence cited in this chapter, as well as that produced by the control-loss literature, supports the view that consistency of objectives and actions, also called *accurate transmission of control,* does not characterize most organizations. Within the loose-coupling paradigm, however, that observation is neither puzzling nor troubling. Given that individual departments have needs for control that must be tailored to their specific tasks, people, histories, and microenvironments, it is desirable that each department follow somewhat different protocols for control. Thus inconsistency or loose coupling through the hierarchy is to be expected and encouraged.

If we invoke the lessons of Chapter Four, we might even suggest that output control in retail stores serves a function similar to that of categories and certification in schools. That is, the taking of measures of output from departments serves to legitimate the activity of the department in the eyes of the larger organization. Thus, we observe great consistency in the manner in which these measures are treated within any one company. At the same time, however, it must be emphasized that this measurement is largely ritual and that it has little bearing on the underlying effectiveness and objectives of the department in question. Rather, departmental effectiveness can be captured only by the more subtle and subjective process of behavior control, and it is through this mechanism that attention to the real objectives is influenced. Since behavior control techniques fail to meet external demands for comparability, precision, quantifiability, and other indications of "rationality," however, they cannot serve as the sole explicit mechanism of control. Thus the two mechanisms exist in a kind of symbiotic relationship, the one providing the legitimating ritual that justifies and protects the other, which produces the real control, which allows the organization to continue to survive in its complex, changing environment.

Appendix 1. Operational Measures.

1. *Output Control Given:* This variable is described in the text of this chapter.

Sample	Mean	SD	N
Department Managers	1.61	.86	215
Assistant Department Managers	1.68	.95	36

2. *Behavior Control Given:* This variable is described in the text of this chapter.

Sample	Mean	SD	N
Department Managers	4.53	2.47	208
Assistant Department Managers	4.57	1.21	36

3. *Output Control Received:*

Sample	Mean	SD	N
Department Managers	1.76	.91	215
Assistant Department Managers	1.39	.77	36
Others (first level)	1.68	.96	215

4. *Behavior Control Received:* This variable is described in the text of this chapter.

Sample	Mean	SD	N
Department Managers	2.39	2.47	214
Assistant Department Managers	3.97	2.80	36
Others (first level)	4.50	1.82	214

5. *Information from Observing:* "How much can you tell by watching the people who report directly to you while they are working?" (1 = I can't tell anything about how well they are doing their job by watching them, 4 = I can tell exactly whether they are doing their jobs properly or not.) For department managers only, in this study. (Mean = 2.40, SD = .59, N = 209.)

6. *Percent Routine:* "What percentage of your time on the job do you spend carrying out routine tasks?" (0–100 percent, in steps of 20 percent.)

Sample	Mean	SD	N
Department Managers	.44	.24	214
Assistant Department Managers	.52	.24	36
Others (first level)	.54	.18	214

7. *Manager's Expertise:* Ability of the department manager, as rated by his first-level subordinates (others). "Regardless of whether or not your supervisor checks often, how familiar is your supervisor with your on-the-job performance?" Asked of others only, for this study. (1 = not familiar at all, 5 = very familiar; mean = 3.51, SD = .54, N = 215.)

8. *Autonomy:* "How often are you given a chance to try out your own ideas on the job?" (1 = never, 5 = always.) For depart-

ment managers only, in this study. (Mean = 3.13, SD = .74, N = 214.)

9. *Interdependence:* "To what extent does your performance depend on how well others do their job?" (1 = almost none, 5 = a very great deal.) For department managers only, in this study. (Mean = 3.43, SD = .59, N = 214.)

10. *Company:* A dummy variable representing membership in either Company 1 or Company 2. Both were full-line, non-discount retail department stores in the midwestern United States. Company 1 had a main store and five branches, departments were drawn from the main store and from one branch. Company 2 was approximately six times the size of Company 1 in sales volume and in number of employees. Departments were drawn from the main store and from two branches. (Mean = 1.73, SD = .45, N = 215.)

11. *Departmental Performance:* "In terms of overall performance, how would you rate your department?" (1 = one of the very best; 5 = below average). For department managers only. (Mean = 1.88, SD = .81, N = 215.)

Appendix 2. Matrix of Zero-Order Correlation Coefficients.

	1	2	3	4	5	6	7	8	9	10	11	12
1. Output control given—D.M.	1.00	-.02	.34[b]	-.04	.68[c]	-.06	.55[c]	.09	.36[c]	.10	-.001	.01
2. Behavior control given—D.M.	208	1.00	.02	.09	-.08	.34[a]	.02	.25	.04	.12[a]	.28[c]	.19[b]
3. Output control received—D.M.	215	208	1.00	.04	.33[a]	-.05	.31[a]	.21	.26[c]	.08	.08	-.01
4. Behavior control received—D.M.	214	208	214	1.00	.08	.05	.18	.05	-.08	.09	.06	.15
5. Output control given—A.D.M.	36	35	36	36	1.00	.05	.49[c]	.14	.29[a]	.20	-.25	.31[a]
6. Behavior control given—A.D.M.	36	35	36	36	36	1.00	-.21	.37[a]	-.07	.33[a]	-.07	.32[a]
7. Output control received—A.D.M.	36	35	36	36	36	36	1.00	.16	.45[b]	.08	.13	.09
8. Behavior control received—A.D.M.	36	35	36	36	36	36	36	1.00	.24	.27	.13	.26
9. Output control received—others	215	208	215	214	36	36	36	36	1.00	.10	.04	.10
10. Behavior control received—others	214	207	214	213	36	36	36	36	214	1.00	.29[c]	.06
11. Information from observing—D.M.	209	207	209	208	36	36	36	36	209	208	1.00	.11
12. Percent routine—D.M.	214	207	214	213	36	36	36	36	214	213	209	1.00
13. Percent routine—A.D.M.	36	35	36	36	36	36	36	36	36	36	36	36
14. Percent routine—others	214	207	214	213	36	36	36	36	214	213	208	213
15. Manager's expertise—others	215	208	215	214	36	36	36	36	215	214	209	214
16. Autonomy—D.M.	214	208	214	214	36	36	36	36	214	213	208	213
17. Interdependence—D.M.	214	207	214	213	36	36	36	36	214	213	209	214
18. Company (dummy variable)	215	208	215	214	36	36	36	36	215	214	209	214

Note: Correlation coefficients in upper right triangle, sample size in lower left triangle. D.M. = Department Managers, A.D.M. = Assistant Department Managers.

[a] $p < .05$

[b] $p < .01$

[c] $p < .001$

Appendix 2 continued on page 288

Appendix 2. Matrix of Zero-Order Correlation Coefficients. (continued)

	13	14	15	16	17	18
1. Output control given—D.M.	.07	-.03	.06	.11	.13a	.06
2. Behavior control given—D.M.	.08	.12	.22c	.13a	.17b	.29c
3. Output control received—D.M.	-.01	-.05	.08	.04	-.02	.08
4. Behavior control received—D.M.	.19	.03	-.01	-.09	.04	.21c
5. Output control given—A.D.M.	-.20	-.01	.23	.11	-.04	.29a
6. Behavior control given—A.D.M.	.30a	.41b	-.20	.04	-.05	.36a
7. Output control received—A.D.M.	-.02	-.13	.15	.15	.03	.16
8. Behavior control received—A.D.M.	.02	.14	.01	-.08	-.04	.23
9. Output control received—others	-.14	-.10	-.07	.01	-.08	.16b
10. Behavior control received—others	.12	.07	.30c	.10	-.004	.33c
11. Information from observing—D.M.	.14	-.05	.25c	.12a	.17b	.19b
12. Percent routine—D.M.	-.04	.08	.01	-.03	.06	.14a
13. Percent routine—A.D.M.	1.00	.58c	.01	.10	-.05	.20
14. Percent routine—others	36	1.00	-.14a	.09	.05	.09
15. Manager's expertise—others	36	214	1.00	.08	-.03	.28c
16. Autonomy—D.M.	36	213	214	1.00	.21c	.08
17. Interdependence—D.M.	36	213	214	213	1.00	.05
18. Company (dummy variable)	36	214	215	214	214	1.00

Note. Correlation coefficients in upper right triangle, sample size in lower left triangle. D.M. = Department Managers, A.D.M. = Assistant Department Managers.

[a] $p < .05$

[b] $p < .01$

[c] $p < .001$

Appendix 3. Output Control Correlations: Original and Recoded Scales.

	Original Scale		Recoded Scale	
Output Control Given by Department Manager, with:				
Output control received by department manager	.70[b]	(51)	.34[a]	(215)
Output control received by others	.23	(48)	.36[b]	(215)
Behavior control given by department managers	.10	(79)	−.02	(208)
Behavior control received by others	.14	(78)	.10	(214)

Note: Number of cases (*N*) in parentheses.

[a]$p < .01$

[b]$p < .001$

11

Organizational Effectiveness and the Quality of Surgical Care in Hospitals

W. Richard Scott
Ann Barry Flood
Wayne Ewy
William H. Forrest, Jr.

For the past several years, we have been studying effectiveness in professional organizations. In particular, we have been examining the relation between the organizational characteristics of hospitals, together with their associated medical staffs and the quality of surgical care. In this chapter, we will describe selected results from our empirical investigations within the context of a more general consideration of some of the conceptual and methodological issues that arise in studying effectiveness in organizations in general and professional organizations in particular.

Because we will draw heavily on data from one of our hospital studies, a brief description of this investigation precedes a discussion of the more general issues.

The Seventeen-Hospital Study

The data base was collected as part of a larger investigation of factors affecting the quality of surgical care in hospitals conducted by the Stanford Center for Health Care Research (1974). Seventeen hospitals were surveyed in the original study, but data from only fifteen are included in some portions of the subsequent analysis, due to missing data from two hospitals. The study hospitals all participated in the Professional Activities Study (PAS) of the Commission on Professional and Hospital Activities (CPHA), a hospital chart-abstracting system that collects and summarizes selected information on all patient discharges from its more than 1,500 member hospitals. Sixteen of the original study hospitals were selected from a sample of all short-term voluntary hospitals participating in PAS as of 1973, the sample being stratified by size, expense ratio, and teaching status. The seventeenth, administratively linked to one of the sixteen, agreed to participate at its own expense. The seventeen study hospitals were not representative of all short-term, acute care hospitals in the United States. In partic-

The overall design and data collection reported here was carried out under Contract PH 42-63-65 with the National Center for Health Services Research, Health Resources Administration, U.S. Department of Health, Education, and Welfare, through the National Academy of Sciences-National Research Council under subcontract MS-46-72-12. The analyses described were carried out under Contract HRA-230-75-0173, with the Health Resources Administration.

We are indebted for assistance to all our colleagues at the Stanford Center for Health Care Research. We especially acknowledge the help of Byron William Brown, Jr., biostatistician, who contributed to statistical aspects of the research and the overall design, and Betty Maxwell, coordinator and administrative assistant, who provided innumerable support services critical to the success of this effort.

Several fellow sociologists assisted in the initial formulation of the study design and in the construction of data-gathering instruments. We acknowledge, with thanks, the contributions of Joan R. Bloom, Donald E. Comstock, Thomas G. Rundall, and Claudia Bird Schoonhoven.

ular, they were larger than the average for this type (304 versus
164 average number of beds). However, they were comparable to
the national average with respect to teaching status and expenses
per patient day. Six of the seventeen study hospitals, or 35 percent,
were affiliated with a medical school or had an approved and active
house staff program while 28 percent of comparable U.S. hospitals
were teaching hospitals in this sense. Study hospitals averaged $113
costs per patient day compared to $115 for similar U.S. hospitals.
Most important, the research team's goal of obtaining substantial
variance within the sample along these important dimensions was
achieved. For the study hospitals, size varied from 99 to 585 beds
and average costs from $78 to $154 per patient day. Ten states and
all major geographic regions within the continental United States
were represented.

Data on individual patients were collected prospectively on
all those undergoing one of fifteen selected surgical procedures.
We attempted to select procedures associated with a large number
of deaths and complications, whether due to high risk or high frequency, to focus on clearly defined procedures amenable to the
staging or estimation of surgical disease and to include procedures
involving a variety of organ systems, surgical subspecialties, and
types of patients. Information pertaining to the patient's condition
both before and after surgery were obtained by a technician trained
by the center staff and stationed in each study hospital. Of the
10,565 patients qualifying for study during the ten-month study
period, about 80 percent (8,593) were included. Losses were due
primarily to patient refusal (56 percent of the patients dropped),
surgeon refusal (19 percent), and lack of critical information (11
percent). The specific procedures studied and the distribution of
patients by procedure and by hospital are reported in Stanford
Center for Health Care Research (1974) and in Scott, Forrest, and
Brown (1976).

Information on the organizational characteristics, relating
both to the hospital and to the corporate organization of the medical and surgical staff, was obtained primarily through structured
interviews conducted by trained interviewers with key hospital and
medical personnel, who acted as expert informants describing the
structure and operation of their units. From twenty to thirty such

interviews were conducted during a two-week visit to each facility. In addition, questionnaires were distributed to several categories of personnel, including staff nurses on surgical wards, operating room staff, anesthetists, surgeons treating study patients, and staff members of key ancillary services such as radiology.

Finally, information on the characteristics of individual surgeons treating study patients was obtained from several sources. Data on education and specialization were obtained from either hospital records or from the American Medical Association (AMA). Surgeons treating study patients were asked to estimate the proportion of their practice carried on in the study hospital. And PAS patient records were utilized to develop, for each surgeon, measures of the total number of operations performed and the proportion of specialized operations performed during 1973. Altogether, 553 surgeons were identified as treating study patients in one of the fifteen hospitals, and some information was available for 98 percent of these surgeons. More detailed information concerning the types of data available and measures developed for surgeon characteristics is reported in Flood (1976). Additional information on specific aspects of the study will be described subsequently as it becomes relevant to the discussion.

Defining and Measuring Effectiveness

There is general agreement that effectiveness refers to the extent to which an organization is successful in realizing its goals. This relatively straightforward definition has become more complex and elusive over time as a consequence of several recent conceptual revolutions. These include the emergence of multiple perspectives or paradigms for analyzing organizations, the development of more complex conceptions of organizational goals, and changes in prevailing assumptions about the unity and coherence of organizations as systems of action. Each of these developments will be briefly described.

At the risk of some oversimplification, it is possible to identify three influential perspectives that have evolved to guide organizational analysis. Each is associated with a somewhat different view as to what are the prime goals of organizations, and hence each suggests a somewhat different conception of what is meant by effectiveness. The first and earliest perspective, the rational system model of organizations, views them as instruments for the attainment of specified goals (Gouldner, 1959). A mechanical model is implied in which goods or services are produced by the organization for external consumption, so that emphasis is placed on measures of productivity (number of units produced in a given time period) or efficiency (number of units of output produced for a given amount of input). The natural system model, developed in reaction to the rational model, views organizations as social units capable of achieving specified goals but simultaneously engaged in other activities required to maintain the unit itself (Etzioni, 1960). Employing an organic model, this perspective places great stress on the capacity of the system to survive. "Support" goals oriented to the maintenance of the system as system are viewed as of equal or greater importance to the more conventional "output" goals stressed by the rational model (Gross, 1968; Perrow, 1970). Specifically, attention is directed to such properties as participant satisfaction (a measure of whether inducements are sufficient to evoke adequate contributions from participants—see March and Simon, 1958), profitability (the excess of returns over expenditures), and survival itself. The third perspective, the open-systems model, views organizations as much more interdependent with environmental factors and as engaged in system elaboration as well as system maintenance (Buckley, 1967). The examination of input, throughput, and output processes of materials, information, and energy is central to the analysis. Effectiveness criteria proposed in the light of this model include adaptability or flexibility (the ability to adjust to changing environments (Georgopoulos and Tannenbaum, 1957) and maximization of bargaining position (as reflected in the ability of the organization to exploit its environment in the acquisition of scarce and valued resources—Yuchtman and Seashore, 1967). Clearly, what criteria of effectiveness are emphasized will depend in part on what perspective is selected to guide conceptualization and analysis.

These perspectives call attention to the different types of goals that may be embraced by or imputed to organizations. A somewhat related conceptual development emphasizes that organizations simultaneously pursue multiple objectives. Simon, with his focus on decision making in organizations, has emphasized that many goals in combination govern choices within organizations. He asserts (Simon, 1964, p. 7), "In the decision-making situations of real life, a course of action, to be acceptable, must satisfy a whole set of requirements or constraints. Sometimes one of these requirements is singled out and referred to as the goal of the action. But the choice of one of the constraints, from many, is to a large extent arbitrary. For many purposes, it is more meaningful to refer to the whole set of requirements as the (complex) goal of the action." This more complex view of goals is reinforced by the emerging view of organizations as composed of collections of subgroups of participants who possess various social characteristics, who are in differing social locations, and who exhibit divergent views and interests regarding what the organization is and what it should be doing. In this view, organizational goals are determined by negotiations among shifting coalitions of participants whose influence in decision making reflects their relative power in the system (see Cyert and March, 1963; Hickson and others, 1971; Pfeffer and Salancik, 1974). This conception of the organization as a political system can be expanded to include outside constituencies who hold goals "for" the organization (Thompson, 1967, p. 127) and who will attempt to see to it that their own interests are served. In this model, we would expect little commonality in the criteria employed by the various parties who assess organizational effectiveness. This expectation is confirmed in a study of small businesses by Friedlander and Pickle (1968), who report relatively low and sometimes negative correlations among effectiveness criteria imputed to owners, employees, creditors, suppliers, customers, governmental regulators, and the host community. They conclude that "organizations find it difficult to fulfill simultaneously the variety of demands made upon them" (Friedlander and Pickle, 1968, pp. 302-303).

Yet another development complicating our conception of effectiveness involves recent challenges to the assumption that organizations necessarily exhibit a unified or consistent set of objectives. The political models just reviewed allow for divergence and conflict among participants but presume their resolution through negotiation and power processes. In the end, the organization is presumed to pursue a single program. Alternative models now being explored suggest the utility of viewing some organizations as "organized anarchies" or as "loosely coupled" systems containing subunits that exhibit a high degree of autonomy and are capable of pursuing inconsistent objectives (see March and Olsen, 1976; Weick, 1976). This conception admits of the possibility that, with respect to any specific criterion of effectiveness, an organization could be both effective and ineffective depending on what component units were being evaluated. All of these and related theoretical issues render the determination of criteria to be employed in the examination of organizational effectiveness a complex and controversial undertaking.

An obvious lesson to be drawn from this review of conflicting conceptions that is applicable to our research on effectiveness in hospitals is that one must be careful not to overgeneralize from our results. Hospitals are multiproduct firms serving many goals, only one of which is patient care. And many types of care are provided in addition to surgical services. Our assessments are based on a subset of surgical procedures somewhat biased in the direction of greater difficulty: Performance on these procedures may not be predictive of performance on others. Another reason to be cautious in any conclusions drawn from our findings concerning relative effectiveness is that our research design picks up patients only after they have been scheduled for surgery. Since for many patient conditions the decision as to whether to operate is both controversial and critical, the design places important limitations on any conclusions we might draw about the quality of the surgical service as a whole. Other important bases for caution in interpreting results from this and similar studies are the many methodological issues that affect all studies of organizational effectiveness. We turn now to a brief review of some of these issues.

One of the most critical methodological decisions to be made in attempting to assess organizational effectiveness is the choice of the type of indicators to be employed. Three general types of indicators have been identified: those based on processes, on structures, and on outcomes (see Paul, 1956; Donabedian, 1966; Suchman, 1967). The advantages and disadvantages of each type will be briefly reviewed. Process measures are widely employed as indicators of organizational effectiveness. Emphasis is placed on the quantity or quality of activities of a given type. As Suchman (1967, p. 61) notes, this type of indicator "represents an assessment of input or energy regardless of output. It is intended to answer the questions 'What did you do?' and 'How well did you do it?'" Some process measures assess work quantity—for example, how many laboratory tests were ordered on the patients treated? Other process measures assess work quality—for example, what proportion of the tests ordered were deemed appropriate given the patient's condition? And still others assess quality control activities—for example, what proportion of the medical charts were reviewed in order to ensure the adequacy of current recording practices? When process measures are used to assess quality, it is important to emphasize that they evaluate conformity to a given standard of performance, but they do not evaluate the adequacy of the standards themselves. They are based on the assumption that it is known what activities are required to ensure effectiveness of performance. Such assumptions are always problematic when the work involved is complex and uncertain, as is the case with surgical care. Structural indicators assess the capacity of the organization for effective performance. Frequently employed measures include assessments of organizational facilities and staff qualifications. This type of measure forms the basis for accreditation reviews. The third type, outcome indicators, focuses attention on the characteristics of materials or objects on which the organization performs. In contrast to process measures, which assess effort, and structural measures, which assess potential or capacity, outcome indicators focus on what effects have actually been achieved. Changes in the patient's health status serve as important outcome indicators for assessing the effectiveness of the patient care program in hospitals. Outcome measures clearly provide important direct indicators of effectiveness but they also present serious problems of interpretation. Outcomes are never pure indicators of performance quality, since they reflect not only the care and accuracy with which work activities were carried out but also the current state of the technology and the characteristics of the organization's input and output environments. Thus, the patient's health status following surgery will reflect not only the quality of care rendered by the surgical staff and hospital personnel but also the current status of medical science with respect to the problem at hand as well as the patient's condition prior to surgery. To be valid indicators of organizational effectiveness, outcome measures need to take into account such factors.

There are varying advantages and disadvantages associated with each of the types of indicators. Each reflects a differing reality, and there may be little correspondence among them. Thus great potential, as reflected by structural measure, may not be actualized in practice; yet accumulated resources in the form of elaborate facilities and highly qualified personnel provide evidence of past performance and present competitive advantage. And careful studies in the area of medical care, for example, suggest that there is little if any correlation between process and outcome indicators of quality of care (Brook, 1973), but both provide important information about organizational performance. Our observation of organizations suggests that each type of indicator appeals to a different organizational constituency: Organizational managers tend to prefer structural measures, since these are most under their control and provide important resources for present and future activities; rank-and-file members of the organization usually prefer process measures because they exercise more control over these aspects of performance; and customers and clients emphasize outcome indicators, caring little for promise or effort but much for the effects achieved. (See Scott, 1977.)

For our study of hospital effectiveness, we decided to employ outcome indicators of effectiveness, assessing changes in the condition of the patient following surgery. Having selected a class of indicators, the specific measures must still be determined. An infinite number of possible measures exists depending on what types of outcomes are to be emphasized—for example, the extension of life versus the quality of life—and at what point in time the measures are taken. We decided to measure the quality of surgical care using measures of both mortality and morbidity and to gather the data for morbidity at the seventh and fortieth day postsurgically or at the time of discharge, if earlier, and on mortality at the fortieth day. Measures of mortality are highly reliable, but mortality is a relatively rare event. For the 8,593 study patients, only 224 or roughly 2.8 percent died within forty days of surgery. A further problem is that mortality is a more likely outcome for some types of surgery than for others, so that its sensitivity as an indicator of effectiveness is highly variable. The forty-day period was selected to balance an interest in obtaining data on mortality over as long a period as might reasonably be attributed to the surgical event against the recognition that causal arguments linking surgical care and outcome weaken with the passage of time. Since some hospitals are known to "improve" their mortality rate by transferring mortally ill patients to other facilities, we followed patients after discharge up to the fortieth day to determine their mortality status. This proved to be a very expensive but worthwhile process, since 25 percent of study patients who died did so after discharge from the hospital but within the forty-day period. Morbidity measures were added to deal with the problem of the insensitivity of the mortality measures to more subtle changes in the health status of patients. Ratings of morbidity were obtained from nurses on the patient care ward on the seventh day. The seventh day was chosen for this assessment to ensure that most study patients would still be hospitalized and to tap postoperative condition early but not immediately following surgery. In addition to these ratings by staff nurses, we recorded the number of catheters, monitors, or other types of life support systems attached to the patient at the seventh day as a more objective indicator of morbidity. Finally, all patients contacted at the fortieth day were asked to report their own perception of their health status on a scale measuring their return to normal functioning.

Two sets of outcome measures were defined on the basis of these data:

Set A: Binary Measures

1. Death within forty days of surgery versus all other outcomes
2. Death within forty days of surgery or severe morbidity at the seventh day versus all other outcomes
3. Death within forty days of surgery or catheters or monitors at the seventh day versus all other outcomes

4. Death within forty days of surgery or severe or moderate morbidity at the seventh day versus all other outcomes
5. Death within forty days of surgery or incomplete return to function at forty days versus all other outcomes

Set B: Interval Measures

6. Mortality scale, with heavy weight given to mortality and slight weight given to morbidity
7. Intermediate scale, with more weight given to mortality and less weight given to morbidity
8. Morbidity scale, with slightly more weight given to mortality than to morbidity

In order to permit valid comparison of outcome rates across hospitals, all of these measures were adjusted to take into account differences in patient condition. The approach used was that of indirect standardization, which involves the computation of estimated probability of each type of outcome for each patient. These estimates were empirically derived through the use of either logistic or linear equations relating variables describing patient condition to each type of outcome measure. Details of these adjustment procedures are reported elsewhere (Stanford Center for Health Care Research, 1974, 1976; Flood, 1976) but will be briefly described here. First, all study patients within a given surgical category were analyzed together, without regard to hospital. The dependence of each type of outcome (for example, death within forty days) on selected prediction variables was then estimated by fitting either a logistic function to the data (in the case of Set A measures) or a linear function (in the case of Set B measures). Prediction variables utilized were the various measures of patient condition, including physical status, stage of surgical disease, age, sex, stress level, and insurance coverage. Second, the coefficients estimated in this manner were then applied to each patient in order to predict, based on his specific characteristics, the probability of each type of outcome. Third, adjusted outcome measures for each patient were obtained by comparing the expected to the observed outcome: For the Set A measures, adjusted outcomes were expressed as ratios of observed to expected outcomes; for the Set B measures, expected outcome scores were subtracted from observed scores. Finally, for some analyses, patient scores were summed across the fifteen operations for all the patients within a given hospital, providing a summary measure of how good were the outcomes experienced in that hospital relative to those outcomes expected based on the characteristics of the patients treated. One further adjustment was made for the Set A measures only. Since the frequency with which the study operations were performed varied considerably among the seventeen hospitals, some estimates were more reliable than others, due to variation in sample size. A Bayesian procedure was employed to adjust all outcome measures for their relative reliability, which had the effect of moving the less reliable estimates toward the middle of the distribution.

Study hospitals were judged to differ significantly in quality of surgical care as measured by adjusted outcomes for six of our eight measures. The first outcome measure, death within forty days, failed to exhibit significant differences among hospitals, primarily because of the small number of deaths observed in the study. The fifth outcome measure, based largely on patient's report of return to function also did not exhibit significant differences. All other measures indicated substantial variation among study hospitals. A reasonable estimate of the extent of these differences is that patients in the poorest hospitals experienced rates of adverse events—mortality, severe morbidity, or moderate morbidity—between two and three times as high as patients in the best hospitals in the sample.

Even though our measures of effectiveness focus on a relatively specific aspect of the performance of the hospital and although we have limited our data set to indicators of outcomes, a number of specific measures have been developed, and many more could be generated. However, it is quite possible that our results and conclusions may vary depending on which measure is selected. To illustrate this possibility, it is instructive to examine at the hospital level the intercorrelations among the outcome measures developed. Table 1 reports Spearman rank order correlations among six of the outcome measures. Correlations among the first three measures, especially 1 and 3, were surprisingly low, given the built-in association among these binary measures as a nested series.

Close examination of Measures 1 and 3 indicate that they were each dominated by different types of surgical procedures: Most of the mortality occurring in the study was accounted for by such operations as amputation of a lower limb and craniotomy, while moderate morbidity was a frequent outcome in the much more common operations, such as prostatectomy and biliary tract surgery. In short, although we had combined data across types of operations to develop a more general measure of quality of surgical care, measures from Set A tended to reflect differences in outcomes among operations as well as differences among hospitals. And one explanation for the absence of any association between Measures 1 and 3 is that hospitals that performed well on types of surgery associated with relatively high mortality rates were not any more likely to perform well on less serious types of surgery. Thus, for these measures, hospitals judged effective by one outcome measure would not necessarily be effective by another. Measures from Set B reduce the built-in association between surgical category and type of outcome in two ways. First, as already noted, the interval measures do not focus on any one outcome or combination of outcomes, but allow each possible outcome to have some (varying) weight in each measure. Second, all of the variables were standard Z scored for each surgical category before being combined into overall measures of surgical quality. This approach gave equal weight to all operations and to all outcomes, focusing attention only on whether hospitals did better or worse than expected. Table 1 reveals that while the different weights employed did give greater or lesser emphasis to different types of outcomes—(note the relatively high level of association between Measures 1 and 6, 2 and 7, and 3 and 8)—they also remained highly intercorrelated (note the high correlations among measures 6, 7, and 8).

　　　Which measure is to be preferred? That would seem to depend on what questions are being asked of the data. If one wished to focus on the quality of surgical care in general, then less serious patient outcomes can be equally revealing and have the advantage of being more numerous so that Measures 3 or 7 or 8 would be preferable. The important point is that different information is provided by each measure, so that thought should be given to the selection of any measure or set of measures.

Table 1. Interrelation of Selected Adjusted Outcome Measures for the Seventeen Hospitals (Spearman Rank Order Correlation).

	Set A: Binary Measures			Set B: Interval Measures		
	1 Mortality only	2 Mortality and severe morbidity	3 Mortality, severe and moderate morbidity	6 Mortality scale	7 Intermediate scale	8 Morbidity scale
1		.45	−.10	.60	.30	.08
2			.34	.68	.67	.43
3				.60	.82	.95
6					.90	.75
7						.93

Explaining Differences in Effectiveness

Given that the study hospitals differed in effectiveness as assessed by one or more measures of adjusted outcomes, how are such differences to be explained? As might be expected, our theoretical approach emphasized organizational variables. Because our indicators of effectiveness relate to quality of surgical care, we focused on those hospital units and personnel most intimately associated with the care of surgical patients—surgeons, the operating room, and surgical wards—as well as the more general features of the hospital context. Our conceptions and data base emphasize that hospitals are comprised of multiple types of organizational units whose structural features may not correspond. We distinguished among hospital-wide organization, organization of the medical and surgical staff, organization of the operating room, and the organization of the individual wards. Measures of such structural characteristics as differentiation, coordination, centralization of decision making, and formalization for each of these types of units revealed relatively low intercorrelations of similar variables across units, suggesting that hospitals may be "loosely coupled" or, at least, highly differentiated organizations (Scott, Forrest, and Brown, 1976, pp. 82-84).

Most of our analyses have been conducted at the individual patient level because we believe that the causal process operates at this level and because this allows us to utilize more specific and accurate data. Patients in hospitals are not "treated" by the entire organizational structure and its associated staff but rather receive care from specific physicians and staff in particular units. Tracking data permits us to assign each patient not only to a specific hospital but also to a particular surgeon and surgical ward. Another reason for preferring the patient level of analysis is to avoid the biases inherent in aggregating these data to the hospital level (see Hannan, Freeman, and Meyer, 1976).

Because we are dealing with professional organizations—organizations in which the central tasks are performed by professionals—it was important that we attempt to determine the extent to which individual professionals (in our case, surgeons) influence the outcome in comparison to the influence of organizational features. It can be argued that surgeons should exert the major impact on adjusted patient outcomes, with hospitals providing a general context within which these individual professionals conduct their activities but exerting relatively little effect on the quality of the work performed. Surgeons are the prototype of the independent professional, trained to exercise discretion and empowered to mobilize the necessary resources to provide quality care. In this view, the hospitals serve, at best, as the "doctor's workshop," a storehouse of facilities, resources and ancillary staff activated and controlled by the individual surgeon. To examine this possibility, a hierarchical two-way analysis of variance was carried out comparing surgeon with hospital effects on adjusted patient outcomes. Appropriate data were available for fifteen hospitals, 553 surgeons, and 7,328 patients for this analysis. The hierarchical version of the analysis of variance was selected to take into account the fact that a given surgeon only practiced in one study hospital. The procedure can be viewed as decomposing any differences found among surgeons into a component for variation among surgeons within a hospital and a component for variation among hospitals, after taking the surgeons into consideration. (For a general discussion of this procedure and computing formulas, see Kempthorne, 1952.) The results of this test showed strongly significant differences among hospitals in the adjusted outcomes of patients using the intermediate scale (Measure 7) after removing the variation in outcomes explained by surgeon differences within hospitals, but no significant differences attributable to individual surgeons within hospitals (Flood and others, 1977). These results are consistent with Freidson's (1970) theoretical arguments that work settings have a stronger impact on professional performance than individual professionals' characteristics, including the skills and values acquired from past socialization. And they are also consistent with the findings of Rhee (1977), who, in a somewhat similar study, examined the effect of physician and hospital characteristics on quality of medical care as assessed by process indicators.

Although the characteristics of individual surgeons may not produce a significant difference in the quality of surgical care once hospital characteristics are taken into account, the question remains as to what features of hospital organization are the most important determinants of quality of care. Analyses directed toward answering this question are by no means completed, but early findings suggest that the organization of the surgical staff is a highly salient feature. Using multiple-regression techniques and after taking into account such general hospital features as size, teaching status, and expenditures per patient (only the latter variable is significantly associated with better quality care for our study hospitals), a great many of the variables used to measure coordination and control within the surgical staff proved to be positively correlated with higher-quality surgical care. Specifically, the greater the proportion of contract physicians—an indicator that Roemer and Friedman (1971) regard as the best single measure of degree of regulation of the medical staff—the more strict the admission requirements for new members of the surgical staff and the greater the power of the surgical staff over tenured surgeons, the better the quality of surgical care as measured by the intermediate scale of outcomes (Measure 7—see Flood and Scott, 1977). These and similar results suggest that the corporate organization of the professional staff is an important factor in the effectiveness of professional organizations.

~~~~~~

12

Uncertainty and Social Influence in Organizational Decision Making

~~~~~~

Jeffrey Pfeffer
Gerald R. Salancik
Huseyin Leblebici

All organizations face the task of allocating scarce resources. In a social setting dominated by large organizations (Boulding, 1953a; Presthus, 1962), these organizational allocation decisions increasingly affect the allocation of society's resources. As Pondy has noted, "To the extent that the social sciences regard the proper use of society's resources as an important problem, the allocation of resources within large organizations through administrative

This chapter was originally published in *Administrative Science Quarterly*, June 1976.

mechanisms becomes an important subproblem" (1970, p. 272). The questions of who makes the allocation decisions and by what criteria are similarly important, as the bases for the allocations become the bases for shaping and stratifying social systems. Resource allocation is an inherently political process, as Lasswell (1936) noted when he described politics as the study of who gets what, when, and how. In spite of the well-established theoretical perspective of decision making (March and Simon, 1958; Cyert and March, 1963), and in spite of the importance of resource allocation decisions made within organizations, there have been few empirical examinations of organizational decision making or resource allocation within organizations. "Although sociologists have devoted considerably more attention to studying the structure and behavior of formal organizations than other social scientists, they have tended not to focus on the resource allocation problem" (Pondy, 1970, p. 271).

In the study of social structures, the basis for the allocation of rewards has been of major concern. A cornerstone of Weber's (1947) theory of bureaucracy was impersonal evaluations of organizationally relevant performance as a basis for promotion and the distribution of rewards within organizations. Udy (1959a; 1962) argued that one of the stages of bureaucratization occurs when organizations become separate from society, so that rewards and status are based on organizationally relevant performance, not on status in the larger social system. Economists, in their theory of business organizations, have posited similar universalistic objective criteria, such as profitability, as the bases for organizational decision making (see Simon, 1959).

More recent writers have argued that organizations do not necessarily make decisions using universalistic, objective criteria, nor even with regard to the welfare of the organization as a whole. Perrow (1972, p. 13) has noted that organizational members are in a continual contest for control over organizational resources and that an inevitable consequence of this struggle is the use of particularistic criteria in decision making—criteria that derive from the particular perspectives or goals of the contending groups. Cyert and March (1963) have argued that organizations are coalitions of interests, with decisions made through a process of bargaining over policy commitments. And Thompson and Tuden (1959) have ar-

gued that the use of computational, bureaucratic decision procedures is limited to the case when there is agreement on both goals
and the connections between actions and consequences.

Bureaucratic versus nonbureaucratic, sponsorship versus
contest (Turner, 1960), universalism versus particularism—all of
these concepts focus on the extent to which relatively bureaucratic,
universal criteria are used in organizational decision making. It is
likely that organizations employ both universalistic and particularistic criteria in their decision making. The purpose of this chapter
is to present one study that directly addresses the issue of the conditions under which universalistic or particularistic criteria are
used more. From various theories in sociology and social psychology, it appears that one of the conditions that affects the use of
particularistic criteria in decision making is the relative uncertainty
associated with the decision. We argue that with the availability of
consensually agreed-on, well-defined objective standards for evaluation, decision-making outcomes will be based more on such standards. Conversely, in the absence of shared objective criteria, processes of social influence will account for more of the variance in
the decision outcomes. This argument is explored with reference
to eight years of National Science Foundation (NSF) grant allocations in four social sciences that vary in the degree of their paradigm development, but we argue that the hypothesis would hold
in a variety of situations in which the uncertainty confronted by
the decision maker varies.

Organizational Decision Making

Examinations of organizational decision making typically
have questioned the validity of rational choice models as descrip-
tors of organizational reality. Cyert, Simon, and Trow (1956), for
instance, took issue with the view that business organizations make
decisions solely on such universalistic criteria as profitability. In a
subsequent article, Cyert, Simon, and Trow (1956), examining four
decisions in three firms, concluded that expectations (forecasts)
were developed to justify the decision that was desired, rather than
having the decision based on the economic forecasts. A similar
point concerning the retrospective nature of meaning was made

by Weick (1969), who noted that new information was integrated using the information and cognitive set one already possessed. Simon (1959) also criticized many of the implicit assumptions underlying models of rational choice. He noted that persons had limited cognitive capabilities and tended to engage in satisficing rather than maximizing behavior as a consequence of these limitations.

Cyert and March (1963) proposed an alternative conceptualization of organizations and organizational decision making. An organization was considered to be a coalition (March, 1962), within which many differing interests were represented. Decision-making procedures were constrained by limited search and information-processing capabilities and were guided by the need to reduce the possible organizational conflict inherent in the differing demands of groups in the coalition. Within this environment, Cyert and March proposed that organizations use standard operating procedures and rely heavily on precedent, attend to goals sequentially, engage in satisficing behavior, and never fully resolve the implicit conflicts arising from the different preferences of various organizational participants.

Cyert and March supported their conceptualization with a simulation model, and simulations of organizational decision making have been virtually the only reported tests of some of the ideas they proposed (Crecine, 1967; Gerwin, 1969). One empirical study is Stagner's survey of 217 executives in 109 companies. The executives reported that "strong divisions within the company may get their way without regard to the welfare of the whole" (Stagner, 1969, p. 12), suggesting that organizational decisions are occasionally based on the particularistic interests of coalitions within the organizations.

Uncertainty and Decision Making

In making decisions concerning the allocation of rewards or resources within organizations, there may be varying degrees of uncertainty present. Recognizing the importance of uncertainty for decision making, Thompson and Tuden (1959) argued that, depending on the nature and extent of social consensus, decision procedures would vary. They noted that computational methods of decision making would probably be employed when there was consensus about goals and consensus about the causal relations between actions and results. If there were no consensus about goals, then the use of universalistic criteria is difficult because there is disagreement about what criteria are appropriate. If there is a lack of consensus concerning causal relations between actions and consequences, then the use of universalistic criteria is difficult because the means of achieving the criteria are not unambiguously perceived. Thompson and Tuden argued that, when goal consensus was lacking, compromise would be the decision strategy employed, while, in the absence of agreement about the connections between goals and actions, judgment would be employed.

That the nature of decision making varies with the degree of relative social consensus or uncertainty has been expressed in both the sociological and social psychological literature. Festinger (1950; 1954), in developing this theory of social comparison, argued that people have a need for self-evaluation and that a person's perceptions and opinions about his own worth and the nature of reality were partly developed through comparison with the capabilities and beliefs of others. The tendency to compare oneself and one's beliefs with others depended on one's relative certainty. Festinger (1950, p. 273) wrote, "It also follows that the less 'physical reality' there is to validate the opinion or belief, the greater will be the importance of the social referent, the group, and the greater will be the forces to communicate." In the absence of objective standards, social comparison is used to stabilize opinions and decide on actions (Festinger, 1954). Or, as Perrow has written, "Competence is hard to judge, so we rely upon familiarity" (1972, p. 11).

In developing theories about social stratification and status, sociologists have also addressed the issue of the use of universalistic versus the use of socially derived criteria. Parsons and Shils (1951) defined universalism in terms of the social relationships that exist among the actors. Blau (1964, p. 265) wrote that "the differentiating criterion is whether the standards that govern people's orientation to each other are *dependent* on or *independent* of the particular relations that exist between them." Blau argued that defining universalism and particularism in terms of social relationships

could, potentially, yield an operational measure of the concept. He
stated that

> The specific differentiating criterion, therefore, is
> whether the value standards that govern the orientations
> and associations among people are *independent or not inde-*
> *pendent of the relationship between their status attributes.* For in-
> stance, if the members of a community, regardless of their
> own age, express highest regard for the maturity of old age,
> or if all age groups tend to value youth most highly, age
> would constitute a universalistic standard. But if most peo-
> ple express a preference for their own age group—the old
> thinking more highly of older people, and the young, of
> younger ones—age would constitute a particularistic stan-
> dard. In other words, attributes that are valued by people
> regardless of whether they possess them reflect universal-
> istic values, whereas preferences for attributes like one's
> own reflect particularistic values [Blau, 1964, p. 266].

Given the theoretical precedent for expecting a relationship
between uncertainty and the use of social criteria in decision making, we can hypothesize that the use of particularistic criteria in
organizational decision making will be a direct function of the uncertainty in the decision situation. Since we define uncertainty as
a lack of consensus about purposes and the means of achieving
them, it should be obvious that the ability of a decision maker to
apply universalistic, objective criteria is impaired. Yet the need to
make a decision remains. The use of particularistic criteria, such
as social similarities and social relationships, provides a means for
making the decision and resolving the uncertainty. As Festinger's
notions of social comparison suggest, when you don't know what
to do because there are no clear objective standards to guide your
behavior, you look around and observe what others like yourself
are doing, and you then employ this social standard to reduce your
uncertainty. It should be noted that this situation does not require
any assumptions about decision makers acting out of either self-
aggrandizement or intentional favoritism. Whether or not these
factors are present in various organizational decision contexts is
irrelevant to our hypothesis that social criteria will be used in decision making as a function of the uncertainty present. This is

because it is unlikely that individual self-interest will vary as a function of uncertainty. Individual self-interest is, we suggest, another factor, orthogonal to uncertainty, that affects the criteria used in decision making.

Decision Making in Science

To test our hypothesis that the use of social influence in organizational decisions varies with uncertainty, we examined National Science Foundation grant allocations. This is a relatively large organization that is fundamentally important in the social system of basic science. It is a public organization, so data about its resource allocation decisions are available. It has elements of both the bureaucratic and coalitional models of organizations, as it is both a government agency and a loose coupling of interest groups vying for scarce monetary resources. Most importantly, grant allocation decisions are made through divisions which represent different scientific disciplines. These disciplines, in turn, vary in the relative consensus and uncertainty associated with their respective paradigms. Consequently, explicit comparisons of relatively similar decisions within the same organization are possible, and these comparisons provide a context for testing our hypothesis concerning the use of social influence.

Lodahl and Gordon (1972) have operationalized the concept of paradigm development in science in a manner consistent with our arguments concerning uncertainty. Paradigm development was measured by the degree of consensus within the field concerning what should or should not be taught and what is good or poor research. A high degree of paradigm development "enhances predictability in at least two ways: (1) it provides an accepted and shared vocabulary for discussing the content of the field; and (2) it provides an accumulation of detailed information (scientific findings) on what has been successful in the past" (Lodahl and Gordon, 1972, p. 61). Given their measurement of the concept of paradigm development, it can be argued that to the extent a field is paradigmatically well developed, uncertainty in decision making concerning that field is reduced.

Decision makers contending with the resource allocation

decisions must ultimately resolve uncertainty and make some decisions. In scientific fields with well-developed paradigms, resource
allocations can be made using the consensually agreed-on standards of evaluation, with less dependence on the particular persons
making the decisions. Conversely, in scientific fields without well-
developed paradigms, or consensus concerning topics, methodologies, or content, objective criteria are (1) unlikely to be widely
shared and (2) unlikely to reduce uncertainty. In these instances,
decisions should depend more on the particular social relationships
existing between the decision makers and those who benefit from
the decisions. The argument is consistent with the findings in social
psychology that, on an individual level, social influence operates
most in situations of social uncertainty (for example, Jones and
Gerard, 1967; Kiesler and Kiesler, 1969). Our argument is that
familiarity, or social influence, will be used along with objective
criteria in decision making and will be used relatively more in scientific fields of less-developed paradigms.

The existing literature in the sociology of science does not,
for the most part, explicitly compare fields for their use of decision
criteria. But those empirical studies that have examined decision
making in science are not inconsistent with the arguments we have
made. Hargens and Hagstrom (1967) examined sponsored versus
contest mobility for 576 natural scientists. They found, after controlling for productivity, that the prestige of the person's doctoral
institution had a significant effect on the prestige of his or her
placement. While the placement impact of doctoral institution
prestige was greatest for new graduates, a significant association
$\gamma = .21$) was also found between the prestige of a person's doctoral
institute and the prestige of his or her affiliation ten years later
(Hargens and Hagstrom, 1967, p. 35). In a study of the mobility
of 682 new Ph.D.s who received their doctorates in 1957, Hargens
(1969, p. 33) found that both regional and prestige-level factors
affected mobility. In a cross-discipline comparison, Hargens observed more inbreeding (hiring of one's own graduates) among the
social sciences and humanities than among the physical and biological sciences. Hargens also found that "Top prestige universities
are more likely to recruit from other top prestige universities in
different regions in the physical and biological sciences (41 percent)

than in the social sciences and humanities (18 percent)" (1969, p. 34). If one assumes that institutional or regional inbreeding is evidence of more particularistic standards, then Hargens' data are consistent with our hypothesis. In the physical sciences, with their greater paradigm development, there is less inbreeding and less within-region hiring than in the social sciences.

Cole and Cole (1973), although concluding that the stratification system in science is highly universalistic, report data on a sample of 120 university physicists that indicate that neither the quality nor quantity of research is highly correlated with the academic rank of the department; rather, the rank of the department where the scientist obtained his doctoral degree is an important determinant of the rank of his current affiliation. These results would tend to indicate that even in the most highly developed sciences, some evidence of the use of nonuniversalistic criteria can be found. And Crane (1965) has reported that, controlling for productivity, scientists at major high-prestige universities received more recognition than scientists at universities that enjoyed less prestige.

The use of social criteria in publication decisions have also been examined by various authors, although again, without cross-discipline comparisons. Yotopoulos (1961) studied three economics journals and found that journals edited at a particular university tended to publish higher than chance proportions of articles by authors from that university. Shamblin (1970) reported a similar finding for sociology. Critiquing a study by Knudsen and Vaughan (1969), he wrote, "The University of North Carolina ranked sixth in publications by faculty and first in publications by recent graduates in *Social Forces*, a journal edited at the University of North Carolina. Additionally, the three top publishing schools in *Social Forces*, the official publication of the Southern Sociological Society, are southern schools that rank low on all other scales, while the authors' (Knudsen and Vaughan, 1969) top four schools rank no higher than eleventh. The University of Chicago ranked first in publications by faculty and first in publications by recent graduates in the *AJS* (*American Journal of Sociology*), the journal edited at the University of Chicago" (Shamblin, 1970, p. 155).

The bias occasionally evident in journal publication does not necessarily indicate intentional favoritism. Similar evidence of particularism can be observed under anonymous reviewing conditions. In fields where there are no universal standards to aid the evaluation process, one could expect similarity in intellectual training to affect decisions. As Crane argued, "First, doctoral training may influence editorial readers to respond favorably to certain aspects of methodology, theoretical orientation and mode of expression in the writings of those who have received similar training. Secondly, both doctoral training and academic affiliations probably influence the personal ties which a scientist forms with other scientists, and these in turn may affect his evaluation of scientific work" (1967, p. 196). Crane concluded that "the academic characteristics of authors of articles selected for publication by scientific journals are similar to the characteristics of the editors of the journals and that anonymity does not affect this relationship" (1967, p. 199). Crane's data, therefore, also are consistent with the argument developed. We have proposed that the social influence process is one of informational social influence, occurring because of the need to reduce uncertainty in low-paradigm fields. In lower-paradigm fields, without consensus on research topics or strategies, backgrounds would affect evaluations more than in high-paradigm fields, regardless of the anonymity of the review process.

In a cross-discipline study, Yoels (1973) reported that "the selection of editors for social science journals is more subject to the influence of 'particularistic' criteria than is the case for the physical and natural sciences" (1973, p. 5). Yoels examined the extent to which editors-in-chief from Columbia and Harvard were likely to select graduates from Columbia and Harvard when making editorial appointments. Since Lodahl and Gordon (1972) report higher paradigm development for the physical and natural sciences, the data developed by Yoels is consistent with the argument made here that social influence will account for more of the decision outcomes under conditions of uncertainty or low paradigm development.

The studies reviewed indicate that the bases for allocations in science is an issue that is both important and unresolved. Those studies that provide any comparisons across fields (Yoels, 1973; Hargens, 1969) indicated that, as hypothesized, particularistic, social influence criteria were more evident in the low-paradigm fields. While the studies reviewed are not inconsistent with our expectations, they were not conducted to test our hypothesis, with explicit attempts to rule out reasonable alternative explanations.

Method and Data

In order to further explore the effect of uncertainty on the use of decision criteria, data were collected on National Science Foundation grant allocations for the period 1964–1971 (National Science Foundation, 1964–1971a). The use of institutional social affiliation as a particularistic criteria is examined by correlating institutional membership on NSF advisory panels with institutional receipt of NSF grants. The hypothesis that social factors will be more evident in decision making as a function of uncertainty is tested by comparing four disciplines that vary in paradigm development, as measured by Lodahl and Gordon (1972): the Division of Economics, the Division of Political Science, and the Division of Sociology and Social Psychology. To distinguish between the two fields in the Division of Sociology and Social Psychology, the principal investigators on grants were identified as being in one field or the other on the basis of American Psychological Association and American Sociological Association directories. Data collected included the name of the investigator, his or her academic affiliation, the amount of the grant, and the length of time of the grant.

By confining the study to four social sciences, the hypothesis is put to a severe test. There are many differences between the physical and social sciences besides the level of paradigm development, including the level of internal and external funding (Lodahl and Gordon, 1973). Restricting analyses to social sciences avoids some of these other differences. Moreover, since there is a greater difference between the physical and the social sciences than among the social sciences in the degree of paradigm development (Lodahl and Gordon, 1972), we have restricted the variance in our independent variable and thus have subjected the hypothesis to a more stringent test.

For a variety of reasons, the unit of analysis employed in this study of resource allocation is the institution rather than the individual investigator. Concepts such as the size of the department only have meaning on an institutional level, and the measure of familiarity used in the study is defined on an organizational level of detail. Further, it is more likely that there are applications from institutions on a more constant basis than from individual researchers, thus making it more plausible to infer that variations in grant allocations reflect variations in decisions rather than merely requests. Individuals operate as agents who both reflect and sustain departmental characteristics of quality. Aggregating the data to the departmental level reduces error variance associated with individual units. This practice is encountered frequently in the literature of the sociology of science where many measures have been defined on an institutional level. A departmental level of analysis is actually less aggregated than the results reported by Crane (1967), Hargens (1969), and Hargens and Hagstrom (1967), all of whom dealt with broad classes of universities.

The dependent variable is the proportion of funds received by each university in each of the four fields separately for each of the eight years studied. If a department received funds at least once during the period, it was assumed to be eligible throughout the period and was included in the sample. During the period 1964 to 1971, sixty departments of political science, eighty-four departments of economics, seventy-two departments of sociology, and ninety-seven departments of psychology (social) received at least one grant from NSF. Within the dependent variable, two components were further identified. Grants for thesis research were separated from grants for other research. The results for total research funds reflect essentially the analysis of grants for nonthesis research, as the amount of grants for thesis research was a very small component of the total (less than 1 percent, for example, in economics). Resource allocations were defined on a proportional basis each year to remove the effects of growth and inflation.

We have argued that there are two contending bases for resource allocation decisions, bureaucratic, universalistic criteria, and particularistic, social influence criteria. Two measures of the bureaucratic criteria were employed. One was the quality of the particular departments assessed by obtaining the department's rank in the 1964 (Cartter, 1966) and 1969 (Roose and Andersen, 1970) lists compiled by the American Council on Education (ACE).[1]

A variety of investigators in sociology have demonstrated a relationship between the Cartter report rankings and other measures of departmental quality, including student-faculty ratios (Janes, 1969; Lavender and others, 1971), hiring patterns (G. R. Gross, 1970; Schichor, 1970), individual prestige (Lightfield, 1971), and research productivity (Knudsen and Vaughan, 1969; Glenn and Villemez, 1970; Lightfield, 1971). Hagstrom (1971) found significant relations between the Cartter rankings and indicators of department size, research production, research opportunities, faculty background, and faculty awards and offices. In economics, Moore (1973) and Siegfried (1972) have observed strong correlations between the rankings of departments in economics and departmental contributions to the major journals.

We are not arguing that the ACE rankings are a perfect measure of objective departmental quality. However, given the extensive literature indicating its correlations with other possible indicators of quality and research scholarship, we argue that this is one of the more adequately validated measures. Moreover, in order for a standard of evaluation to be universalistic, it is only necessary that it be equally accepted regardless of social relationship, not that it be perfectly valid as a measure. Using Blau's (1964, p. 266) discussion, as long as age is equally valued by all, it is universalistic, regardless of whether or not age is, objectively, a valid indicator of wisdom, ability, and so on. In the present instance, it is likely that the Cartter report rankings are generally accepted—indeed, one of the concerns expressed was that the publication of these rankings would freeze the evaluations and opinions scientists had of the various institutions.

The other objective criterion is department size, estimated by the number of faculty within each professorial rank (and in total) as measured in 1966 (American Council on Education, 1966). If research dollars were being distributed on the basis of proportionality, then the larger the faculty, the more research funds the institution would receive. Thus, the size of the faculty in the field at a given institution is included as an additional control variable.

Consistent with Blau's (1964) discussion of particularism as the effect of the social relationship existing between a judge and the object of judgment, the indicator of nonbureaucratic criteria used for this study is the university department's representation on the National Science Foundation advisory panels (National Science Foundation, 1964–1971b). Listings of persons who had served as reviewers of proposals were also sought but were said not to be a part of the public record. The hypothesis is that a university department's representation on an advisory panel increases the probability that the department will receive money and the amount of money received. Because of the limited number of advisory panel positions open in any given year, sampling restriction problems are present in this measure. Consequently, a more reliable measure of social influence or familiarity is the department's proportional representation over all eight years. This aggregation introduces biases of its own and we will report both aggregated and cross-lagged individual year path analyses.

As a measure of the degree of paradigm development in the four social sciences, we take the results reported in Lodahl and Gordon's Table 1 (1972, p. 60), in which the four social sciences as well as various physical sciences were ranked in terms of their degree of paradigm development using survey data collected from scientists in the various fields. In terms of paradigms, economics was ranked as the most developed, psychology second, sociology third, and political science as least developed.

Results

Our analysis of the impact of departmental size, quality, and social influence is based on both data aggregated over the eight-year period and a panel analysis of the relationship between advisory panel membership and grant allocations. For the aggregated analysis, the proportion of grants received, proportional representation on advisory panels, and the national rankings were averaged for the period 1964–1971.

Figure 1 presents path diagrams of the relationships among the variables for each of the four social sciences. The argument is that size of the department is positively related to the national rank of the department, and that both size and rank affect the membership on advisory panels. All three factors, size, rank, and panel membership, may, in turn, influence the receipt of research grants.

In Figure 1, it is evident that in all four social sciences, the coefficient of the variable for panel membership is at least twice its standard error.

While Figure 1 indicates that, as predicted, there is a significant effect of panel membership on grant allocations, in order

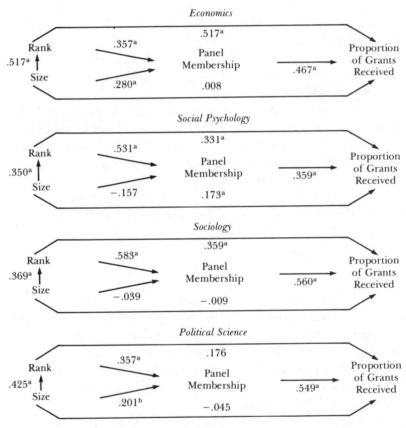

a > Two times the standard error.
b > One and one half times the standard error.

Figure 1. Path Diagrams for Aggregated Data Analysis of Relationships Among Variables.

to test whether the magnitude of this effect varies over the social sciences being examined, unstandardized regression coefficients were computed. These regressions are presented in Table 1. Since the highest rank is one, rank enters with the expected sign. The results in Table 1 indicate that the formulation as tested accounted for a substantial amount of the variance in grant allocations.

Except in the case of social psychology, size is not statistically significant. For the two variables of national rank and panel membership, we tested for the homogeneity of the regression coefficients using a covariance analysis. The null hypothesis that the regression coefficients are the same for the four social sciences is rejected for both the rank and panel membership variables (for the national rank coefficient, $F = 21.605$, $df. = 3/303$, $p < .005$; for the panel membership coefficient, $F = 7.39$, $df. = 3/303$, $p < .005$). By inspection of Table 1, it is evident that the direction of the difference is consistent with our hypothesis.[2] Eliminating social psychology, since size in that case was statistically significant, the coefficients are still not equivalent by the covariance analysis (for panel membership, $F = 5.764$, $df. = 2/209$, $p < .005$; for national rank, $F = 3.012$, $df. = 2/209$, $p < .05$).

The aggregate data analyses support the hypothesis that bureaucratic, universalistic criteria are used relatively more in de-

Table 1. Regressions Estimating Proportion of Dollars Obtained Aggregated over the Period 1964–1971.

Field	Constant	National Rank	Panel Membership	Size	r^2
Economics	2.71	−.0508 (.0071)	2.48 (.378)	−.0009 (.0078)	.76
Social Psychology	1.41	−.0192 (.0057)	2.014 (.514)	.0172 (.0086)	.42
Sociology	2.66	−.0448 (.0117)	3.61 (.568)	−.009 (.016)	.65
Political Science	2.57	−.0356 (.025)	6.92 (1.50)	−.014 (.037)	.40

Note: Coefficients are the unstandardized regression coefficients. Numbers in parentheses are the standard errors of the coefficients.

cision making in fields with more highly developed scientific paradigms, where the uncertainty associated with such decision making is less and is reducible through the application of consensually shared, well-learned judgment criteria.

Cross-Lagged Path Analysis. There are two problems with the preceding analysis that are overcome with a cross-lagged path analysis. One problem is the potential bias from aggregation over time (Hannan, 1971). A cross-lagged analysis on yearly data avoids this bias. A cross-lagged analysis also allows testing our hypothesized model against the alternative that resource allocations lead to panel membership. It is quite plausible that NSF advisory panel members are selected to evaluate research proposals because of their own experience in doing grant research. Departments with a history of awards would then have a higher probability of being represented on the panels, which also could account for the observed relationship between panel membership and grant awards. Cross-lagged analysis permits exploring whether panel membership tends to lead resource allocations or resource allocations tend to lead panel membership.

The causal model estimated is displayed in Figure 2. Heise (1970) has argued that cross-lagged path analysis provides a more valid examination of causality in panel data than either simple cross-lagged correlations or analyses of difference scores. For our analysis, grants at time t are examined with regard to the relative influence of panel membership and grants at time $t - 1$.

The cross-lagged path model estimated puts our hypothesis to a severe test. Annual estimates of an institution's social influence are less reliable than the aggregate estimates, as already discussed, which tend to decrease the correlations between panel member-

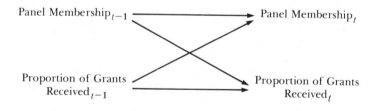

Figure 2. Cross-Lagged Path Model.

ships and grants. Further, since panel membership is an imperfect measure for social influence but grants are well measured, the variable for grants in year $t - 1$ is more likely to be significant, since in a path analysis, the variable with the most measurement error is likely to show the least effect, other things being equal (Meyer, 1973). And, by introducing grants received in the preceding year as a control variable, we have introduced a very strong statistical control. Allocation decisions are frequently based on precedent (Davis, Dempster, and Wildavsky, 1966), and, in the case of research grants, on the histories of institutions and individuals. A preceding year's grants should be one of the best possible proxy measures of the institution's research competence and eligibility, assuming only a limited turnover of faculty in a one-year period. The measure represents another indicator of an institution's worthiness for grants and would be the logical choice for those who argue that each year's grant decisions represent the application of universalistic standards of scientific worth.[3]

With eight years of data, we have seven regressions for each of the two dependent variables, panel membership and grants, for each of the four fields, or fifty-six regressions in all. These regression results are presented in Table 2.

The results displayed in Table 2 provide some support for the arguments made. First, it is important to note that except in the case of political science, the standard errors on both the grants and the panel membership coefficients are quite stable over time. If the standard errors were unstable, then the measures may be unreliable and the pooled standard errors may be meaningless estimates, reducing confidence in the validity of the previously discussed covariance analysis. Second, in more than one half of the instances panel membership in the preceding year is significantly associated with grants in the current year, even after controlling for grants received in the preceding year. And third, a significant amount of variance in grant allocations is still explained using these unaggregated data.

The results also indicate that, for these data, it is not possible to reject either the argument that panel membership leads grant allocations or that grant allocations lead panel membership. The former relationship is statistically significant at less than the .05

Table 2. Multiple-Regression Equations from Cross-Lagged Path Analysis.

Economics (N = 84)

$Grants_{65}$ = .578 + 1.63 $Panel_{64}$ + .331 $Grants_{64}$ R = .53
               (.580)   (.085)

$Grants_{66}$ = .499 + 2.02 $Panel_{65}$ + .313 $Grants_{65}$ R = .57
               (.578)   (.091)

$Grants_{67}$ = .601 + 1.60 $Panel_{66}$ + .233 $Grants_{66}$ R = .37
               (.698)   (.139)

$Grants_{68}$ = .414 + 2.09 $Panel_{67}$ + .275 $Grants_{67}$ R = .58
               (.449)   (.078)

$Grants_{69}$ = .651 − 1.42 $Panel_{68}$ + .593 $Grants_{68}$ R = .64
               (.508)   (.080)

$Grants_{70}$ = .176 + 1.87 $Panel_{69}$ + .521 $Grants_{69}$ R = .62
               (.528)   (.127)

$Grants_{71}$ = .400 + 1.16 $Panel_{70}$ + .510 $Grants_{70}$ R = .77
               (.344)   (.058)

$Panel_{65}$ = −.023 + .698 $Panel_{64}$ + .034 $Grants_{64}$ R = .85
               (.056)   (.0082)

$Panel_{66}$ = .100 + .527 $Panel_{65}$ + .0087 $Grants_{65}$ R = .47
               (.123)   (.019)

$Panel_{67}$ = .067 + .603 $Panel_{66}$ + .010 $Grants_{66}$ R = .57
               (.107)   (.021)

$Panel_{68}$ = .074 + .380 $Panel_{67}$ − .009 $Grants_{67}$ R = .49
               (.076)   (.013)

$Panel_{69}$ = .031 + .435 $Panel_{68}$ + .093 $Grants_{68}$ R = .71
               (.111)   (.017)

$Panel_{70}$ = −.000 + .465 $Panel_{69}$ + .059 $Grants_{69}$ R = .66
               (.086)   (.021)

$Panel_{71}$ + .046 + .541 $Panel_{70}$ + .033 $Grants_{70}$ R = .62
               (.095)   (.016)

Social Psychology (N = 97)

$Grants_{65}$ = .693 + 2.16 $Panel_{64}$ − .049 $Grants_{64}$ R = .44
               (.467)   (.084)

$Grants_{66}$ = .423 + 3.75 $Panel_{65}$ + .129 $Grants_{65}$ R = .69
               (.492)   (.094)

$Grants_{67}$ = .384 + .846 $Panel_{66}$ + .483 $Grants_{66}$ R = .63
               (.360)   (.084)

$Grants_{68}$ = .300 + 2.65 $Panel_{67}$ + .221 $Grants_{67}$ R = .55
               (.497)   (.094)

$Grants_{69}$ = .808 + .081 $Panel_{68}$ + .217 $Grants_{68}$ R = .23
               (.624)   (.100)

Grants_{70} = .021 + 1.42 Panel_{69} + .733 Grants_{69} R = .68
                 (.470)   (.089)

Grants_{71} = .354 + .896 Panel_{70} + .501 Grants_{70} R = .57
                 (.493)   (.083)

Panel_{65} = .058 + .447 Panel_{64} − .0055Grants_{64} R = .49
                 (.086)   (.016)

Panel_{66} = .043 + .454 Panel_{65} + .086 Grants_{65} R = .56
                 (.132)   (.025)

Panel_{67} = .089 + .371 Panel_{66} + .011 Grants_{66} R = .51
                 (.075)   (.018)

Panel_{68} = .065 + .399 Panel_{67} − .0071Grants_{67} R = .44
                 (.085)   (.016)

Panel_{69} = .042 + .694 Panel_{68} + .0281Grants_{68} R = .65
                 (.092)   (.0147)

Panel_{70} = .023 + .672 Panel_{69} + .047 Grants_{69} R = .70
                 (.077)   (.014)

Panel_{71} = .059 + .558 Panel_{70} + .0079Grants_{70} R = .61
                 (.076)   (.013)

Sociology (N = 72)

Grants_{65} = 1.00 + .210 Panel_{64} + .250 Grants_{64} R = .30
                 (.859)   (.103)

Grants_{66} = .637 + 2.75 Panel_{65} + .239 Grants_{65} R = .58
                 (.619)   (.078)

Grants_{67} = .652 − .782 Panel_{66} + .659 Grants_{66} R = .55
                 (.549)   (.121)

Grants_{68} = .940 + 1.20 Panel_{67} + .276 Grants_{67} R = .38
                 (.741)   (.112)

Grants_{69} = 1.14 − .682 Panel_{68} + .266 Grants_{68} R = .25
                 (.880)   (.126)

Grants_{70} = .744 + .661 Panel_{69} + .359 Grants_{69} R = .32
                 (.888)   (.141)

Grants_{71} = .686 + .901 Panel_{70} + .363 Grants_{70} R = .47
                 (.743)   (.096)

Panel_{65} = .057 + .368 Panel_{64} + .021 Grants_{64} R = .51
                 (.098)   (.0117)

Panel_{66} = .126 + .616 Panel_{65} + .021 Grants_{65} R = .46
                 (.148)   (.018)

Panel_{67} = .098 + .276 Panel_{66} + .052 Grants_{66} R = .55
                 (.083)   (.018)

Panel_{68} = .052 + .330 Panel_{67} + .036 Grants_{67} R = .50
                 (.010)   (.015)

Panel_{69} = .042 + .612 Panel_{68} + .050 Grants_{68} R = .70
                 (.103)   (.015)

(table continued on p. 326)

$$\text{Panel}_{70} = .065 + \underset{(.093)}{.623} \quad \text{Panel}_{69} + \underset{(.015)}{.014} \text{ Grants}_{69} \qquad R = .64$$

$$\text{Panel}_{71} = .063 + \underset{(.087)}{.412} \quad \text{Panel}_{70} + \underset{(.011)}{.049} \text{ Grants}_{70} \qquad R = .67$$

Political Science ($N = 60$)

Grants and Panel regressions for 1965 were not computed because of the small size of the program in 1964.

$$\text{Grants}_{66} = 1.24 + \underset{(2.66)}{9.08} \quad \text{Panel}_{65} - \underset{(.056)}{.015} \text{ Grants}_{65} \qquad R = .41$$

$$\text{Grants}_{67} = 1.22 + \underset{(1.55)}{1.74} \quad \text{Panel}_{66} + \underset{(.110)}{.130} \text{ Grants}_{66} \qquad R = .20$$

$$\text{Grants}_{68} = .940 + \underset{(.900)}{1.14} \quad \text{Panel}_{67} + \underset{(.098)}{.289} \text{ Grants}_{67} \qquad R = .41$$

$$\text{Grants}_{69} = .953 + \underset{(1.06)}{2.67} \quad \text{Panel}_{68} + \underset{(.111)}{.217} \text{ Grants}_{68} \qquad R = .45$$

$$\text{Grants}_{70} = 1.30 - \underset{(1.63)}{.182} \quad \text{Panel}_{69} + \underset{(.253)}{.243} \text{ Grants}_{69} \qquad R = .13$$

$$\text{Grants}_{71} = .763 + \underset{(1.22)}{1.57} \quad \text{Panel}_{70} + \underset{(.098)}{.300} \text{ Grants}_{70} \qquad R = .39$$

$$\text{Panel}_{66} = .086 + \underset{(.180)}{.568} \quad \text{Panel}_{65} + \underset{(.0038)}{.011} \text{ Grants}_{65} \qquad R = .49$$

$$\text{Panel}_{67} = .105 + \underset{(.137)}{.773} \quad \text{Panel}_{66} - \underset{(.0097)}{.0047} \text{Grants}_{66} \qquad R = .60$$

$$\text{Panel}_{68} = .000 + \underset{(.075)}{.429} \quad \text{Panel}_{67} + \underset{(.0081)}{.028} \text{ Grants}_{67} \qquad R = .69$$

$$\text{Panel}_{69} = .160 + \underset{(.172)}{.486} \quad \text{Panel}_{68} - \underset{(.018)}{.0049} \text{Grants}_{68} \qquad R = .36$$

$$\text{Panel}_{70} = .116 + \underset{(.099)}{.642} \quad \text{Panel}_{69} - \underset{(.015)}{.0031} \text{Grants}_{69} \qquad R = .66$$

$$\text{Panel}_{71} = .066 + \underset{(.104)}{.521} \quad \text{Panel}_{70} + \underset{(.0084)}{.012} \text{ Grants}_{70} \qquad R = .56$$

Note: Coefficients presented are the unstandardized regression coefficients. The numbers in parentheses are the standard errors of the respective coefficients.

level of probability in sixteen out of twenty-eight regressions, while the latter is significant in fifteen out of twenty-eight regressions. What is occurring is that frequently both panel memberships and grants are related to panel memberships and grants in the following year, when the two variables are entered simultaneously in a multiple-regression equation.

Although the cross-lagged analyses are consistent with the

finding of an effect of panel membership, an inspection of the results across scientific fields indicates that there are not significant differences in the expected direction. The model, as estimated, does not control for another indicator of quality, national rank, and grants in the preceding year may already capture some of the effects of particularism, thereby diminishing the effect of panel membership. However, it is likely that the biggest problem is that, because there are few panel positions for any single year, the measure of social influence is likely to have error associated with it. Aggregating over time probably reduces this error. A clearer test of the hypothesis would involve a setting in which there were enough positions in each year to avoid measurement problems and to permit a panel analysis to be performed on an annual basis. Journal editorships and article publication in chemistry, sociology, and political science were examined by Pfeffer, Leong, and Strehl (1977). Consistent with the results reported in the present study, they found that there was a stronger effect of editorial board composition on articles published in the following year in the two social sciences, sociology and political science, compared with chemistry, a field with a more highly developed paradigm.

Differences in the Stability of Grant Allocations. Another way of examining the impact of social influence operating in differentially uncertain contexts is to consider the stability of the distribution of grants over time. If decisions were made in the context of stable shared norms of scientific worth and patterns of faculty turnover were similar for the four fields, then grants in the four fields should be equally stable. If, on the other hand, the criteria applied in decision making vary with the composition of each year's panel, then there should be more instability in fields that rely on multiple particularistic standards. The average year-to-year stability (correlations) of grant allocations for 1964–1971 was .50 in economics, .40 in social psychology, .36 in sociology, and .22 in political science. These correlations are significantly different from one another (by a z transformation, chi-square = 22.20, $df. = 3, p < .005$) and are perfectly related to the relative paradigm developed for the four fields.

While the four fields differ significantly in the stability of grant allocations, they are stable on other dimensions. The rank order correlation between the 1964 and 1969 American Council on Education rankings is .93 in economics, .85 in sociology, .96 in psychology, and .89 in political science. There is some evidence that research output may be just as stable. W. J. Moore (1973) examined article production in nine major economics journals from ninety-four programs in economics. He reported that the correlation between article output during the period 1958–1968 and the period 1968–1971 was .89 (W. J. Moore, 1973, p. 14). Thus, not only are the national rankings stable, but also, at least in economics, research productivity is relatively stable across institutions over time. Since departmental size is also relatively stable, it is clear that the instability in grant allocations cannot be related to instability in departmental size, national rank, or, probably, research productivity.

The relative stability of grant allocations in the four fields, therefore, is quite consistent with the argument being developed. The allocation of grants in economics, with the more developed paradigm, is the most stable, while grant allocations are least stable in political science. These data, coupled with the results already presented, indicate that low paradigm development creates uncertainty in the decision-making process, and, as hypothesized, this uncertainty is reduced by the use of particularistic criteria.

Discussion

Influence, operating through social comparison processes, has been used in the past to explain the extent to which individuals will conform to group norms and seek group affiliation (Festinger, 1950; 1954). We have argued that social influence operates not only through the individual's need for social referents and social comparison but also has an effect on decision outcomes when uncertainty is present that cannot otherwise be resolved. In the absence of universal bureaucratic standards or criteria, particularistic criteria, deriving from existing social relationships, are more likely to influence decision outcomes. To observe this result, we need to impute no motives to the decision makers except the need to actually make the decision. We are arguing that social influence is inevitable in decision-making situations of great uncertainty.

These arguments were illustrated in a study of grant allocations made by the National Science Foundation in four social sciences during the period 1964–1971. But, of course, these issues are relevant to and can be pursued in a variety of contexts, including examining the criteria affecting promotion, hiring, and pay in academic departments, and the acceptance of papers in academic journals. In nonacademic contexts, one might compare the evaluation of employees in jobs that differ in terms of the visibility of their output, or the criteria that are used in making purchase decisions for equipment that varies in its uncertainty. In each of these contexts, we would hypothesize that social influence will account for decision outcomes more to the extent that uncertainty is present in the decision situation.

Because universalism is such a strongly held norm in science (Zuckerman, 1970), the results presented here may bother some scientists. We have thus considered many alternative explanations for the data, and we will discuss a sampling of these. As the reader will see, however, these explanations all fail to account for at least one aspect of the results we have presented.

Alternative Hypotheses. One hypothesis is simply that advisers favor their own institutions. This hypothesis is at variance with the fact that care is taken to lessen the possibility that panel members are involved in decisions concerning their own institutions. More importantly, the hypothesis does not account for the fact that panel membership is more strongly related to grant allocations in fields with lower paradigm development.

It might be argued that the association between panel membership and grants occurs because panel membership is itself based on the receipt of past grants. This argument, however, is inconsistent with the facts that the effect of panel membership varies over the four fields and that, even controlling for grants in the preceding year, panel membership generally has a statistically significant effect on grant allocations.

Yet another hypothesis might be that grants are rewards distributed to those who have served on advisory panels. While this would account for the observed lag structure between panel membership and grants, it would not account for the differential application of this reward system across fields.

And we can consider three slightly more sophisticated alternative hypotheses.[4] The first is the following: Institutional representation on advisory panels increases the probability that individuals at the represented institutions will submit more proposals. Assuming the same level of quality and the same level of acceptance, the result would be a higher proportion of dollars received. This hypothesis, however, does not account for why this effect would be stronger in political science than in economics. Further, the hypothesis does not suggest why the effect of panel membership should operate with a one-year lag structure.

It has also been suggested that applicants from the represented institutions engage in informal communication with the institution representative about proposals, resulting in prescreening by the representative to reduce submissions of unqualified proposals. Thus, assuming no difference in the overall quality of proposals, this will result in submission of more qualified proposals from the represented institutions and therefore increase the probability of receiving a grant. One could expect differences between disciplines if one posited that paradigm development is related to uncertainty and that the more uncertain fields would make more use of this informal communication process. At this point, however, the hypothesis is merely explicating one possible mechanism by which social familiarity affects decision outcomes. To the extent that the field has a less-developed scientific paradigm, it is quite plausible to suggest more informal communication, both on the part of the grant applicants and on the part of the judges. As Festinger (1954) has persuasively argued, uncertainty not tractable by objective standards does produce more communication.

The final alternative is that panel members are selected on the basis of their empirical research competence, presumably correlated with the competence of their institutions. Competence in doing large-scale empirical research, however, may be differentially correlated with national rankings of the departments across the fields. One might argue that in political science and sociology, theoretical work and library research are more prevalent, while in economics, perhaps, scholarship requires undertaking large-scale research projects that are data oriented. Thus, one might argue, American Council of Education rankings are more highly correlated with grant allocations in economics because quality in economics departments is based on doing empirical research. But this hypothesis can also be rejected. Clearly, one measure of research competence and preference for doing empirical research is the actual grants received, according to this argument. Yet, we have seen that controlling for grants received in the previous year, panel membership lagged one year still has a significant effect on allocations.

It is possible to think of almost limitless potential explanations for the observed results. Such post hoc explanations have the advantage, of course, of having the data available, and even then, as we have seen, they frequently fail to account for the observed pattern of results. Further, the explanation developed in this chapter is well founded in the literature on social influence processes (for example, Smith, 1973), is generalizable to other contexts, and is parsimonious.

Conclusion

It is likely that the degree of uncertainty in the decision situation is not the only factor that affects which criteria are employed. The consequences of the decision, or its importance, the visibility of the decision and the process by which it is made, and the scarcity of the rewards or resources being allocated all might also affect the influence of criteria on decision outcomes. It is argued that to the extent decision outcomes are consequential, as in the allocation of resources that are important or large in amount, there is more incentive for participants to use social influence and social relationships to influence decision outcomes. This is true also with regard to the scarcity of what is being allocated. In the absence of scarcity, there is no allocation problem at all. It is only when resources are scarce that social influence is likely to become important (see Salancik and Pfeffer, 1974). If there were enough funds to be distributed to practically all applicants, then there would be no correlation between panel membership and allocation decision outcomes. And, of course, the visibility of the allocation process and its outcomes will tend to ensure that more objective, bureaucratic criteria are employed. However, since the situation may still have uncertainty, this visibility will shift the focus of the social influence process to the decision among competing criteria, rather than directly among competing candidates or proposals.

With the empirical concern given to elements of bureaucracy in formal organizations, it seems that more attention should be paid to the nature of the criteria used in organizational decision processes. As Pondy (1970) suggested, the criteria and outcomes associated with resource allocation within organizations have important effects on the larger society.

Notes

1. Of course, there are not separate departments of social psychology. The assumption was made that the rankings and size of the psychology departments would adequately approximate the social psychology component of these departments. This was the only feasible way to undertake the analysis.

2. When the multiple regressions are computed with size omitted, the coefficients for the variables of national rank and panel membership in social psychology fall, as expected, between the values for the variables in economics and in sociology.

3. A previous year's grants to an institution is not a perfect proxy measure of scientific merit. Multiple and contradictory factors can contribute to the correlation of grants from one year to another. For instance, while precedence may lead to a positive correlation between grants in one year and grants in another, it is also possible that departments that have received funds in one year may have less need of funds subsequently, leading to a negative correlation. Social norms operating in departments may lead departmental members to repeat the successes of their colleagues; learning from failing colleagues, however, may result in departments that fared poorly in one year striving even harder for success in the next year. Despite these complications, a preceding year's grants is still a good proxy control variable. It permits testing the argument of those who contend that grants are good representations of the evaluation process of NSF decision makers operating under objective standards. The argument is that each year's grants represent allocations to the most deserving contenders, regardless of advisory panel membership. If a significant correlation between membership and grants obtains when the influence of "merit" itself is statistically controlled, the support for the social influence argument is strong. And, this procedure biases the analysis against our own causal model. We have argued that any year's grants represent both components: merit, based on universalistic standards, and social influence, based on particularistic standards of similarity between the judges and the judged. Consequently, by introducing a previous year's grants along with panel membership, some variance that otherwise might be attributed to panel membership will be associated with the previous year's grants, which measures both universalistic and some component of particularistic outcomes.

4. These alternative hypotheses were suggested by anonymous reviewers.

Part Three

~~~~~~

Implications

~~~~~~

In the first of the two concluding chapters, John Freeman (Chapter Thirteen) points out that the choice of the appropriate unit of analysis in organizational research is much more than an academic exercise. Inferences about the locus of causation of behavior in organizations depend greatly on how inclusive the unit of analysis is. The more inclusive the unit, the greater the likelihood of identifying causal elements at the macroscopic level, but the greater the loss of microscopic detail. Definitions of organizational birth, reorganization, and demise also affect inferences about environmental effects. The more stringent the definitions, the more meager the effects. In the final chapter John Meyer (Chapter Fourteen) shows that the range of environmental variations affecting organizations may be much greater than variations in organizations themselves. Meyer argues that conceptions of the environment must be extended to include characteristics of entire societies, that environments not only affect organizations but often generate their structures independently of technical requirements, and that evaluation of organizations is often no more or less than ritual conformity to societal myths about rationality.

I believe that concern with the unit of analysis and with the range of environmental effects on organizations reflects a distinctly sociological perspective. Economic models treat firms as bounded by markets, and psychology examines the behavior of individual people in organizational settings, focusing relatively little attention on units larger than work groups. But the sociological approach to organizations views boundaries as both permeable and variable over time, introducing elements of complexity and realism in organizational research. For economics, the environment is described sufficiently by prices, and for psychology the environment is as much enacted as it is reacted to. The sociological approach, in contrast, views organizations as very much determined by the structure of the larger social systems in which they operate as well as by demands of the immediate task environment. Our aim is not to reject economic and psychological approaches to organizations but to indicate that sociologists tend to raise questions somewhat different from those arising out of other disciplinary perspectives.

Marshall W. Meyer

13

The Unit of Analysis in Organizational Research

John H. Freeman

When this book's authors first met as a group, Scott brought up an issue that was to recur on many subsequent occasions. In describing the research he and John Meyer were doing on schools, he said there was reason to doubt whether they were studying organizations at all. As represented in Chapter Nine of this volume, their studies had shown that schools are not characterized by hierarchical authority structures, do not control participation, or manifest the regularity of activity that one normally associates with the term *organization*. This struck me as important at the time because Hannan and I were just beginning our research on school district administration. I had been asking myself why districts, as opposed to schools and classrooms on one hand and state educational systems on the other, should be worth studying. The easiest and most common answer to this question is that the data are available at the district level. That is, the reason for studying districts is that people who deal with education in practical capacities use districts as sources of information. Under many circumstances, one has a *choice* of unit boundary. In this chapter, I am going to consider that choice, using the other chapters as illustrations.

Going back over these chapters, we find a rather dazzling diversity. Various authors have written about finance agencies, schools, corporations, school districts, stores in department store chains, hospitals, and government research foundations. Each produces a variant of the same basic problem—how to bound the organization in such a way that observed units are unambiguously separable from each other and from their environments in both time and space.

Development of the Field and Exacerbation of the Problem

It is one of the more homely truisms of scientific research that one pays a price for asking more complicated questions. As one's theories become more ambitious, the data needed to test them become more difficult to obtain. As designs are elaborated, the avenues multiply through which errors can enter. In recent years, surveys of organizations have become common. Open-systems perspectives dominate the field. And longitudinal designs are becoming more common. These developments have reinforced each other. When one does case-study research, focusing on single points in time or on brief periods, the technological and environmental factors are constant. They figure so prominently in open-systems theories partly because they are more variable in the data sets produced by the designs used to research them.

In conducting a survey, one first chooses a population to be surveyed, and this is a population of units. One must decide whether one is studying households, housewives, people in general, or organizations. After making such a choice, one develops rules for deciding whether or not a problematical case falls within the population of interest. Are infants "people" according to one's theoretical interest? Are local offices of larger firms "organizations"?

These questions do not arise as serious matters when one is dealing with a closed-systems perspective using static case-study methods. If one is studying interpersonal processes within a single organization, one samples people and the common problem encountered in defining the population is full-time versus part-time employment (in work organization), as well as active versus inactive membership (in voluntary associations). If one admits the permeability of organizational boundaries in one's theory, one cannot treat those boundaries so cavalierly. In particular, one faces the serious possibility that "openness" of the system will itself be an important variable. Organizations with highly permeable boundaries are more deeply and extensively penetrated by other organizations, and it becomes difficult to decide where one ends and another starts. Furthermore, if one sees the environment as a repository for exogenous variables (that is, "causes" taken as primary in the theory), interpenetration of organizations breaks down the exclusivity of exogenous variation. A system of very porous organizations may have more unit character than any one of them taken alone. In consequence, the research begins to assume case-study characteristics with a closed-system perspective. For example, one might conduct a study in which environmental effects on some focal organization are viewed as coming from what Evan (1966) calls the "organization set." If the focal organization is found to be very permeable, so that where it stops and members of its organization set start is difficult to determine, environmental factors become internal characteristics of the set that now forms the real operative unit of analysis. And this unit has not been studied in terms of its environment.

A second complexity introduced into organizational research in recent years is longitudinal analysis of structure. How does one recognize organizational beginnings and endings? Researchers use legal and financial definitions. It is clear that the social arrangements that identify organizations for theoretical purposes may persist long after bankruptcy. And organizations may change their goals, technology, location, personnel and control structures while maintaining the same name and a continuing legal existence. If one cannot determine beginnings and endings for organizations, one cannot define survival (or failure to survive). Most theories dealing with effectiveness use the threat of failure as the driving force that links goals and behavior. Without a definition of beginning and ending, such theories are untestable and remain vacuously teleological.

So there are problems of boundary definition in both space and time. Open-systems perspectives and longitudinal research designs exacerbate them. In the following section, I take up a particularly difficult boundary problem in space, the hierarchical clustering of organizational units and choice of level. Several of the authors in this book have been wrestling with this problem in their own work, and their example is instructive.

Part or Whole? Organizations as Hierarchical Systems

In addition to their structuring as hierarchies when attention is focused on authority, organizations can be seen as hierarchical in the sense described by Herbert Simon (1962). They are Chinese boxes, systems within systems, and this gives them a partly decomposable quality that in turn creates a fundamental unit problem. Many of the "organizations" commonly studied are parts of larger organizations. In the finance agencies studied by Marshall Meyer (Chapters Three and Eight), we find organizational units that are parts of larger government structures, units that perform highly variable functions, frequently change their names, experience turnover of high-level officials, and operate within a constraining legal-political context. This raises problems of conceptualization of the phenomena under study. For instance, one might ask whether agency chiefs have the legal authority to manipulate the structures of their departments. So far as civil service is concerned, it is clear that they do not, and this affects the level of formalization. Similarly, one might wonder if the reorganizations Meyer studies are the result of political and legal processes operating at the municipal (or county) level. In short, when leadership changes and a department of finance reorganizes, is this part of a more general upheaval, or is it peculiar to the finance department? The answer to this question affects the locus of causation. If one's research is conducted at the local level, one may be missing the most important causal variables. In this situation, then, *misspecifying the unit leads to misspecifying the model used to analyze the data.*

A second problem involves the organization's *human popu-*

lation. Who is a participant, and who is not? At first glance, this seems to be a simple issue. Either one works for General Motors, or one does not. There are two complications, however. A *measurement* problem involves organizational size. Do two half-time employees count the same as one full-timer? Most researchers answer affirmatively and study full-time equivalents.

A related issue involves deciding whether or not to include *lower participants*. Are "raw materials" for people-processing organizations (for example, students in schools) most fruitfully viewed as part of the organization or what it works on? Are members of voluntary associations the functional equivalents of production workers, as Akers and Campbell (1970) imply? Hannan and I (Chapter Seven) treat enrollments of school districts as indicators of demand for services, a kind of environmental variation. From our point of view, when a family moves into a school district's territory, the school-age children of that family lay claims for services on the district, just as they lay claims on the police department and fire department for services. From Etzioni's (1961) point of view, those additional students are lower participants, in the same theoretically defined category as blue-collar workers. A major status difference between pupils and blue-collar workers lies in the fact that the business firm controls participation. It has the right to deny employment to blue-collar workers, but the school district cannot deny admission to pupils who live within its service area. The point here is that control over participation is an important unit property on which definitions are often based. A loss of control over participation is seen in many contexts as a loss of "corporateness."[1]

Finally, the hierarchy problem sometimes takes the form of shifting the *attribution* of phenomena to more or less inclusive levels. In the authority hierarchy, subordinates pass the buck, bumping responsibility to successively higher levels. In more general terms, the consequences of organizational action do not always manifest themselves at the same level for which it is appropriate to view the phenomena themselves. For example, Hirsch (1975) compared the profitability of the recording and pharmaceuticals industries and concluded that firms in the recording industry are less profitable because they are unable to control entry. The pharmaceutical industry is more difficult to enter, and this creates a more profitable market. An alternative explanation is that both are profitable, but the recording industry requires less capital to enter. The firms in that industry attempt to hide profits by reporting them through parent companies (such as Columbia Broadcasting System, the parent of Columbia records).[2] Since most record companies are subsidiaries and most pharmaceutical firms are not, this "bumping" phenomenon may be the true mechanism explaining the observed difference. Whether or not this is true is not important here. The point is that both credit and blame can be shifted up and down a hierarchy. In an earlier (Freeman, 1975) paper, I argued that this same process may well occur when one is looking at ratios of administrators to production workers in local units. What seems to be a reduction in that ratio may actually be a shifting of administrative functions to higher levels. A greater pressure on such a function may result in pushing it up rather than local expansion. Another way of looking at this is to note that increasing functional load creates functional turf that aggressive higher authorities may use to increase their own responsibilities and rewards.

Less inclusive organizational units at any time often pool the consequences of their previous actions through collective organization. This is most likely when those consequences occur at the same time, and this may have little to do with when the original actions were taken. So, for example, shoe manufacturers combine in trade associations to lobby in government agencies and in Congress. They seek assistance in withstanding the consequences of their own previous decisions on issues of design, technology, and organization. In particular, these consequences amount to an inability to compete with imports.

In Chapter Five, Ouchi describes types of business firms that vary according to the extensiveness of obligation between individual and organization. Some firms make narrowly defined demands on their employees and make few promises to them. Both firm and employee ask "What have you done for me lately?" Others embrace not only the employee for most of his adult life but also his family. Ouchi views this as a property of the system—of the firm as a whole. But it is open to question how one treats the observations on which empirical investigation is based. If a firm's top executives say the company's policy is paternalism (for this is what Ouchi is talking about) and one observes in a particular sales office a "What have you done for me lately?" pattern, we could easily imagine the participants attributing this inconsistency to the firm and its policies, to the conditions under which that office works, or to the personalities of the people who work in that office. The sources of data are not unaffected by the attribution process.

Continuity and Change

Organizations, like all other social units, display continuity over time, but at the same time they exhibit variables or sets of variables that change at relatively more rapid rates. One researcher's structure (for example, a more or less highly centralized authority system) is another's process (for example, delegation of authority). All structures are the end result, or the chosen moment, of a process. When one is doing cross-sectional research, it is not difficult to ignore this fact. Since the variables are not represented as changing in the data, the researcher may mix them together or separate them according to his or her interests. The researcher rarely considers the implied assumption that causal relations among variables have run their course at the time of study (for example, the system has settled down to an equilibrium). In doing cross-sectional research, one assumes that the independent variables have changed at some previous point in time and that the effects of those changes have occurred by the time the researcher takes his measurements. As Coleman points out (1968), one would understate the effects of the independent variables if this were not the case.

However, when one's research is longitudinal the rates of change of the variables in the study are of crucial importance in distinguishing the boundaries of units. Any unit, if viewed in a sufficiently long-term context relative to the rates of change in variables of interest, can be seen to exhibit impermanence. And, when attention is focused on very brief periods of time, stability in structural features of the organization seems so great as to approach constancy and hence these features are irrelevant.

In the study of school districts reported in Chapter Six,

Hannan and I had two problems that depended on the rate of change in the variables under study. The first of these involved the lag structure. The shorter the time lag and the period of time covered by the change term, the more serially correlated errors overwhelm the estimates, and the more difficult it becomes to observe hypothesized differences between growth and decline in school districts even if they are "really" there. As time spans become longer, fewer and fewer districts are continuously growing or declining and one loses cases. Furthermore, it is obvious that if the period is lengthened sufficiently, the effects of decline must "catch up" with the effects of growth. As the number of students approaches zero, the number of administrators reaches zero sooner or later.

A second problem involves the creation and destruction of school districts. Because districts are unifying (elementary and high school districts merge), they constantly are both dropping out of and appearing in the population. The longer the time span under consideration, the more difficult it becomes to perform analyses that are generalizable to any population at a single point in time. All of this presumes that one has arrived at a decision about treating the results of merger processes as "new districts." We chose to eliminate both districts created by merger during the time period under study and those which disappeared as distinct districts.

The studies of finance agencies conducted by M. Meyer and Brown (Chapters Three and Eight) involve similar issues. In Chapter Three, they are concerned with changes that occur in various historical periods and the ways in which broader-system phenomena affect the units under study—effects of "history," if you will. The problem is more difficult to solve than those just discussed, because the degree of structural change observable in any short period of time (for example, a year or two) ranges from triviality to complete reorganization. In the research underlying both chapters, they had to decide when a new organization replaced the old one. This decision is particularly nettlesome when one believes, as they do, that causal relationships producing slow or moderate rates of change can be treated as linear but that these relationships become discontinuous or at least curvilinear during periods of "reorganization."

If one is to have a unit that is recognizable over time, one has to define it through reference to invariant properties or to variables that change slowly relative to those under investigation. One has to decide in advance, then, which variables are to be taken as part of the causal process of interest and which will be used to define the unit. If this is not done, specific design and analysis questions become intractable. For example, one would find it difficult to decide which points in time to use for observations (that is, sampling in time). One would find it difficult to specify whether or not the functions linking the variables in the model are linear or, if not, what sort of curvilinearity to anticipate. The lag structure would also be difficult to specify. And finally, it would be difficult for others to find comparable data sets to use in replicating the study, or bases for reliable comparisons between the study in question and other studies in the literature.

To this point, we have identified two forms of boundary problems in organizational research. The first involves boundaries in space where the researcher has difficulty deciding how to separate different organizations. Hierarchical systems of organizations create many potential boundaries and, to the degree that the entire system is decomposable, the choice may seem arbitrary. The second problem involves beginnings and endings of organizations. Unit properties result from a constellation of variables that change at rates intermediate between variations so rapid as to be irrelevant to the process at hand and variations so slow as to provide context but not cause. In the following section, we take up concrete methodological issues that are of general relevance but that have not been analyzed in terms of unit problems to date.

Specification and Estimation

Although we have considered the two boundary problems separately, they are interconnected, because the rates at which variables change are in part a function of the inclusiveness of the unit that they characterize. While not always the case, it is generally true that variables at lower levels of analysis change at least as rapidly as variables at higher levels and usually change a good deal faster. This will obviously be the case when macro properties are measured as aggregates of micro properties. For example, when organizational conflict is defined as conflict incidents per capita or something like that, the mean will change at a rate approaching the rates of change of the individual scores being aggregated to the degree that the micro changes are correlated. When they occur at different times, the macro change will be spread out over time and will perforce occur more slowly.

There are sound theoretical reasons for expecting variables describing processes conceputalized in more inclusive ("macro") terms to change more slowly than micro process variables, even when the former are not aggregates of the latter. As Barnard (1938, pp. 232–233) suggests, it is common for decision-making theorists to assert that decisions made higher up in the authority hierarchy cover longer spans of time. And these decisions tend to be those which pertain to the organization as a whole. The higher one goes in the hierarchy, the more decisions have long-run perspective and the more inclusive they become so far as consequences are concerned. The results of these decisions, then, are changes in variables that are likely to take years to work themselves out. At lower levels in the authority hierarchy, where decisions pertain to smaller units or perhaps only to single persons, the variables that change as a result of decision can be expected to continue their changes for shorter periods of time.

Finally, while less inclusive units are affected by or are part of changes that occur in more inclusive units, the reverse is not necessarily the case. Consequently, most events that occur in the whole also affect its parts. The parts, then, must change at least as rapidly as the whole. And, for actions of the parts to affect the whole, a great deal of change is often required before the whole responds. Put plainly, it is often the case that lower-level units have to make two jumps for every one they can provoke from the whole.

This association between inclusiveness of unit and rate of change in variables exacerbates problems of model specification. In general, specification involves the choice of variables to be included in the model and the functional form attributed to them (for example, linearity assumptions). The boundaries chosen in space and time encourage the researcher to select some variables for study and discourage the selection of others. If he draws unit

boundaries that are too narrow, given the causal process of interest, it is likely that variables characterizing the macro structure will
be constant or nearly constant, and it is likely that they will be ignored. Spuriousness is an obvious risk under such circumstances.
The issue is not whether spuriousness occurs because unit boundaries are drawn in one way rather than another, but whether the
theorist-researcher will notice the true causal variable.

When the researcher focuses his attention on units inclusively defined, he may ignore the variables whose rates of change
make them appear as incomprehensible detail—noise—or he may
aggregate them. In the latter case, he is likely to lose track of causal
priority, because the aggregation procedure obscures the sequence
of change. As a result, he will be tempted to view every variable
as a potential cause of every other variable. He will find it easy to
make plausible arguments for causal effects running in both directions and for the suggestion of feedback loops. This loss of re-
cursiveness carries with it the likelihood of underidentification with
its indeterminate linkage between empirical observation and theory.

Definition of unit boundaries also affect the independence
of observations made on those units. If the value on the dependent
variable measured for one case depends on the value measured for
another, the observations are not independent and estimation will
be biased. When this problem occurs over time, its consequence
will be autocorrelated disturbances. When it occurs because boundaries in space are improperly drawn, "overreplication" as in Galton's Problem (Naroll, 1968) and its consequence, restriction of
variance, may result.

Autocorrelated disturbances occur when unrecognized variables are causing some of the variation in the dependent variable
at an early point in time, and disturbances are correlated with the
independent variables in the model at some later point in time.
Normally, this happens when the unrecognized causal variables
change slowly relative to the time span over which measurements
are made. When researchers ignore independent variables because
they are changing very slowly and seemingly can have no effect,
autocorrelation problems are likely. In Chapter Seven, growth and
decline processes in California school districts were analyzed. With
panel data, discounting the existence of autocorrelated distur-

bances is difficult.[3] If one is looking at variations in size of the supportive component or in number of administrators as a function of enrollments, an obvious causal agent is financial strength of the district. It is reasonable to argue that changes in finances from t_0 to t_1 affect the supportive component at t_1 apart from increases or decreases in enrollments over that time. If one does not include financial variables in the model and if they are changing slowly (as they probably are), t_0 levels of financial support will be correlated with errors in the model used to predict supportive component at t_1, and this biases the estimates of the effects of enrollments. Such an error would be almost certain if the unit were defined at the school level, because finances vary at the district level, although this was not the problem in Chapter Seven. One is likely to say, "Given some level of financing, shifts in enrollments are likely to place strains on the administrative staffs of schools, requiring them to hire more clerical personnel and thereby increasing the supportive component size." The point is that one cannot make the *ceteris paribus* assumption implied by the word *given,* and this problem is *more* likely when the unrecognized cause (finances in this case) changes slowly relative to the period between t_0 and t_1.

Galton's Problem involves cross-sectional research in which the units of analysis are derived from some single unit or small number of original units. Consequently, one may think one has some large number of units in one's sample but actually only have one (in the extreme case). For anthropologists, this issue is salient because it seems reasonable to argue that diffusion processes spread the cultural traits of a small number of forebearer cultures around the globe. In organizational research, this same problem occurs when one is studying local offices or subunits of some larger organization. Even if the local units have the authority to vary their structures, correlations created by common "ancestry" lead to problems of inference.

Both these problems involve the pattern of causation over time and the obscuring of nonindependent observations by the lagged effects of changes in those causal variables. In many instances, the simple observation is that most of the variation in the independent variable occurs longitudinally, but the changes are simultaneous for all the units studied. A case in point is Pennings'

(1975) recent study of stock brokerage organizations in which environmental variables seemed to have no effect on structure. His sample consists of the local office of a *single* stock brokerage house. It is obvious that most variations in market-related environmental variables (stock averages, volume, and so on) vary longitudinally, not across offices. And, as Pennings says, it is also likely that local offices are not free to adjust their internal structures as they will. Headquarters no doubt exerts influence over how local offices are set up. Consequently, one would not expect to find cross-sectional effects of environmental variables.[4]

Independence problems are not limited to systems in which subunits are branches of larger units. They also occur in the relationships *between* organizations. If one follows the logic of Thompson and McEwen's argument (1958), earliness of one organization's entrance into the goal-setting process of another affects the latter's independence. As one moves from bargaining through co-optation to coalition, observation of the goal-setting process shows less and less independence among the units. One would also expect the structural characteristics of one organization to reflect those of its partners to an increasing degree as the scale increases.

Hawley (1968, p. 334) points out that the flow of resources through a set of organizations places constraints on structure such that organizations receiving resources tend to mimic the structures of the organizations from which the resources come. The more exclusive this flow is (that is, the greater the proportion of the total coming from any single organization), the stronger this effect should be. If this is true, the web of organizations may itself be the most appropriate unit of analysis because observations made on its constituent organizations may not be independent of one another.

A similar consideration arises when the outcomes of competitive processes are considered, Hannan and I (1977) have argued that organizations competing for resources often differentiate as a result of the process. This is a form of survival failure but is most significant in that it produces a destruction of the competitive process itself. Failers adopt specialized functions in the broader system. This is Durkheim's basic explanation for the division of labor in society (1933, pp. 266–275). An alternative is combination (organization) of organizations to resist the survival failure consequences of competition. When this occurs, it is the system of organizations that is selected for or against, and the unit boundary has been expanded. When organizations divide up resources by differentiation or by acting in concert, thereby specializing along lines other than functional, the result is a loss of independence in the statistical sense.

One final set of issues involves measurement and the common use of reputational or other attribute-based organizational measures. Almost all studies of power in organizations are based on reports by organizational participants of organizational properties. The results are generally aggregated. Essentially, each individual participant's report is treated as an observation, and the aggregation process is intended to reduce errors of inference by averaging out random measurement errors. It does so only when the problem in observation is reliability. Bias is not discounted by such a procedure. The process also fails to perform its intended function when observations are not themselves sampled randomly from a universe of possible observations. This is common when informants are not randomly selected from the set of relevant informants. So, for example, a researcher may choose to study a structural or technical variable that pertains to a macro structure (extent of functional differentiation) and to measure it through the use of interviews. If these interviews are conducted only with top management personnel, the expected averaging-out process will not function if the views of those managers are nonrandomly distributed. In this situation, the boundary problem involves how much informants know about what they are asked to measure.

A second measurement problem involves aggregation of observations on lower-level properties and representing them as an average or other standardized score. For example, organizations may be said to have an "average span of control" when the property being observed is span of control associated with an organizational position. One might just as easily posit an organizational property called "organizational hair length" or "organizational happiness." If an organization is more than the sum of its parts, it is erroneous to define its structural properties as simple aggregates of those parts. Aggregation error is almost certain to occur when the variables *change* at lower (disaggregated) levels but are measured as macrostructural averages. The reason for this is that differences in the dependent variable occur because those changes are not perfectly coincidental in time or omnipresent across subunits, and the resultant variation is treated as if it were the same as in the previous discussion—random measurement error.

So what determines the consequences of measurement problems vis-à-vis the boundary problem is the same as in the specification and estimation problems. The issue revolves around the degree to which units defined more narrowly and less inclusively display changes in the dependent variable that occur in the same way *across* subunits and *over time*.

Suggestions for Defining Organizational Boundaries

The arguments in previous sections have stressed the importance of the dependent variable and of basing analyses on the maximum amount of variance (excluding measurement error). It is not surprising, then, that the suggestions in this section are based on this same notion. In general, when changes in the dependent variable occur simultaneously, and result from changes in the same independent variable(s), the subunits can be treated as a macro unit. It is this simultaneity of change and the operation of correlated causes that produce the unified pattern of action that we generally use to infer unitary properties. And under such circumstances economy of effort in conducting the research and in constructing explanations (that is, Occam's Razor) will be furthered by defining units more inclusively.

Often changes occur at different times for the same reason or at the same time for different reasons. In other words, the two conditions just mentioned will not both hold. In this case, the decision depends on the research design. Longitudinal research brings the timing of changes in the dependent variable into center stage. Defining boundaries inclusively when changes in subunits on the dependent variable are sporadic will probably result in biased es-

350

timates of causal effects because the lag structure of the model will be difficult to determine and, for the same reason, choice of measurement interval will be complicated.

One set of variables that will ordinarily produce changes that are correlated among subunits over time pertains to what Thompson (1967) called "pooled interdependence." One can often anticipate the level of analysis appropriate to a given research problem when that problem focuses on the common reward or cost and the expected degree of "pooling" in the organization. If all the organization's members and all its subunits share a common fate with regard to some process, it will make sense to define the unit inclusively. So, for example, one might be studying competition with attention focused on the consequences of failure to compete successfully. If such failure can be expected to have deleterious consequences for all organizational units at the same time, it makes sense to adopt the more macro definition.

A series of unit considerations pertain to the boundary in space, and particularly to the hierarchical boundary problem. An organization will seek to maintain its control over participation. This was a central element in Weber's original definition of the corporate group (1947, p. 145). Aldrich (1971) has recently argued that this criterion may prove useful in dealing with unit problems. In general, a wide variety of dependent variables will be correlated across subunits when the criteria regulating participation are applied at higher levels. So, for example, universities may impose admissions and hiring standards on their departments. As a result, it would be erroneous to analyze the departments as statistically independent units so far as variables rooted in personnel are concerned. It would be misleading to search for causes at the departmental level, if that meant ignoring university-wide variables (which are cross-sectionally constant at the departmental level).

A similar set of dependent variables involves processing information and maintaining secrecy. All organizations attempt to maintain control over how information about their internal operations is disseminated. To the degree that this control is vested in higher authorities, one might be tempted to view the organization in question as a subunit. In particular, this has consequences for control phenomena, since they normally depend heavily on how feedback and command are carried out. Breaking points in the flow of communication indicate structural boundaries that may be appropriate for unit definition when the (dependent) variables under investigation characterize the information processes within those boundaries.

Each of these suggestions operates by increasing the likelihood that within the unit changes in the dependent variable will occur at the same time and for the same reasons. The result should be increased theoretically relevant between-unit variance, but this should not be confused with observed variance. One maximizes observed variance by experimental manipulation, or by stratified sampling procedures. When independent and dependent variables are conceptualized as pertaining to different units of analysis, the *dependent* variable determines the level of analysis and serves as the guidepost for defining unit boundaries.

Notes

1. See Aldrich (1971) for a detailed treatment of authority and the importance of control over entrance and exit for determining unit boundaries.

2. This idea was suggested by Robert A. Meyer in a personal communication.

3. Current work on that problem deals with autocorrelated disturbances through the use of pooled cross sections and time series. When the original study was conducted, too few panels were available to permit the application of this technique.

4. Much of the discussion was prompted by comments made by Jeffrey Pfeffer in a personal communication.

14

Strategies for Further Research: Varieties of Environmental Variation

John W. Meyer

The preceding chapters develop perspectives and empirical analyses that vary widely. But there is agreement on certain core issues. The common ideas suggest lines to be pursued in further research, as well as some methodological strategies that ought to be employed in such research. I discuss these themes in three areas: First, research is proposed on the environmental origins of organizational structures. Second, the preceding chapters suggest some lines of inquiry on the internal structures of organizations. Third, a few new perspectives on organizational effects are proposed.

A main theme throughout the discussion to follow centers on the complex ways in which organizations are affected, constructed, maintained, controlled, and evaluated by their environments. We are concerned, throughout this book, with much more than the traditional closed-systems models of organizations. We go beyond even the more contemporary open-systems models that see organizations as adapted to their environments in complex ways. Our views on the relations between organizations and environments transcend such formulations—organizations are constructed by their environments (J. Meyer and Rowan), selected by them (Hannan and Freeman), and react to the larger features of these environments (Ouchi and Jaeger). Internally, the histories of organizations are in good part constructed by the histories of their environments (M. Meyer and Brown, J. Meyer and Rowan, Hannan and Freeman, M. Meyer). In short, a main theme of the studies in this book is that the real unit of theoretical analysis in organizational research is often the structure of the wider environment itself (Freeman).

This can all be said quite abstractly. Its real significance for research, however, lies in the fact that environments are seen to possess many more dimensions of interest than are typically considered. The following discussion suggests a sustained attention to the implications for organizations of many different kinds of environmental variations. It also suggests a wide range of distinct processes by which environments create and shape organizations.

Environments and Organizational Structures

Recent organizational research has emphasized the technological origins of organizations and their structures. Production systems create interdependencies among people and activities that create pressures for effective coordination. Variations among technologies, then, create variations in organizational structure. In the extreme version of this idea, formal organizations are created by the pressures of complex technical procedures that expand in modern society. Research on this line looks for variations in technology, in the hope of finding that these variations greatly affect organizational structure. Findings provide some encouragement, but effects are often weaker than have been anticipated.

Our work does not really attack a technological view so

much as it calls attention to the other main source of variation in organizational structure: the environments of organizations.[1] Many different ideas developed earlier suggest that we should study variations among organizational environments and their impact on organizational structure. Such a view is not unique to our work. What perhaps *is* novel is the variety of properties of organizational environments to which we call attention and the variety of processes by which these properties affect organizations. For instance, we suggest studies of the consequences of the following properties of organizational environments.

First, we suggest studying the consequences of *cultural values* (see Ouchi and Jaeger). Cultures emphasizing diffuse interpersonal solidarity will tend to create organizations that have low vertical and horizontal mobility, infrequent work evaluations, elaborate rituals of group and organizational community, relatively fixed but implicit definitions of roles, and the dominance of rules of seniority and status. Cultures emphasizing individual task achievement will create organizations with high mobility, explicitly defined roles, frequent and output-based evaluations, and few rituals of diffuse solidarity. The main idea here goes beyond assertions that bureaucratization occurs more frequently in cultures with universalistic and achievement-oriented values. Many variants of modern culture can produce rationalized organizations—but the level at which rationalization occurs may vary. In more individualistic cultural settings, the roles and actions of individuals are organized on a technically rational basis. In societies with more emphasis on status and solidarity, rationalization may tend to occur at higher organizational levels, with individual status and group membership seen as relatively fixed and with outputs measured and controlled at the level of the organization as a whole (or even the whole institutional system in which it is embedded).

Research on this question must compare technically similar organizations operating in different cultural contexts. The structures of factories or hospitals performing quite standardized tasks may vary systematically with broader social definitions of the nature of people, groups, and social actions. In American society, for instance, even religious organizations tend to subject their functionaries to the rites of technical rationality, evaluating them in terms of individual output (funds raised, attendance obtained, groups of parishioners organized) and subjecting them to patterns of high mobility.

Second, we suggest studying the consequences of *societal patterns of associational life* (Ouchi and Jaeger). Organizations evolving in social contexts with dense associational patterns will tend to have high mobility and technically specialized roles. On the other hand, when associational life in the environment is weak, emergent organizations will reflect broader types of solidarity, as in the traditional political bureaucracies described by Weber and others, and will emphasize technical activity less. Again, relevant research must compare technically similar organizations operating in community and societal contexts that vary on denseness of associational ties.

These two general environmental arguments together offer an explanation for the peculiar characteristics of many American organizations. A culture emphasizing task achievement and a social structure dense with associational life allows very specialized organizations with high mobility and weak internal solidarity to emerge and survive with surprising stability. In other societies, with cultures emphasizing solidary group life and structural networks of great intensity and little density (for example, strong extended families, clans, ethnic groups, status groups, and the like), *fewer organizations* may emerge (technical activity held constant), and those that do are likely to be buttressed by status structures and solidarities enabling them to compete with their environments for loyalty. The possibilities for multitudes of casual organizations created by the features of American life noted by de Tocqueville may in another society emerge only with the more dramatic efforts of a Mao Tse-tung and a Cultural Revolution. Put differently, the destruction of the traditional order of diffuse political bureaucracy may in fact enable the rapid expansion of the modern organizational society. Depending on the cultural and associational context, one organizational form replaces another. Obviously, such ideas can only be properly tested with comparative data or with data over substantial periods of time. We must find macrosociological environmental variation to study.

Third, we suggest studying the consequences of *the political and institutional structure of the environment* (see chapters by Pfeffer;

M. Meyer and Brown; J. Meyer and Rowan). In large part, the
successful establishment of rationalized organizations depends on
the environmental legitimacy and power conferred on the components of those organizations. Occasionally, organizational roles
and units are created by independent internal invention in response to urgent coordinative and technical problems. But most
commonly organizations arise and become structurally elaborated
by incorporating roles and units already given meaning and authority in the wider environment—in other, similar organizations,
in particular organizational units in the environment or in the social context as an institutional system. Thus, when sales departments, research and development departments, or personnel departments become widely known as appropriate components of
organizations, given organizations are more likely to adopt and incorporate them. These units are given more power and acquire
more legitimacy inside the organization because of their status outside it. Thus it arises that societies with elaborately rationalized institutional rules—with hosts of technical professions, with elaborate technological myths, and with complex and rationalized systems
of law and state organization—generate much more formal organization, even with technical work activity held constant. To
study this idea, research comparing the rise and survival of formal
organizations—and organizations of great complexity—in different contexts is again required. This can be done either through
comparative research or through the analysis of secular trends in
a given social context. What kinds of societies, for instance, generate rationalized psychiatric counseling professions and build them
into the structures of organizations? How is it that organizational
subunits devoted to evaluation or to evaluation research are generated? Clearly, the processes here are environmental in the first
instance—environmental rules and pressures make evaluation necessary and define the forms it can take. Similarly, the spread of
modern rationalized systems of accounting may in part derive from
factors internal to organizations but must be heavily influenced by
environmental pressures. If the accounting practices and structures of American organizations are heavily influenced by American tax laws, research across countries or time should be able to
find very substantial variations in these structures.

Thus the existence and structure of given types of organization depend on environmental institutions and organizational structures. Organizations and their internal units derive legitimacy, power, and authority from their status in social environments. This happens in two ways: First (see J. Meyer and Rowan), the social validity of a given unit—a professional group, a technical procedure, or a departmentalized function—is often defined more importantly in the environment than by internal technical efficacy. A safety department, for instance, may be essentially required by external rules, and a planning department may be necessary to satisfy investors or donors. The power of a finance department and its functionaries may depend on their status in the environment, as is the case with a research and development department. The authority of economists or operations researchers may depend greatly on the legitimacy and status their professions and credentials have in the environment. But, second (see Pfeffer; M. Meyer and Brown), legitimacy and meaning aside, the power and resources a given organization unit has may directly depend on its links to the environment—on the organizational dependencies on the environment that it controls or mediates.

These theories make the empirical prediction, for instance, that organizational personnel departments arise and become more powerful in environments in which (1) the personnel professions and practices are highly legitimated, located in established academic fields, and prescribed by laws and prestige systems and (2) labor markets and occupational definitions are organized in increasingly complex ways.

To study such questions, comparative research incorporating environmental variation is again necessary. Time series analyses of the rise of given types of organizational units in response to environmental changes are called for. So are analyses comparing the structures of technically similar organizations in different environments.

Fourth, we suggest studying the consequences of *environmental variation and competition*. The preceding arguments, as with most lines of thought in the literature, build in two assumptions open to question. One, environments are depicted as stable, with fixed values, rules, and sets of opportunities. Two, each organization of a given type is treated as freely responding in isolation to its environment. Hannan and Freeman call both assumptions into question, and suggest some interesting consequences.

In the first place, environments in any given domain may provide resources and pressure that vary over time (and at any one point in time), defining *many* possible niches for organizations and altering these niches. Organizations emerging and surviving in highly variable environments are more likely to maintain structures that pursue multiple purposes, with relatively low internal interdependent differentiation and low structural rigidity. Their status structures are likely to be flexible, with high rates of mobility (both internal to the organization and between the organization and the environment).

Second, organizations do not emerge in a given environment in isolation. Their existence and survival depend on their competitive situation vis-à-vis other organizations in the same environment. Our earlier arguments, for instance, suggest that environmental rules make it advantageous for every institution of higher education to be like Harvard. But this may be a very unsuccessful strategy for a given school competing in an environment already filled to carrying capacity with a Harvard. It follows, therefore, that the extant distribution of organizations of higher education will reflect not only the environmentally defined desiderata but also the outcome of competitive processes.

These ideas lead to the conclusion that environments generate not simply individual organizations but *distributions* of organizations across sets of variables. Future research must emphasize studies in which independent variables characterize environments by the distribution of resources and pressures they provide (not only central tendencies). And such research must examine dependent variables that characterize not only individual organizations but populations of organizations.

Studies of Internal Organizational Structure

The ideas just discussed also suggest research on the internal linkages of organizational structures. These linkages are seen as depending on properties of organizational environments. Two main ideas—closely related—are suggested. One is the assertion that modes of evaluation and control are carried through the organization from its relation to its environment (see Ouchi; Ouchi and Jaeger). Organizations whose relations to the environment are defined in terms of measurable outputs and exchanges are likely to employ output control and evaluation on *internal* subunits and individuals up and down the hierarchy. Here as elsewhere the studies in this book emphasize environmental rather than purely technical factors as core determinants of organizational structure. The general assertion here is obviously open to empirical test: Is it the case that organizations are more likely to employ output controls internally if they are themselves under such controls, holding technology constant? And are given output controls more likely to spread within such organizations? To examine this idea, research could compare hospitals, or schools, or subunits of business firms, or firms themselves. Some firms produce highly measurable outputs in highly competitive environments, while others have monopoly positions or produce outputs that are difficult to measure and evaluate.

A second line of argument (see J. Meyer and Rowan; J. Meyer and others; Pfeffer and others) pursues the same theme: Organizations that are primarily dependent on conformity to institutional rules rather than on the production of particular measured outputs tend to take on ceremonial characteristics. That is, they dramatize their public formal structures but tend to *loosely couple* these structures to technical activity. This involves evaluating and controlling individuals and subunits by inspection of their credentials or status—or, at most, of some public aspects of their work processes—and the avoidance of output inspection and control. That is, the internal structures of organizations that exist in highly institutionalized environments tend to be ceremonial reflections of those environments, rather than closely coordinated systems of output-directed activity. Schools, for instance, maintain the standardized apparatus of fields and grades and credentialed teachers. But they do not seem to inspect the work or outcomes of this structure carefully (J. Meyer and Rowan). The importance of this idea lies in its ability to explain the commonly noted separation of the more formalized and the more "work-related" (sometimes called *informal*) aspects of organizational life. For instance, the instructional work of a school often proceeds very differently from the specifications of the formal curriculum. This kind of gap has long been known to characterize many types of organizations. Research on this issue must, again, compare technologically similar organizations operating in contexts that differ in their institutionalized controls over organizations. For instance, do firms that rely entirely on Defense Department funding for difficult-to-measure activities tend to stress personnel credentials and formal status definitions rather than work- or outcome-related measures, in their evaluation and control of individuals and subunits? Do managers of political bureaucracies try to avoid getting detailed information on the work or outputs of their subordinates?

These ideas return to some of the classic issues in the field of organizations and redress some imbalances in current discussions of these issues. What is the nature of organizational authority? And how is control exercised? Clearly, in the modern world authority is justified in terms of rationality, and control is exercised by rationalized methods. But what is the rationality involved? Is it the rational pursuit of the immediate goals of technical production as held by the organization itself (or by particular organizational decision makers)? This is the "rationality" of current organizations theory—in it, authority is by and large Weber's authority of expertise, and control is the coordination of reciprocally and sequentially interdependent outputs (Thompson, 1967). But what if the rationality around which the organization is built has little to do with the efficient production of certain outputs—and instead is the rationality of the sovereign, little impeded by technical constraints? Here is the delegated authority of office, the control through pooled interdependence. And the calculus of the organizational actor is no longer around the efficient attainment of immediate productive ends but involves conformity to the rational prescriptions of the sovereign—perhaps conformity in technical activity but, in any event, public and ceremonial conformity. Is this not the situation of the manager of the school, the hospital, the public bureaucracy, the church, or many other organizations? One may protest that many organizations—for instance, business firms in capitalistic society—are under the rationalizing pressure of the market or other output controls rather than under the controls of the ceremonial rules of the sovereign. But many firms are in at least partial monopoly situations or depend on licenses or privileges from the state. And most components of modern firms are not under strict output controls. How is a firm to assess the true contribution of its production to its safety department, personnel department, environmental engineers, research engineers, planners, finance department, economic advisers, or organizational consultants? Is the value of such units to the firm not assessed ceremonially?

Many of the chapters in this volume touch on this crucial issue (Chapters Two, Three, Four, Five, Eight, Nine, Ten, Twelve, and Thirteen), and all of them in one way or another conclude that the rationality of organizational life may importantly be determined by the rationality built into the environments of organizations. In the work of J. Meyer and Rowan, Ouchi and Jaeger, and J. Meyer and others, the process is direct—organizations ape the legitimating rationality of the environment. In the work of Pfeffer, M. Meyer and Brown, M. Meyer, and Pfeffer and others, the process is political—power and resource distributions inside the organization are determined by power distributions outside it. In the chapters by Hannan and Freeman, the possibility is left open that organizations are at any one point in time rigid ossifications and that the overall process occurs through selection and the creation of new appropriate organizational forms in the environment.

In one way or another, all these arguments provide a return to the issue with which this review began—the societal determinants of organizational structure. And all these arguments provide a basis for an agreement on the future of organizational structures in postindustrial societies. Let us take it as axiomatic that *in postindustrial societies, rationalized states expand their dominance over more and more aspects of social life, increasing centralization and homogeneity in these domains.*

If this is true, it follows from the preceding arguments that we should expect organizations to become: (1) Increasingly reflective of rules institutionalized in states, (2) increasingly homogeneous within given domains, (3) increasingly organized around the rituals of conformity to wider institutions, (4) decreasingly structurally determined by the constraints of technical activity, and (5) decreasingly held together by output controls, employing instead the more ritualized controls of credentials, process controls, and the controls of group solidarity.

If we assume, further, that institutionalized state and societal structures in given domains are relatively stable,[2] it further follows from the preceding arguments that typical postindustrial organizations will be more structurally stable and will survive longer than has heretofore been characteristic of organizations in modern society. Postindustrial organizations, then, may slowly be returning to some of the forms of traditional premodern political bureaucracies, with great emphasis on solidarity, fairly low personnel turnover, relatively rigid but inexplicitly defined structure, the elaboration of rituals of status and credentials, low rates of internal mobility, and diffuse social relationships. There should be important differences too: The traditional political bureaucracies (for example, as was the Prussian Civil Service) were built on prerationalized social systems made up of primordial status groups, ethnic groups, clans, families, and so on. Postindustrial bureaucracy, reflecting the rationalized society, is built on the modern professionalized division of labor as institutionalized in society. The flexibility and universalism of this social system may make possible some modifications on more traditional political bureaucracy. For instance, the elaborated and specialized division of labor may make more complex and multidimensional organizational forms possible, less dependent on simple unidimensional hierarchy. It may also enable higher rates of mobility among organizations, as professionalized actors fit automatically in appropriate slots in many organizations.

In certain respects, these ideas lead to clear research design suggestions: We should trace the features of organizational histories as they respond to changes in the environment (particularly the structure of the state) over time, and we should study variations in organizational structure as they are affected by comparative variations in the structure of the environment and the state. Is it true, for instance, that organizations in more advanced postindustrial societies are likely to have high stability and great survival value? Is it true that they tend, in their internal structures, to shift away from the direct evaluation of individuals and subunits on output criteria, increasingly employing instead the criteria of conformity in structure and process to rationalize social *rules* built into society and the state?

In other respects, the research problem here cannot be put in terms of clear research designs. We need to link up our descriptive knowledge of modern organizations, in which the ceremonial pageantry of organizational life is apparent and routinely understood, with our theoretical models, in which it is an anomaly, a source of errors, or a series of exceptions to be explained away. Current organization theory is constructed around the pretense that most of the organizations of the modern world—government bureaus, schools, hospitals, monopoly firms, armies, professional organizations, and so on—are unusual and anomalous. We construct, with increasing elaborateness, models of organizational structure and organizational action that reflect a dying world: the world of the autonomous organization surrounded by free labor, capital, and commodity markets, using determinate technologies to produce outputs of known properties and market-determined value. We adapt these models by incorporating in them more and more forms of uncertainty, giving them quite complex mathematical structures. And we ignore the obvious fact that postindustrial society creates vast new forms of certainty, which organizations may obtain by the mere process of conformity to environmental specifications. Organization theorists sit in universities—highly stabilized and ritualized structures that are much more dependent on ceremonial and political congruence with their environments than on any aspect of technical efficiency—and imagine that the world outside is still that of a nineteenth-century factory. As with other outmoded forms of social life in complex societies, rational models of organization and action may make their last stand in the ideologies of academics in ivory towers.

Effects and Effectiveness

Organizational life and current organizational theory and research are moving in opposite directions. Organizations themselves, as we have discussed throughout this book, become increas-

ingly insulated from technical work and criteria of technical efficiency. Increasingly, they are controlled by institutional rules and
internal and external political processes. And increasingly they are
de facto monopolies or in conformity with rules that themselves
have monopoly power. Schools and states and hospitals and armies
and even economic organizations derive their power from their
institutional and political environments, rather than from competition in technical production. Their outputs are increasingly
defined institutionally, rather than technically. Schools and their
environments measure graduates (not learning), hospitals and their
environments assess patient-days (not cures), government bureaus
exchange very abstractly measured services with society, and firms
produce products (and, increasingly, services) whose meaning and
value decreasingly have simple market-determined worth. Internally, such organizations function by conformity to abstract rules
and internal and external political relations, rather than in terms
of the maximization of known technical production functions.

In reaction to these changes, organization theory and research become increasingly focused on the problem of technical
efficiency and effectiveness, searching for the grail of rationality
in an increasingly political, bureaucratic, and institutional world.
New myths of technical rationality arise—"evaluation research,"
"Program Planning Budgeting Systems" (PPBS), "organizational
development," and so on. These are all efforts to apply the rhetoric
of rationality to increasingly complex and increasingly institutionalized systems. With the breakdown of the classic market controls
over organizational production, organization theory and research
attempt to preserve as doctrines the older rules and justifications
or organizational control and legitimacy. As known products and
production functions disappear, myths and arbitrary accounting
devices appear. In fact, much current research on organizations
(see typical articles in the *Administrative Science Quarterly*) is in fact
a celebration of the myths of rationality or a discovery of new devices for giving these myths vitality in organizational domains
where they have grown opaque. Instead of analyzing organizational structures, we researchers spend too much time supporting
the myths of rationality by creating ceremonial production func-

tions—rulelike pretenses to technical rationality to apply to invisible activities and outputs.

Our own work leads to a skeptical view of these efforts. We see organizations more as competing *politically* for *institutional legitimacy* in contemporary environments and less as competing *technically* for *market advantages*. Organizational outputs are increasingly institutionally defined by the environment and are increasingly defined at highly aggregated and abstracted levels. The rhetorical claims for technical efficiency may be useful political devices for organizations to employ, but they are no longer the main structures by which organizations are controlled and legitimated.

Thus, the organizational effects and effectiveness that really operate in social life to regulate organizational survival are matters of political agreement and social definition negotiated between organizations and their environments. A school can become defined as an effective organization if it properly classifies and processes students according to environmental rules: Instructional outcomes may be immaterial (J. Meyer and Rowan). Hospitals' success in their environments presumably has little to do with their medical effects on patients: They are reimbursed for following standardized medical and patient care procedures and for the number of patients they manage and the number of days and procedures they apply to these patients.

It is important to understand that the utilization, by organizations and their environments, of highly ritualized measures of output and evaluation is not necessarily to be seen as distorted or inefficient. Especially in situations where "true" outputs are difficult to measure, or technologies unclear, or effects dependent on the levels of commitment or faith by participants, the use of ceremonialized criteria may have important benefits. It signals the commitments of the parties, it defines otherwise invisible purposes and standards, and it brings in the whole wider public community as an implicit witness to otherwise unstable and obscure bargains.

Two research implications of these ideas follow. First, we should study more carefully the social processes by which organizational environments create and apply definitions of effectiveness to organizations. We should not assume that it is simply our task as researchers to create and define appropriate organizational outcomes but should rather come to understand how such definitions are managed in the real world. Reforming relations between organizations and their environments is undoubtedly laudable, but it is the task of organizational research to understand these relations, in the first instance. The chapters in this book suggest that the following variables are relevant in understanding why both organizations and their environments are inattentive to outcome assessments of organizational effectiveness, and why they increasingly employ structural (or ceremonial) measures and definitions: (1) The environment itself may be a highly institutionalized organizational structure, utilizing its own rules of rationality in managing organizations (M. Meyer and Brown; J. Meyer and Rowan), and (2) actual organizational outcomes may be uncertain or invisible in definition, leaving coordination in the hands of social agreements (Ouchi and Jaeger; Pfeffer and others) and/or political processes (Pfeffer).

A second research implication here is that we should study the consequences of the current waves of development of interest in technical effectiveness—the current concern with evaluation research and the ongoing traditions of empirically investigating organizational effects. Do these traditions really operate to create new local adaptations in organizations, in conformity with structures and techniques proven "successful"? Or do they rather function as politically legitimating devices, more important for their existence than for their findings, and as environmentally utilized devices for formulating new institutional rules in terms of which to regulate organizations? Consider, for instance, the possible future history of lines of research such as that reported by Scott and Flood. Will hospitals ever be directly subjected to such research-created devices of assessment? Is it not more likely that the findings of such research will enter into the wider political environments of hospitals, creating new sets of standards and regulations that will be institutionally imposed on subsequent generations of hospitals? The view taken in the studies in this book tends to side with the latter argument. Studies of organizational effectiveness are not likely, by and large, to improve the capacity of local organizations to act with technical efficiency. They are more likely to create new social definitions of the "effective" organization—definitions that themselves will be applied in a rulelike way by organizational environments (in particular, by the state).

Thus we again return to the point that in modern societies rationality is less a property of technical action and structure within formal organizations than it is in an institutionally defined and organized set of recipes for action, by which local organizations survive by conforming. And thus we return to the main theme of this book: We are wary of conceptions of organizations as rationally adapting to their environments and imagine that organizations are in good part more passive creatures of these environments, systems of social conformity and political conflict along lines laid out and bounded by the larger social structures of the environment.

Conclusion

The main research implication of our studies, then, is that future studies should investigate variations in organizational structures as they are affected by variations among environments. We need, in organizations research, many more comparative studies —comparisons of technically similar organizations in different institutional and competitive environments, be they cities, countries, industries, or time periods. If organizations are indeed social products of their environments, we must study empirically how they vary in structure among such environments.

Notes

1. The distinction between environments and technologies is not as clear as it might seem, since technologies are usually environmentally created and institutionalized, from the point of view of any given organization. By technologies, we mean chains of interdependent purposive activity. By environments, we mean the collection of external rules and networks of organized interests that impact on a given organization. In many cases, a technology—whatever its origins—is clearly built into a given organization and controlled by the organization. This especially tends to be the case when the interdependent activities and their products are socially visible and subject to clear, known causal rules. In other cases—those which we tend to emphasize in this chapter—technologies are collections of activity where causal texture is not intrinsically highly visible. In such instances, organizational technologies are often highly dependent on environmental definition and prescription; that is, on social fiats external to the organization. This point is emphasized in this chapter: It makes the distinction between environment and technology even less clear and adds force to the point that we are less involved in an attack on ar-

guments that organizations arise around technologies than we are involved in stressing the environmental origins of both organizational structures and technological rules.

      2. In the long run, this assumption probably makes sense: State bureaucracies and bureaucratic requirements probably impose great stability on the domains they manage. In the short run, the point is not so convincing: The rapid changes and inconsistent rules of units of the American federal bureaucracy seem in recent years to have been a source of turbulence and instability in many organizational environments. In such environments, Hannan and Freeman argue, very flexible organizational units arise, not highly stabilized ones.

References

Abegglen, J. C. *The Japanese Factory: Aspects of its Social Organization.* New York: Free Press, 1958.

Acland, H. "Parents Love Schools?" *Interchange,* 1975, *6,* 1–10.

Aiken, M., and Hage, J. "Organizational Interdependence and Intraorganizational Structure." *American Sociological Review,* 1968, *33,* 912–930.

Akers, R., and Campbell, F. L. "Size and the Administrative Component in Occupational Associations." *Pacific Sociological Review,* 1970, *13,* 241–251.

Aldrich, H. E. "Organizational Boundaries and Interorganizational Conflict." *Human Relations,* 1971, *24,* 279–287.

Aldrich, H. E. "Technology and Organizational Structure: A Reexamination of the Findings of the Acton Group." *Administrative Science Quarterly,* 1972, *17,* 26–43.

Aldrich, H. E., and Pfeffer, J. "Environments of Organizations." *Annual Review of Sociology,* 1976, *2,* 79–105.

Aldrich, H. E., and Reiss, A. J. "Continuities in the Study of Ecological Succession: Changes in the Race Composition of Neighborhoods and Their Businesses." *American Journal of Sociology,* 1976, *81,* 846–866.

American Council on Education. *American Universities and Colleges.* Washington, D.C.: American Council on Education, 1966.

369

"America's Oldest Companies." *Nation's Business,* July 1976, *64,* 36–37.

Angell, R. C. *The Moral Integration of American Cities.* Chicago: University of Chicago Press, 1951.

Angell, R. C. "The Moral Integration of American Cities, Part II." *American Journal of Sociology,* 1974, *80,* 607–629.

Argyris, C. *Personality and Organization.* New York: Harper & Row, 1957.

Argyris, C. *The Applicability of Organizational Sociology.* Cambridge, England: Cambridge University Press, 1972.

Ariès, P. *Centuries of Childhood: A Social History of Family Life.* New York: Knopf, 1962.

Arrow, K. J. *Limits of Organization.* New York: Norton, 1974.

Bailyn, B. *Education in the Forming of American Society.* Chapel Hill: University of North Carolina Press, 1960.

Baker, E. C., "The Technology of Instructional Development." In R. M. W. Travers (Ed.), *Second Handbook of Research on Teaching.* Chicago: Rand McNally, 1973.

Baldridge, J. V. *Power and Conflict in the University.* New York: Wiley, 1971.

Barnard, C. I. *The Functions of the Executive.* Cambridge, Mass.: Harvard University Press, 1938.

Bendix, R. *Work Authority in Industry.* New York: Wiley, 1956.

Bendix, R. *Nation Building and Citizenship.* New York: Wiley, 1964.

Berliner, J. S. *Factory & Manager in the U.S.S.R.* Cambridge, Mass.: Harvard University Press, 1957.

Bidwell, C. "The School as a Formal Organization." In J. G. March (Ed.), *Handbook of Organizations.* Chicago: Rand McNally, 1965.

Blalock, H. M., Jr. *Social Statistics.* New York: McGraw-Hill, 1972.

Blau, P. M. *The Dynamics of Bureaucracy.* Chicago: University of Chicago Press, 1955.

Blau, P. M. *Exchange and Power in Social Life.* New York: Wiley, 1964.

Blau, P. M. "The Hierarchy of Authority in Organizations." *American Journal of Sociology,* 1968, *73,* 453–467.

Blau, P. M. "A Formal Theory of Differentiation in Organizations." *American Sociological Review,* 1970, *35,* 201–218.

Blau, P. M. "Interdependence and Hierarchy in Organizations." *Social Science Research*, 1972, *1*, 1–24.

Blau, P. M., and Duncan, O. D. *The American Occupational Structure.* New York: Wiley, 1967.

Blau, P. M., Heydebrand, W. V., Stauffer, R. E. "The Structure of Small Bureaucracies." *American Sociological Review*, 1966, *31*, 179–191.

Blau, P. M., and Schoenherr, R. A. *The Structure of Organizations.* New York: Basic Books, 1971.

Blau, P. M., and Scott, W. R. *Formal Organizations.* San Francisco: Chandler, 1962.

Bolton, J. E. *Small Firms: Report of the Committee of Inquiry on Small Firms.* London: Her Majesty's Stationery Office, 1971.

Boulding, K. E. *The Organizational Revolution.* New York: Harper & Row, 1953a.

Boulding, K. E. "Toward a General Theory of Growth." *Canadian Journal of Economics and Political Science*, 1953b, *19*, 326–340.

Bradburn, N. M. *The Structure of Psychological Well-Being.* Chicago: Aldine, 1969.

Brook, R. H. *Quality of Care Assessment: A Comparison of Five Methods of Peer Review.* DHEW Publication No. (HRA) 74-3100. Washington, D.C.: Bureau of Health Services and Research Evaluation, 1973.

Buckley, W. *Sociology and Modern Systems Theory.* Englewood Cliffs, N.J.: Prentice-Hall, 1967.

Burns, T., and Stalker, G. M. *The Management of Innovation.* London: Tavistock, 1961.

Buttrick, J. "The Inside Contracting System." *Journal of Economic History*, 1952, *12*, 201–221.

Callahan, R. E. *Education and the Cult of Efficiency.* Chicago: University of Chicago Press, 1962.

Campbell, J. P., and others. *Managerial Behavior, Performance, and Effectiveness.* New York: McGraw-Hill, 1970.

Caplow, T. "Organizational Size." *Administrative Science Quarterly*, 1957, *1*, 484–505.

Cartter, A. M. *An Assessment of Quality in Graduate Education.* Washington, D.C.: American Council on Education, 1966.

Chandler, A. D., Jr. *Strategy and Structure.* Cambridge, Mass.: M.I.T. Press, 1962.

Child, J. "Organizational Structure and Strategies of Control: A Replication of the Aston Study." *Administrative Science Quarterly,* 1972a, *17,* 163–177.

Child, J. "Organizational Structure, Environment and Performance: The Role of Strategic Choice." *Sociology,* 1972b, *6,* 1–22.

Child, J. "Strategies of Control and Organizational Behavior." *Administrative Science Quarterly,* 1973, *18,* 1–17.

Churchill, B. C. "Age and Life Expectancy of Business Firms." *Survey of Current Business,* 1955, *35,* 15–19.

Coch, L., and French, J. R. P. "Overcoming Resistance to Change." *Human Relations,* 1948, *1,* 512–532.

Cohen, E. G., and others. "Organization and Instruction in Elementary Schools." Technical Report No. 50. Stanford, Calif.: Center for Research and Development in Teaching, Stanford University, 1976.

Cohen, E. G., and others. "Technology and Structure in the Classroom: A Longitudinal Analysis of the Relation Between Instructional Methods and Teacher Collaboration." Unpublished paper, Center for Research and Development in Teaching, Stanford University, Stanford, Calif. 94305, 1977.

Cohen, M. D., March, J. G., and Olsen, J. P. "Garbage Can Model of Organizational Choice." *Administrative Science Quarterly,* 1972, *17,* 1–25.

Cole, J. R., and Cole, S. *Social Stratification in Science.* Chicago: University of Chicago Press, 1973.

Cole, R. *Japanese Blue Collar: The Changing Tradition.* Berkeley: University of California Press, 1971.

Cole, R. "Functional Alternatives and Economic Development: An Empirical Example of Permanent Employment in Japan." *American Sociological Review,* 1973, *38,* 424–438.

Coleman, J. S. "The Mathematical Study of Change." In H. M. Blalock, Jr., and A. B. Blalock (Eds.), *Methodology in Social Research.* New York: McGraw-Hill, 1968.

Coombs, P. H. *The World Educational Crisis.* New York: Oxford University Press, 1968.

Corwin, R. G. *Militant Professionalism*. New York: Appleton-Century-Crofts, 1970.

Crane, D. "Scientists at Major and Minor Universities: A Study of Productivity and Recognition." *American Sociological Review*, 1965, *30*, 699–714.

Crane, D. "The Gatekeepers of Science: Some Factors Affecting the Selection of Articles for Scientific Journals." *American Sociologist*, 1967, *2*, 195–201.

Crecine, J. P. "A Computer Simulation Model of Municipal Budgeting." *Management Science*, 1967, *13*, 786–815.

Crozier, M. *The Bureaucratic Phenomenon*. Chicago: University of Chicago Press, 1964.

Cubberly, E. P. *Public School Administration*. Boston: Houghton Mifflin, 1916.

Cyert, R. M., Dill, W. R., and March, J. G. "The Role of Expectations in Business Decision-Making." *Administrative Science Quarterly*, 1958, *3*, 307–340.

Cyert, R. M., and March, J. G. *A Behavioral Theory of the Firm*. Englewood Cliffs, N.J.: Prentice-Hall, 1963.

Cyert, R. M., Simon, H. A., and Trow, D. B. "Observation of a Business Decision." *Journal of Business*, 1956, *29*, 237–248.

Dahl, R. *Who Governs?* New Haven, Conn.: Yale University Press, 1961.

Davis, O. A., Dempster, M. A. H., and Wildavsky, A. "A Theory of the Budgetary Process." *American Political Science Review*, 1966, *60*, 529–547.

Deal T. E., Meyer, J. W., and Scott, W. R. "Organizational Influences on Educational Innovation." In J. V. Baldridge and T. E. Deal (Eds.), *Managing Change in Educational Organizations*. Berkeley, Calif.: McCutcheon, 1975.

Dibble, V. K. "The Organization of Traditional Authority: English County Government, 1558 to 1640." In J. G. March (Ed.), *Handbook of Organizations*. Chicago: Rand McNally, 1965.

Dill, W. R. "Environment as an Influence on Managerial Autonomy." *Administrative Science Quarterly*, 1958, *2*, 409–443.

Donabedian, A. "Evaluating the Quality of Medical Care." *Milbank Memorial Fund Quarterly*, 1966, *44*, (Part 2), 166–203.

Donham, W. B. "Foreword." In E. Mayo, *The Social Problems of an Industrial Civilization*. Boston: Graduate School of Business Administration, Harvard University, 1945.

Dore, R. *British Factory–Japanese Factory*. Berkeley: University of California Press, 1973.

Doreian, P., and Hummon, N. P. "Estimates for Differential Equation Models of Social Phenomena." In D. R. Heise (Ed.), *Sociological Methodology 1977*. San Francisco: Jossey-Bass, 1977.

Dornbusch, S. M., and Scott, W. R. *Evaluation and the Exercise of Authority: A Theory of Control Applied to Diverse Organizations*. San Francisco: Jossey-Bass, 1975.

Dowling, J., and Pfeffer, J. "Organizational Legitimacy: Social Values and Organizational Behavior." *Pacific Sociological Review, 1975, 18,* 122–136.

Downey, H. K., Hellriegel, D., Slocum, J. W. "Environmental Uncertainty: The Construct and Its Application." *Administrative Science Quarterly, 1975, 20,* 613–629.

Downs, A. *Inside Bureaucracy*. Boston: Little, Brown, 1967.

Dreeben, R. "The School as a Workplace." In R. M. W. Travers (Ed.), *Second Handbook of Research on Teaching*. Chicago: Rand McNally, 1973.

Duncan, R. B. "Characteristics of Organizational Environments and Perceived Environmental Uncertainty." *Administrative Science Quarterly, 1972, 17,* 313–327.

Durkheim, E. *The Division of Labor in Society*. G. Simpson, Trans. New York: Free Press, 1933.

Durkheim, E. *Suicide*. New York: Free Press, 1951.

Elton, C. *Animal Ecology*. London: Sidgwick & Jackson, 1927.

Etzioni, A. "Two Approaches to Organizational Analysis: A Critique and a Suggestion." *Administrative Science Quarterly, 1960, 5,* 257–278.

Etzioni, A. *A Comparative Analysis of Complex Organizations*. New York: Free Press, 1961.

Evan, W. M. "The Organization Set: Toward a Theory of Interorganizational Relations." In J. D. Thompson (Ed.), *Approaches to Organizational Design*. Pittsburgh: University of Pittsburgh Press, 1966.

Evans, P. B. "Multiple Hierarchies and Organizational Control." *Administrative Science Quarterly*, 1975, *20*, 250–259.

Fantini, M., and Gittell, M. *Decentralization: Achieving Reform.* New York: Praeger, 1973.

Fayol, H. *Administration Industrielle et Générale.* Paris: Durod, 1916.

Festinger, L. "Informal Social Communication." *Psychological Review*, 1950, *57*, 271–282.

Festinger, L. "A Theory of Social Comparison Processes." *Human Relations*, 1954, *7*, 117–140.

Field, A. "Educational Reform and Manufacturing Development, Massachusetts 1837–1865." Unpublished doctoral dissertation, University of California, Berkeley, 1972.

Flood, A. B. "Professionals and Organizational Performance: A Study of Medical Staff Organization and Quality of Care in Short-Term Hospitals." Unpublished doctoral dissertation, Stanford University, 1976.

Flood, A. B., and Scott, W. R. "Professional Power and Professional Effectiveness: The Power of the Surgical Staff and the Quality of Surgical Care in Hospitals." Paper presented at the meeting of the Pacific Sociological Association, Sacramento, Calif., April 21–23, 1977.

Flood, A. B., and others. "Effectiveness in Professional Organizations: The Impact of Surgeons and Surgical Staff Organization on the Quality of Care in Hospitals." Paper presented at the meeting of the American Sociological Association, Chicago, September 5–9, 1977.

Form, W. H. "The Social Construction of Anomie: A Four-Nation Study of Industrial Workers." *American Journal of Sociology*, 1975, *80*, 1165–1191.

Franklin, J. L. "Down the Organization: Influence Processes Across Levels of Hierarchy." *Administrative Science Quarterly*, 1975, *20*, 153–164.

Freeman, J. H. "Environment, Technology and the Administrative Intensity of Manufacturing Organizations." *American Sociological Review*, 1973, *38*, 750–763.

Freeman, J. H. "The Unit Problem in Organization Research."

Paper presented at the annual meeting of the American Sociological Association, San Francisco, August, 25–29, 1975.

Freeman, J. H., and Brittain, J. "Union Merger Processes and Industrial Environments." *Industrial Relations*, 1977, *16*, 173–185.

Freeman, J. H., and Hannan, M. T. "Growth and Decline Processes in Organizations." *American Sociological Review*, 1975, *40*, 215–228.

Freeman, J. H., and Hannan, M. T. "Reply to Kaufman." *American Sociological Review*, 1976, *41*, 748–749.

Freeman, J. H., and Kronenfeld, J. E. "Problems of Definitional Dependency: The Case of Administrative Intensity." *Social Forces*, 1974, *52*, 108–121.

Freidson, E. *Profession of Medicine*. New York: Dodd, Mead, 1970.

French, J. R. P., and Raven, B. "The Bases of Social Power." In D. Cartwright and A. Zander (Eds.), *Group Dynamics*, (3rd ed.) New York: Harper & Row, 1968.

Friedlander, F., and Pickle, H. "Components of Effectiveness in Small Organizations." *Administrative Science Quarterly*, 1968, *13*, 289–304.

Friedman, M. *Essays on Positive Economics*. Chicago: University of Chicago Press, 1953.

Gause, G. F. *The Struggle for Existence*. Baltimore, Md.: Williams & Wilkins, 1934.

Georgopoulos, B. S., and Tannenbaum, A. S. "A Study of Organizational Effectiveness." *American Sociological Review*, 1957, *22*, 534–540.

Gerwin, D. "A Process Model of Budgeting in a Public School System." *Management Science*, 1969, *15*, 338–361.

Glenn, N., and Villemez, W. "The Productivity of Sociologists at 45 American Universities." *American Sociologist*, 1970, *5*, 244–252.

Goffman, E. *Interaction Ritual*. Garden City, N.Y.: Doubleday, 1967.

Goode, W. J. "A Theory of Role Strain." *American Sociological Review*, 1960, *25*, 483–496.

Gordon, G., and Becker, S. "Organizational Size and Managerial Succession: A Re-Examination." *American Journal of Sociology*, 1964, *70*, 215–222.

Gouldner, A. W. *Patterns of Industrial Bureaucracy.* New York: Free Press, 1954.

Gouldner, A. W. "Organizational Analysis," In R. K. Merton, L. Broom, and L. S. Cottrell, Jr. (Eds.), *Sociology Today.* New York: Basic Books, 1959.

Graen, G., Dansereau, F., Jr., and Minami, T. "Dysfunctional Leadership Styles." *Organizational Behavior and Human Performance,* 1972, 7, 216–236.

Graicunas, V. A. "Relationship in Organizations." *Bulletin of the International Management Institute,* 1933 (March), 183–187.

Granovetter, M. S. "The Strength of Weak Ties." *American Journal of Sociology,* 1973, 78, 1360–1380.

Griffith, E. S. *A History of American City Governments: The Progressive Years and Their Aftermath, 1900–1920.* New York: Praeger, 1974.

Gross, E. "Universities as Organizations: A Research Approach." *American Sociological Review,* 1968, 33, 518–544.

Gross, G. R. "The Organization Set: A Study of Sociology Departments." *American Sociologist,* 1970, 5, 25–29.

Gross, N., and Herriott, R. E. *Staff Leadership in Public Schools: A Sociological Inquiry.* New York: Wiley, 1965.

Grusky, O. "Corporate Size, Bureaucratization, and Managerial Succession." *American Journal of Sociology,* 1961, 67, 261–269.

Grusky, O. "Managerial Succession and Organizational Effectiveness." *American Journal of Sociology,* 1963, 69, 21–31.

Gulick, L., and Urwick, L. (Eds.). *Papers on the Science of Administration.* New York: Institute of Public Administration, 1937.

Hage, J., and Aiken, M. "Routine Technology, Social Structure and Organizational Goals." *Administrative Science Quarterly,* 1969, 14, 366–376.

Hagstrom, W. O. "Input, Outputs, and the Prestige of University Science Departments." *Sociology of Education,* 1971, 44, 375–397.

Haire, M. "Biological Models and Empirical Histories of the Growth of Organizations." In M. Haire (Ed.), *Modern Organization Theory.* New York: Wiley, 1959.

Hall, R. H. "The Concept of Bureaucracy: An Empirical Assessment." *American Journal of Sociology,* 1963, 69, 32–40.

Hall, R. H. *Organizations: Structure and Process.* Englewood Cliffs, N.J.: Prentice-Hall, 1972.

378   References

Hall, R. H., Haas, J. E., and Johnson, J. N. "Organizational Size, Complexity and Formalization." *American Sociological Review*, 1967, *32*, 903–912.

Halpern, S. *Drug Abuse and Your Company*. New York: American Management Association, 1972.

Hamblin, W. "Leadership and Crises." *Sociometry*, 1958, *21*, 322–335.

Hannan, M. T. "Problems of Aggregation." In H. M. Blalock, Jr. (Ed.), *Causal Models in the Social Sciences*. Chicago: Aldine-Atherton, 1971.

Hannan, M. T. "The Dynamics of Ethnic Boundaries." Unpublished manuscript, Department of Sociology, Stanford University, Stanford, Calif. 94305, 1975.

Hannan, M. T. "Modeling Stability and Complexity in Networks of Organizations." Paper presented at the annual meeting of the American Sociological Association, New York, August 30–September 3, 1976.

Hannan, M. T., and Freeman, J. H. "Environment and the Structure of Organizations." Paper presented at the annual meeting of the American Sociological Association, Montreal, August 26–30, 1974.

Hannan, M. T., and Freeman, J. H. "Obstacles to Comparative Studies." In P. S. Goodman, J. M. Pennings, and Associates, *New Perspectives on Organizational Effectiveness*. San Francisco: Jossey-Bass, 1977a.

Hannan, M. T., and Freeman, J. H. "The Population Ecology of Organizations." *American Journal of Sociology*, 1977b, *82*, 929–964.

Hannan, M. T., Freeman, J. H., and Meyer, J. W. "Specification of Models for Organizational Effectiveness." *American Sociological Review*, 1976, *41*, 136–143.

Hannan, M. T., and Young, A. A. "Estimation in Multi-Wave Panel Models: Results on Pooling Cross-Sections and Time Series." In D. Heise (Ed.), *Sociological Methodology 1977*. San Francisco: Jossey-Bass, 1977.

Hargens, L. L. "Patterns of Mobility of New Ph.D's Among American Academic Institutions." *Sociology of Education*, 1969, *49*, 18–37.

Hargens, L. L., and Hagstrom, W. O. "Sponsored and Contest Mobility of American Academic Scientists." *Sociology of Education,* 1967, *40,* 24–38.

Hartmann, H. *Authority and Organization in German Management.* Princeton, N.J.: Princeton University Press, 1959.

Hawley, A. H. "Ecology and Human Ecology." *Social Forces,* 1944, *22,* 398–405.

Hawley, A. H. *Human Ecology: A Theory of Community Structure.* New York: Ronald Press, 1950.

Hawley, A. H. "Human Ecology." In D. L. Sills (Ed.), *International Encyclopedia of the Social Sciences.* New York: Macmillan, 1968.

Heise, D. R. "Causal Inference from Panel Data." In E. F. Borgatta (Ed.), *Sociological Methodology, 1970.* San Francisco: Jossey-Bass, 1970.

Hendershot, G. E., and James, T. F. "Size and Growth Determinants of Administrative Ratios in Organization." *American Sociological Review,* 1972, *37,* 149–153.

Henderson, C. R. "Specific and Combining Ability." In J. W. Gowens (Ed.), *Heterosis.* Ames: Iowa State College Press, 1952.

Henderson, C. R. "Selection Index and Expected Genetic Advance." In *Statistical Genetics and Plant Breeding.* Publication No. 982. Washington, D.C.: National Academy of Sciences, 1963.

Hickson, D. J., Pugh, D. S., and Pheysey, D. C. "Operations Technology and Organization Structure: An Empirical Reappraisal." *Administrative Science Quarterly,* 1969, *14,* 378–395.

Hickson, D. J., and others. "A Strategic Contingencies Theory of Intraorganizational Power." *Administrative Science Quarterly,* 1971, *16,* 216–229.

Hinings, C. R., and others. "Structural Conditions of Intraorganizational Power." *Administrative Science Quarterly,* 1974, *19,* 22–44.

Hirsch, P. M. "Organizational Effectiveness and the Institutional Environment." *Administrative Science Quarterly,* 1975, *20,* 327–344.

Hobbs, N. (Ed.). *Issues in the Classification of Children: A Sourcebook on Categories, Labels, and Their Consequences.* San Francisco: Jossey-Bass, 1975.

Holdoway, E. A., and Blowers, T. A. "Administrative Ratios and

Organizational Size." *American Sociological Review,* 1971, *36,* 278–286.

Hollander, E. O. *The Future of Small Business.* New York: Praeger, 1967.

Holt, J. C. *How Children Fail.* New York: Pitman, 1964.

Homans, G. C. *The Human Group.* New York: Harcourt Brace Jovanovich, 1950.

Hopwood, A. G. "An Empirical Study of the Role of Accounting Data in Performance Evaluation." *Empirical Research in Accounting: Selected Studies,* Supplement to the *Journal of Accounting Research,* 1972, *10,* 156–182.

Hummon, N. A. "Notes on Blau's 'A Formal Theory of Differentiation in Organizations.'" *American Sociological Review,* 1971, *36,* 297–303.

Hummon, N. P., Doreian, P., and Teuter, K. "A Structural Control Model of Organizational Change." *American Sociological Review,* 1975, *40,* 812–824.

Hutchinson, G. E. "Concluding Remarks." *Cold Spring Harbor Symposium on Quantitative Biology,* 1957, *22,* 415–427.

Hutchinson, G. E. "Homage to Santa Rosalia, or Why Are There So Many Kinds of Animals?" *American Naturalist,* 1959, *93,* 145–159.

Illich, I. *Deschooling Society.* New York: Harper & Row, 1971.

Janes, R. W. "The Student-Faculty Ratio in Graduate Programs of Selected Departments of Sociology." *American Sociologist,* 1969, *4,* 123–127.

Johnson, R. T., and Ouchi, W. G. "Made in America (Under Japanese Management)." *Harvard Business Review,* 1974, *52,* (5), 61–69.

Jones, E. E., and Gerard, H. B. *Foundations of Social Psychology.* New York: Wiley, 1967.

Kahn, R. L., and others. *Organizational Stress: Studies in Role Conflict and Ambiguity.* New York: Wiley, 1964.

Kasarda, J. D., and Janowitz, M. "Community Attachment in Mass Society," *American Sociological Review,* 1974, *39,* 328–339.

Katz, D., and Kahn, R. L. *The Social Psychology of Organizations.* New York: Wiley, 1966.

Katz, M. *The Irony of Early School Reform.* Boston: Beacon, 1968.

Kaufman, R. L. "The Solution and Interpretation of Differential

Equation Models: Comment on Freeman and Hannan." *American Sociological Review*, 1976, *41*, 746–748.

Kelsall, R. K. *Higher Civil Servants in Britain*. London: Routledge & Kegan Paul, 1955.

Kempthorne, O. *The Design and Analysis of Experiments*. New York: Wiley, 1952.

Kiesler, C. A., and Kiesler, S. *Conformity*. Reading, Mass.: Addison-Wesley, 1969.

Kimberly, J. R. "Environmental Constraints and Organizational Structure: A Comparative Analysis of Rehabilitation Organizations." *Administrative Science Quarterly*, 1975, *20*, 1–9.

Kimberly, J. R. "Organizational Size and the Structuralist Perspective: A Review, Critique, and Proposal." *Administrative Science Quarterly*, 1976, *21*, 571–597.

Knudsen, D. D., and Vaughan, T. R. "Quality in Graduate Education: A Re-evaluation of the Rankings of Sociology Departments in the Cartter Report." *American Sociologist*, 1969, *4*, 12–19.

Kolarska, L. "Interorganizational Networks and Politics: The Case of Polish Industry." Unpublished manuscript, Academy of Science, Warsaw, Poland, 1975.

Kriesberg, L. "Careers, Organizational Size, and Succession." *American Journal of Sociology*, 1962, *68*, 355–359.

Lasswell, H. D. *Politics: Who Gets What, When, How*. New York: McGraw-Hill, 1936.

Lavender, A. D., Mathers, R. A., and Pease, J. "The Student-Faculty ratio in Graduate Programs of Selected Departments of Sociology: A Supplement to the Janes Report." *American Sociologist*, 1971, *6*, 29–30.

Lawrence, P. R., and Lorsch, J. W. *Organization and Environment*. Boston: Graduate School of Business Administration, Harvard University, 1967.

Lazarsfeld, P. F., and Menzel, H. *On The Relation Between Individual and Collective Properties*. In A. Etzichi (Ed.), *Complex Organizations*. New York: Holt, Rinehart and Winston, 1961.

Leeds, R. "The Absorption of Protest: A Working Paper." In W. W. Cooper, H. J. Leavitt, and M. W. Shelly (Eds.), *New Perspectives in Organization Research*. New York: Wiley, 1964.

Levin, S. A. "Community Equilibrium and Stability: An Extension of the Competitive Exclusion Principle." *American Naturalist,* 1970, *104,* 413–423.

Levine, S., and White, P. E. "Exchange as a Framework for the Study of Interorganizational Relationships." *Administrative Science Quarterly,* 1961, *5,* 583–601.

Levins, R. "Theory of Fitness in a Heterogeneous Environment. I. The Fitness Set and Adaptive Function." *American Naturalist,* 1962, *91,* 361–378.

Levins, R. *Evolution in Changing Environments.* Princeton, N.J.: Princeton University Press, 1968.

Lieberson, S., and O'Connor, J. F. "Leadership and Organizational Performance: A Study of Large Corporations." *American Sociological Review,* 1972, *37,* 117–130.

Light, I. H. *Ethnic Enterprise in America.* New York: World, 1972.

Lightfield, E. T. "Output and Recognition of Sociologists." *American Sociologist,* 1971, *6,* 128–133.

Lipset, S. M., Trow, M., and Coleman, J. *Union Democracy.* New York: Free Press, 1956.

Lodahl, J., and Gordon, G. "The Structure of Scientific Fields and the Functioning of University Graduate Departments." *American Sociological Review,* 1972, *37,* 57–72.

Lodahl, J., and Gordon, G. "Funding the Sciences in University Departments." *Educational Record,* 1973, *54,* 74–82.

Lortie, D. C. "Observations on Teaching as Work." In R. M. W. Travers (Ed.), *Second Handbook of Research on Teaching.* Chicago: Rand McNally, 1973.

Lowin, A. "Participative Decision Making: A Model, Literature Critique, and Prescriptions for Research." *Organizational Behavior and Human Performance,* 1968, *3,* 68–106.

MacArthur, R. H. *Geographical Ecology: Patterns in the Distribution of Species.* Princeton, N.J.: Princeton University Press, 1972.

MacArthur, R. H., and Levins, R. "Competition, Habitat Selection and Character Displacement in Patchy Environment." *Proceedings of the National Academy of Sciences,* 1964, *51,* 1207–1210.

McCall, G. J., and Simmons, J. L. *Identities and Interactions.* New York: Free Press, 1966.

McEachern, W. A. *Managerial Control and Performance.* Lexington, Mass.: Heath, 1975.

McFarland, D. D. "Organizational Structure as Generated by a Branching Process." Unpublished paper, 1972.

McGregor, D. *The Human Side of Enterprise.* New York: McGraw-Hill, 1960.

Mann, F. C., and Hoffman, L. R. *Automation and the Worker: A Study of Social Change in Power Plants.* New York: Holt, Rinehart and Winston, 1960.

March, J. G. "The Business Firm as a Political Coalition." *Journal of Politics,* 1962, *24,* 662–678.

March, J. G., and Olsen, J. P. *Ambiguity and Choice in Organizations.* Bergen, Norway: Universitetsforlaget, 1976.

March, J. G., and Simon, H. A. *Organizations.* New York: Wiley, 1958.

Marschak, J., and Radner, R. *Economic Theory of Teams.* New Haven, Conn.: Yale University Press, 1972.

Maslow, A. H. *Motivation and Personality.* New York: Harper & Row, 1954.

Mason, K. O., and others. "Some Methodological Issues in Cohort Analysis of Archival Data." *American Sociological Review,* 1973, *38,* 242–258.

May, R. M. *Stability and Complexity in Model Ecosystems.* Princeton, N.J.: Princeton University Press, 1973.

Mayo, E. *The Social Problems of an Industrial Civilization.* Boston: Graduate School of Business Administration, Harvard University, 1945.

Merton, R. K. "Bureaucratic Structure and Personality." *Social Forces,* 1940, *17,* 560–568.

Merton, R. K. *Social Theory and Social Structure.* (2nd ed.) New York: Free Press, 1957.

Merton, R. K., and others. (Eds.). *Reader in Bureaucracy.* New York: Free Press, 1952.

Meyer, J. W. "The Charter: Conditions of Diffuse Socialization in Schools." In W. R. Scott (Ed.), *Social Processes and Social Structures.* New York: Holt, Rinehart and Winston, 1970.

Meyer, J. W., and Rowan, B. "Notes on the Structure of Educational Organizations." Paper presented at the annual meeting of the American Sociological Association, San Francisco, August 1975.

Meyer, J. W., and Rowan, B. "Institutionalized Organizations: Formal Structure as Myth and Ceremony." *American Journal of Sociology*, 1977, *83*, 440–463.

Meyer, J. W., and Rubinson, R. "Education and Political Development." *Review of Research in Education*, 1975, *3*, 134–162.

Meyer, J. W., and others. "The Impact of the Open Space School Upon Teacher Influence and Autonomy: The Effects of an Organizational Innovation." Technical Report No. 21. Stanford, Calif.: Center for Research and Development in Teaching, Stanford University, 1971.

Meyer, J. W., and others. "The Degree of Linkage between District, School, and Classroom." Technical Report No. 50. Stanford, Calif.: Center for Research and Development in Teaching, Stanford University, 1976.

Meyer, M. W. "The Two Authority Structure of Bureaucratic Organizations." *Administrative Science Quarterly*, 1968, *13*, 211–218.

Meyer, M. W. "Some Constraints in Analyzing Data on Organizational Structures." *American Sociological Review*, 1971, *36*, 294–297.

Meyer, M. W. *Bureaucratic Structure and Authority*. New York: Harper & Row, 1972a.

Meyer, M. W. "Size and Structure of Organizations: A Causal Analysis." *American Sociological Review*, 1972b, *37*, 434–440.

Meyer, M. W. "Population and Organization: Some Further Thought on the Relationship Between Size and Structural Differentiation." Paper presented at the 68th annual meeting of the American Sociological Association, New York, August 27–30, 1973.

Meyer, M. W. "Organizational Domains." *American Sociological Review*, 1975, *40*, 599–615.

Michels, R. *Political Parties*. New York: Free Press, 1949. (Originally published 1915.)

Miles, M. B. "Planned Change and Organizational Health." In J. V. Baldridge, and T. E. Deal (Ed.), *Managing Change in Educational Organizations*. Berkeley, Calif.: McCutcheon, 1975.

Mitau, G. T. *State and Local Governments: Politics and Processes*. New York: Scribner's, 1966.

Mohr, L. "Organizational Technology and Organizational Structure." *Administrative Science Quarterly*, 1971, *16*, 444–459.

Monod, J. *Chance and Necessity.* New York: Vintage, 1971.

Moore, M. H. "Policy Toward Heroin Use in New York City." Unpublished doctoral dissertation, Harvard University, 1973.

Moore, W. J. "The Relative Quality of Graduate Programs in Economics, 1958–1972: Who Published and Who Perished." *Western Economic Journal,* 1973, *11,* 1–23.

Mousseau, J. "The Family, Prison of Love: A Conversation with Phillipe Ariès." *Psychology Today,* 1975, *9,* (3), 52–54.

Nakane, C. *Japanese Society.* (rev. ed.) Middlesex, England: Penguin Books, 1973.

Naroll, R. "Some Thoughts on Comparative Methods in Cultural Anthropology." In H. M. Blalock, Jr., and A. B. Blalock (Eds.), *Methodology in Social Research.* New York: McGraw-Hill, 1968.

National Civil Service League. *A Model Public Personnel Administration Law.* Washington, D.C.: 1970.

National Science Foundation. *Grants and Awards.* (Annual.) Washington, D.C.: U.S. Government Printing Office, 1964–1971a.

National Science Foundation. *Annual Report,* Washington, D.C.: U.S. Government Printing Office, 1964–1971b.

Nelson, D. *Managers and Workers.* Madison: University of Wisconsin Press, 1975.

Nerlove, M. "Further Evidence on the Estimation of Dynamic Economic Relations from a Time-Series of Cross-Sections." *Econometrica,* 1971, *39,* 341–358.

Nielson, F. "The Interrelationships of Educational and Economic Institutions: Pooling of Cross-Sections and Heteroscedasticity." Unpublished paper, Department of Sociology, Stanford University, Stanford, Calif. 94305, 1974.

Nielsen, F., and Hannan, M. T. "The Expansion of National Educational Systems: Tests of a Population Ecology Model." *American Sociological Review,* 1977, *42,* 479–490.

Norr, J. L., and Norr, K. L. "Societal Complexity on Production Techniques: Another Look at Udy's Data on the Structure of Work Organizations." *American Journal of Sociology,* 1977, *82,* 845–853.

Ouchi, W. G. "The Relationship Between Organizational Structure and Organizational Control." *Administrative Science Quarterly,* 1977, *22,* 95–113.

Ouchi, W. G., and Johnson, J. B. *Integrating the Organization with the Society*. Stanford Research Paper No. 367. Stanford, Calif.: Graduate School of Business, Stanford University, 1977.

Ouchi, W. G., and Maguire, M. A. "Organizational Control: Two Functions." *Administrative Science Quarterly*, 1975, *20*, 559–569.

Parsons, T. *The Social System*. New York: Free Press, 1951.

Parsons, T. "Suggestions for a Sociological Approach to the Theory of Organizations, I." *Administrative Science Quarterly*, 1956, *1*, 63–85.

Parsons, T., and Shils, E. A. *Toward a General Theory of Action*. Cambridge, Mass.: Harvard University Press, 1951.

Patchen, M. "Alternative Questionnaire Approaches to the Measurement of Influence in Organizations." *American Journal of Sociology*, 1963, *69*, (1), 41–52.

Paul, B. D. "Social Science in Public Health." *American Journal of Public Health*, 1956, *46*, 1390–1396.

Pennings, J. M. "The Relevance of the Structural-Contingency Model for Organizational Effectiveness." *Administrative Science Quarterly*, 1975, *20*, 393–410.

Penrose, E. T. *The Theory of the Growth of the Firm*. New York: Wiley, 1959.

Perrow, C. "Hospitals: Technology, Structure and Goals." In J. G. March (Ed.), *Handbook of Organizations*. Chicago: Rand McNally, 1965.

Perrow, C. "A Framework for the Comparative Analysis of Organizations." *American Sociological Review*, 1967, *32*, 194–208.

Perrow, C. "Departmental Power and Perspective in Industrial Firms." In M. N. Zald (Ed.), *Power in Organizations*. Nashville, Tenn.: Vanderbilt University Press, 1970.

Perrow, C. *Organizational Analysis: A Sociological View*. Belmont, Calif.: Wadsworth, 1970.

Perrow, C. *Complex Organizations: A Critical Essay*. Glenview, Ill.: Scott, Foresman, 1972.

Pettigrew, A. M. *The Politics of Organizational Decision-Making*. London: Tavistock, 1973.

Pfeffer, J., and Leblebici, H. "The Effect of Competition on Some Dimensions of Organizational Structure." *Social Forces*, 1973, *52*, 268–279.

Pfeffer, J., Leong, A., and Strehl, K. "Paradigm Development and Particularism: Journal Publication in Three Scientific Disciplines." *Social Forces,* 1977, *55,* 938–951.

Pfeffer, J., and Salancik, G. R. "Organizational Decision Making as a Political Process: The Case of a University Budget." *Administrative Science Quarterly,* 1974, *19,* 135–151.

Pfeffer, J., and Salancik, G. R. "Organizational Context and the Characteristics and Tenure of Hospital Administrators." *Academy of Management Journal,* 1977, *20,* 74–88.

Phillips, J. C. *Municipal Government and Administration in America.* New York: Macmillan, 1960.

Pondy, L. R. "Effects of Size, Complexity, and Ownership on Administrative Intensity." *Administrative Science Quarterly,* 1969, *14,* 47–60.

Pondy, L. R. "Toward a Theory of Internal Resource-Allocation." In M. N. Zald (Ed.), *Power in Organizations.* Nashville, Tenn.: Vanderbilt University Press, 1970.

Pondy, L. R. "A Minimum Communication Cost Model of Organizations: Derivation of Blau's Laws of Structural Differentiation." Unpublished paper, 1975.

Presthus, R. *The Organizational Society.* New York: Knopf, 1962.

Pugh, D. S., and others. "Dimensions of Organization Structure." *Administrative Science Quarterly,* 1968, *13,* 65–106.

Pugh, D. S., and others. "The Context of Organization Structures." *Administrative Science Quarterly,* 1969, *14,* 91–114.

Ramirez, F. O. "Societal Corporateness and Status Conferral." Unpublished doctoral dissertation, Stanford University, 1974.

Reich, C. A. *The Greening of America.* New York: Random House, 1970.

Reissman, L. *The Urban Process.* New York: Free Press, 1964.

Rhee, S. "Relative Importance of Physicians' Personal and Situational Characteristics for the Quality of Patient Care." *Journal of Health and Social Behavior,* 1977, *18,* 10–15.

Roemer, M. I., and Friedman, J. W. *Doctors in Hospitals: Medical Staff Organization and Hospital Performance.* Baltimore, Md.: Johns Hopkins University Press, 1971.

Roethlisberger, F. J., and Dickson, W. J. *Management and the Worker.* Cambridge, Mass.: Harvard University Press, 1939.

Rogers, D. *110 Livingston Street.* New York: Random House, 1968.

Roose, K. D., and Andersen, C. J. *A Rating of Graduate Programs.* Washington, D.C.: American Council on Education, 1970.

Rubinson, R. "The Political Construction of Education." Unpublished doctoral dissertation, Stanford University, 1974.

Rushing, W. R. "Effects of Industry Size and Division of Labor on Administration." *Administrative Science Quarterly,* 1967, *12,* 273–295.

Salancik, G. R., and Pfeffer, J. "The Bases and Use of Power in Organizational Decision Making: the Case of a University." *Administrative Science Quarterly,* 1974, *19,* 453–473.

Salancik, G. R., Pfeffer, J., and Kelly, J. P. "A Contingency Model of Influence in Organizational Decision Making." *Pacific Sociological Review,* in press.

Sampson, S. F. *"Crisis in a Cloister."* Unpublished doctoral dissertation, Cornell University, 1969.

Schein, E. *Process Consultation.* Reading, Mass.: Addison-Wesley, 1969.

Schichor, D. "Prestige of Sociology Departments and the Placing of New Ph.D.'s." *American Sociologist,* 1970, *5,* 157–160.

Scott, W. R. "Organizational Structure." In A. Inkeles (Ed.), *Annual Review of Sociology.* Vol. 1. Palo Alto, Calif.: Annual Reviews, 1975.

Scott, W. R. "Effectiveness of Organizational Effectiveness Studies." In P. S. Goodman, J. M. Pennings, and Associates, *New Perspectives on Organizational Effectiveness.* San Francisco: Jossey-Bass, 1977.

Scott, W. R., Forrest, N. H., Jr., and Brown, B. W., Jr. "Hospital Structure and Postoperative Mortality and Morbidity." In S. M. Shortell and M. Brown (Eds.), *Organizational Research in Hospitals.* Chicago: Inquiry Book, Blue Cross Association, 1976.

Selznick, P. *TVA and the Grass Roots.* Berkeley: University of California Press, 1949.

Selznick, P. *Leadership in Administration.* New York: Harper & Row, 1957.

Shamblin, D. H. "Prestige and the Sociology Establishment." *American Sociologist,* 1970, *5,* 154–156.

Short, J. F. *The Social Fabric of the Metropolis.* Chicago: University of Chicago Press, 1971.

Sidey, H. "The Presidency." *Time*, July 28, 1975, p. 8.

Siegfried, J. J. "The Publishing of Economic Papers and Its Impact on Graduate Faculty Ratings, 1960–1969." *Journal of Economic Literature*, 1972, *10*, 31–49.

Simon, H. A. "Theories of Decision-Making in Economics and Behavioral Science." *American Economic Review*, 1959, *49*, 253–283.

Simon, H. A. "The Architecture of Complexity." *Proceedings of the American Philosophical Society*, 1962, *106*, 467–482.

Simon, H. A. "The Organization of Complex Systems." in H. Patee (Ed.), *Hierarchy Theory: The Challenge of Complex Systems*. New York: Braziller, 1973.

Simon, H. A. "On the Concept of Organizational Goal." *Administrative Science Quarterly*, 1964, *9*, 1–22.

Simon, H. A., and Bonini, C. P. "The Size Distribution of Business Firms." *American Economic Review*, 1958, *48*, 607–617.

Smith, P. B. *Groups Within Organizations*. New York: Harper & Row, 1973.

Srole, L., and others. *Mental Health in the Metropolis: The Midtown Manhattan Study*, New York: McGraw-Hill, 1962.

Stagner, R. "Corporate Decision Making: An Empirical Study." *Journal of Applied Psychology*, 1969, *53*, 1–13.

Stanford Center for Health Care Research. *The Study of Institutional Differences in Postoperative Mortality*. Report to the National Academy of Sciences, National Research Council. Springfield, Va.: National Technical Information Service, 1974.

Stanford Center for Health Care Research. "Comparison of Hospitals with Regard to Outcomes of Surgery." *Health Services Research*, 1976, *11*, 112–127.

Starbuck, W. "Organizational Growth and Development." In J. G. March (Ed.), *Handbook of Organizations*. Chicago: Rand McNally, 1965.

Stinchcombe, A. L. "Bureaucratic and Craft Administration of Production." *Administrative Science Quarterly*, 1959, *4*, 168–187.

Stinchcombe, A. L. "Social Structure and Organizations." In J. G. March (Ed.), *Handbook of Organizations*. Chicago: Rand McNally, 1965.

Stogdill, R. N., and Coons, A. E. *Leader Behavior: Its Description and Measurement*. Columbus: Bureau of Business Research, Ohio State University, 1957.

Suchman, E. A. *Evaluative Research.* New York: Russell Sage Foundation, 1967.

Suleiman, E. N. *Politics, Power, and Bureaucracy in France.* Princeton, N.J.: Princeton University Press, 1974.

Sumner, W. G. *Folkways,* Boston: Ginn, 1907.

Tannenbaum, A. S. *Control in Organizations,* New York: McGraw-Hill, 1968.

Taylor, F. W. *The Principles of Scientific Management.* New York: Harper & Row, 1911.

Templeton, A. R., and Rothman, E. A. "Evolution in Heterogenous Environments." *American Naturalist,* 1974, *108,* 409–428.

Terreberry, S. "The Evolution of Organizational Environments." *Administrative Science Quarterly,* 1968, *12,* 590–613.

Thibaut, J. W., and Kelley, H. H. *The Social Psychology of Groups,* New York: Wiley, 1959.

Thompson, J. D. *Organizations in Action.* New York: McGraw-Hill, 1967.

Thompson, J. D., and McEwen, W. J. "Organizational Goals and Environment: Goal-Setting as an Interaction Process." *American Sociological Review,* 1958, *23,* 23–31.

Thompson, J. D., and Tuden, A. "Strategies, Structures, and Processes of Organizational Decision." In J. D. Thompson and others (Eds.), *Comparative Studies in Administration.* Pittsburgh: Pittsburgh University Press, 1959.

Tönnies, F. *Gemeinschaft and Gesellschaft.* (C. Loomis, Trans.) New York: American Book Company, 1957. (Originally published 1887.)

Tosi, H., Aldag, R., and Storey, R. "On the Measurement of the Environment: An Assessment of the Lawrence and Lorsch Environmental Uncertainty Scale." *Administrative Science Quarterly,* 1973, *18,* 27–36.

Trist, E. L., and Bamforth, K. W. "Some Social and Psychological Consequences of the Longwall Method of Goal-Getting." *Human Relations,* 1951, *4,* 3–38.

Tullock, G. *The Politics of Bureaucracy.* Washington, D.C.: Public Affairs Press, 1965.

Turk, H. "Interorganizational Networks in Urban Society: Initial

Perspectives and Comparative Research." *American Sociological Review*, 1970, *35*, 1–19.

Turner, R. H. "Sponsored and Contest Mobility and the School System." *American Sociological Review*, 1960, *25*, 855–867.

Tyack, D. B. *The One Best System*. Cambridge, Mass.: Harvard University Press, 1974.

Udy, S. H., Jr. "'Bureaucracy' and 'Rationality' in Weber's Organization Theory." *American Sociological Review*, 1959a, *24*, 791–795.

Udy, S. H., Jr. *Organization of Work*. New Haven, Conn.: Human Relations Area Files Press, 1959b.

Udy, S. H., Jr. "Administrative Rationality, Social Setting, and Organizational Development." *American Journal of Sociology*, 1962, *68*, 299–308.

Udy, S. H., Jr. *Work in Traditional and Modern Society*. Englewood Cliffs, N.J.: Prentice-Hall, 1971.

U.S. Congress. "An Act to Regulate and Improve the Civil Service of the United States." In *United States Statutes at Large*, 1881–1883, *22*, 403–407. Washington, D.C.: U.S. Government Printing Office, 1883.

U.S. Congress. "An Act to Amend the Social Security Act, and for Other Purposes." In *United States Statutes at Large*, 1939, *84*, 1360–1402. Washington, D.C.: U.S. Government Printing Office, 1939.

U.S. Congress. "An Act to Reinforce the Federal System by Strengthening the Personnel Resources of State and Local Governments." In *United States Statutes at Large*, 1970–1971, *84*, 1909–1929. Washington, D.C.: U.S. Government Printing Office, 1971.

U.S. Senate Committee on Governmental Operations. *More Effective Public Service: The First Report to the President and the Congress by the Advisory Council on Intergovernmental Personnel Policy–January, 1973*. Washington, D.C.: U.S. Government Printing Office, 1974.

Warren, R. L. *The Community in America*. Chicago: Rand McNally, 1972.

Weber, M. *Wirtschaft and Gesellschaft*. 2 vols. Tübingen, Germany: J. C. B. Mohr, 1925.

Weber, M. "Bureaucracy." In H. Gerth and C. W. Mills (Eds.), *From Max Weber: Essays in Sociology*. New York: Oxford University Press, 1946.

Weber, M. *The Theory of Social and Economic Organization*. (A. M. Henderson and T. Parsons, Trans.) New York: Free Press, 1947.

Webster, W. "Organizational Resistance to Statewide Educational Reform." Paper prepared for Conference on Schools as Loosely Coupled Systems. Palo Alto, Calif., November 21, 1976.

Weick, K. E. *The Social Psychology of Organizing*. Reading, Mass.: Addison-Wesley, 1969.

Weick, K. E. "Educational Organizations as Loosely Coupled Systems." *Administrative Science Quarterly*, 1976, *21*, 1–19.

Weston, J. F., and Mansinghka, S. K. "Tests of the Efficiency Performance of Conglomerate Firms." *Journal of Finance*, 1971, *26*, 919–936.

Whisler, T. L. *Information Technology and Organizational Change*. Belmont, Calif.: Wadsworth, 1970.

Whittaker, R. N., and Levin, S. (Eds.). *Niche: Theory and Application*. Stroudsberg, Pa: Dowden, Hutchinson & Ross, 1976.

Whyte, M. K. "Bureaucracy and Modernization in China: The Maoist Critique." *American Sociological Review*, 1973, *38*, 149–163.

Williamson, O. *Corporate Control and Business Behavior*. Englewood Cliffs, N.J.: Prentice-Hall, 1970.

Williamson, O. *Markets and Hierarchies: Analysis and Antitrust Implications*. New York: Free Press, 1975.

Winter, S. G., Jr. "Economic 'Natural Selection' and the Theory of the Firm." *Yale Economic Essays*, 1964, *4*, 224–272.

Wirth, L. "Urbanism as a Way of Life," *American Journal of Sociology*, 1938, *44*, 1–24.

Woellner, E. H. *Requirements for Certification*. Chicago: University of Chicago Press, 1972.

Woodward, J. *Industrial Organizations: Theory and Practice*. London: Oxford University Press, 1965.

Yoels, W. C. "The Structure of Scientific Fields and the Allocation of Editorships on Scientific Journals." Paper presented at the

68th annual meeting of the American Sociological Association, New York, August 27–30, 1973.

Yotopoulos, P. A. "Institutional Affiliation of the Contributors to Three Professional Journals." *American Economic Review*, 1961, *51*, 665–670.

Yuchtman, E. and Seashore, S. E. "A System Resource Approach to Organizational Effectiveness." *American Sociological Review*, 1967, *32*, 891–903.

Zald, M. N. "Who Shall Rule: A Political Analysis of Succession in a Large Welfare Organization." *Pacific Sociological Review*, 1965, *8*, 52–60.

Zald, M. N. "Political Economy: A Framework for Analysis." In M. N. Zald (Ed.), *Power in Organizations*. Nashville, Tenn.: Vanderbilt University Press, 1970.

Zuckerman, H. "Stratification in American Science." *Sociological Inquiry*, 1970, *40*, 235–257.

Index

Abegglen, J. C., 17, 113, 114, 369
Accounting, 356; and manager behavior, 268
Accounting departments. *See* Finance departments
Accreditation reviews, 297
Acland, H., 89, 259, 369
Adaptation perspective, 132
Adaptive function, 158, 159–161
Administration departments. *See* Finance departments
Administrative overhead, 10, 11
Administrative Science Quarterly, 4
Administrator succession, 45
Advisors to NSF, 316–332
Aerospace industry, 128
Affiliation in society, 110, 111, 125–130
Affirmative action departments, 49
Age of organization. *See* Era of origin
Aides for teachers, 255
Aiken, M., 5, 33, 44, 48, 76, 369, 377
Akers, R., 339, 369
Aldag, R., 33, 390
Aldrich, H. E., 2, 19, 137, 171, 200, 266, 350, 351, 369
Allocation of resources, 306, 307; at NSF, 316–328; and paradigms, 313; and precedent, 323; uncertainty in, 309–312

American Council on Education (ACE), 317, 318, 328, 330, 331, 369
American Medical Association (AMA), 293
American Sociological Association (ASA), 78
"America's Oldest Companies," 168, 370
Andersen, C. J., 317, 388
Angell, R. C., 111, 370
Argyris, C., 4, 11, 39, 200, 370
Aries, P., 127, 370
Arizona and organizational form, 116
Arrow, K. J., 10, 370
Assessments, finance departments making, 201
Aston group, 5, 7, 19
Auditors' offices. *See* Finance departments
Authority, 227; nature of, 360
Autonomy, 296; operational measure of, 285, 286; in schools, 240; of teachers, 250; zero-order correlation coefficients for, 287, 288

Bailyn, B., 93, 370
Baker, E. C., 235, 370
Baldridge, J. V., 42, 370
Bamforth, K. W., 112, 390
Barnard, C. I., 344, 370

395

Bayesian procedure, 301
Becker, S., 204, 376
Behavior control, 38–42, 270, 271; and accounting data, 268; antitransmission of, 275; correlation of, 271–275; and interlevel transmission, 279; monitoring of, 266, 267; operational measures of, 284–286; paths for variables, 272, 274; regression on behavior control by supervisors, 281; significance of, 284; zero-order correlation coefficients, 287, 288
Bendix, R., 17, 92, 370
Berliner, J. S., 17, 370
bias and cross-lagged analysis, 322
Bidwell, C., 76, 81, 84, 259, 370
Blalock, H. M., Jr., 231, 370
Blau, P. M., 3–5, 7, 9, 10, 24, 25, 33–35, 39, 49, 52, 69, 92, 141, 142, 145, 177, 178, 205, 310, 311, 318, 370, 371
Bloom, J. R., 291
Blowers, T. A., 8, 379
Bolton, J. E., 167, 371
Bonacich, E. M., 52
Bonini, C. P., 150, 389
Boston and organizational form, 116
Boulding, K. E., 142, 306, 371
Boundary-spanning activities, 204
Bradburn, N. M., 371
Breweries, study of, 42
Brittain, J., 146, 376
Brook, R. H., 298, 371
Brown, B. W., Jr., 290, 292, 303, 388
Brown, M. C., 12, 27, 51–77, 342, 353, 356, 357, 366
Buckley, W., 294, 371
Budgets: regressions of size of budget and demand variables, 226; and teachers, 251. *See also* Finance departments
Bureaucratization, 11–13, 51–77; and educational institutions, 47, 89, 92, 93; and environment, 53, 54; and formalism in, 63–69; and hierarchy, 69–71; measures of, 317, 318; preconditions of, 51, 52; and schools, 89, 92, 93
Burns, T., 5, 9, 31, 33, 133, 371
Buttrick, J., 12, 371

California, 116; and merit system, 56, 57; and public schools, 177–199
Callahan, R. E., 88, 371
Campbell, F. L., 339, 369
Campbell, J. P., 203, 371
Capacity: and carrying capacity, 146, 180, 181, 191–196; and excess capacity, 153–155; and niche theory, 153, 154
Caplow, T., 10, 142, 371
Career path, by type of organization, 120
Carrying capacity, 146, 180, 181, 191–196
Cartter, A. M., 317, 318, 371
Case studies, 3
Causal relationships, 214–223; and bureaucracies, 12; and change, 345; and cross-lagged path model, 322; and recursive causal models, 7, 8; and time series approach, 8
Census data, 167
Centralization, 39, 40–47; and formalization, 70; in schools, 89; and task routineness, 48
Chandler, A. D., Jr., 8, 372
Change in organizations, 45, 341–343; and causal effects, 345; and conflict, 344; dollars obtained from NSF, 321; and environment, 71–73, 75; and longitudinal analysis, 349, 350
Chicago, University of, 314
Child, J., 16, 34, 44, 47, 372
China and work organization, 113, 116–130
Choice of units, 136–139
Churches, 110, 111, 354, 355
Churchill, B. C., 167, 372
City finance agencies, study of, 51–77
Civil service, 12; history of, 55–59; legal authority in, 338; and origins of organization, 63–68; stability of, 223
Closed versus open systems, 10, 18, 21–28, 200, 228, 229, 336, 337
Clubs, 110, 111
Coalitional models, 34, 36–38, 307
Coch, L., 40, 372
Cohen, E. G., 90, 233, 237, 248, 252, 254, 372

Cohen, M. D., 15, 34, 198, 372
Cole, J. R., 314, 372
Cole, R., 114, 121, 372
Cole, S., 233–263, 314, 372
Coleman, J., 112, 382
Coleman, J. S., 183, 185, 341, 372
Collective organization, 340
Columbia Broadcasting Systems, 340
Columbia University, 315
Commission on Professional and Hospital Activities (CPHA), 291
Communication, 38, 41; and isomorphism, 143
Community matrix, 148, 189
Comparative studies, 9, 18, 357; from case studies, 4; cross-national comparisons, 17; of educational organizations, 105, 106; quantitative studies, 5, 6
Competition, 143–151; and centralization of power, 44; coefficients of, 147, 181, 188; and natural selection theory, 31, 32; and principle of competitive exclusion, 147
Complexity, 48
Comptrollers' offices. See Finance departments
Computers, 44; changes brought by, 202; control of, 213, 214; finance departments using, 206; Q-coefficients of turnover of operation of, 213–215; turnover of control of, 207
Comstock, D. E., 291
Conflict and change, 344
Connectedness of structure and goals, 15
Consistency of objectives, 295, 296
Consonance hypothesis, 30–36
Construction firms, 162, 163
Consumer affairs departments, 49
Contest mobility, 313
Contextual analysis, 4
Contingency theory, 18, 30, 33, 36
Continuity in organizations, 341–343
Control, 264–289; chart of transmission of, 273, 274; of employees by type of organization, 119; and loose coupling, 283, 284; model of, 145, 146; and observation, 276; of population

participation, 339; rationalized methods of, 360; transmission (see Transmission). See also Behavior control; Outputs
Coombs, P. H., 78, 92, 372
Coons, A. E., 204, 389
Coordination needs, 177, 178
Coping with uncertainty, 35, 42
Corwin, R. G., 103, 373
Cost-benefit analysis, 202
County finance agencies, 51–77
Coupling. See Loose coupling
Craft-administered organizations, 162, 163
Crane, D., 314, 315, 317, 373
Crecine, J. P., 309, 373
Cross-lagged path technique, 214; of NSF grants, 322–327
Cross-sectional research: and change, 341; and Galton's Problem, 346
Crozier, M., 15–17, 42, 137, 373
Cubberly, E. P., 88, 373
Cultural differences, 15–17, 354, 355
Cummins Engine Company, 115
Cyert, R. M., 26, 34, 37, 42, 132, 155, 295, 307–309, 373

Dahl, R., 228, 373
Dansereau, F., Jr., 203, 377
Darwin-Lotka law, 171
Darwinism, 132
Data: census, 167; for school study, 237–241; used in California public school systems study, 186, 187
Data-processing facilities: finance departments controlling, 202; and growth of organization, 225
Davis, M., 233
Davis, O. A., 323, 373
De facto segregation in schools, 245, 246
de Tocqueville, A., 355
Deal, T. E., 81, 233, 247, 373
Decentralization. See Centralization
Decision making: decentralization of, 70; familiarity, 313; by type of work organization, 117, 118
Demand variables and budget size, 226
Dempster, M. A. H., 323, 373

398

Index

Department managers. *See* Supervisors
Dependency, 180, 181
Dibble, V. K., 15, 53, 373
Dickson, W. J., 23, 387
Differentiation, 10, 49, 50; and era of origin, 68, 69. *See also* Subunit power
Dill, W. R., 31, 373
Discipline patterns in schools, 257
Discontinuities in ecological analysis, 140–142
Diversity in system, 149
Divisions of finance departments, 207
Divorce, 111, 127
Donabedian, A., 296, 373
Donham, W. B., 112, 374
Dore, R., 114, 374
Doreian, P., 145, 146, 181, 374, 380
Dornbusch, S. M., 81, 90, 265, 374
Dowling, J., 95, 107, 374
Downey, H. K. 33, 374
Downs, A., 265, 374
Dreeben, R., 81, 259, 374
Duncan, O. D., 92, 371
Duncan, R. B., 31, 33, 374
Durkheim, E., 111, 144, 347, 374
Dynamic structure, 181

Ecology of organizations, 131–171
Economics and concentration of ownership interests, 16, 46, 47
Educational materials, 251
Educational organizations, 40, 78–109; and accountability, 80, 89; and accreditation, 94–96; activities and outcomes decoupled from structure, 98–101; administrators' authority, 83, 84; bureaucratic control of, 47, 89, 92, 93; and California public schools, 177–199; and comparative studies, 104–106; as coordinated organizations, 233–263; corporate control of, 92–94; and costs, 99–101; and credentials, 93, 94; curriculum, 82, 83; data for study of, 237–241; decentralist stance, 89; and decoupling, 98–101; de facto segregation in, 245, 246; and enrollments, total effects of, 192, 193; and evaluation of, 81, 82, 88, 89, 241, 242; and face work,

102; funds for, 246; and goal displacement, 90, 91; homogeneity in, 258, 259; and ideologies, 236; and illegitimacy of, 94–96; and inspection of instructional activity, 96–98; intensity of interaction in, 190; and lack of coordination over technical interdependencies, 83; and localism, 97, 98; and logic of confidence, 101–103; loose coupling of, 79, 81, 259; national development of, 92–94; as nonorganizations, 335, 336; and pluralistic setting, 100, 101; and principals (*see* Principals of schools); and pupil-teacher ratios, 178, 179; and rationality, 108; and reformers, 88; and research propositions, 104–109; and ritual classifications, 79, 84–87, 93–95; and rules, 40, 260, 261; and saving face, 102; and student classifications, 85, 86; and teachers (*see* Teachers); and testing, 96–98; and topic classifications, 86
Efficiency of organization, 15, 294
Elton, C., 139, 374
Emergency Employment Act, 57, 58
England, education in, 236
Environment: and adaptation perspective, 132; and bureaucratization, 53, 54; and change of organizations, 71–73, 75; coarse-grained environments, 157–164; and contingency theory, 33; and era of origin, 59–69; fine-grained environments, 157–164; and growth and decline in public school systems, 177–199; and origins of organizations, 62, 63; and size, 71–73
Equations: and linear differential equations, 182, 183. *See also* Lotka-Volterra equations
Era of origin, 59–69; and formalization, 63–68; and structure, 68, 69
Errors in measures, 348
Estimations, 182–186
Etzioni, A., 294, 339, 274
Europe and type of work organization, 116–130
Evaluation: of employees by type of or-

ganization, 118; of schools, 81, 82, 88, 89, 241, 242; of teachers, 256
Evan, E. M., 337, 374
Evans, P. B., 265, 266, 283, 275
Excess capacity, 153–155
Expandability of organizations, 141, 142
Expansion of markets, 149
Experience rating, 16
External influence, 46, 212
Ewy, W., 290–305

Faculty. *See* Teachers
Failure of small businesses, 167
Fantini, M., 89, 375
Fayol, H., 23, 375
Federal regulation in local government personnel practices, 55–59
Festinger, L., 310, 311, 328, 330, 375
Field, A., 93, 375
Field development, 336–338
Finance departments, 200–232; demand for services of, 214; size of, 206, 207; structural change tabulations, 230; study of, 51–77; and subgroup performances, 16
Financial variables in models, 346
Fitness, 141; Levin's fitness set theory, 166; and niche theory, 153, 156–163
Flood, A. B., 290–305, 366, 375
Flow of resources, 347
Form, W. H., 111, 375
Form of organization, 138, 171
Formalization: and decentralization, 70; and era of origin, 63–68; and hierarchy, 69–71
Forrest, W. H., Jr., 290–305
Fortune 500, 167
France, ministry of education in 17, 236
Franklin, J. L., 266, 283, 375
Freeman, J. H., 6, 8, 11, 13, 27, 36, 50, 52, 131–199, 304, 333–353, 358, 361, 375, 376, 378
Freidson, E., 305, 376
French, J. R. P., 40, 48, 372, 376
French bureaucratic patterns, 17, 236
Friedlander, F., 295, 376
Friedman, J. W., 29, 144, 305, 376, 387
Functionalism, 35, 132
Fundamental parameters, 185, 186

Galton's Problem, 346
Gause, G. F., 147, 170, 171, 376
Gemeinschaft and Gesellschaft, 116
Generalism, 152–166
Generalized least squares estimators, 184
Genetic structure, 138, 140
Georgopoulos, B. S., 294, 376
Gerard, H. B., 313, 380
Gerwin, D., 309, 376
Gittell, M., 89, 374
Glenn, N., 318, 376
Goals: and contingency theory, 34; and independence, 347
Goffman, E., 96, 102, 376
Goode, W. J., 114, 376
Gordon, G., 204, 312, 315, 316, 319, 376, 382
Gouldner, A. Q., 3, 24, 112, 204, 268, 294, 377
Graduate Record Examination, 97
Graen, G., 203, 377
Graicunas, V. A., 142, 377
Granovetter, M. S., 377
Grants: and finance departments, 206. *See also* National Science Foundation
Griffith, E. S., 12, 57, 377
Gross, E., 294, 377
Gross, G. R., 318, 377
Gross, N., 241, 259, 377
Growth of organization: and dataprocessing, 225; model of, 145, 146
Grusky, O., 200, 204, 205, 377
Gulick, L., 2, 23, 377

Haas, J. E., 33, 378
Hage, J., 5, 33, 44, 48, 76, 369, 377
Hagstrom, W. O., 313, 317, 318, 377, 379
Haire, M., 142, 377
Halaby, C., 200
Hall, R. H., 9, 33, 200, 377, 378
Halpern, S., 111, 378
Hamblin, W., 46, 378
Hannan, M. T., 8, 11, 13, 27, 36, 50, 52, 131–179, 181, 304, 335, 339, 342, 347, 353, 358, 361, 376, 378, 385
Hargens, L. L., 313–317, 378, 379
Hartmann, H., 17, 379
Harvard University, 315, 358

Harwood study, 40
Hawley, A. H., 136, 143–146, 164, 165, 170, 171, 347, 379
Hawthorne Plant of Western Electric Company, 23
Heise, D. R., 214, 322, 379
Hellriegel, D., 33, 374
Hendershot, G. E., 8, 379
Henderson, C. R., 185, 379
Henry, N., 200
Herriott, R. E., 241, 259, 377
Heteroscedasticity, 184, 185
Heydebrand, W. V., 34, 35, 371
Hickson, D. H., 5, 15, 16, 19, 27, 32, 42, 43, 48, 295, 379
Hierarchy and formalization, 69–71
Hinings, C. R., 42, 44, 379
Hirsch, P. M., 339, 340, 379
Historical studies, 8, 9; and bureaucratization, 51–77; of civil service movement, 55–59; closed to open systems, 21–28; and events affecting organizations, 61; of finance departments, 201, 202; and origins of bureaucracy, 12, 13; rational to social models, 21–28
Hobbs, N., 86, 379
Hoffman, L. R. 113, 383
Holdoway, E. A., 8, 379
Holistic concern of employees, 120
Hollander, E. O., 167, 380
Holt, J. C., 81, 380
Homans, G. C., 111, 380
Hopwood, A. G., 265, 268, 380
Hospitals, 290–305; chief administrators, tenure and characteristics of, 45; morbidity measures in, 298, 299, 301; as multiproduct firms, 296; outcome measures of, 297–303; and Spearman rank order correlations, 301–303; surgeons (*see* Surgeons); and table of outcome measures, 303
Hummon, N. A., 101, 380
Hummon, N. P., 145, 146, 181, 374, 380
Hutchinson, G. E., 140, 152, 380

IBM, 115
Ideal type of American work organization, 116–130
Illich, I., 94, 380

Independence: and goal-setting, 347; of observations, 345
Independent teachers, consensus among, 356, 357
Indicators, 296, 297
Individual preferences, 3, 4, 15–17, 36, 37, 50
Individual responsibility, 118
Inertial pressures, 133–135, 164
Influence, 315; and conformity to group norms, 328; determinants of, 42–45; incentives to use, 331; and representation, 319
Information: capacity to process, 44; control of, 38, 41
Input measurement, 267, 297
Inside contracting system, 12, 13
Insularity of leaders, 212, 213, 227
Interdependence of departments: and control, 279; operational measure of, 286; and schools, 255; zero-order correlation coefficients for, 287, 288
Interfirm mobility, 121, 123
Intergovernmental Personnel Act, 55, 56, 61
Interpersonal skills of school suprintendents, 249
Interviews with Japanese and American employees, 114–130
Intili, J. K., 233–263
Investments by finance departments, 201
Isomorphism, 143, 144, 151, 152, 164
Israel, education in, 236

Jaeger, A. M., 26, 110–130, 353–355, 359, 361, 366
James, T. F., 8, 379
Janes, R. W., 318, 380
Janowitz, M., 111, 113, 125, 380
Japan: feudal culture in, 121; and interview with employees of Japanese firms, 113–130; type of work organization, 116–130
Johnson, J. B., 117, 386
Johnson, J. N., 33, 378
Johnson, R. T., 114, 123, 380
Jones, E., 313, 380

Kahn, R. L., 114, 205, 380
Kasarda, J. D., 111, 113, 125, 380

Katz, D., 205, 380
Katz, M., 93, 380
Kaufman, R. L., 183, 380
Kelley, H. H., 268, 390
Kelly, J. P., 42, 388
Kelsall, R. K., 17, 381
Kempthorne, O., 304, 381
Kiesler, C. A., 313, 381
Kiesler, S., 313, 381
Kimberly, J. R., 10, 76, 177, 381
Knievel, E., 113
Knudsen, D. D., 314, 318, 381
Kodak Company, 115
Kolarska, L., 113, 381
Kriesberg, L., 204, 381
Kronenfeld, J. E., 178, 376

Lag structure and change, 343
Lagged measure of leadership, 209
Lasswell, H. D., 381
Lavender, A. D., 318, 381
Lawrence, P. R., 5, 9, 31, 33, 37, 49, 265, 381
Lazarsfeld, P. F., 4, 381
Leaders: accounting data and behavior of, 268; autonomy of, 208, 212, 213; demand variables for, 217, 220, 221; hypotheses concerning, 216; recruitment of, 228; and size of environment, 216, 218; structural variables, autocorrelations of, 209; structure of, 200–232; supervision, regressions of, 224; and supervisors (see Supervisors); turnovers of, 208–212, 227
Leblebici, H., 33, 44, 46, 306–332, 386
Leeds, R., 49, 381
Length of employment, by type of work organization, 117
Leong, A., 327, 387
Levi Strauss, 115
Levin, S. A., 149, 381
Levine, S., 132, 382, 392
Levins, R., 152–164, 171, 382
Lieberson, S., 203, 228, 230, 382
Light, I. H., 130, 382
Lightfield, E. T., 318, 382
Lipset, S. M., 9, 112, 382
Lockheed, aid to, 169
Locus of causation, 338

Lodahl, J., 312, 315, 316, 319
Longitudinal analysis, 8, 9, 336–338; and change, 341; and market-related environments, 347; and timing of change, 349, 350
Loose coupling, 15, 37, 79, 129, 296; in complex organizations, 266; and control-loss paradigm, 283, 284; educational organizations, 79, 81, 259; existence by, 265; hospitals as, 303; to technical activity, 359
Lorsch, J. W., 5, 9, 31, 33, 37, 49, 265, 381
Lortie, D. C., 81, 235, 259, 382
Lotka-Volterra equations, 147, 148, 165, 169
Lowin, A., 40, 382

MacArthur, R. H., 171, 382
McCall, G. J., 96, 382
McEachern, W. A., 46, 47, 382
McEwen, W. J., 347, 390
McFarland, D. D., 10, 383
McGregor, D., 23, 26, 383
Maguire, M. A., 39, 82, 267, 277, 280, 386
Managers. See Supervisors
Mann, F. C., 113, 383
Mann, H., 88
Mansinghka, S. K., 16, 392
Mao Tse-tung, 355
March, J. G., 15, 26, 28, 34, 36, 37, 79, 81, 132, 155, 198, 259, 266, 294–296, 307, 309, 372, 373, 383
Marschak, J., 138, 383
Maslow, A. H., 126, 383
Mason, K. O., 76, 383
Massachusetts and merit system of appointment, 56, 57
Mathers, R. A., 381
Maxwell, B., 291
May, R. M., 169, 383
Mayo, E., 23, 26, 112, 115, 383
Measures, 348, 349; errors in, 348; ritualization of, 365
Medical facilities. See Hospitals
Membership in groups, 111
Menzel, H., 4, 381
Merit hiring, 12, 13, 55–59; entry level employees hired by, 63–65

Merton, R. K., 24, 39, 115, 383
Meyer, J. P., 52
Meyer, J. W., 10, 15, 27, 28, 40, 52, 78, 109, 129, 171, 173, 175, 198, 200, 233–266, 304, 333, 335, 352–368, 373, 383, 384
Meyer, M. W., 1–19, 27, 44, 51–77, 173, 175, 178, 200–232, 334, 338, 342, 353, 356, 357, 366, 384
Meyer, R. A., 351
Michaels, R., 198, 384
Miles, M. B., 89, 384
Military bases, 128
Minami, T., 203, 377
Minnesota Mining and Manufacturing (3M), 115
Mitau, G. T., 57, 384
Mobility, 120, 121, 123; and culture, 355; in postindustrial organizations, 362; and prestige, 313
Model Public Personnel Administration Law of 1970, 58
Models of organizational processes, 229, 294; closed versus open systems, 21–28; competition model, 180–182; continuous-time partial adjustment model, 181; control model, 145, 146; cross-lagged path model, 322; financial variables in, 346; growth model, 146; and multivariate techniques, 7; politics and administrative rationality, 178, 179; of postindustrial organizations, 363; rational to social models, 21–28; rational system model, 294; recursive causal modeling, 7, 8; specification of, 344–349; type Z model, 15
Mohr, L., 32, 384
Monod, J., 138, 385
Monopolies, 364
Moore, M. H., 111, 318, 385
Moore, W. J., 328, 385
Morbidity measures, 298, 299, 301
Mortality, measures of, 298, 299, 301
Mousseau, J., 385
Multinational corporations, 17
Multiple regression approach, 6, 7; of cross-lagged path analysis of NSF grants, 324–326; and hospitals, 305
Municipal Finance Officers Association

of the United States and Canada, 201

Nakane, C., 114, 385
Naroll, R., 345, 385
National Cash Register, 115
National Institute of Education (NIE), 78
National Science Foundation (NSF), 52, 173, 316–328; allocation of grants by, 311–316; cross-lagged path analysis of grants from, 322–327; dollars obtained from, 321; publications by, 385; stability in grants from, 327, 328
Natural selection theory, 31, 32
Natural system model, 294
Neighborhoods, importance of, 110, 111
Nelson, D., 8, 12, 385
Nerlove, M., 184, 185, 385
Newness, liability of, 167
New York: and merit system, 56, 57; work organizations in, 116
New York State Board of Regents, 97
Niche theory, 151–164, 181, 191
Nielson, F., 146, 181, 185, 385
Nonindustrial societies, 17
Normative theories of structure, 29–36
Norr, J. L., 17, 385
Norr, K. L., 17, 385
North Carolina, University of, 314
NSF. *See* National Science Foundation

Observations, 279; and change, 343; independence of, 345; standardized score for, 348, 349; subordinates and control, 276; zero-order correlation coefficients from, 287, 288
Occam's Razor, 349
O'Connor, J. F., 203, 228, 230, 382
Oldest companies, survival of, 168, 370
Olsen, J. P., 15, 26, 28, 34, 79, 81, 198, 259, 296, 372, 383
Open systems models, 10–18, 21–28, 200, 228, 229, 294, 336, 337
Operative causality and change, 223
Optimization, 144
Organizations in Action, 9
Origin of organization. *See* Era of origin
Ouchi, W. G., 15, 26, 39, 82, 110–130,

173, 176, 264–289, 340, 341, 353–355, 359, 361, 366, 380, 385, 386

Outcomes, 16; in hospitals, 297–305; indicators of, 297, 298; social influence affecting, 331

Outputs, 270, 271; correlation of, 271–275; definition of, 364, 365; internal use of, 359; legitimation by, 284; monitoring of, 266, 267; operational measures of, 284–286; original scales for, 289; paths for variables, 272, 274; and rational model, 294; and recorded scales, 289; and religious organizations, 354, 355; research output, stability of, 328; of retail stores, 268, 269; ritualized measures of, 365; and supervisors, 272, 274, 275; transmission of, 270; zero-order correlation coefficients, matrix of, 287, 288

Overreplication, 345

Ownership, concentration of, 46, 47

Panel members on NSF boards, 316–332

Panel studies. *See* Longitudinal analysis

Paradigms: and allocation of resources, 313; in science, 312; in social sciences, 319

Parsons, T., 95, 111, 132, 310, 386

Patchen, M., 265, 386

Paternalism of mines and plantations, 112, 113

Patients. *See* Hospitals

Paul, B. D., 296, 386

Peer groups, 16

Pendleton Act, 55, 56

Pennings, J. M., 32, 346, 347, 386

Penrose, E. T., 155, 386

Per capita growth, model of, 146

Performance and structural contingency theory, 30–36

Perrow, C., 9, 25, 33, 37, 42, 83, 200, 235, 236, 294, 307, 310, 386

Personnel agencies, study of, 35

Personnel procedures: causes and consequences of, 51–77; and era of origin, 63–69; and formalization, 63–69

Pettigrew, A. M., 38, 41, 42–44, 386

Pfeffer, J., 2, 15, 26, 29–50, 52, 95, 107,

171, 173, 174, 198, 295, 306–332, 351, 355, 357, 359, 361, 366, 369, 374, 386–388

Pheysey, D. C., 5, 19, 32, 379

Phillips, J. C., 57, 387

Physicians. *See* Surgeons

Pickle, 295, 376

Poland and work organization, 113

Political appointees, leaders as, 212

Politics, 15–17, 36–46, 177–199, 338, 355, 356

Polymorphism, 160

Pondy, L. R., 6, 10, 306, 307, 331, 387

Pooled interdependence, 350

Populations: change in, 342; choosing of, 336; and ecology, 11, 13, 14, 131–171; problems involving, 338, 339

Postindustrial organizations, 361–363

Power, 15–17; constraints on, 44; determinants of, 42–45; link between power and structure, 45, 46. *See also* Centralization of power

Presthus, R., 306, 387

Prestige of scientists, 313, 314

Price, J. L., 200

Principals of schools: consensus among, 243, 257; and evaluation of schools, 241, 242; influence on districts, analysis of reports on, 248; as informants, 238–241; role definitions for, 260; in strong districts, 247–250; teachers' agreement with, 250–257; variance analysis of responses of, 244, 245

Probability samples, 6

Procedural systems, 154, 155

Process measures, 296–298

Procter and Gamble, 115

Productivity, model of, 294

Professional Activities Study (PAS), 291, 293

Professionals and excess capacity, 154

Profits, maximization of, 144

Program Planning Budgeting Systems (PPBS), 202, 364

Progressive movement, 57

Protest absorption, 49

Public health agencies, 32

Public relations departments, 49

Public schools. *See* Educational organizations

Publication by professionals, 314, 315, 327

Pugh, D. S., 5, 9, 19, 25, 32, 69, 76, 379, 387

Pupil-grouping, 242

Purchasing of new equipment and influence determinants, 42

Purpose of organizations, 11

Q-coefficients of turnover of computer operations, 215

Quality control, 297

Quantitative research, 3–6, 9, 10, 52

Radner, R., 138, 383

Ramirez, F. O., 92, 97, 387

Rational models, 21–28, 294, 308, 354

Rationality, 15, 35, 36; and bureaucratization, 51; and control, 360; and coordination, 177, 178; and educational reformers, 88, 108; myths of, 364

Raven, B., 48, 376

Recruitment of leaders, 228

Recursive causal modeling, 7, 8

Reform movement, 12, 57; and education, 88

Reich, C. A., 28, 387

Reiss, A. J., 137, 369

Reissman, L., 113, 387

Religious organizations, 110, 111, 354, 355

Reorganization and leaders, 210

Research methods, 2–9, 104–109

Resources: and allocation (*see* Allocation of resources); control of, 37, 47; and ecological model of competition, 145; flow of, 347

Responsibility of individuals, 118

Retail stores output, measures of, 268, 269

Rhee, S., 305, 387

Ritualized measures of outputs, 365

Robinette, P., 52

Roemer, M. I., 305, 387

Roethlisberger, F. J., 23, 387

Rogers, D., 81, 89, 388

Roose, K. D., 317, 388

Rothman, E. A., 171, 390

Routinization. *See* Tasks

Rowan, B., 15, 27, 28, 40, 78–109, 129, 198, 259, 265, 353, 356–366, 383, 384

Rubinson, R., 92, 93, 97, 384, 388

Rules, 40, 41; for schools, 40, 260, 261

Rundall, T. G., 291

Rushing, W. R., 6, 388

Salancik, G. R., 36, 42–45, 295, 306–332, 387, 388

Sampson, S. F., 18, 388

San Francisco Bay Area elementary schools, study of, 81–83, 90, 173

Schein, E., 388

Schichor, D., 318, 388

Schoenherr, R. S., 5, 7, 10, 25, 35, 69, 142, 205, 371

Scholastic Aptitude Test, 97

School districts, 36

Schools. *See* Educational organizations

Schoonhoven, C. B., 291

Science, decision making in, 312–316

Scientific management, 12

Scott, W. R., 16, 21–28, 39, 81, 90, 141, 142, 173, 175, 177, 233–263, 265, 290–305, 335, 366, 371–375, 388

Seashore, S. E., 294, 393

Segmental institutions, schools as, 235–237

Segmented concern of employees, 120

Selection, theory of, 131–171

Self-evaluation, need for, 310

Selznick, P., 3, 24, 27, 112, 132, 204, 388

Shamblin, D. H., 314, 388

Shils, E. A., 310, 386

Short, J. F., 113, 125, 388

Sidey, H., 110, 389

Siegfried, J. J., 318, 389

Simmons, J. L., 96, 382

Simon, H. A., 37, 42, 132, 150, 169, 265, 266, 294, 295, 307–309, 338, 373, 383, 389

Simulation models, 309

Size of organizations, 7; and bureaucratization, 52, 53; and centralization of power, 44; and contingency theory,

33; and differentiation, 49, 50; and effect on structure, 142; and environmental demands, 71–73; and era of origin, 68, 69; and expandability of organizations, 141, 142; and national rank of department, 319–321; of NSF grant departments, 318; and quantitative research, 10; and structural differentiation in organizations, 10; and survival, 150, 151
Slocum, J. W., 33, 374
Small businesses, failure of, 167
Smith, P: B., 331, 389
Social clubs, 110, 111
Social comparison theory, 310
Social influence. *See* Influence
Social models, 21–28
Social sciences, paradigm developments in, 319
Social Security Act, 55, 56
Societal preferences, 16, 17, 355
Society: and education, 92–94; and work organizations, 110–130
Sociology, 308, 310
Southern Sociological Society, 314
Spearman rank order correlations, 301–303
Specialism: and niche theory, 151–164; in schools, 234, 235; versus generalism, 13, 14
Specification of model, 344–349
Sponsored mobility, 313
Srole, L., 111, 389
Stability of organizations, 59; and leadership, 203, 222; and postindustrial organizations, 362; in NSF grants, 327, 328; presumption of, 357; of schools, 259
Stackhouse, A., 233
Stagner, R., 309, 389
Stalker, G. M., 5, 9, 31, 33, 133, 371
Standardized score and observations, 348, 349
Stanford Center for Health Care Research, 291–305, 389
Starbuck, W., 76, 389
State control mechanisms, 149, 150
State finance agencies, 51–57
Statistics, 6, 7

Status, 227, 260, 358
Stauffer, R. E., 34, 35, 371
Steinem, G., 113
Stinchcombe, A. L., 6, 9, 19, 27, 52, 59, 61, 132, 145, 162, 167, 389
Stock brokers, 32
Stogdill, R. N., 204, 389
Storey, R., 33, 390
Strategic contingencies' theory, 42, 43, 48
Stratification system in science, 314
Strehl, K., 327, 387
Structural contingency theory, 30–36
Structural measures, 297
The Structure of Organizations, 7, 10
Student classifications, 85, 86
Stull Act, teacher evaluations under, 242
Subgoals, 16, 17
Substitutability, 48
Subunit power, 42, 43, 49, 50; and adaptation perspective, 132; creation of, 49; of finance departments, 207
Suchman, E. A., 296, 297, 390
Suleiman, E. N., 17, 390
Sumner, W. G., 111, 390
Superintendents of schools: and evaluation of schools, 241, 242; influence of, 248–250; as informants, 239–241
Supervision: and demand variables, 227; and leadership, regressions of, 224
Supervisors: expertise of, 279; operational measures of, 285; output control, 272, 274, 275; regression on behavior control by, 281; watching subordinates, 276; zero-order correlation coefficients for expertise of, 287, 288
Support goals, 294
Surgeons: proportion of practice in study hospital of, 293; tracking data for, 304
Surgical care. *See* Hospitals
Systems analysis, 202

Tables: affiliation in society, 125; American type of work organization, 117; budget size and demand variables, regressions of, 226; carrying capacity and estimated niche parameters,

Tables (Continued)
191; control, transmission of, 273, 274; cross-lagged path analysis of NSF grants, 324–326; data processing and size of organization, 225; demand variables for leadership, regressions of, 217, 220, 221; enrollments in public schools, 192; formalization measures, 64, 66, 67, 70, 71; and functionally differentiated schools, 234, 235; funds for schools, 246; high versus low performing departments, transmission in, 278; influence on school districts, analysis of reports on, 248; Japanese type of work organization, 117; mean size and era of origins, 68; original scale for output controls, 289; personnel components in equilibrium, predicted levels of, 193; principals' answers, variance analysis of, 244, 245; public schools and estimated competition coefficients, 188; Q-coefficients of turnover of computer operations, 215; recorded scale for output controls, 289; responsiveness parameter, 195; school districts and means of selected variables, 187; Spearman rank order correlation in hospitals, 303; structural change tabulations, 230; structural variables by leadership, autocorrelations of, 209; supervision and leadership, regressions of, 224; supervisors, regression on behavior control by, 281; teachers' responses, analysis of variance for, 253, 254; zero-order correlation coefficients for control, 287, 288
Tannenbaum, A. S., 39, 294, 376, 390
Tasks: and centralization of power, 44; and control, 279, 280; and power of persons, 47–49; specialization of, 48, 49; and structure, 33; substitutability of, 48; zero-order correlation coefficients for, 287, 288
Taxes and organizations, 201, 356
Taxonomy, 9
Taylor, F. W., 12, 23, 390
Teachers: control over instruction, 90,

91; and decision-making participation, 257; evaluations of, 81, 82, 242, 256; and independent teachers, 256, 257; and logic of confidence, 101–103; meetings of, 246; principals' agreement with, 250–257; as professionals, 90, 103; questions asked to, 239; and ritual classifications, 79, 84, 85; status of, 260; as team members, 242, 255; variance for, responses, analysis of, 253, 254
Teaching hospitals, study group as, 292
Technology: and contingency theory, 18; as determinant of structure, 18, 19; impact of, 9, 32; of schools, 235, 236; and structural contingency theory, 32, 33
Templeton, A. R., 171, 390
Tennessee Valley Authority, 24
Tenure of department head, 218
Terreberry, S., 205, 390
Teuter, K., 145, 146, 181, 380
Thesis research grants, 317
Thibaut, J. W., 268, 390
Thittaker, R. N., 392
Thompson, J. D., 7, 9, 15, 16, 25, 34, 35, 42–45, 49, 107, 114, 132, 154, 204, 231, 265, 295, 307–310, 347, 350, 360, 390
Time series approach. See Historical studies
Tönnies, F., 111, 116, 390
Tosi, H., 33, 390
Tracking data for hospital patients, 304
Traditions in organizations, 366
Transaction cost approach, 13, 14
Transmission, 264, 265; chart of, 273, 274; in high versus low performing departments, 277, 278; and interlevel transmission, 279; of output control, 270
Trist, E. L., 112, 390
Trow, D. B., 42, 308, 373
Trow, M., 112, 382
Tuden, A., 307–310, 390
Tullock, G., 265, 390
Turk, H., 137, 390
Turner, J. H., 52
Turner, R. H., 308, 391

Turnover of leaders, 208–212, 227, 362
Tyack, D. B., 88, 93, 103, 391
Types of work organizations, 116–130

Udy, S. H., Jr., 9, 17, 25, 100, 112, 116, 307, 391
Uncertainty, 33, 42, 43; in resource allocation, 309–312
Unified objectives, 295, 296
U. S. Civil Service Commission, 55
Universalism: definition of, 310, 311; as norm, 329
Universities: and amalgamated organizations, 160, 162; subunit power in, 42
Urwick, L., 2, 23, 377
Utah International, 115

Values and leadership, 204
Vaughan, T. R., 314, 318, 381
Variations in environments, 352–368
Vertical structure of bureaucracies, 218
Villemez, W., 318, 376
Volunteers as teachers aides, 255

Warren, R. L., 113, 125, 391
Wayne, J., 113
Webb, E. J., 264

Weber, M., 2, 9, 11–13, 23, 34, 39, 51–53, 56, 74, 115, 116, 132, 203, 204, 307, 350, 360, 391, 392
Webster, W., 83, 392
Weick, K. E., 15, 26, 28, 37, 79, 81, 129, 198, 259, 265, 309, 392
Western work organizations, 116–130
Western Electric company, 23
Weston, J. F., 16, 392
Whisler, T. L., 392
White, P. E., 132, 382
Whittaker, R. N., 152, 392
Whyte, M. K., 113, 392
Wildavsky, A., 323, 373
Williamson, O., 10, 13, 16, 19, 265, 392
Winter, S. G., Jr., 142, 144, 392
Wirth, L., 111, 392
Woellner, E. H., 85, 392
Woodward, J., 9, 19, 25, 31–33, 392
Work organization and society, 110–130

Yoels, W. C., 315, 392
Yotopoulos, P. A., 314, 393
Yound, A. A., 184, 378
Yuchtman, E., 294, 393

Zald, M. N., 45, 134, 393
Zuckerman, H., 329, 393